All-New Hints

from Heloise

All-New Hints

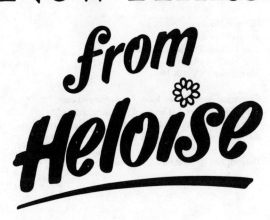

A Household Guide
for the '90s

A Perigee Book

Perigee Books
are published by
The Putnam Publishing Group
200 Madison Avenue
New York, NY 10016

Printed in the United States of America

Quality Printing and Binding by:
Berryville Graphics
P.O. Box 272
Berryville, VA 22611 U.S.A.

ACKNOWLEDGMENTS

What would I do without my everfaithful research editor, Marcy Meffert, who smooths out the lumps and bumps for me; my King Features editors Merry Clark, who gives me guidance and laughs, and Sandy Klink, who keeps me within the borders; and Roger Scholl of The Putnam Publishing Group, who has been patient and gentle when giving me directions!

If you have a hint you would like to share with me, don't hesitate to write to me at the address below. However, because of the volume of mail I receive, not every letter can be answered personally.

Heloise
P.O. Box 79500
San Antonio, TX 78279

—Heloise

To Mr. Thurston Twigg-Smith, President and Publisher, and Mr. Buck Buchwach, Executive Editor of the *Honolulu Advertiser,* who over 30 years ago gave my mother, the original Heloise, a chance to start her column. Also to my dear, wonderful father, Mike Cruse, who told her she could do it, gave her emotional and business support, and to this day helps me run the office.

Thank you, gentlemen.

—Heloise

CONTENTS

CHAPTER 5. PLANTS AND YARD CARE   155

CONTENTS ————————————————————— *17*

CHAPTER 13.   LEAVING THE HOME
                 BEHIND   367

INTRODUCTION

When the "Hints from Heloise" newspaper column began thirty years ago, one mention of using cocoa butter to help heal a minor burn or using boric acid to rid your house of roaches caused a "run" on these items in drugstores. The reader reaction is the same today. Every time I mention using white iodine to strengthen fingernails, my pharmacist asks me to please let him know about it ahead of time, because he just can't keep it on the shelves. So, although the column has spanned several decades, Heloise fans are still as loyal and numerous as ever, if not more so!

The fan of thirty years ago was a "housewife," but today's fan is anyone, young or old, male or female, whose life-style demands saving time, money, and energy.

When my mother began this column thirty years ago, one of her carpet cleaning hints came from the Orient, where she lived with my military-career father. Some of her Chinese friends showed her how they cleaned their carpets by rubbing them with the cut side of cabbages which had been chopped in half. Yes, it works, but you need a ton of cabbages!

As the Heloise fans grew to the millions, Mother's kitchen cupboards became famous, for they had been rendered nearly paintless from testing so many readers' cleaning solution hints. My jeans and sneakers were always game for testing reader hints; most worked but some were disasters!

I grew up with Heloise hints, as did most of America, and this is certain: Although the times, the hints, and the fans may have changed, the need for hints is greater than ever before. The sources of information for hints have evolved, so I have to consult with experts in a wide range of fields, major manufacturers, government agencies, and consumer information services.

For example, I can't suggest rubbing carpets with cabbages anymore. While most people had wool carpets thirty years ago, today's carpets are into second and third generations of improved man-made fibers and blends of fibers, and each has its own peculiarities.

I don't test cleaning hints on my cupboards. With the vast selection of paints, varnishes, and other finishes used today, my only recourse, if I'm to provide valid Heloise hints, is to call a paint and varnish research facility or a professional association to find out what cleaning preparation will work on which surface.

Just as the way we keep house has changed, the keepers of houses have changed. People who used to run vacuum cleaners and mixers are using microwave ovens and computers. Instead of just watching our television sets, we tape and view movies with our VCRs.

Throughout this new Heloise hints book, you'll find that tips on dealing with the new products and technology that are a part of our homes and life-styles have been included, along with some of the classic Heloise helps readers have enjoyed for thirty years.

Our homes are filled with hi-tech electronics that help us live well if we use them efficiently, but hi-tech has to help us instead of making our lives more complicated.

Perhaps computers are the most prominent of the new hi-tech electronics in American homes. Adults who didn't learn about computers in school have been pushed into the computer age by their jobs. Many adults learn about computers from their children, who view them as ordinary classroom equipment, on the same level with the pencils and Big Chief tablets their parents used in "the olden days." Most of us who work on computers don't care about their inner workings; we just want to know how we can get the most use from them. We don't need information overload—when you ask somebody for the time, you don't want an explanation of how a watch works. I've attempted to include a wide variety of advice and suggestions on how you can use your home computer, if you own one, to help in the organizing and running of daily life—from grocery lists and menu planning to record keeping and more.

In fact, the "Hints from Heloise" column and this book are produced on computers and the copy is circulated via modem to computers in three cities: San Antonio, where I have my office; New Orleans, where my research editor, Marcy Meffert, lives; and New York, where my King Features editors, Merry Clark and Sandy Klink, work. We will share what we've learned about juggling computer data later in the book.

As we approach the 1990s, over 55 percent of today's women work outside as well as in their homes. For these women, time is more valuable than money. They aren't likely to recycle such things as egg cartons, aluminum foil, and other containers, nor do many of them sew or spend most of their time cooking or cleaning. (I should note that when the Heloise column began, aluminum foil was a new, wonderful household aid!) Today's busy part-time homemakers haven't the time, energy, or desire to do the "extraordinary" tasks accomplished by full-time homemakers.

Whether or not we personally approve of these changes, we can't escape reality; changes have occurred and are here to stay. Women are making choices, and whether we are full-time or part-time homemakers we must respect those choices. Also, we have to recognize that for those who work outside the home, household chores are often shared with spouses, children, roommates, and hired help.

While those who stay home may seem to have the time to do it all, they need help too. A big Heloise hug to the unsung heroes who also contribute their time and energy outside the home, volunteering time to their communities and getting paid in thank-you certificates and plaques instead of money.

Whether they work for money or thank-yous, working women need help, and not all of them are getting it. *Working Mother* magazine (February 1988 issue) reported on a survey that revealed that few of the 2,811 women interviewed got regular help from spouses or children. Of these women, 77 percent prepared dinner and 64 percent cleaned up afterwards without help. Only 17 percent of husbands, 6 percent of eldest daughters, and 5 percent of eldest sons cleaned up after dinner as a regular chore. Of these women, 92 percent did laundry regularly and only 25 percent had children or husbands who regularly did laundry. Some children are being recruited for housework; this magazine survey revealed that eight-year-olds were using microwave ovens and vacuum cleaners and eleven- and twelve-year-olds were using washers and dryers. A Johnson's Wax survey of 1,409 households revealed that women still do about 84 percent of the housecleaning and that women, ages twenty-five to forty-four, spend about 6.8 hours a week on housework, while men spend only 2.4 hours a week doing housework.

You don't need any more numbers to see why so many women feel tired, overworked, and underappreciated. Getting rid of that tired, worn-out excuse "I don't know how" is the best way to get help and therefore have more time "to smell the daisies."

Which brings me to the reason for writing this new Heloise hints book. In addition to tips on how to do things better, more quickly, and more economically, you'll find that some of the information in this book is very basic, such as how to iron or what exactly to do when cleaning a room.

I'm hoping that whoever is in charge of running the household—and not all the in-charge people are women—will be able to use this book when writing notes to household helpers—for example, "Please start [the laundry, supper, cleaning the bathrooms, etc.]. See page _____ in *All-New Hints from Heloise.*" The pages to use for a particular job can be paper-clipped and the specific way of doing a chore can be highlighted so that the helper knows exactly what to do.

I hope the in-charge person will make a copy of the stain removal section, then thumbtack it to the wall above the washer so that all members of the household can get their own stains out before the stains have set. A copy of the room cleaning steps can be tacked on a bedroom door.

Now, we all know that not everyone lives in the so-called nuclear family with two parents and 1.7 or 2.5 children, a dog, two cats, and a bowl of fish or cage of gerbils. Many men and women are choosing to remain single or marry much later in life. *Over 50* magazine, for example, reports that twenty-two million people over fifty live alone by choice. This book will help people who are on their own for the first time, whether they are students, formerly married people, or others who have been previously uninvolved with the responsibilities of caring for themselves.

The housekeeping priorities for people who don't live in a nuclear family differ from those who do. Moreover, as a result of changing priorities, lifestyles have changed. People whose moms slaved for hours in the kitchen to entertain guests are likely to serve some store-bought deli treat—before they go out to a restaurant dinner. The emphasis in entertaining has shifted to one of expediency and convenience.

"Priority" is a major buzzword today. In a sense, my hints have always been about priorities. Do you want to spend your time cleaning the bathroom tiles with a toothbrush? Or would you rather visit a friend or read a book? You make the choice; you set your own priorities.

"Clean" to some people means uncluttered; to others, it's totally and antiseptically spotless and shining. To still others, "clean" is a four-letter word, something to be avoided whenever possible.

When I travel throughout the country, people often teach me new words. For example, in the northeastern part of the United States, some people use a very descriptive word for the kind of frantic cleanup that goes on in a house between the time you see someone walking toward your door and the time that person rings your doorbell. The word is "scurryfunge." In some areas they "red up the house," meaning "ready up the house for company."

Most of us don't feel the need to present an aura of super cleanliness to anyone anymore. Much of the time, we're just too tired to "scurry," but every now and then we do "funge," whether we "red up the house" for company or just for ourselves.

Doing a funge may be a constructive solution when we've had a really bad, problem-filled week and need to vent our frustrations upon something. Dirt bashing is always a good way to work off some steam (which, by the way, cleans and presses things well).

The point is that we spend less time cleaning and more time in other areas of our so-often busy lives. Cleaning can be done as it is needed, and each person's level of what is "clean" is different. One benefit of my new book is that everyone can take exactly what he or she needs—and skip what doesn't fit into today's busy schedule.

I know my mother would like this book and the new "into the 1990s" approach I've begun to take in the "Hints from Heloise" column, because she was always looking for ways to make all chores easier and life more pleasant.

I just know she is up there on a cloud of nylon net smiling, because angels' wings really are made of nylon net!

CHAPTER 1

Saving Time in the Kitchen

Family Kitchens

The kitchen has been called "the heart of the home" because for most families it's the center for nourishment of both soul and body.

Some of the best communication between friends and family occurs when people work together on meal preparation and even on cleanup, neither of which is a chore when it's shared.

People who remember the days before dishwashers remember that washing and drying dishes was an opportunity for the "washer" and the "dryer" to talk, maybe not about important things, but to make the kind of small talk that binds people together.

Have you ever noticed at parties that a lot of the fun and real getting-to-know-people goes on in the kitchen?

When we designed our home, we designed the kitchen to have the traffic pattern of people flow and to be large enough so that we could entertain in the kitchen. Even the center island is larger than normal—it's about 5 feet by 6 feet and 41 to 42 inches high, which makes it leaning height—so I can put out chips and dip, and people are comfortable in the kitchen.

How many children do their homework at the kitchen table while one of their parents fixes dinner? And how many kitchen tables have been the scene of such happy family memories as coloring Easter eggs, making Christmas cookies, and the best unifier of families, a daily meal together in which events of everyone's day are shared?

Many people, including me, have desks or work areas in their kitchens to make household planning and management convenient, and it sure seems more pleasant. A lot of people also use their kitchen tables as home offices. I'm known to do some of my best work right here.

Whatever goes on in your kitchen, I know that the hints gathered for this chapter will help you to spend less time on chores and more time on pleasant kitchen activities.

Appliances

They slice, dice, chop, stir, wash, dry, clean, cool, heat; and, like the human helpers in our lives, appliances need some TLC (tender, loving care).

We keep our human helpers going by saying "please" and "thank you" and "You sure did a good job." We keep our appliances going with maintenance. And, just as some humans need more encouragement than others, some appliances need more pleases and thank-yous than others.

The most important tip I can give you about all appliances is to read the booklet that comes with each appliance.

Manufacturers spend a lot of money researching and developing their products and they provide printed materials with them so that you will know how to properly use and trouble-shoot these products. You paid for the research and development and the resulting booklets when you paid for the appliance, so you might as well get your money's worth by at least glancing through the instruction and help booklets.

• Put appliance instruction booklets, guarantees, and warranties in a three-ring binder or accordion folder, or assign one special drawer in the kitchen for them. Keep the instruction booklets, guarantees, and warranties for all of your appliances in one place so that you can get them easily.

In the following table, I've listed the appliance; then the average number of years it can be expected to function; and then, in parentheses, the low and high numbers of years the appliance functions. These life expectancies are based on the first owner's length of use time and don't necessarily mean that the appliance is worn out.

• If your brand of appliance has not lasted as long as the average, you may want to buy a different brand the next time. And, naturally, if your brand has lasted longer than the average, you'll surely want to buy the same brand next time.

• If your appliance conks out at an age that is near the maximum, it may be more economical to buy a new one than to have it repaired—most likely over and over again, until you've spent enough money to have bought a new appliance.

Here are, according to appliance, the average, minimum, and maximum life expectancies (in years):

APPLIANCE LIFE EXPECTANCIES

Appliance	*Average*	*Minimum*	*Maximum*
Air conditioner (room)	11	8	14
Blanket (electric)	8	7	10
Can opener (electric)	7	5	10
Charcoal grill (outdoor)	6	3	9
Clock (electric)	8	5	10
Clothes washer	12	9	14
Compact hi-fi system	6	5	7
Corn popper	5	4	7
Desk calculator	7	5	10
Dishwasher	11	8	14
Dryer			
Electric clothes dryer	13	11	16
Gas clothes dryer	14	12	16
Electric fan	16	11	22
Fax machine	8	7	10
Floor polisher	11	4	13
Furnace			
Electric furnace	18	15	22
Gas furnace	16	13	20
Garbage disposal	10	7	12
Hair dryer	4	2	6
Home-security alarm system	14	10	17
Humidifier	8	6	11
Ice-cream maker (electric)	9	7	10
Iron	9	6	12
Lawn mower (power)	8	5	10
Microwave oven	11	10	14

APPLIANCE LIFE EXPECTANCIES (*Continued*)

Appliance	*Average*	*Minimum*	*Maximum*
Percolator (electric)	6	5	9
Personal computer	6	5	10
Range			
Electric range	15	13	19
Gas range	15	11	18
Refrigerator	13	11	18
Shaver (electric)	4	3	5
Smoke detector	10	8	15
Styling comb (electric)	4	3	5
Telephone answering machine	5	3	5
Television (color)	8	6	10
Television (projection)	7	5	7
Toaster	8	5	9
Toothbrush (electric)	3	1	3
Trash compactor	10	8	13
Typewriter (electric)	8	7	9
Vacuum cleaner	11	4	12
Videocassette recorder	7	6	8
Waffle iron	10	5	11
Water heater			
Electric water heater	12	8	17
Gas water heater	10	5	13
Snow thrower	10	6	12

Dish-Washing

Dishwasher Efficiency

• To get maximum dishwasher efficiency, start by choosing the right detergent. Shake the box of powdered detergent; if you can't hear the granules rattling inside, don't buy it. Lumpy dishwasher detergent won't dissolve well enough to do its job.

• Find a better place to store detergent than under the kitchen sink, where it's moist and warm—it is the worst place to store powdered dishwasher detergent.

• If you find that the larger box of the powdered dishwasher detergent does get lumpy, you might want to consider buying smaller boxes, because you'll use them up more quickly and they won't go bad.

Getting Sparkling Clean Dishes and Glassware

If you follow the directions in the booklet that came with your dishwasher and you still get enough film and water spots to feel like you're in a TV detergent commercial, it's probably because the water isn't hot enough.

Some machines have built-in "boosters" that heat the water when it's in the machine; if yours does not have a booster, here are some tips:

• To test if your hot water is hot enough to dissolve dishwasher detergent and help your dishwasher do its job, run hot water in your sink until it's the hottest it can get. Then, fill a tall glass and put a tablespoon of dishwasher detergent in. If the detergent dissolves before it gets to the bottom, the water is hot enough.

• DO let the water run from the faucet until it's hot before you run the dishwasher. Keep the water heater setting at 120 degrees Fahrenheit. If the heater is set for 140 to 160 degrees, the water is too hot; children and even adults have been scalded by hot bath water, often with serious consequences.

• DON'T run the dishwasher while the washing machine is running and during or after baths unless you have more than one water heater. (Running the dishwasher—clothes washer too—during baths in homes with limited water pressure can be harmful to the health of relationships. Nobody wants cold water to suddenly spew out on a shampoo-lathered head! Also, fluctuating hot water flows can burn if the hapless bather adjusts the shower to the hot water flow during the washer's fill cycle.)

• DO try different detergents. Some people may get better results with the new, thick liquid dishwasher detergents. Also, different brands of detergent seem to work better in one part of the country than another because of variances in water hardness. The one Mom used when you were home may not work in the city you live in. Use your coupons to try the smallest size of a new brand to see which works best in your area.

• If you have softened water, don't forget to use less than the full recommended amount of detergent. Using too much detergent can etch your glasses, causing them to look cloudy and "dirty," and nothing will make them clear again.

• Glasses will also become etched from improper loading or overloading of the dishwasher, a blocked filter, a spray arm that doesn't move as it should, or any other situation that prevents water from adequate washing and rinsing. If the proper water action is blocked, detergent will remain on the glassware too long and will not rinse off completely, thereby etching your glassware. I wash and dry my best crystal by hand. It takes only a few seconds to do this.

• However, if your glasses are cloudy because of hard water buildup, soak them in warm vinegar, then try to wash off the cloudy part. (Read on to find the two-step method for cleaning the dishwasher and its contents.)

• If you have an older-model dishwasher, you may need to rinse the dishes well before loading them.

• Starchy foods such as rice seem to cause the most trouble if you don't rinse dishes before loading the dishwasher. Also, dishwasher efficiency depends upon how long you've let food dry on the dishes.

• DO check your dishwasher filter regularly (if your model has one) and keep it clean. The cleaner the filter, the cleaner the dishes. If the filter is dirty, food particles will recirculate over your clean dishes.

• Also, check the bottom of the dishwasher door if you have a front-loading dishwasher. Use a wadded paper towel or thick sponge to protect your hands when you wipe this area because some dishwasher doors have sharp bottom edges. And, I've found broken glass and even a missing spoon!

You will be surprised at the gunk (mostly hardened fats and oils) that accumulates here. It is more likely to accumulate when the dishwater isn't hot enough and can ultimately damage the seal in some washers.

• If you rinse all of your dishes before loading, you'll surely have family members confused about whether dishes in the dishwasher are clean or dirty. One good signal is to put one cup right side up when you load the dishwasher. This cup will get filled with water during the cycle and you'll know that the dishwasher has been run.

• Some people like to put magnets on the front with little notes that say, "Wash me" or "I'm washed." Some of the new models have green lights that glow if the dishwasher has gone through its cycle.

Cleaning Your Dishwasher

Wait! Don't skip this section because you think this is a useless chore or a chore to totally avoid.

Often the reason your dishwasher won't clean properly is that it needs a cleaning beyond its own self-washing. Also, sometimes a real ogre of a landlord who's determined to keep your apartment damage deposit will have one less point to pick on if you put a sparkle on the appliances. Sparkling appliances help sell your house, too.

• Dishwasher stains can be removed by wetting the stains and sprinkling instant powdered orange breakfast drink or powdered lemon drink on them. The citric acid removes the stain. Let it stand for at least one hour.

Then, wipe a bit off to see if the stain has disappeared. If it has, load the dishwasher; add the dishwasher detergent, and let it run through the cycle.

• An easy way to clean the entire dishwasher, if it looks generally grungy, is to put citric acid or powdered orange or lemon drink in the detergent cup and let the washer run through its normal cycle.

• Here's a two-step method to get the dishwasher and its contents clean and sparkling.

CAUTION: Never combine the bleach and vinegar for a one-step process. It's dangerous! Also, DO NOT put gold-trimmed dishes, glassware, or silverware in the dishwasher when you use this process, because it damages such trim and objects.

Step one: Pour one cup of bleach into a bowl and set the bowl on the bottom rack of the dishwasher. Run it through the "wash" cycle only. Do not dry. If your dishwasher can't be stopped after a cycle, then punch the "cancel drain" button.

Step two: Fill the bowl again, this time with one cup of vinegar. Let the dishwasher run through the entire cycle this time.

Your dishes will be sparkling clean, and the discolorations, film, and mineral buildup on the interior of your dishwasher should have disappeared; if not, repeat steps one and two.

Trouble-Shooting

• Before you call a repairman to fix an improperly working dishwasher, check the following:

Has the circuit breaker tripped or a fuse blown?

Is the water hot enough? Check the temperature on your water heater.

Make sure the filter-strainer is clean.

Washing Dishes by Hand

Some things just don't go into the dishwasher. Also, not everyone has a dishwasher that operates on electricity. Some "dishwashers" are run by human energy.

• Dip washed dishes in a vinegar water bath to rinse them clean.

• To help protect your fine crystal, line the sink with a thick dish towel or washcloth. Be sure to wear rubber gloves, because you can rinse glasses with hotter water that way, which means they dry faster.

• If you spray glass baking dishes with oven cleaner, let them stand for about 30 minutes; you'll get the burned-on grease off and have sparkling clean dishes again. This is especially important if the glass dishes are used with silver holders, where burned-on gunk looks doubly bad.

• Soak dishes and pans with dried egg or milk in cold water. Hot water actually cooks these foods onto their containers and makes cleaning more work.

• Soak gunky dishes in hot, soapy water as you are preparing a meal for family or guests and you won't have as much scraping to do during the final cleanup. Just fill the sink with water and then add utensils, pots, and dishes as you finish with them.

• CAUTION: Never drop knives into a sink full of dishwater, because you might cut your hand while you're groping around for dishes.

• If you have lost something in the dishwater, use a drinking glass to peer through the suds to see what's in the bottom of the sink.

• If you break a glass, let the water drain out and use a paper towel to retrieve it so you don't cut your hand.

• Have an extra sink strainer handy to accommodate the extra dishes you use when you have company. If you have people drying dishes as you wash, you can put one strainer on each side of the sink and ease the traffic congestion in the kitchen. (With two strainers, you can also give the more fragile pieces to the more careful dish dryers, especially if you have children helping you!)

• Make a spare strainer and avoid clutter in your cupboards: Cover several layers of newspaper with a clean towel; the newspaper will absorb the dripping water and keep it from flowing across your countertops.

• If you are washing stacks of dishes, put the whole stack into the dishwater at one time so that the bottom ones soak while you swish off the top ones. This is much easier than putting a stack of dishes beside the sink and putting dishes one at a time into the dishwater for washing.

Refrigerator and Freezer Care

Sometimes we take our appliances for granted, but can you imagine life now without a refrigerator or freezer?

Like our other appliances, refrigerators and freezers have lives of their own. And, if we are to keep them in good shape, we have to take time to properly care for them.

Cleaning and Defrosting Refrigerators and Freezers

• CAUTION: Be sure you unplug the refrigerator before doing any major cleaning.

• When junk and lint collect under the refrigerator, simply attach an old stocking or nylon net to the end of a yardstick or broom handle with a rubber band. Carefully slip it under the refrigerator and move the stick from side to side. If you don't do this regularly, get ready for a shock the first time a repair person moves your appliance from its usual spot. Accumulated dust and dirt can interfere with the air circulation around, and therefore the self-cooling system of, the coils and motor; you can also use your vacuum cleaner to pull the dust off from the bottom front of the refrigerator coils.

• DO pull out the refrigerator/freezer at least three or four times a year so that you can scrub the floor and vacuum the condenser coils at the back and bottom of the appliance. More expensive refrigerators may have the back coils enclosed within their walls, but they still need cleaning underneath.

• DON'T forget the inside of the refrigerator and freezer. The best time to clean the interior is the day the trash is being picked up and before you go grocery shopping.

• When you wash and rinse frost-free or automatic-defrost refrigerator parts, you can use hot, sudsy water and hot rinse water on metal and porcelain parts, but since plastic and glass can crack from sudden changes in temperature, use lukewarm water for washing and rinsing these parts.

• Don't use strong-scented detergents for washing plastic refrigerator/freezer parts, because they may retain the odors.

• Defrost refrigerators or freezing compartments when frost buildup is about one-fourth inch thick. Cooling efficiency decreases when frost buildup is greater than a quarter of an inch, and energy use increases because the engine runs more.

• Keep the food you've removed from the freezer in a cooler or in a laundry basket lined with newspapers. Cover the laundry basket with more newspapers and put ice cubes on top. Or line your kitchen sink with newspapers. Place the frozen food there and top it with newspapers to help insulate it.

• CAUTION: Never poke at ice with an ice pick, because you could puncture the coils.

• Also, if you use one of those electric defrosters, be careful to keep it away from plastic meat trays or the freezer door, because the heat can melt plastics.

• Wipe out the freezer with detergent, borax, or baking soda solution, then rinse and wipe dry. Then set the controls and plug it in again. (You unplugged the fridge/freezer for defrosting, right?)

• Prevent frost buildup by not overloading refrigerators and by opening the door as seldom as possible, especially in hot weather.

• Covering all cooked foods and liquids not only prevents spills and transfer of odors to other foods but helps prevent humidity buildup.

• Door gaskets that are clean last longer. Always wipe the door gasket with borax or baking soda solution only. Strong detergents or bleach can cause deterioration and result in a bad seal.

• Test your refrigerator door seals by closing the door over a piece of paper or a dollar bill so that it's half in and half out of the appliance. If you can pull the paper or bill out easily, the seal may need replacing, or the latch, if there is one, may need adjusting.

• The painted metal exterior of refrigerators and freezers should be cleaned with mild detergent or appliance polish only. Strong spray-on–wipe-off cleaners tend to ultimately remove the paint from metal.

Storing Food in the Refrigerator

• I like to save various sizes of jars and buy clear plastic containers on sale to use for storing my leftovers; it helps everyone see what's there. I try to keep them in the front and always on the same shelf so that I can have easy access to them and they don't get lost when somebody does the refrigerator shuffle. (The refrigerator shuffle is a dance some people do during the TV commercial go-get-a-snack break.)

• I've developed a system of keeping certain things in the door shelves, and using certain shelves like assigned parking spaces for specific foods. For example, the dairy products, such as milk, yogurt, and cheese, are kept on the top shelf, leftovers are kept on the second shelf, and so on.

• If you find food way in the back of the refrigerator that's grown "hairy and green" and has left a terrible odor in the refrigerator, you can freshen the fridge by washing it with a mixture of one tablespoon of baking soda to the wash water. For a wonderful aroma add some lemon extract or a teaspoon of vanilla in clean water, then wipe the interior thoroughly.

• Always keep baking soda or a cup of fresh charcoal in the back of the refrigerator to keep it smelling fresh and clean. When you move and expect to have your refrigerator/freezer closed up for several days on a van or in storage, tossing in a handful of baking soda, charcoal, or unused ground coffee in a cloth bag (or knotted knee-high or pantyhose leg) will prevent your being greeted by a musty odor the first time you open your appliance. (This is a favorite among military families, whose appliances are frequently in storage while they go to new stateside or overseas duty stations.)

Cleaning Kitchen Ranges

Continuous-Cleaning and Self-Cleaning Ovens

Let's face it, if 10 is the highest rating on your Fun Things to Do Chart, cleaning the oven is rated at best a −93, but somebody's gotta do it.

However, this most dreaded chore has been made much less horrible and even bearable by "continuous-cleaning" and "self-cleaning" ovens. Whether you have either of these or a standard oven, like it or not, your oven has to be cleaned, if only to prevent oven grease fires or the unpleasantness of filling your oven and house with smoke and spoiling the flavor of whatever you're cooking. Also, if the oven and its thermostat are covered with baked-on grease, the thermostat may not accurately determine the oven's temperature.

Many people are confused by the difference between continuous-cleaning and self-cleaning ovens.

• A self-cleaning oven provides for the removal of soil during a separate high-heat cycle. This means you have to set the cycle for cleaning when needed.

• A continuous-cleaning oven gradually reduces oven soil on a specially treated surface to a "presentable" clean condition during normal baking or broiling operations. Each time you cook, the oven burns off dirt and grease. You'll need to clean up large spills to keep the oven looking good.

• NEVER use any kind of cleaning aid in a continuous-cleaning or self-cleaning oven. The finish will be removed. Once that happens, the oven will no longer clean itself. Do all wiping up with ordinary detergent and water or window cleaner.

• In self-cleaning ovens, use a plain water–dampened sponge or paper towel to wipe up the ash that remains in the bottom after the cleaning process has finished.

• If you choose to clean the oven racks in a self-cleaning oven cycle, be prepared to have them become discolored and dull finished. If the appearance of the oven racks is of no importance to you, you can clean them in the oven. Some stove booklets instruct you to wipe the sides of the racks and the grooves in which the racks slide with salad oil after cleaning so that the racks will slide more easily without scratching the oven walls.

• The racks will not come clean in some ovens. To clean them, take them outside, if possible, put them in a large heavy-duty plastic trash bag and spray them with an oven cleaner or ammonia. Then, close it tight. You can clean your racks in the bathtub with this method, but make doubly sure the bag is sealed tightly.

No matter where you do the cleaning, keep the racks in the bag overnight. The next day spray them off with a hose and use a steel wool pad to get any hard-to-remove grease spots off. Rinse in the sink or tub with hot water.

CAUTION: ALWAYS turn on the vent and/or open a window to protect yourself from fumes and ALWAYS keep children and pets away from such cleaning projects!

• Many people try to experiment with cleaning other greasy kitchen things in the oven during the self-cleaning cycle. Remember that these ovens get as high as 500 degrees Fahrenheit and sustain that temperature for more than an hour. A friend of mine tried to clean greasy barbecue grill lava briquets during the cycle. The result was an oven full of flaming grease to contend with. Fortunately for her, the rush of air into the oven when she opened the oven door (to spray the fire with a kitchen extinguisher) put the fire out.

• When you are dealing with extreme temperatures and strong chemicals, follow the directions given for them to the letter and don't get too creative. You may get results you haven't bargained for!

Cleaning Standard Ovens

Manufacturers recommend cleaning this type of oven with a commercial oven cleaner. You must be very careful using these, because most of them contain lye and nitrogen compounds, which can cause burns.

• When you use oven cleaners, be sure to wear rubber gloves and have plenty of circulating fresh air. The fumes are dangerous to inhale; keep children and pets away from the area. To be on the safe side, protect yourself by wearing a face mask or at least eyeglasses.

• Don't spray near any electrical connections, heating elements, or the thermostat.

• Try not to spray on an unprotected hot (because of being lit) oven light bulb; the bulb may shatter.

• If your oven isn't too grimy, try baking soda. Sprinkle some on a damp cloth and scrub.

• The best advice is to clean up any spill as it happens. It is easier to clean one layer of gunk than several old, hard-as-asphalt layers.

• You can get most of the burned food off if you pour some salt on the spill; allow the oven to cool; wipe clean.

• To prevent further spillovers when baking "bubbly" things, put a sheet of heavy aluminum foil or a cookie sheet in the bottom of the oven. If you have an electric oven, you must place the aluminum foil under the heating coils. Cover food when possible and cook at the lowest temperature to prevent splattering.

Cleaning Range Tops

Keeping range-top burners and reflectors clean makes them reflect heat more efficiently, saving energy.

• Sponge range-top surfaces with hot water and let dry. Stainless-steel surfaces should be towel-dried to prevent water spots. Harsh scouring powders will scratch chrome, so use metal polishes made especially for chromium and soft metals when you need to do serious cleaning (more than a wipe-up).

• To keep the stainless steel surface really sparkling and shiny, clean it with a window cleaner or full-strength vinegar, or with a dab of ammonia on a sponge. Or, to really cheat, put a little cooking oil on a paper towel and wipe over all surfaces, then polish.

• Electric coil units are self-cleaning; they burn off spills when turned on high heat. But turn on the vents and open windows when you do this, even if it's just for a few minutes.

• Gas burners, drip trays, burner rims, and other removable parts of the range top can be soaked in strong detergent solutions such as one half to one cup of laundry or dishwasher detergent added to a gallon of hot water and dissolved. Rinse well after soaking and dry with a towel.

• CAUTION: Gas burners must be drained and dried before you replace them so that residual water will not divert the flow of gas.

• To thoroughly dry the gas burner, use a hand-held hair dryer on high to get to any places you can't reach so that you remove all moisture.

Microwave Ovens

Isn't it great that in this world of hurry, rush, and hurry again, it no longer takes hours to prepare meals?

While microwave ovens don't completely replace conventional ovens and range tops, they certainly make life easier.

• Cooking times vary according to the wattage. For example, the lower the wattage, the more slowly the food cooks. If you're not sure of your microwave oven's wattage, here's a simple test.

Put ice in a two-cup measure and add one cup of water. Stir for about two minutes or until the ice stops melting and the water is very cold. (Your objective is to have extremely icy, the coldest possible, water without actually using ice itself.) Remove the ice and put the cold water into a one-cup microwave-safe glass measure. Put it in the microwave oven uncovered, on the high setting, until the water begins to boil.

If your oven has 600 to 700 wattage, the water will boil in less than 3 ½ minutes. If it takes 3 ½ to 4 ½ minutes to boil, the wattage output is 500 to 600 watts. If it takes longer than 4 ½ minutes, the wattage output is less than 500 watts.

• Use the temperature and time for the meal you're preparing suggested in the cookbook that comes with your microwave oven. The manufacturers know what they are talking about. They have tested and tested these recipes to get the right times and temperatures for specific food portions—why not use their research?

Microwave Oven Utensils

Many wonderful microwave-safe glass, plastic, and ceramic dishes and utensils are made specifically for the microwave oven, and using paper plates and towels diverts even more kitchen time to personal "put your feet up and rest" time, because it eliminates cleanup.

Some people think that any container that is not metal may safely be used in the microwave oven, but this is not true.

For example, if, when you heat water in a mug for tea or instant coffee, the handle becomes too hot to hold, the mug is probably not recommended for a microwave oven. You can boil water, as I do, in a microwave-safe glass measuring cup. The handle doesn't get hot even when the water is still bubble-boiling in the measuring cup.

• Here's a test from the Association of Home Appliance Manufacturers to determine if a dish is microwave-safe:

Place a glass measuring cup of water next to the empty dish to be tested. (Never metal or gold-trimmed dishes!) Heat on full power for one minute, then check the temperature of the dish.

If the dish is cool and the water very warm, the dish can be used. If the dish is slightly warm, it can be used for short-term cooking only. If the dish is hot and the water is cool, do not use the dish. A hot dish means that the utensil is absorbing the rays instead of permitting them to pass through, as they should for safe cooking.

• Certain plastic containers and dishes cannot be used. For example, the foam trays on which meat is sold at the store and fast food containers will melt at high temperatures.

• Never use dishes with gold or silver trim or trademark signatures on the bottom (metallic); it may cause arcing (sparks) and discoloring, and the dishes may break.

Arcing occurs when an electric current flows from the microwave wall to the metal in the oven. It causes a popping sound and a light flash that could damage the microwave oven.

• Some instruction booklets say that you should NEVER use glass jars, not even canning jars, which withstand high temperatures, because they can break due to microwave action on the curved edge at the top of the jar. I have not had this happen, but perhaps it's better to be safe than sorry, as the old saying goes, and to use another container for heating things.

• CAUTION: If you heat babies' bottles in the microwave oven, always shake the bottle after heating to mix well. You must always test a few drops on the inside of your wrist to feel the temperature. The bottle may feel only warm on the outside, but the milk on the inside may be scalding hot.

• ALWAYS remove all lids carefully by first tilting them with the open side AWAY from your face; escaping steam burns skin. Position your hands so that they are not burned by steam or spillovers. Be especially cautious when you've put plastic wrap over a dish or container; always open the wrap so that steam escapes away from your face or, for that matter, away from anyone who is watching you cook.

• When you boil water for cocoa, tea, or instant coffee in the cup from which you'll drink it, be aware that stirring or dropping in a tea bag can cause the water to bubble over the edge of the cup if the microwaves are still active in the water. The water is less likely to bubble over if you wait a few seconds before making your beverage.

• Be careful not to run the microwave oven with the tea bag in it. I know of one case where the metal staple in the teabag ruined the microwave oven.

• Always place larger, thicker pieces of food to the outside of the container and smaller, thinner pieces toward the center. Using round plates and baking dishes will make you do this automatically.

• When placing several dishes in a microwave oven at the same time, place one dish in the center and all the other dishes around it.

• If your microwave oven doesn't have a built-in rotator, be sure to rotate and stir the food often, or buy one when you find a sale. Rotating the food is often the key to successful cooking.

• Cover the dish with a microwave-safe lid or plastic wrap; it can help promote even cooking by trapping the heat and steam inside.

• As you do with other appliances, it's important to wipe up spills when they occur. The microwave oven surface is easy to clean. If soil doesn't just wipe off, try heating a bowl of water, so that the steam will soften the spills, then wipe clean. Wipe around the door seal, door surface, or frame frequently to maintain a good seal.

• If your microwave oven needs a serious cleaning, put two tablespoons of either lemon juice or baking soda in a cup of water in a microwave-safe four-cup bowl. Let the mixture boil in the microwave oven for about five minutes so that steam condenses on the inside walls of the oven. Then wipe off the walls, inside of the door, and door seals.

I love my microwave oven and experiment with different dishes all the time. I'm sure you will too.

Garbage Disposals

If you own a garbage disposal, you know how they speed cleanup. Here are some tips on keeping that disposal grinding and flushing away for many years.

• ALWAYS run lots of water while using it and for a few seconds after use. This is the most important instruction for using a disposal. My husband, who is a plumbing contractor, has told me that if the garbage disposal ever backs up, it's my fault because I always forget to run a lot of extra water. If you don't run enough water when using your disposal, food waste will back up into the disposal and damage the unit, not to mention clog the plumbing.

Disposal Odors

• Sometimes odors can occur; I call them bad breath in the kitchen. Here's how you can sweeten the disposal.

Fill an ice tray with water with one-half cup of white vinegar added; then freeze. (Don't use that tray for your drinks; mark it.) Put the vinegared ice cubes down the garbage disposal about once a week; they will freshen it and clean the disposal and clean off the blades as well.

CAUTION: Be sure your disposal is of a good, sturdy quality if you do this. The less expensive brands may not have the capability of chopping up the ice cubes.

• You can also grind orange and lemon rinds to get rid of odors, which is a real time-saver because you were probably going to grind them up just to get rid of them!

• Check the garbage disposal gasket (the rubber piece that fits in the drain hole). If you can remove it, take it out and clean it thoroughly. If not, put on rubber gloves, be sure the disposal has no chance of being turned on, stick your hand down the disposal, and scrub underneath. That will help eliminate a lot of the bad odor.

• If you add other foods when you are grinding up tough, stringy stuff, you won't be as likely to get a garbage jam in the disposal. However, under no circumstances do you put artichoke leaves, asparagus, or very stringy vegetables or food down the garbage disposal. You're only asking for trouble.

• NEVER use hot water while using the disposal, just cold water and plenty of it so that you'll flush the waste all the way down and prevent odors from coming back to haunt your kitchen.

• NEVER use drain cleaners in the disposal, because they may damage it.

• Occasionally, flush the disposal drain by filling up your sink with water and then draining the sink with the disposal running.

CAUTIONS:

• NEVER put your hand or any non-grindable object down the disposal while it is running. Keep the cover on it at all times until ready to use.

• DON'T position your head directly over the disposal when you turn it on. If a knife or spoon or any utensil has fallen into the disposal without your knowledge, turning the disposal on could turn the utensil into a dangerous projectile when the disposal force shoots it out of the opening.

• To unjam a garbage disposal: Look carefully at the disposal. There's usually a red restart button. Press it and then turn the garbage disposal on, and many times this will do the trick. You may have to try this once or twice. If this does not work, place a broom handle or a very sturdy stick into the disposal and turn it counterclockwise to try to unjam the motor. Pull the stick out, run water, flip the switch, and see if that does it.

Appliances

Often the problems we have with appliances result from misuse or lack of cleaning. Here are some hints for best appliance use and care:

• Some appliances such as electric fry pans or roasters may not heat properly when plugged into extension cords. Try plugging such appliances directly into the wall socket.

• CAUTION: Always unplug appliances for cleaning or servicing. Never immerse a whole appliance, and never immerse the electrial components, in water unless the manufacturer specifically states you can do so.

• Coffee percolator stems can get clogged, effecting the ability to perk and affecting the coffee taste. Clean the stem with a small round brush. You can also make a super long cotton swab by wetting the end of a wooden shish-kebab stick and twisting it in a wad of cotton to clean the inside of the stem.

• To avoid coffee grounds from getting into the percolator stem while you fill the basket with coffee, hold your finger over the stem.

• Off-tasting coffee in a drip coffee maker can mean there is too much hard-water mineral deposit accumulating in the brew chamber. To clean a drip coffee maker, run the fullest measure the pot allows of white vinegar through the cycle, followed by a cycle or two of the fullest measure of fresh water. (Some coffee maker brands have you run the vinegar through twice, or have you unplug the coffee maker to make the vinegar work longer. Check your manual for instructions.)

• To avoid wasting vinegar that has been used to clean a coffee maker, collect the filtered vinegar in a coffee pot after it has run through and store it in an empty jar. The vinegar can be used again in cleaning the coffee maker a couple of times. (You can also use the stored vinegar to clean and "sweeten" drains, etc.)

• Avoid having to clean your coffee maker by brewing your coffee with distilled water. This will make for better coffee, too.

• If the tray in the bottom of your toaster is covered with crumbs, the thermostat won't work properly to give your toast the shade of brown you want. Also, crumbs at the bottom of the toaster can catch fire. Usually there is a latch on the bottom of the toaster that pops the tray open so that you can clean it.

• To catch drippings and crumbs in a toaster oven, place a piece of aluminum foil on the bottom of the "catch" tray. (Check the manufacturer's instructions first, however.)

• Quick-clean your blender or food processor by half-filling it with water and adding a drop or two of liquid dishwashing detergent; run it a few seconds, rinse, and let dry.

• If you have a hand-held European-style blender, fill a deep bowl or large glass with water and a dash of liquid detergent, cover, whirr it a few moments, rinse, and let dry.

• Blenders operate best if only two-thirds full. A blender that is too full may not operate at all.

• Never attempt to slice or grate hard frozen cheese or other frozen foods with your food processor or slicer. The processor blades are likely to break.

• Electric can openers need clean cutters to work well. Clean the blade with a scouring pad or scrubber. Or you can use an old toothbrush. Clean blades not only help your opener work more efficiently, they are more sanitary as well.

• Waffle-iron grids can accumulate burned-on grease. To clean metal grids place an ammonia-soaked paper towel or napkin between them, and leave it overnight. Then clean with steel wool. If you have non-stick grids, follow manufacturer's instructions.

• New or recently cleaned grids can stick. Before using them, grease with unsalted fat and preheat thoroughly before pouring on batter.

• If your vacuum cleaner has lost suction, check to see if the bag is too full or if objects are caught in the intake mechanism.

• Use a seam-ripper or a single-edged razor blade to cut across the hairs and threads that get wound around a vacuum cleaner's or carpet sweeper's rotating brush.

Kitchen Cleaning Tips

Countertops

• Never use abrasive cleansers on plastic laminated tops; they scratch and eventually remove the finish. If stains occur, squeeze fresh lemon juice over them; allow the juice to soak about 45 minutes. Then sprinkle baking soda over the lemon juice and rub with a soft cloth.

• A solution of mild dish-washing liquid and water does the daily cleanup job. Just wash, rinse with clear water, and your countertop should look good for a long, long time.

• You can also clean countertops by pouring club soda on the counter and wiping up the soda with a soft cloth. Then rinse with warm water and wipe dry. You can finish the job on dull-finished countertops by polishing the countertops with a plastic laminate cleaner, which gives them a low luster.

• Shiny-finish countertops will stay shiny if you apply lemon oil about once a week and wipe dry. It not only cleans but preserves the finish.

Chopping-Block Countertops

• Tiny knife cuts are natural wear for these tops, because they are made to be cutting surfaces. They must be scrubbed with soap and water. Small crevices can harbor bacteria, so occasionally you may want to disinfect the counter or chopping block with a mild bleach solution (two to three tablespoons of bleach to a quart of water). Rinse well always, and then rejuvenate the surface with a thin coat of mineral oil; let it soak for a half an hour and buff.

• A baking soda scrub will also clean chopping blocks and will also remove stains and some light burn marks. Rinse, then rub with oil as above.

Tile Countertops

Although a lot of people think that the grout between tiles will stain and always look dirty, tile is really easy to keep clean.

• Grout is no problem at all if you seal it with a grout sealer, found in tile stores. Follow the directions on the box. You may have to repeat the process once a year.

• The grout between kitchen tiles can start to look very grungy. You can make a mild bleach solution—two tablespoons to a quart of water—and dab at just the grouting with a cotton swab to bleach out the grout.

• Wash tiles with dish-washing liquid and water or vinegar and water when the they look grimy. You get best results if you scrub tiles with a nylon brush or nylon net. Just wash, rinse, and then step back to admire your handiwork. Then take a break; you deserve it for making your tiles look so great!

• For a quick fix, you can use typewriter correction fluid, which comes in a variety of colors in addition to white. This also works in the bathroom.

• If you've always wanted hand-painted wall tiles, such as those in decorator shops, but can't afford to rip out your old tiles and replace them, try putting decals on your tiles. You can either make a border of decal tiles or make your own design by alternating decal tiles with plain tiles. When you change colors (and then the decals on the tiles), you can buy a decal remover kit where decals are sold.

I have also used decals on bathroom walls. They can be applied to glossy or semi-glossy paint. Three butterflies were applied so that they looked as if they were fluttering across the bathroom toward the window.

• If you have artistic talent or artistic friends, you can use acrylic paints or waterproof markers to draw murals or decorations on your walls. Just be sure the drawing is done with waterproof materials, or you'll have some really "drippy" designs when you wipe off the walls!

I took several colored waterproof markers and drew wispy willow trees on my bathroom walls rather than repainting the whole thing. When I get tired of this, I'll simply spray it with a sealer and paint over it.

Kitchen Sinks

• Stainless-steel sinks should never be cleaned with abrasive cleaners, which will scratch the surface; you'll never be able to get the sink to look good again.

• If you feel you must use a powdered cleanser, be sure to rub WITH the grain of the stainless steel rather than in circles or in the opposite direction.

• To clean stainless steel sinks, use baking soda; even some liquid cleansers may scratch surfaces. ALWAYS read those labels! Just sprinkle some baking soda in the sink and scrub with a damp cloth. Vinegar is great for removing water spots and attacking gunk buildup.

• Wipe the sink dry after each use. To keep the sink shiny or for a hurry-up sparkle, wipe it with a little oil or vinegar on a soft, clean cloth.

• White and light-colored porcelain sinks sometimes need a good whitening treatment to get rid of accumulated stains. Try pouring liquid bleach into the bottom (enough to cover the bottom), then fill the sink with cold water. Let it soak for at least one-half hour. Tell your family what's going on and watch out for children or pets, especially sneaky cats who drink from sinks, so that they won't be accidentally harmed by the bleach.

• Never use any kind of bleach on colored porcelain sinks, because it fades the colors. Clean colored porcelain sinks with mild liquid detergents, baking soda, or vinegar.

• CAUTION: Powdered abrasive cleansers and mild liquid cleansers can still be abrasive enough to wear off the glaze of your kitchen or bathroom sink. This is very important to remember, because once the glaze is gone, your sink will never be shiny again and it will be harder and harder to keep clean.

Pots and Pans

• Aluminum pans can be kept shiny by filling them to the brim with water, adding two tablespoons of cream of tartar, then letting the water boil. The shine comes back in a few minutes.

• To clean a stained aluminum pot "automatically," try cooking tomato sauce in it. The acid brings back the aluminum shine and gets rid of most dark stains. If you have no plans to cook with tomato sauce, you can also clean aluminum pots by adding two tablespoons of white vinegar to boiling water.

• DO NOT use any type of ammonia or bleach-based cleaner on aluminum; it will cause pitting.

Cast-Iron Cookware

Most serious cooks say that cast iron is the best cookware you can use. It may take a little more work to take care of cast iron, but it's worth it. I have several cast-iron pots and skillets that have been passed on to me from my mother. They are more than 60 years old but still cook better than any other skillets I've used.

• Most new cast-iron skillets have been seasoned, but in case you've bought one that has not, here's what to do.

First wash it with sudsy water, then rinse with hot water and dry well. Slather on a thick layer of unsalted vegetable shortening over the inside and outside of both the pot and lid. Cover the pot with the lid, set it on a cookie sheet, and bake it in an oven at 250 degrees Fahrenheit for 1 ½ hours. Swab the grease around occasionally with a dry cloth or paper towel to keep the surface of the pot evenly coated.

After baking the pot allow it to cool, then wipe out any excess grease. Buff to a sheen with a dry, clean cloth or paper towel.

• If you have an old cast-iron skillet that has become rusty, all you need to do is reseason it. First remove all the rust by using a scouring pad, then wash and dry. Season as described above.

• You can season and reseason a cast-iron skillet by using it to deep fry. You'll be boiling the oil into it.

• Never let the skillet soak in soapy water. As soon as you have finished using it and it has cooled, wash it quickly in soap and hot water, using a mild dish-washing liquid, or run lots of hot water on it and scrub with a nylon net scrubber.

• If food particles have become baked on, remove with a nylon scrubber. Never use a harsh cleanser or metal scouring pads, which will scratch the surface.

• Rinse the pan after washing, then place it on the burner on medium high for a few seconds to dry it. Don't keep it on the burner long; if it starts smoking, the seasoning will be removed.

• Rub the pan with a light coating of vegetable oil when it is completely dry and before storing. Place a heavy grocery bag (or paper plate or coffee filters) above and below the pan if you're stacking it in a cupboard.

• Every now and then, you need to clean the grease that gets burned onto your iron skillet and sticks to the bottom and sides like asphalt on a road. Many people simply put the iron skillet into the fire of a barbecue grill after they've finished cooking so that the grease just burns off as the coals burn down and go out. The skillet needs to stay in the hot fire for about an hour.

CAUTION: Don't touch the skillet until you are absolutely sure it has burned off and cooled. And don't try to cool it with cold water; it will crack the iron. After it's cool, reseason the skillet as noted in this section.

It really doesn't take that long to season an iron skillet. Seasoning should be done at least once a year so that your skillet can last you a lifetime and beyond—consider how many of us have inherited iron skillets from our mothers and grandmothers.

• If you haven't been lucky enough to inherit a good cast-iron skillet, buy one at an antique store, flea market, or garage sale, where you can find one that has been cooked in and seasoned for years and years.

Non-Stick Pans

• Never use metal utensils on non-stick surfaces of pots, pans, and other cooking equipment, because they scratch easily. Even when the tags say you can use metal utensils, it's still better to use plastic or wood to save the surfaces from scars.

• Non-stick surfaces are very easy to keep clean; just soak them in hot, sudsy water and clean with a nylon scrubber. DON'T ever use abrasive cleaners, and especially don't use steel wool.

• If you have a heavily soiled or discolored non-stick pan, just fill the pan with water and add two tablespoons of bleach or dishwasher detergent. Simmer the solution in the pan to loosen the crusty stuff.

• CAUTION: DO be very careful not to let non-stick pots and pans burn dry. The fumes can contain a poison that is especially hazardous to babies and small animals, and deadly to pet birds.

• As with anything else, if you take care of your non-stick cookware, it will last a long time.

Enamelware

• Enamelware is usually made with a metal base; the outside and inside may be coated with porcelain enamel, or the outside may have an epoxy enamel, acrylic enamel, or polyurethane finish. This cookware washes well in the dishwasher, but must never be scoured with powders or steel wool. Porcelain enamels may be scratch-resistant, but you shouldn't use any abrasives until you check the manufacturer's directions carefully. Soak pans with burned-on food in water and then scrub with nylon scrubbers.

Glass Cookware

• Commercial cleaners are available for ceramic and glass cookware and ceramic tops on ranges.

• You can get burned-on foods off by soaking the cookware in hot, sudsy water. If you've burned starchy or sugary foods, try adding baking soda to the soak; scrub with more baking soda and a nylon scrubber.

• Burned-on grease can be removed with ammonia.

• Coffee and tea stains will come out if soaked in a solution of two tablespoons liquid chlorine bleach per cup of water or two tablespoons automatic dishwasher detergent to a pot of warm water.

• Mineral deposits on range-top cookware will come off if you boil full-strength vinegar in the pot for about 15 minutes. (Pour this used vinegar down your kitchen drain to clean and sweeten it.)

• CAUTION: Never scrub glass cookware with a highly abrasive cleanser or a steel wool pad, because it can eventually weaken the glass to the point where it will crack if used at too high a temperature.

Cleaning Silver

Sterling silver cries out to be used instead of being hidden in drawers. The tiny scratches that occur naturally when it's used produce what is called the "patina."

• Wash silver in hot, sudsy water, rinse, and buff dry with a soft cloth.

• Sterling silver, except for knives with cemented handles, can be washed in dishwashers.

• Silver plate, which is normally treated just like sterling, should not be washed in the dishwasher.

• Silver gets tarnished faster when it is exposed to eggs, salad dressing, and other foods that contain sulfur. Salt will corrode silver. Infrequently used items can be wrapped in silver cloth (cloth treated with silver nitrate), plastic bags, or plastic wrap. Do not wrap silver with rubber bands—the rubber can discolor the silver.

• Many commercial polishes are available.

CAUTION: Using quick-dip cleaners can eventually permanently damage your silver.

• The following cleaning method is quick but not for all silver pieces and should be used only occasionally.

Place aluminum foil in the bottom of a cooking pot. (Aluminum pots may get darkened if used for this process.) Add enough water to cover the silver pieces. For each quart of water, add one teaspoon of salt and one teaspoon of baking soda. Bring solution to boil. Add silver. Boil two to three minutes or until the tarnish is removed. Remove silver, rinse, and buff dry with a soft cloth.

The quick and easy way that I do this is to put a piece of aluminum foil at the bottom of the kitchen sink, fill the sink with hot, hot tap water, and then do the rest of the procedure.

CAUTION: The above method leaves a dull white luster and removes the dark accents in design crevices, which is usually not desirable. It may also soften the cement of hollow-handled flatware.

Cleaning Tin

Most tin utensils are solid tin. Tin-plated iron items will rust if the plating is worn away by polish. Because unpolished tin absorbs heat better than polished, most tinware is not polished.

• Remove rust by rubbing with 0000 steel wool that has been dipped in mineral or vegetable oil.

For more on cleaning and polishing metal surfaces, see Chapter 3, "In and Around the House."

Cleaning Copper and Brass

Tarnish can be removed with commercial cleaners or with some of the home-made cleaners listed below. Those made with lemon juice or vinegar will give copper and brass a bright finish; the oil and rottenstone cleaner will give these metals a soft luster.

• Saturate a sponge or cloth with vinegar or lemon juice; sprinkle salt on the sponge; and then rub metal, rinse, and dry.

• Rub metal with a paste made by adding flour to the salt and vinegar or lemon juice; rinse; and dry.

• Make a thin paste from rottenstone (an abrasive powder available at hardware stores) and an oil such as cooking or salad oil. Wipe off excess oil after rubbing; polish with a clean cloth.

Home Pest Control

Roach Extermination Formula

• Whenever my roach recipe is published I get an avalanche of mail from people who forgot to clip it from their newspapers. So here it is—you'll never have to clip it again.

It doesn't matter where you live—hot climate or cold—you're bound to find roaches. They are difficult to eliminate, but you can keep control of them using the following boric acid formula. I have found it does a great job, and my readers agree.

ROACH EXTERMINATION FORMULA

¼ cup shortening or bacon drippings
⅛ cup sugar
 8 ounces powdered boric acid
½ cup flour
½ small onion, chopped (optional)
   Enough water to form a soft dough

Mix the shortening and sugar together until they form a creamy mixture. Mix together the boric acid, flour, and onion and add to the sugar and shortening.

Blend well, then add water to form a soft dough. Shape the mixture into small balls or just drop a small amount of it into an opened small plastic sandwich bag.

The mixture will stay soft for a longer period of time if placed in bags. When they harden it's time to replace them.

Variation
I prefer to make a dry mixture that is easy to apply.

Mix powdered boric acid with an equal or larger amount of flour, cornmeal, or sugar. For example: 4 ounces of boric acid mixed with 4 to 8 ounces of sugar, flour, or cornmeal.

Place the boric acid balls or the powdered mixture throughout the house. Put them under your kitchen and bathroom sinks, near the pipes; under the dishwasher, refrigerator, and stove; where you store paper grocery bags and paper goods. Remove your wall plates and sprinkle the mixture behind the outlets. Put some in the garage. Place some under your deck. Put some under your water heater and in the closet.

In short, sprinkle this powder or place dough balls in the out-of-the-way places where roaches like to hide. After they walk through it, they groom themselves and become poisoned.

• When we built our house, I had this formula mixed in large batches and put in between the walls.

• You can buy small quantities of powdered boric acid (4, 8, or 12 ounces) at drugstores, pharmacies, or grocery stores. To buy larger quantities (50 pounds or more), look in the telephone book Yellow Pages under "Chemical Distributors," some of which sell boric acid. (Most commercial products for killing roaches contain boric acid.)

CAUTION: Keep the mixture away from small children and pets. Boric acid can be poisonous if ingested in sufficient quantities. It can cause diarrhea, cramps, and vomiting.

• If your child or pet does swallow some, immediately call your local poison control center for instructions.

• Why not write down the phone number of the poison control center in your area right now! Or, if you have a programmable phone, designate a poison control center button, just as you've programmed a 911 or other emergency button. Teach children to use the emergency numbers (use pictures to identify the numbers for very young children), but make sure they understand that emergency numbers are not for play; emergency phone operators answering joke calls are being taken away from real emergency calls, and children should be taught the seriousness of calling these numbers.

Weevil Extermination

Weevils don't cause as much worry as roaches, but they are just as unwanted in the kitchen.

It's best to keep them from becoming established in your cupboards. As noted in the food storage section (Chapter 2), storing flour, cornmeal, grits, and other grains in jars or sealed plastic bags or containers prevents weevils from migrating from one food package to another.

• Putting newly bought starchy foods into the freezer for at least 7 days or just storing such foods in the freezer or refrigerator is one way to control weevils, because freezing kills larvae.

Here are some old wives' tales that work.

• Sticking in a few dried bay leaves into the flour, cornmeal, and so forth, containers helps repel weevils, and I've found that putting a few sticks of unwrapped spearmint gum on cupboard shelves or sprinkling black pepper where staples are kept discourages weevils, roaches, and other bugs.

• Once weevils have taken up residency in your cupboards, you'll have to take some pretty drastic measures to get rid of them. I've learned that there are 18 different species of weevils, each having its own food preference. Some parts of the country have flying as well as crawly insect invaders, with the corresponding different species.

• Here's how to get rid of weevils and other cabinet invaders. (Warning: This process is a chore if ever there was one!)

First, take everything out of your cabinets and destroy every visibly infested box or bag. You may feel that this is wasteful, but in the long run it's cheaper than continually throwing out infested food.

Be sure to check every single box of staples, including flour, meals, cereals, dried fruits, spices, dry pet food, pasta products, dry beans, peas, etc.

Next, take the boxes in which you have not seen any weevils and put them into the freezer for four days at zero-degree temperature or in an oven at 150 to 160 degrees Fahrenheit for 30 minutes. DO NOT SKIP THIS STEP. Freezing or heating will destroy the weevil eggs, which you cannot see and which will hatch and reinfest your cupboards if they are not destroyed.

The third step is to scrub shelves with hot, sudsy water using a stiff bristled brush and paying special attention to cracks, crevices, and undersides of shelves, where weevils or eggs are likely to be hidden, ready to reinfest everything after you've cleaned up.

Before returning anything to your cabinets, spray shelves, crevices, and cabinet walls with an insecticide that says it kills weevils or whatever unwelcome insects have established a village in your cabinets. Allow cabinet doors to remain closed for three to four hours. The alternative to spraying cabinets is to close up the kitchen, cover all food, get children and pets out of the house, and use a fogger type of insecticide according to directions given on the can.

After doing all of the above, put everything into sealable glass jars before returning foods to the shelves. Glass or clear plastic containers will allow you to see if foods are reinfested and prevent weevils from migrating to other parts of the cabinets.

• My best advice is to buy small quantities of staples—enough for a few weeks—and get into the habit of freezing them before using. Open each food package when you get home from the store and return any infested items (with sales slip) without delay.

• I understand that the small brown "German" roaches often lay their eggs in the grocery store brown paper sack stacks and when they hatch, the babies feed on the glue used in manufacturing paper sacks. Therefore, wherever you store stacks of brown paper grocery sacks, you are likely to have roach infestation.

• See section on gardening and the storage of insecticides (page 162).

I can't emphasize this enough: ALWAYS store chemicals where children and pets can't get to them, and when you throw away used containers of chemicals, bag them carefully so that children and pets can't get at them. We want to avoid tragedies!

Coffee and Tea Beverages

Coffee

Grinding your own coffee beans and creating your own special "house blends" is fun. Freezing coffee (whole beans or ground) in a well-sealed container or zipper bag is a great way to preserve flavor. Also, you can keep various kinds of coffee in the freezer and have different blends every day. I like to mix blends of decaffeinated and caffeinated coffees for a milder brew.

• Try adding about one-fourth to one-half teaspoon of instant coffee to spaghetti sauce. It gives the sauce a nice, less acid flavor and adds a bit of brown color to the bright red tomato sauce that makes it look more homemade-cooked-for-hours.

• If you don't feel like reheating leftover coffee in the microwave oven, make yourself a glass of iced coffee from your morning pot's leftovers for a tasty coffee break during the day. I like iced coffee as a treat with a dash of cinnamon or nutmeg.

• If you like café au lait (coffee with boiled milk), you can make it instantly by heating milk in a microwave-safe mug in the microwave oven and then pouring hot coffee into the boiled milk. It's not the famous Café du Monde of New Orleans, but it's a pretty good substitute. Canned skim milk makes especially good quickie no-pans-to-wash café au lait, and saves a few fat calories too.

Tea

• Tea bags hold dried tea leaves but do not protect the flavor unless individually wrapped and sealed in plastic or foil. Tea is considered a fragrant herb, and whether you buy loose tea or tea bags, tea should be stored in a container with a tightly fitting lid.

• When you buy tea, the number of tea bags per pound tells you how strong the tea is. Most teas are sold with 200 bags to the pound; if you usually get one to two cups per bag from such a tea, then you may get four cups per bag from a tea that has 150 bags per pound and may need two bags for one cup if the tea has more than 200 bags per pound.

• When you use tea bags in a teapot, take the paper tags off to avoid having them drop into the pot and adding a paper taste to the tea. You can also keep the tags out of the tea by tying or looping the strings to the teapot or cup handle. You may be able to clip the tag to the rim or handle of your cup with a spring clothespin.

• Tea concentrate for a large crowd can be prepared ahead of time. Here's how to make 40 to 50 cups of tea.

1. Bring 1 ½ quarts fresh, cold water to a rapid boil.
2. Remove water from heat and immediately add one-fourth pound loose tea. Stir to immerse leaves and then cover. (Double this recipe for 80 to 90 cups.)
3. Let stand five minutes. Strain into a teapot until ready to use.
4. To serve this concentrate as hot tea, bring out a pot of boiling fresh water, right from the boiling kettle, pour about two tablespoons of tea concentrate into each cup, and fill up with hot water. The strength of the tea depends upon the water-tea ratio.

If you are using this concentrate for iced tea, add 50 percent more tea to allow for melting ice—that is, use six tea bags or six teaspoons of tea for four glasses of iced tea.

• Use leftover hot tea for iced tea, or freeze "tea cubes" to cool your next cup of hot tea or glass of iced tea.

• If you make a pitcher of iced tea and the tea becomes cloudy, add a small amount of boiling water and stir, and the tea will clear up. Some teas are sold especially for iced tea and these teas are less likely to get cloudy.

• Sun tea is not only an energy saver (yours and electrical power). It tastes better too, and can be made with any kind of tea.

1. Put the appropriate number of tea bags (about the same number of bags for the amount of water as for hot tea) into a glass container (quart or gallon).
2. Fill with fresh cool water and put the container on a sunny patio or doorstep where it will be safe from curious pets and children. Depending upon the weather, you'll have tea by noon or certainly 4 P.M. tea time.
3. Pour over ice and add flavorings of choice.

• If you are in a hurry, make "sun tea" in your microwave oven by boiling water in a glass jar or pitcher, then tossing in the appropriate number of tea bags and letting the tea steep on the kitchen counter for a couple of hours until it reaches the right strength. I once tried to speed this process along by simmering the tea bags in the pitcher in the microwave oven, but it was a mess because the bags broke and I had to strain the tea to use it. So, better let the tea steep naturally.

• You can boil water in the cup in the microwave oven for tea or coffee in three to four minutes, then add instant coffee or a tea bag for one-cup ease.

• CAUTION: If you add the tea bag or stir the instant coffee with a spoon immediately (within a second or two) after removing the cup from the microwave oven, the water is likely to bubble over because of the microwaves' action in the cup. Wait a few seconds before adding more action to the cup, and put the cup where spillovers won't burn you.

• When you are buying herb teas, read the labels to be sure what sorts of ingredients have been combined. You don't want to drink herbs you're allergic to. Also, some of the properties of certain herb tea ingredients may have effects you haven't bargained for, especially if you drink excessive amounts.

For example, many herb teas contain caffeine, which you may be trying to avoid. Some contain chicory and other herbs that are mild laxatives and that could cause distress if you drank too much. Some herbs (tonka beans, sweet clover, and other plants) are coumarins (substances that prevent blood clotting) and could be dangerous to some people when consumed in excess (several pots daily).

Leftovers

Leftovers are great time and money savers. They can be popped into the microwave or conventional oven whenever you need a quick meal and cooking is the farthest thing from your mind.

Don't hesitate to serve the same foods two days in a row. If it's a nutritious meal on Monday, it will be a nutritious meal on Tuesday, and may even taste better. If your family rebels, there are ways to disguise almost any food. When you look into your refrigerator, don't think of the food as leftovers; think of it as the beginning of your next meal—build around it and consider it a bonus.

Being Creative with Leftovers

• One of the ways to disguise leftovers is to add some fresh ingredients or spices. The leftover stew that's enough for only two might become a hearty soup, enough for four, if fresh or canned stewed tomatoes, some frozen or canned mixed vegetables, and noodles or rice are added. Some casseroles, stews, and pot roasts actually taste better the next day, after their flavors have blended. Texas chili is always better the second and third day.

• You can make a hot dish using accumulated leftover vegetables. A combination of vegetables and macaroni, and that last wiener or slice of meat, can be put into a pan with a can of beef vegetable soup. If you are using a lot of leftovers, you may want to add a bouillon cube to flavor the soup and possibly corn starch to thicken the sauce.

I once read in a French cookbook that just about anything you add water to will taste better if you add bouillon instead. Many types and flavors of bouillon are available. Some of the gourmet department liquid bouillons also add color to stews and soups.

• To save time, you can prepare your own TV dinners by cooking extra portions and then freezing them. You can freeze individual portions in plastic zipper-type freezer bags or on ready-to-heat-and-eat-from plates. Keep three-sectioned heavy paper plates on hand or heavy plastic plates, found on sale, to freeze leftover portions to be reheated in the microwave oven. Fill each plate with one serving, place it in a freezer-safe plastic bag, and freeze. Aluminum plates can be used for leftovers that will be reheated in conventional ovens.

• Try freezing larger amounts of leftovers in a plastic-lined bowl. When the food is frozen, remove the contents from the bowl and put them in a freezer-safe bag. This way you haven't lost a bowl to the freezer, and this also helps save valuable freezer space.

• Using the plastic bag or foil and this idea, you can also freeze casseroles in the same casserole in which they will be heated so that the block of food will fit into its proper cooking container. Always date everything you put into your freezer; it's so easy to lose track of time.

Keeping Track of Stored Leftovers

You should date all leftovers in the refrigerator so you won't end up throwing them away because you don't know how long they have been stored. Tape an 8″ × 11″ sheet of fairly stiff plastic to the inside of a cupboard door. Cut little squares from a roll of masking tape and stick them on the plastic. When you need a date sticker, remove one of the squares and write the date on it (i.e., 5 for the fifth of that month or 25 for the twenty-fifth—there will really be no need for a month on refrigerator leftovers because, we hope, you won't have anything left over for that long). When the dish used is empty, replace the date sticker on the heavy plastic to be reused; it's all marked and ready for the next leftover!

• Always put leftovers on the top shelf or in the same area of your refrigerator. Even consider marking the area "Leftovers." This way, they'll never be overlooked or forgotten. One of my favorite hints is to put them in glass jars so that I can see what I have to work with when I'm holding a "combination-of-leftovers gourmet event."

Cooking and Cleanup

It can't be said too often: We need to have help from the people we live with, and we need to take shortcuts when we can. Otherwise, we won't have time and energy left to enjoy the people and events in our lives that make us happy.

• Here's a good thawing tip to help teenagers and other cooks' assistants to remember to take items out of the freezer for dinner: Tape a memo sheet on the door and write down the item to be taken out. This easy reminder will prevent dinner delays while you quick-thaw something for dinner. Or, take the meat out of the freezer the night before and let it thaw in the refrigerator during the day so that it will be ready when you are ready to cook.

• If you have little ones who seem to demand most of your time in the late afternoon instead of the morning, try cooking that night's meal in the morning, when you have more time and may be in the kitchen anyway.

• Most of our days begin and end in the kitchen anyway, so if you take a few minutes the night before to plan what you'll have the next evening, it will take only a little while the next morning to put it all together. Be sure to refrigerate the dinner preparations properly so that you can reheat them safely when dinnertime rolls around.

Cooking Tips

• Cook ground meat thoroughly. This is very important because it's handled so often in the preparation and packaging process that it can quickly develop bacteria. Do not eat raw ground meat.

Steak tartare is the exception to this rule, but you should eat it only if you can be certain that the meat has been freshly ground and properly handled before it was served. You have to decide if you trust the chef or friend who serves it in a restaurant or at home.

• Never put cooked meat, chicken, or seafood on a platter that you have used for uncooked meat, chicken, or seafood unless the platter has been carefully washed. Bacteria from raw meat can be transferred to the cooked meat.

• Plastic cutting boards are safer than wooden cutting boards because they aren't likely to harbor bacteria from foods. If you use a wooden cutting board, clean the board with a mixture of two teaspoons of chlorine bleach and one teaspoon of vinegar to a gallon of water. Reseason the wooden board by rubbing it with mineral oil. If you use salad oil for reseasoning, it's likely to become rancid and you won't be able to use the board anymore. (This same process applies also to unfinished wooden utensils and salad bowls.)

• Onions: If you put onions into the freezer 15 minutes before use or into the fridge the day before, you'll reduce the spray of onion oils that vaporize when you cut them, and your eyes won't cry.

• Garlic: If you like fresh garlic or garlic-flavored oil, try this. Buy fresh garlic, peel all of the cloves at one time, then immerse them in light sesame or safflower oil in a glass jar. The oil seals the garlic from the air, and some sources say it will keep without refrigeration up to six weeks. I still think it's better to keep it in the fridge. If the cloves turn pale brown, the flavor is being lost. The bonus here is that you not only have garlic ready to use, but you have garlic-flavored oil for cooking or salads. Just keep replacing the oil you take from the jar.

• Sour cream substitute: The texture and flavor is not exactly the same, but if you need a substitute for sour cream in a pinch, combine six ounces of cottage cheese with one teaspoon of lemon juice in a food processor or blender until it's smooth. Plain, unflavored yogurt can also substitute for sour cream in many recipes.

Microwave Oven Cooking Tips

• To adapt your recipes to microwave cooking, find a similar dish in the cookbook that came with your microwave oven to determine cooking time, dish size, and proportions of ingredients to use.

• Adding a large amount of liquid to a dish lengthens the cooking time, so you need to reduce the amount of liquid to about half that used in a conventional recipe. Also, if the container is sealed in plastic wrap, very little liquid will evaporate.

• Since you will be using less liquid, reduce the amount of salt in your recipe.

• Because alcohol flavors are very unstable in microwave cooking, you will need to increase the proportion of wine in cooking liquids to get the flavor you want.

• Garlic cooks out very quickly, so increase the amount you use.

• Dried herbs and pepper flavors will be intensified, so reduce the amount of these ingredients. However, you need to increase the amount of fresh herbs.

Using Spices and Herbs

You can be creative with spices and herbs. It doesn't take much time to toss in a pinch of this and a few leaves of that to put a bit of zip into otherwise plain food. For quick flavors try adding the following:

• One-fourth teaspoon of allspice to simmering chicken or turkey stock to get the wonderful fragrance of cinnamon, cloves, and nutmeg.

• Allspice to cream soups or a pinch sprinkled over citrus fruits.

• Basil to tofu or tempeh marinades.

• A pinch of basil to peas, green beans, eggplant, zucchini, macaroni. And sprinkle it on cut tomatoes or cucumbers.

• One medium bay leaf to a six-serving recipe of soup, chicken or meat stew, spaghetti sauce, venison.

• A dash of cayenne to Hungarian goulash or anything else you want to bite you back!

• Garlic rubbed on pork, sprinkled with caraway seed and brown sugar before roasting.

• Chili powder to perk up sloppy joes, eggs, or cottage cheese.

• Dried chives on cottage cheese or on your cream-cheese sandwich. Also on your baked potato, omelet, and cucumber or lettuce salad. Chives are good when combined with any herbs.

• One teaspoon celery seed to one cup French dressing.

• Chervil to potato salad.

• A dash of cinnamon in dark wild-game gravies.

• A pinch of cloves to sweet potatoes or sliced buttered carrots.

• Cumin to potatoes, rice, and bread.

• Curry powder to egg salad and to barbecue sauce for grilled chicken or salmon, and to beef pot pies.

• Cardamom to curries, and acorn or butternut squash; also, a pinch into baked custard.

• Cayenne into coleslaw.

• Cilantro into scrambled eggs.

• Dill into salads, sour cream, cottage cheese, and omelets, and on salmon.

• A pinch of fennel into coleslaw and cooked cauliflower.

• Ginger into kale or collard greens, carrots, beets, and tomato soups, and with miso.

• Marjoram into soups, salads, and tofu or tempeh stir-fries.

• Mint to cold steamed squash, cauliflower, and potato or bean salad.

• Mustard powder into coleslaw, potato or bean salad, vegetable soups, and cream sauces.

• A pinch of crumbled rosemary to mashed potatoes.

• Tarragon into lentil or split-pea soup.

• Thyme into omelets, tomato dishes, and lentil or split-pea soup.

Cleanup

• To clean up more easily when cooking spaghetti, macaroni and cheese, scalloped potatoes, or meat loaf, line the baking dish with aluminum foil (but only if you're cooking in the regular oven, not in the microwave oven!). After dinner remove the foil, and there's no more fretting over scrubbing an encrusted food dish. If there are leftovers, wrap the aluminum foil over the food, label it, and place in the freezer.

• When a pot is layered with thick scorched or caramelized food, try boiling a mixture of one tablespoon of baking soda per cup of water in the pot to lift that mess off.

For more cleanup tips, see Chapter 12, "Entertaining."

Utensils

• If you keep cooking utensils in a kitchen drawer, you can identify them more easily by turning the handles to the back of the drawer. This way you can find the tool you want.

• To make chopped eggs easily, after slicing them in an egg slicer place the slices crosswise and slice again. You can also use the egg slicer for slicing fresh mushrooms. Placed stem up, two or three small ones can be sliced at a time. The slices are thicker than those produced by a food processor and are more uniform.

• When the edges of plastic utensils get a bit rough or burred, file them down with a fresh emery board. You can cut away the rough edges of rubber and plastic scrapers with good kitchen shears. You save on having to purchase new spatulas and turners, and prevent scratching those expensive non-stick-surface pans.

• Some of the best kitchen shears I know are blunt-ended surgical shears, available in medical supplies stores. You have to be careful where you put your fingers when you are working because they are extremely sharp, but you'll also be able to disjoint a chicken (raw or cooked) faster than with a knife. These shears can also make quick snips in the fatty edges of steaks and chops, even after they are already in the pan and starting to curl up (because you forgot to snip).

Of course, you already knew that the fatty edges of steaks and chops must be snipped in two or three places before frying and broiling to prevent their curling up into a difficult-to-serve cup-o-chop or steak cup. One might argue that when the meat curls up into a cup it holds sauces better, but if it's curled up, it won't brown and cook properly.

• Another all-purpose tool that you can buy at medical supplies stores is forceps. These pointy-nosed, handle-locking medical "pliers" (actually a doctor's version of needle-nosed pliers) will retrieve things from small openings (drawstrings from pajamas, drape cords from the rods, bobby pins or jewel stones from crevices); will hold small objects for placement (jewel stones, decals) when they are being glued; and help in a variety of crafts. They clamp on to things you'd usually use tweezers to grasp and hold them until you release the handles. They also can be used to fix jewelry clasps and bezels.

• Spaghetti grabbers, sold in most kitchen utensils departments, are terrific multi-use utensils. They are either ten-fingered plastic "hands" on a handle or wooden utensils that have several pegs on a broad flat "spoon" end of the handle. Both are handy, but the plastic grabbers are the most versatile because they'll grab just about any food in the kitchen that has to be manipulated while it's in hot water or oil. (CAUTION: Extremely hot oil might melt the plastic grabbers.) Use a spaghetti grabber to:

1. Stir/separate cooking noodles and then lift pasta out of the pot.
2. Remove the bouquet garni (bag of spices) from soups and stews before serving.
3. Remove the meat/chicken/turkey hunks from soup for deboning and then to return the boned meat to the pot without splashing.
4. Remove vegetables from the pot-roast pan and arrange them on the platter.
5. Pull one batch of boiling anything out of the water when you intend to reuse the boil for more batches, as when you are boiling fresh shrimp.
6. Pull out the soft potatoes and leave the undone ones in the pot for more cooking when you are boiling potatoes for salad.
7. Break up tuna fish and stir it into pasta salad without totally smashing ingredients.
8. Fish soaking utensils out of hot, sudsy water, especially if you think you've tossed a knife into it.

And on and on, whenever you need an extra hand that doesn't mind a dip in hot water or oil so that you can pull just about anything out of bubbling hot liquid and put any lumpies into liquid without splashing.

And if nobody is looking, you can use it to scratch that unreachable place between your shoulder blades!

• Spring (colored metal, wood, plastic) clothespins are helpful everywhere in the house. They hold skirts on hangers, notes on curtains, mail to mailboxes, and in the kitchen they pinch bags shut, hold coupons and recipe cards together, clip a recipe to a nearby object so it's easily read, clip a dish towel to your blouse when you need an apron and are in too much of a hurry to get one, clip a towel around a child's neck for an instant bib, and . . . need I say more? Keep a bunch in the kitchen clipped to any convenient object.

• Use a tea or spice ball to hold the bouquet garni of spices when you make soup or stew—nobody will ever bite into a stray whole pepper ball, and you won't have to fish around with your spaghetti grabber for those bay leaves that lurk in the murky depths of pots.

• If you have long hair that gets in your way while you are busily cooking or cleaning in the kitchen, cut four to six one-inch slashes (like an asterisk) across the center of a plastic lid (nut, baking powder, chip can) and poke your hair through it for a ponytail. It's not glamorous but will do until you are finished with your work and can put yourself together again in your usual gorgeous style. This idea could help at the beach when your hair is wet and blowing in the wind.

• For a cute holder in which to store your small kitchen utensils, cover a coffee can (large size) or other similar container with leftover wallpaper. If you haven't cut up the lid for a ponytail holder, you can put it on the bottom of the can to protect it from wet counter spills.

CHAPTER 2

Saving Supermarket Dollars

Saving money at the supermarket goes beyond using coupons, shopping the specials, and knowing how to pick out the best from the display. In addition to saving money, shopping efficiently also saves time. And, if you store your food, cook it, and use up leftovers efficiently, you get the utmost for the time and money you spend at the supermarket.

Saving Time and $$$ by Planning Ahead

We all hate to sit down and write lists, but I have found that planning ahead, making lists, and taking a little time to organize really does save time, not to mention money, in the long run.

Even the busiest person needs to sit down and sip a cup of tea or coffee once in a while, and if you're the kind of person who needs an excuse to take a break, use list-making time as your excuse! You may even find that by getting organized you'll have saved enough time to have a bona fide, pleasant, uplifting "fun break."

We all feel happier when we are running our homes and schedules instead of having our homes and schedules run us.

Menus and Shopping Lists

• Meal planning doesn't have to be a boring chore. If you make separate index cards for each dinner you prepare for a few months, menu planning becomes a simple matter of pulling out enough index cards for the number of meals you'll be shopping for; your food shopping list is always ready-made!

• If you are lucky enough to have a family computer, you can keep all sorts of menu files that can be called up and printed whenever you're ready to shop. It really saves time to keep a master shopping checklist to print out which will remind you to check for those things you usually forget. You can keep track of what you buy and then revise your list and run off a supply of lists every three months or so.

• Another ready-made grocery list is the sale page from your newspaper. Just check off on the ad page the items you need, and jot down items that aren't in the ad. Grocery ads help you plan menus around things that are on sale, which saves money!

• Save time and money by planning weekly menus before you shop. Shopping for one week eliminates those short but time-consuming treks to the store; menus not only discourage expensive impulse buying, they also eliminate having to make that daily decision of what to fix for dinner.

• Save time by going to the store early Saturday morning before it becomes crowded or shop at any time you've noticed is unpopular at your store, such as during sports events or popular TV shows. Waiting in long lines at the checkout counter is just one more tedious thing that can be avoided if you plan ahead.

• While bargain shopping is a good practice, time is money and a full day of bargain shopping and wasting gas in an attempt to save a dollar or two is usually not a bargain at all.

Coupons

• When making a shopping list, place a "C" next to items that have a coupon to be redeemed, to make couponing easier for you.

• Or, if you are shopping with a roommate, spouse, or child, make two lists—one for coupon items and one for regular shopping. Have one person go off with the coupons and a separate cart; then both of you can meet at the checkout counter in half the usual shopping time. Reading the coupon requirements is not only fun for kids, but it teaches them how to be aware of details. If you're having a child do the coupon hunt, always offer an incentive by making sure that some of the coupons are for favorite cereals and other goodies.

• When grocery stores accept double coupons, check the newspaper section to see how many coupons will be useful to you. If there are a lot, you can save money by buying another copy of the paper.

• I keep a few coupons for items I frequently use and need in my purse at all times. The money they save really does add up.

• Keep a box handy when you read newspapers or magazines. When you see coupons, tear out the entire page and put it in the box. When your children are bored or watching television, they can cut them out.

• Go through your coupons every other month and pull out those due to expire in the next two months, then clip these together and put them in front of the others. If there's no expiration date, write the word "none" across the coupon. Also, when you clip a coupon out of a newspaper or magazine, you can underline the expiration date or mark it with a highlighter pen. This helps to organize coupons and helps the cashier find the expiration date, saving the cashier's time and yours.

Coupon Holders

Keep all of your coupons in one place instead of scattered around the house. There are many different ways to organize them.

• One way that works well is to arrange your coupon file in the order of the supermarket's aisles. I use an accordion-style canceled check file to avoid the bulk of a recipe file box.

• A spare napkin holder can keep coupons in one place and can also hold your shopping list.

• An old checkbook cover is also a handy holder.

• Those little wallets that traveler's checks come in are good coupon holders. Holes can be punched at the end of each coupon so that you can fasten them to the metal brads. And they fold up nice and snug.

• You can hold a legal-size envelope on the refrigerator with a magnet, then write your grocery list on the envelope and place coupons to be redeemed inside it. Don't waste money on a new envelope; it can be recycled from "junk mail." You might as well get some use from it!

• A plastic recipe box is large enough to handle hundreds of coupons. Use the index card dividers to separate food groups.

• You can also keep coupons in a large metal or plastic lunch box, using file box dividers to separate coupons into groups. The lunch box fits into the seat portion of the shopping cart and makes handling coupons easy.

• You can use a clothespin to hold coupons you plan to redeem; this will leave your hands free for shopping.

• When clipping coupons, why not take some of the money you save and give it to a charity or perhaps to a friend who is struggling?

• Take extra coupons to work to share with your fellow workers.

• Tuck coupons for baby products in with baby shower gifts.

• Treat yourself. Keep track of the money you save couponing and then spend it when you're on vacation, use it for gifts to yourself or others, or spend it on something you want but don't need.

Shopping Trips

If you organize your shopping trips, you'll save time as well as money and gas. For example, you can buy several weeks' worth of supplies on double-coupon days or when your favorite brands are on sale.

Most of us use certain products more frequently than others. It helps to know how much of a product you use over a period of time so that you can stock up without overstocking when there's a sale.

• Date such products as they are put to use, so that you'll know how long it takes to use them up. For example, if you find that you use about six tubes of toothpaste and eleven bottles of shampoo in one year, you can safely buy those amounts of toothpaste and shampoo.

I don't date food items that I will consume in short periods of time, but I do date such items as a large jar of jelly, aluminum foil, instant and regular coffee, salt, and pepper.

• When I run errands all day, I put a plastic laundry basket in the trunk of the car and put my packages in the basket. Small bags don't get lost, and you can carry in the basket with all the bags in one trip when you get home.

• Put an inexpensive foam cooler in the car, and you can put frozen foods in it when you grocery shop. Then you don't have to worry if you need to make extra stops en route home and you won't have to pass up a good buy on milk or meat; and ice cream will be in better shape too.

• If you keep transparent tape in the glove compartment of your car, on shopping days you can attach a piece of tape to the top of your shopping list when you leave your car and then stick the exposed half of the tape onto the middle of the grocery cart handle. Your list will be easy to read; it won't get lost and you'll have both hands free to shop. Don't forget to remove it from the cart when you're through!

• If you have friends who meet for a weekly card game, tennis, or whatever, do your shopping together on that day and take turns driving. One car going for weekly groceries sure beats several when it comes to saving gas, and you have the added bonus of pleasant company. You and your friends also can buy in bulk and then split for extra economy.

• Another tip to make shopping more pleasant is to remember that the shopping carts that work, the ones that don't have wheels with minds of their own, are the carts left in the parking lot by previous shoppers! Take one with you when you enter the store and make dozens of store employees happy at the same time.

• Higher-priced items in the store are usually placed at eye level; you'll save money if you look up, down, and sideways at all the brands of the product you want.

• Always compare weights and volume, not just the size of the package. A box or jar may be bigger but still contain the same contents. Also, the giant economy size may not cost less per ounce, pound, etc. Many people carry small calculators to avoid supermarket math, and some stores have price per ounce or piece actually posted on the shelf.

• When you have bought several six-packs of canned soft drinks encased in the popular plastic rings, it saves room in the shopping cart if you place the six-pack with three cans on each side of the grocery cart's edge, letting them hang by the plastic holder. They'll hang there securely and take up little cart space.

• Always purchase meat and poultry last and refrigerate them as soon as possible when you get home.

• To save time in the grocery checkout line, place meat packages in clear plastic bags (from produce section) so that their price labels show through the unprinted side of the bag. The clerk can see clearly the price and code and can ring up items more quickly, without the other groceries getting messy.

Buying Produce

Anyone who gardens knows how to buy produce, because watching things grow teaches you to observe what's old and what's fresh.

For example, broccoli with little yellow flowers trying to poke through the green heads is older than broccoli that has no flowers. The same goes for asparagus, which also "flowers" when it's mature.

• You can tell how long asparagus, lettuce, and other vegetables that have obvious cut ends have been in the store just by looking at the cut end. Is it a fresh cut or is it brown and, in the case of asparagus, somewhat dry?

• When you see delicate leaves on the ends of carrots or radishes, you know they didn't just get off the turnip truck yesterday; they are sprouting and, therefore, old.

• The rule of thumb is don't press your thumb into produce, because such bruising causes a lot of waste and spoilage that the rest of us shoppers end up paying for.

Other shopping rules are:

• Buy in season (grocery ads and specials will indicate this).

• Buy the best quality you can afford but avoid overpriced out-of-season foods.

• Don't buy too-ripe or too-green produce because, in most cases, flavor will never reach its peak.

• Be wary of oversize fruits, which may not taste as good as they look (except for Bing cherries and blueberries, where bigger is better).

Some of the following information on buying fruits and vegetables is from my own experience, but I checked with the experts too. Some of the information is from a book called *Buying Produce* by Jack Murdich (Hearst Books, New York, 1986), who is an experienced produce buyer, and some of it is from the U.S. Department of Agriculture.

Buying Fruits and Berries

Many fruits and berries used to be luxury foods, available only if you grew them in your own backyard or lived in areas of the country where they were grown. Otherwise, if they were available at all, the costs were prohibitive.

The kiwi is a good example. Not only were these fuzzy brown, yummy fruits rare in markets, they were so expensive that few people would even try them. One small kiwi (and all are relatively small for the price) used to cost more than $1 each. Now that kiwis are grown commercially and shipped throughout the U.S., they can even be found as "specials" priced reasonably for just about anyone's fruit salad.

It takes time and trial and error to learn how to select the best of those fruits, berries and melons that are relatively new to supermarket displays. Here are tips to help you:

• Gooseberries: These look like green grapes and can be eaten raw, but are usually made into jam or pies and are seldom seen in stores.

• Guavas: Available from December to February, guavas are light green or yellow. They are plum-shaped; the flesh is white to dark pink. Unless tree ripened, they are tart. They are usually made into jelly.

• Kiwis (or kiwifruit): Available from May through November when grown in California, and from November through May when imported from New Zealand. Buy fairly firm kiwis and ripen them at room temperature for about a week. A kiwi that is about as soft as a ripe plum is ready to eat. Tip: If a kiwi is in this stage at the store, it may be bruised and ready to deteriorate.

Some people like to sprinkle kiwi, after it's been peeled and sliced into rounds, with lime juice and eat it as is; others use it for chocolate fondue, and it is also glazed for topping pastries. If you like yogurt, then kiwi and any kind of berries or vanilla-flavored low-fat yogurt is a tasty and fairly low-calorie dessert.

• Kumquats: They peak from December to May, are very tart, and contain a lot of seeds. Few people like to eat them raw, and they are usually used for marmalade. Buy firm, orange fruit and store it in the fridge. Don't buy green kumquats; they won't ripen to an acceptable flavor.

• Loquats: They peak from mid-March to May and are usually too expensive to be more than just a "taste" item. They look like small, fuzzy apricots and have three or four pits.

• Lychees (lychee nuts): You are not likely to find these in regular supermarkets because they're very expensive. They are about as big as a golf ball and have a rough, tough inedible skin which fades from strawberry color to dusty pink after it is picked. The light green flesh surrounds an inedible nut. The edible part of one lychee is about the same as two or three grapes. Both fresh and dried lychees are sold in Oriental communities as gifts.

• Mangoes: In season from January through September, they peak in May, June, and July. Ranging in size from a few ounces to four pounds, several types of mangoes are available in the United States. Some mangoes are fibrous and stringy, but three types are recommended: the Haden (yellow-skinned with a red cheek when ripe); the Kent (large, green-skinned, with reddish cheek); and the Keitt (large, green, with or without red cheek). Flat, kidney-shaped mangoes are usually fibrous and sour.

Tree-ripened mangoes are the sweetest, and imported mangoes are usually ready to eat when bought at the market. Florida mangoes are picked hard and need a week at room temperature to ripen. Buy unbruised fruit. You can peel and slice mangoes and serve them alone or in fruit salad.

• Papayas: In season year-round, papayas are usually light green when harvested; they ripen to a golden yellow. The flesh is yellow or orange-pink.

Buy firm, pale green or pale yellow fruit and ripen it at room temperature. It's better not to refrigerate papayas.

• Passion fruit: About as big as an egg. Its inedible skin is usually purple but can be red and gold; the flesh is yellow. I used to pluck them from the trees in Hawaii when I was a child and eat them until I was stuffed.

• Persimmons: Domestic persimmons are available from October to January; Chilean ones are sold in the spring. Ripe persimmons look like shiny, acorn-shaped, deep orange tomatoes.

Eating an unripened persimmon can cause you to pucker more than you'll ever know or want to remember. The old wives' tale about freezing unripe persimmons so that they will be ripe and edible when they thaw is true. Buy firm, colorful persimmons and ripen them for several days at room temperature. When the skin is shriveled (blistered skin is not yet ripe) and has lost its color, the fruit can be eaten. The skin can be eaten if you wish.

• Pineapples: Available year-round, pineapples are jetted in from Hawaii or shipped from Latin America. Generally, Hawaiian pineapples are the sweetest and juiciest, because Latin American pineapples are picked while too green to have reached their full sugar content. The tags will tell you where the pineapples have been grown. Buy the largest pineapple in the display that is firm and shows some color.

• Pomegranates: Although some have yellow skin, most commercially grown pomegranates have red, leathery skin. The flesh is made up of juicy red kernel clusters, and each kernel has a seed that is optionally edible. They peak in October and November and need no refrigeration, although fridge storage will help them last longer.

It's interesting to know that the Egyptians used pomegranate juice for ink and dyeing fabric—a warning not to dribble any of the juice on your clothing!

• Prickly pears: These are the fruit of the cactus and are not actually pears, although they are more or less pear-shaped. Although most are deep red, some are pale yellow, orange, or pink. Buy large fruit, ripen at room temperature, then refrigerate.

You have to be determined to eat prickly pear because its skin is covered with barbs and the pulp has lots of seeds, which are edible but very hard to chew. Most prickly pear in the market has been singed to remove the barbs. To eat it, cut off the top and bottom and then cut it from end to end so that you can peel off the inedible skin. You will be rewarded by a tasty, juicy fruit.

• Star fruit (carambolas): Relatively new to our markets, star fruit peak from September to January. They look like five-pointed starfish and most come from Hawaii and the Caribbean islands, although some are grown in the United States. The deeper the yellow color of the fruit's waxy-looking edible skin, the less tart the fruit. They can be eaten raw, used in jams and jellies, and included in fruit punches.

• Watermelons: They peak from June through August. The way to select all watermelons is the same: The only way to be certain of a watermelon's ripeness is to cut a plug or to buy one that is cut in half or quarters. Sometimes, melons that have been displayed in very hot sun at roadside stands will be sun damaged—almost mushy, as if cooked. (This is also true of tomatoes.) Ask to have the watermelon plugged so you can see what's inside.

Buying Vegetables

It's no secret that I love vegetables and only rarely eat meat. Veggies—raw, steamed, stir-fried—please the eye as well as the palate, and, as medical research is showing, the fiber from vegetables and grains may be our best ally against numerous diseases, including cancer of the colon, a disease almost unknown in parts of the world where people eat an abundance of fruits, vegetables, and grain and very little meat. Dietary fiber intake is becoming important in the control of diabetes as well. Plus, if you are trying to lose weight, veggies fill you up without filling you with lots of calories, unless you smother them in sauces or butter.

Modern farming and shipping give us a variety of vegetables throughout the year, and like fruit, many vegetables and herbs which we can buy at any supermarket were almost unknown or totally unknown by our grandmothers and even our mothers.

Combinations of vegetables are available in the frozen-food sections, but fresh vegetables are becoming more popular because they are so readily available and priced so reasonably these days.

Here are some tips to help you get your money's worth when you buy vegetables, which, until recently, were not always available in supermarkets.

Unless otherwise noted the vegetables listed are available year-round and should be kept refrigerated.

• Anise (sweet fennel): Usually out of season in hot weather, anise has fernlike green foliage that looks a bit like fresh dill weed. The greens can be chopped and used for seasoning. Buy fresh, green foliage and crisp-looking bulbs for a sweet licorice flavor.

• Avocados: Most avocados used to be sold very firm and took a long while to ripen; now many are ready to use when bought, but because they are so ripe they are often bruised at the market.

To quick-ripen avocados in half the natural time, put the avocado into a brown paper bag with a tomato and then put the bag in the warmest part of the house. The natural ethylene gas from the avocado and tomato plus warmth is what speeds up ripening.

To test for ripeness, put the avocado in the palm of your hand. A Florida avocado is ready to serve if it yields to slight pressure. Let a California avocado ripen one more day after this test. Florida avocados are usually twice as big as California ones and have a lower calorie count. California avocados have a more nutlike flavor and a richer, creamier flesh. According to some avocado fans, the difference between California and Florida avocados is like that between ice cream and ice milk, with the Florida product being the ice milk.

Cut avocados turn dark when exposed to air. Sprinkle the surface with fresh lemon or lime juice and use as soon as possible. If you only use a half avocado, leave the pit in the unused half. Here in Texas, we put the pit into avocado dip when we refrigerate it to prevent darkening.

Avocados don't ripen in the fridge, and refrigeration will make the flesh turn black. You can freeze pureed but not whole or cut avocados.

• Broccoli: Broccoli should be firm, green, and not yellow or budded with yellow flowers. Some broccoli has a slightly purple cast to the buds and this is a mark of quality.

• Celeriac (knob celery): Used as a cooked vegetable or raw in salads, celeriac is usually sold in bunches with three knobs and green tops attached. Larger knobs tend to be woody; buy smaller ones. If the greens are fresh, they can be used for soup. It's easy to peel after cooking. If served raw, you'll need to sprinkle it with lemon juice because it discolors when cut.

• Kale: A curly-leafed member of the cabbage family, kale tastes much like cabbage when it's cooked. Buy crisp, dark green or slightly blue leaves. Wilted, limp, or yellow leaves are old. When you see pink, purple, or white-hearted kale, it's ornamental and usually too expensive to eat.

• Kohlrabi: This looks like pale green beets but grow above the ground. Buy kohlrabi that is the same size as beets to avoid getting a woody, overmature one. It should look crisp; if the leaves are wilted/yellow, don't buy it. The leaves, if green and fresh, can be cooked like spinach. Kohlrabi is served cooked or raw.

• Mustard greens: Although these are popular in the South, they aren't often eaten in the rest of the United States. Buy dark or light green leaves, which may have a bronze cast. If limp and yellow, they are old; don't buy them. They are wonderful when cooked and seasoned the old-fashioned way, which is to cook the living heck out of them after adding salt, pepper, bacon drippings, or bits of ham.

Chinese mustard greens have white stems, green leaves, and a slightly bitter flavor. They are usually stir-fried or used in soups.

• Okra: This native African vegetable is like the little girl in the nursery rhyme: When she was good, she was very, very good, but when she was bad, she was horrid. When okra is overcooked it is really horrid—it's gluey and slimy.

Buy velvety, small (less than 2½ inches—bigger ones are woody and stringy) pods, then bake, boil, or fry them in various ways. Okra is popular in Cajun dishes, and in the South it's often fried after being rolled in cornmeal. If you cook it in water, especially in an aluminum pot, add lemon juice to prevent discoloration of the okra and the pot.

Chinese okra *(sing gwa)* is dark green and about an inch in diameter and about 12 inches long. It is often used with seafood dishes.

• Peppers: Either sweet or hot, peppers come in many sizes, shapes and colors. Immature peppers are green; mature peppers can be red, yellow and purple. Generally speaking, the redder the pepper, the sweeter the flavor and shorter the storage time. To tell the difference between hot and sweet peppers, you need to know their names. For example, chili, jalapeño, cayenne, pulla and serrano are hot peppers. Bell and California Wonders are sweet peppers.

HINT: Wear rubber gloves when handling hot peppers; they can really irritate your skin. Some people say it's the seeds that are hot, and some say it's the veins in serrano peppers that are hottest. Whatever's the hottest, wear rubber gloves (the thickest possible) to protect your hands. And don't ever rub your eyes!

• Swiss chard: Sold in bunches, chard should have crisp green leaves, not wilted ones that are turning yellow. Popular for cooking, even when over-cooked, Swiss chard will keep its texture and color and won't get dull and slimy like spinach. Bok choy is an Oriental type of Swiss chard.

Buying Staples

When you are buying canned goods and other products, the cheapest may not be the best buy. With so many brands of everything on the market, the best buy depends upon your personal taste and the way you'll use the product. Generic canned vegetables may be just fine for adding to soups or stews, but may not be tasty and attractive when served as a separate course at dinner.

The basic guidelines for quality of brands of any product are these: national name brands; private labels/house brands; economy brands; and generics, or "no-names."

• National name brands: These are usually the most expensive; if they have been around for several years, they are bound to have good quality because competition is so keen that national name-brand products that aren't as good as their competition aren't likely to survive.

• Private labels/house brands: The prices of these are 10 to 20 percent lower than national brands; the quality is comparable, although the taste—for example, of soups—may not be the same as that of a national brand. However, many store brands are produced by national manufacturers for the large chains.

• Economy brands: These are sold at about 25 percent less than national brands; they are a type of house brand and are generally a bit lower in quality than national or house brands. Supermarket chains usually have their own house and economy brands.

• Generics: Often with yellow, white, or other plain labels and plain black letters designating contents, these products can be production overages from processing plants but are more likely to be lower-quality fruits, vegetables, and so on or end runs in the production line. The quality can vary greatly from one purchase to another; the price will always be well below that of the other labels. I certainly think these are good buys for things like paper plates, napkins, bubble bath for the kids, and anything where quality isn't important and saving money is.

Storing

Food costs too much to waste it by improper storage, but waste isn't the only reason you should store food properly. The Centers for Disease Control (CDC) estimates that as many as four million people get bacterial infections that cause diarrhea, fever, and vomiting, and as many as two thousand people die annually from common food poisoning. Most salmonella poisoning is traced to contaminated meat, poultry, eggs, or milk, but the bacteria can also be harbored in other foods that come in contact with contaminated water or foodstuff. For information on salmonella and other food poisoning, you can call the U.S. Department of Agriculture's hot line, 1-800-535-4555. Put your tax dollars to good use.

Generally, you should keep foods in cool, dry places, and avoid overloading your refrigerator (which prevents it from cooling food properly). The temperature in the refrigerator should be 42 to 44 degrees Fahrenheit in its warmest part and 40 degrees or less in its coldest part (other than the freezer).

Cereals, Flour, Grains

• When I buy raw cereals, flour, rice, and certain packaged foods, I put them into glass jars to prevent bug traffic from one food to the other. I save the cooking instructions and put them into the jar or tape them on the outside. Big ol' gallon pickle jars are my favorites.

• If you put foodstuffs made from grain, especially flour and cornmeal, into the freezer for at least 7 days after bringing them home, any visible or invisible infestations will be destroyed and you won't have to share your groceries with uninvited crawling creature "guests."

• The FDA recommends storing cornmeal in the refrigerator, especially in the summer.

Spices

• Spices and most canned and packaged foods should be stored in a cool, dry place and not above the stove. Because heat rises, the shelves above the stove are pretty warm when the stove is in use and, if you have a gas stove with a pilot light, the heat will be constant. Spices especially will lose their flavor if stored near heat. Like other foods, color and odor changes indicate loss of quality. For best use, buy the smallest quantity.

The FDA and cooking experts say that keeping spices and herbs frozen or refrigerated is the best way to preserve flavor.

• The next-best way is in a cool, dry, dark cupboard, where most of us keep them.

• You can keep track of the age of spices by marking the date of purchase on a strip of masking tape and sticking it to the bottom of the container.

• If you grow your own herbs for drying or if you like to make your own spice mixtures, you can use clean, dry baby food jars to store them.

• If you're short on cupboard space, nail or glue the jar lids to the underside of a shelf so that you can just unscrew jars from their lids when you use spices.

Canned Goods

• If you are on a low-fat diet, keep unopened cans of soup or chili in the refrigerator. After the food is sufficiently chilled, you can easily skim off the congealed fat, then heat as usual. You'll never miss the fat and the flavor will be as good as before.

• Canned goods should be kept in a dry, cool room with a temperature of about 70 degrees Fahrenheit. Never store canned goods near steam pipes, furnaces, kitchen ranges, or in the garage, because both freezing and too much heat will affect the quality of canned goods.

Nonacid canned foods are safe in the above conditions for two to three years, with some vegetables such as potatoes keeping as long as five years. Acid foods, such as tomatoes and all fruits, are safe for about 18 months.

• If you see rust or discoloration on a can at the seam or anywhere else or if a can bulges at either end, throw out the can without opening it and certainly without handling or tasting it. Consider any discolored or off-odor food to be spoiled and poisonous; discard it and make sure children and pets can't get at it.

• CAUTION: Whenever you are in doubt about the age of canned foods or they even hint at being spoiled, it always makes sense to be cautious and throw them out. No amount of money saved is worth taking a chance of making yourself sick.

In fact, never taste-test any type of questionable food, whether it's canned, home-cooked, carry-out, or even fresh from the market. Always throw out foods that you suspect may be spoiled. When in doubt, throw it out!

• Dispose of spoiled or questionable foods carefully. Seal them in containers. If possible, flush spoiled foods down the disposal or toilet to keep them away from pets who might raid your garbage. To prevent garbage jamming in the pipe of your garbage disposal, be sure to always run lots of water when you turn it on. Let the water run a few seconds after turning it off to thoroughly flush out the pipes.

Fresh Vegetables

• Eating fresh vegetables as soon as possible ensures getting maximum food value from them. Vegetables should be stored in the refrigerator; most refrigerators have crisper drawers for this purpose. (See storage times listed elsewhere in this chapter.)

• However, if you have a garden or access to large quantities of certain vegetables, you may want to freeze the surplus. Except for green peppers or onions for seasoning, most vegetables need to be blanched (put in boiling water for several minutes) before freezing to prevent deterioration.

• Tomatoes have a high water content and tend to collapse when thawing, thus losing their juice. A lot of people freeze surplus garden tomatoes anyway. They are easy to peel (hold under running water for a minute or so and the peel comes off) and then easy to pop, still frozen, into soups, stews, and sauces.

• Potatoes need to be cooked before freezing.

• Lettuce, cabbage, onions, celery, and carrot sticks will lose crispness and get limp and tough, and therefore can't be eaten raw if frozen, but are fine for soups, stews, and casseroles.

The U.S. Department of Agriculture (USDA) has many fine booklets on canning, preserving, and freezing that can be obtained by calling the USDA's local office or your local Cooperative Extension Agent. Look in the government section (blue in some cities, but not all) of your phone book under the federal government listings for the USDA or under your state listings for your local county Cooperative Extension Agent.

Eggs

• The American Egg Board tells us that fresh eggs can be stored in their cartons in the refrigerator as long as five weeks and that the store carton is the best container for storage. Contrary to what we would think, the shell is porous; it does allow odors to penetrate.
    The reason the store carton is the best container is that if you take the eggs out of the carton and put them in the egg holder in the door, every time you open and close the door the eggs are subject to temperature variation and to movement, which causes them to spoil more quickly.

• Eggs can be stored eight to ten days if hard-cooked in shells, and two to four days for egg whites in a covered container or egg yolks covered with water.

• Eggs cannot be frozen in their shells, but raw whole eggs, whites, and yolks and hard-cooked yolks can be frozen. Follow the directions below.
    Egg whites should be sealed tightly in a freezer container that is labeled with the number of whites and the date.
    To freeze whole eggs or yolks, add either ⅛ teaspoon salt or 1½ teaspoon sugar or corn syrup for each four yolks or two whole eggs. In addition to the date and number of yolks or whole eggs, note whether you've added salt or sugar to the eggs so that you'll know if they can be used for main dishes.
    Thaw frozen eggs overnight in the refrigerator or under cool running water. Yolks and whole eggs should be used as soon as they're thawed; thawed whites will have better volume when beaten if they are kept at room temperature for about 30 minutes.

Cheeses

• Store cheeses in the refrigerator. Some American cheeses will crumble if frozen, which is fine if you plan to use them in a sauce or as a salad topping, but not so fine if you want slices.

• Sliced cheeses can be refrigerated in their original film wrappers. You can wrap cheese with waxed paper or plastic and then with foil before refrigerating it. Processed cheese, cheese food, and spreads sold in sealed jars or packages keep without refrigeration but must be refrigerated after you open the containers.

• Cheeses are classified as very hard (for grating), hard, semisoft, soft, and also as ripened or unripened cheeses.

Very hard cheeses include Asiago old, Parmesan, Romano, sapsago, and Spalen. Hard cheeses include cheddar, granular or stirred curd, Caciocavallo, Swiss, Emmentaler, and Gruyère. Among the semisoft cheeses are brick, Muenster, Limburger, Port du Salut, Trappist, Roquefort, Gorgonzola, blue, Stilton, and Wensleydale. Soft cheeses include Bel Paese, Brie, Camembert, cooked, hand, and Neufchâtel (as made in France). The above cheeses are all ripened cheeses.

Among the unripened cheeses are these soft cheeses: cottage, pot, baker's, cream, Neufchâtel (as made in the United States), mysost, primost, and fresh ricotta.

• Generally, ripened cheeses keep longer than unripened cheeses, and you can buy enough to last for several weeks. Most soft unripened cheeses are perishable, so it's best to buy only as much as you'll use in a short time.

Meat, Poultry, Seafood

• Take a tip from the fish market: Store all seafood on ice in the refrigerator. If you put fish, shrimp, and other seafood on ice in a colander, and then put the colander in a water-catching pan or dish, the seafood won't get water-logged by soaking in melted ice if it has to wait several hours before going to pot or pan.

• Use fresh seafood the day you buy it. When you have to freeze it, freeze it as soon as possible IMMERSED IN WATER, in sealed containers, to best preserve flavor. Clean milk cartons or zippered plastic bags are good containers for fish.

• If you buy fresh shrimp to freeze in the raw stage at home, remove the heads from the shrimp before freezing. Fat in shrimp heads will become rancid even in the freezer and spoil the taste of shrimp. You can also freeze cooked and shelled shrimp for use as hors d'oeuvres.

• Many people like to soak thawed frozen fish in milk for several hours before cooking, because milk tends to take away any "fishy" taste (or "gamey" taste from game fish) that may have developed. Blot the milk from the fish and prepare as planned. You can thaw frozen shrimp in salted cold water.

• Refrigerate unfrozen raw meat, poultry, and fish; keep commercially frozen stuffed poultry in the freezer until you cook it. Cold cuts should be refrigerated promptly and never kept for more than two or three hours in the temperature danger zone (see FDA recommendations below).

Temperature Danger Zone

Bacteria grow and toxins are produced when food is not cooled and refrigerated properly. The U.S. Department of Agriculture tells us to keep hot foods hot (above 165 degrees Fahrenheit) and cold foods cold (below 40). The danger zone for food is between 40 and 140 degrees, the temperature range in which bacteria grow rapidly. Food that has been kept in the temperature danger zone for more than two or three hours may not be safe to eat. This includes food that is kept in the oven at danger zone temperatures.

Either serve food after cooking or refrigerate it promptly. You can refrigerate hot foods if they will not raise the refrigerator temperature above 45 degrees F. Letting foods cool down to room temperature before refrigerating them is no longer recommended. This old wives' tale is a hangover from the days of iceboxes when hot foods would melt the ice chunk. If you place the hot food on the coldest shelf of your refrigerator, it will cool down quickly. Give the dish some air space to help it cool down faster and make sure you don't put the hot dish next to butter, margarine, jelled cranberries, or anything else that will be easily affected by the heat.

Storage Limits for Keeping Food

If foods are properly handled before purchase and stored in the average, properly working refrigerator, the following times are the storage limits suggested by the U.S. Food and Drug Administration's "FDA Consumer" and various U.S. Department of Agriculture publications and *Good Housekeeping* magazine.

• Apples and cherries: Store without washing in a crisper or moisture-resistant wrap. Apples keep about one month; citrus fruits, two weeks; most other fruit, five days, except pineapple, which keeps about two days. Canned and cooked fruits (in covered container) keep one week; unopened canned fruit keep one year; dried fruit, six months.

- Baby foods (covered, in original can or jar): Two to three days.

- Bananas: Should not be refrigerated.

- Beef, fresh: Variety meats such as heart and liver, one to two days in the refrigerator; ground beef, one to two days; chops, steaks, three to five days; sausages, one to two days; roasts, three to five days.

  Frozen beef: Variety meats, one to two months; and sausage, one to two months; ground beef, three to four months; chops, six to nine months; steaks, six to twelve months; roasts, six to twelve months.

- Berries and cherries (in crisper or moisture-proof wrapping): Three days.

- Bread: Commercially frozen, baked bread can be frozen for three months; for unbaked bread, check label.

- Butter (margarine): In the refrigerator, one to two weeks; freeze nine months.

- Casseroles, stews: Three to four days in the refrigerator; freeze cooked meat dishes, two to three months; and cooked pastry dishes, four to six months.

- Cheeses: Opened cream cheese, two weeks; cottage cheese, ten to thirty days; opened Swiss, brick, processed, three to four weeks.

- Chicken (Poultry): Refrigerate two to three days; freeze for nine to twelve months. Chicken livers will keep one to two days in the refrigerator, three months frozen.

- Custards, custard sauces, cream-filled pies or cakes (on coldest shelf): Two to three days.

- Fish: Fresh fish, shellfish (all wrapped loosely) are best if kept only twenty-four hours in the refrigerator. Cooked fish and shellfish (covered or wrapped), canned fish and shellfish (opened, covered), one day.

- Fruit juices (in covered container): Three to four days.

• Gravy: Can be kept one to two days in the refrigerator and can be kept frozen up to one month.

• Ice cream (sherbert): One month in the freezer.

• Ketchup: Unopened, twelve months on the shelf; refrigerate after opening.

• Lettuce: Unwashed, head lettuce keeps five to seven days in the refrigerator crisper; washed and drained, three to five days.

• Lunch meats: Can be refrigerated three to five days. (Always look at the date on the package.)

• Mayonnaise, salad dressing: Unopened on the shelf, two to three months; in the refrigerator after opening, six to eight weeks.

• Meats: Generally, processed or cured meats (such as sliced ham) keep one week in the refrigerator, one to two months in freezer. Bacon and franks will keep three to five days in fridge; bacon keeps one month in the freezer; franks, one to two months. Ground meat (loosely wrapped) is best kept only twenty-four hours in the refrigerator; fresh poultry (wrapped loosely) can be kept one to two days.

• Milk: Keeps about five days in the refrigerator. Cream in carton keeps one week; one week for evaporated milk (in opened can). (Always check the date on the carton when buying milk or cream.)

• Pasta: Dried pasta has a shelf life of two years.

• Peanut butter: Best kept refrigerated. Keeps 6 months unopened; two months after opening.

• Pork: Fresh, three to five days for chops, one to two days for ground; three to five days for roasts. Frozen, three to four months for ground; three to four months for chops; four to eight months for roasts.

• Potatoes: Store in cool, dry place but not in the refrigerator.

• Rice, white: Up to two years if kept in a tightly closed container, in a cool, dry place; brown, one year.

• Soups: Can be refrigerated for one to two days; freeze for one to four months.

• Sugar: Granulated sugar keeps two years in a tightly closed container. Brown sugar keeps four months.

• Vegetables: Store-bought frozen vegetables can be kept up to eight months in the freezer; fresh vegetables, from one to seven days in the refrigerator.

Root vegetables (carrots, rutabagas, etc.) keep up to two weeks in the refrigerator.

Fresh vegetables, salad greens (in crisper or moisture-proof wrapping) keep up to five days.

Leftover vegetables (in covered container) and canned vegetables (in original can or other covered container) keep three days in the refrigerator.

Refreezing

Generally, if a food is safe to eat and is only partially thawed, it's safe to refreeze it, but any food which has an off-odor or color should be discarded.

• Foods that have partially thawed, that still contain ice crystals and have been held no longer than one or two days at refrigerator temperatures can be refrozen, but you should use all refrozen foods as soon as possible.

• Refrozen foods will never have the same quality as fresh or never-thawed frozen foods. They lose texture, appearance, and flavor, and may also lose food value. Ice cream and uncooked baked goods, especially, will deteriorate in texture and taste if refrozen. Most of my sources recommend discarding thawed ice cream.

• If you've thawed meat, fish, and poultry in the refrigerator, you can refreeze them within 24 hours of defrosting. However, stews, casseroles, and other combination dishes that have been thawed should not be refrozen.

• If you have a power failure which accidentally thaws foods over a period of days, you can refreeze foods only if they still have ice crystals in them. The exceptions are fruit and juice concentrates.

• If food has thawed completely (either by accident or by choice of the cook), or has warmed to room temperature and been kept at room temperature for more than two hours, throw it out.

Fruit and juice concentrates will ferment if they are spoiled by thawing and being kept at room temperatures. Always discard any fruit with an "off" flavor.

Special-Care Foods

• Eggs and any uncooked or cooked foods containing eggs should be refrigerated.

• Creams, custards, meringue pies, and foods with custard fillings—including cakes, cream puffs, and eclairs—should not be kept at room temperature. Cool slightly and then refrigerate. If such foods are taken on picnics, keep them in a cooler. Salads and sandwiches made with salad dressings containing eggs or milk products and little vinegar or other acids also need refrigeration.

• Caviar, that extra-elegant treat, needs special care because it is highly perishable. It should be removed from the refrigerator 15 minutes before eating and the lid should be removed only at the last moment. Unopened, a container of fresh caviar may be stored in the refrigerator for up to four weeks. Serve caviar in its original container placed in a bed of ice. If the caviar is oversalted, serve it with chopped hard-cooked egg; if it is fishy, serve it with chopped onion; if it is somewhat sour, serve with lemon juice.

By the way, here's some information to use when you play trivia board games: The caviar names such as Beluga, Sevruga, Osetrova, and Sterlet tell you which sturgeons produced it. Caviar tins are labeled with the name of the district where the fish was caught. "Malosol" means that the caviar is only slightly salted. It comes from the Russian words *malo* ("little") and *soleny,* ("salted").

Champagne and Wine

If you buy caviar, you'll probably buy champagne to enjoy with it (although some people like vodka with caviar). In France, all sparkling wine labeled "Champagne" can come, by law, only from the Champagne region. American vintners are not prevented from calling their sparkling wines "champagne." German sparkling wine is *Sekt*, and in Italy it's *spumante*.

• Champagne is ready to drink when you buy it and need not be saved for aging.

• Champagne should not be opened so that it shoots out of the bottle like Old Faithful geyser in Yellowstone National Park, unless, of course, you are a ballplayer celebrating a World Series win.

The best way to open a bottle of champagne is to put a napkin or handkerchief between your hand and the bottle. (This protects your hand if the bottle breaks and keeps the heat of your hand from the narrowest point on the bottle and therefore the point of most pressure from the bubbly inside.)

Remove the foil, then the wiring, keeping the bottle pointed away from yourself and not at anyone else. (The cork can pop out once the wiring is off. This is especially true for a bottle that has been jostled en route to opening.)

As you hold the cork in one hand, twist the bottle gently away from the cork with the hand protected by the napkin. If the cork doesn't ease out, you'll have to carefully push it away from the bottle with your thumb. Sometimes running warm water over just the neck of the bottle will help. If you keep the bottle at a 45-degree angle during this procedure, more of the champagne's surface will be exposed to the atmosphere and therefore the champagne will be less likely to have pressure built up at the bottle neck and will be more likely to remain in the bottle until you can pour it and enjoy.

• While we're on the subject of champagne, here's some champagne measure language for you to use when you play guessing board games and which will help you shop when you have a party.

A half-pint (1–2 glasses) is called a split
⅛ gallon (2–3 glasses) is a pint
¼ gallon (5 glasses) is a quart (a bottle)
2 quarts (10 glasses) is a magnum
4 quarts (21 glasses) is a jeroboam
6 quarts (31 glasses) is a rehoboam
8 quarts (41 glasses) is a methuselah
12 quarts (62 glasses) is a salmanasar
16 quarts (83 glasses) is a balthazar
20 quarts (104 glasses) is a nebuchadnezzar

• If you are buying champagne for the future, it's better to buy bottles of less than a magnum size. They last longer. Keep dated records of where and when you bought champagne and wine, then record any comments after you open and taste it.

Champagne is meant to be drunk within a short period of time. Therefore, do not buy champagne to keep and store away for five or ten years at a time. And most important, do not store the champagne in the refrigerator. (Purists think that champagne can absorb odors from other foods in the refrigerator over a long period of time. In addition, the cork, in cold temperatures, will eventually shrink, allowing the bubbles to escape and the wine to go flat.) Store it in a cool, dark place on its side. Then put it in the refrigerator or in a bucket of ice water two hours before serving.

• Wine that is capped instead of corked is wine that is ready to drink when you buy it; enjoy!

• Whether your taste is for sparkling or still (nonbubbly) wines, proper storage of wine will preserve the flavors you've spent your hard-earned money to buy.

• Remember that wine that doesn't require aging or that you will drink soon can be stored standing up for a short time, but wine that is to be aged should be stored lying down to keep the cork damp so that no air can reach the wine. You can set notched boards at right angles to your storage shelves to let bottles lie on their sides without clanging into each other.

• Accordion-type wooden wine racks can be installed in any type of cabinet or bookcase to hold wine bottles on their sides and in the dark, as nature demands.

• If you buy a case of wine, the case can be placed on its side in a cool basement for storage. Wine boxes (cases) can be inserted into cabinets to hold stored wine bottles on their sides.

To make your own wine "rack":

• Construct a concrete-block "student" bookcase by layering blocks with sturdy boards and then stacking wine bottles, which have been inserted into mailing tubes, on the shelves.

• Or stack clay tubular drain tiles against a cool cellar wall to hold wine bottles. The tiles can be supported on the sides of this "wine rack" if they are placed wall to wall or within a bookcase or other sturdy frame.

• Or fit two sturdy pieces of wood, which have been fitted with grooves so that they are joined diagonally to form an X, into a square cabinet and then insert wine bottles in the spaces.

• Most oenophiles (wine experts) agree that the ideal temperature for a wine cellar should be 55 to 60 degrees Fahrenheit, with 45 to 70 degrees as the outer limits. Keeping the temperature constant is even more important than the exact temperature.

• Humidity prevents the corks from drying out and allowing the wine to evaporate or spoil. Too much humidity, however, will allow fungus to grow. The best humidity level is 75 percent.

• Remember that wine can "breathe" through the cork, and therefore cellar odors can be absorbed by the wine.

• Wine rests better in the dark, and it doesn't like vibrations, especially if it is an aged wine. Keep your stored wine away from laundry machines or other vibrating equipment.

• If you are moving during very hot or very cold weather, you will need to insulate the wines. My sources advise me that when you are moving at any time, wrap the wine bottles in about a one-inch thickness of newspapers for shipping; once they are moved, let the bottles rest undisturbed for at least a month before they are opened.

CHAPTER 3

In and Around the House

Sometimes we top-clean and sometimes we get an uncontrollable urge to clean up every speck, spot, and smudge in the house.

Although we may do a thorough type of cleaning only at Christmas, Easter, or when we are moving out of a house or apartment, we do need to top-clean often. For most people, that means at least once a week. We all know that if you keep things reasonably clean, you don't need to do serious cleaning as often. For example, a carpet that's vacuumed frequently won't develop dirty traffic paths that need shampooing as quickly as one that is seldom vacuumed. Bathroom fixtures that are cleaned frequently don't accumulate excessive hard water deposits and stains. And, of course, clean things (any things) last longer.

You can prevent unnecessary cleaning if you get rid of clutter as a habit, if you organize proper storage systems and places, and if you can get the people you live with to cooperate and help. You can reduce the amount of dirt in the house by confining eating and messy projects to easily cleaned areas, by wiping up spills as soon as possible, and by controlling household pests. (I don't mean people here!)

If you are among the millions of Americans who live alone, you can't delegate cleaning chores unless you hire someone. If you are one of the almost thirty million working couples in the United States or one of the many families with children under eighteen in which both parents work, you have even less time to clean.

Few people can keep up the pace of working at two jobs—home and outside the home—forever. Many people have developed systems for more equitable sharing of housework. For example, working couples alternate chores each Saturday or Sunday—one person cleans, the other does the week's laundry and grocery shops; the next week they trade jobs, and so on.

Many families either rotate certain chores from person to person or use the "job jar" system, in which different jobs are written on pieces of paper and drawn on a certain day so that the "winner" gets a chore by chance.

Whatever system is used, I know that this book can help. The page number on which the appropriate cleaning tip is printed could be written on the job jar assignment note. Parents who leave notes designating certain chores to be done by children after school can also note the page on which appropriate instructions for that chore are given. Favorite cleaning hints can be marked with a highlighter pen so that the chore person of the day can find them easily.

It's often difficult to get a system going, especially when everyone is used to "good ol' mom" (or whoever is the usual family cleaner) doing everything. However, if everyone pitches in, everything gets done faster and everyone, including "good ol' mom" or "good ol' whoever," gets a bit more self time. (Self time is when you read a book, call a friend, exercise, meditate, or do anything else that gives you pleasure and renews your spirit.)

Rewards work, no doubt about it. After a housework session, whether it's a top cleaning or a serious and even under-the-rug cleaning, all the workers deserve something special—a movie, dinner out, a picnic, anything that's fun, and the reward system applies whether you live alone, as a couple, or in a family.

Who knows, when you get more people into the cleaning act, you may develop better ways of getting jobs done, which, of course, you'll want to send to my Heloise's column so that others can benefit too.

Whenever you are cleaning, always follow directions on products. Read labels before buying products appropriate to the type of cleaning you will do. Many cleaning products are poisonous or flammable or both. Store them away from kitchen ranges, radiators, or furnaces, and ALWAYS store cleaning products out of the reach of small children, never under the kitchen sink.

Bathrooms

Cleaning the bathroom is a terrible chore to most people. But think about this: The bathroom is usually the smallest room of the house, so there is really less total area to clean, whether you measure it in cubic feet or square feet of surfaces. Isn't that a nice thought?

We have to accept the fact that no matter how spotless we make them, bathrooms don't stay pristine clean unless locked shut. But there are ways of making this chore less tedious, and some of them are listed below.

Cleaning Tiles and Bathroom Fixtures

• One of the easiest ways I know to quick-clean a bathroom, especially one with tile walls and floor, is to get a bunch of paper towels and a spray bottle of commercial window cleaner or the homemade one described below.

• Make your own all-purpose cleaner and shiner (mix and store in an empty plastic quart bottle) by adding two tablespoons of vinegar or two tablespoons of sudsy ammonia and filling the bottle with water. Be sure to label this clearly as your homemade cleaner so it doesn't get used for other purposes.

Clean from the top down, changing paper towels as you go and saving all the wet ones to do the floor. Do mirrors, sink area, wall tiles, the outside and rim of the bathtub, toilet tank and seat, and finally the floor. (Most plastic and painted wood toilet seats and many wall paints can be cleaned with liquid window cleaner. Test an inconspicuous place first to make sure.)

• Wash the floor with the used towels and more sprays of cleaner, wiping it with dry towels as you back out of the room to avoid putting footprints on the wet floor. It helps if you get dust and hairs off the floor first, but it's not absolutely necessary.

Close the shower curtain to cover the tub, throw a rug over the heavy traffic patch of the floor, and you have a shiny, clean bathroom. (Clean the tub or shower stall some other day, when you aren't in such a rush.)

• You can make your own ceramic-tile cleaner from common household ingredients. Mix one-fourth cup baking soda, one-half cup white vinegar, and one cup ammonia in a bucket.

Add one gallon of warm water and stir until the baking soda dissolves. Apply with a sponge or scrub brush. You'll need to mix a fresh batch for each cleaning, because this is not a "keeper."

CAUTION: Wear rubber gloves, because this is a bit unkind to your skin and nails.

• A variation of the cleaner above, which can be used for serious scrubbing or heavy-duty grout cleaning, is the following paste made from three cups baking soda and one cup warm water. In a medium-size bowl, mix to a smooth paste and then scrub it into the grout with a damp sponge or toothbrush. Rinse thoroughly afterward. Always mix a fresh batch for each cleaning.

• Cleaning things with baking soda really makes your fingernails white. This is a good cleaning job to do after you've done some craft or project that stains the undersides of your fingernails or have been digging in the garden without wearing gloves. You can clean two messes with one paste! Follow up with hand lotion.

• Here's another quickie cleaner for tiles and shower doors. Spray tiles or glass shower doors liberally with any brand of pre-wash spray. Wait a few minutes, then rub the scum away with a damp sponge. (If you use a petroleum or oil-based pre-wash spray, be sure to rinse or wash out the bottom of the tub or shower stall carefully, as it can be slippery.)

Rinse the area thoroughly and dry with a towel.

• Do family members leave squished-out toothpaste all over the sink? Take a wet sponge or dirty washcloth and use the toothpaste to clean the sink and fixtures. Rinse the sink and toss the washcloth into the laundry.

• You can remove most mildew from the grout between tiles by rubbing it with an old toothbrush or nail brush dipped in laundry bleach. (Don't use abrasive powders or steel wool pads, because they'll scratch the tile.)

Rinse with clear water after cleaning.

• You can also remove mildew from the grouting between tiles by dabbing a toothbrush in powdered cleanser, wetting it, and scrubbing it in between the tiles, then letting it sit for a few moments before rinsing off.

• If some brown spots remain no matter what you do, you can camouflage stained grout with a white fingernail pencil or white typewriter correction fluid.

• To keep tiles and shower doors looking shiny, spray them with your favorite furniture spray and shine with a soft cloth or paper towels.

Of course, the tiles must be clean before you use this, or you'll just end up with a mucky mess. And again, be sure that the floor of the tub or shower is completely clean, as it can be slippery.

Cleaning the Toilet Bowl

Almost everyone who moves around from apartment to apartment, house to house, will occasionally find a bathroom that has escaped not only regular real cleaning, but also minimal care! If you find yourself in an apartment or house that was previously inhabited by someone with toilet-cleanophobia (the fear of cleaning toilets), the first tip in this section may help.

• Sprinkle one-fourth cup sodium bisulfate (sodium acid sulfate from hardware store or drugstore) into a wet toilet bowl for a single scrubbing and flushing.

CAUTION: Wear rubber gloves. Also, don't use this acid with chlorine bleach, because the resulting fumes are toxic.
Let it stand for 15 minutes; then scrub and flush as usual.

• In some parts of the United States, the only way to completely avoid rust-stained toilet bowls is to not have toilet bowls, and who could live with that!

Rust stains under a toilet bowl rim will sometimes yield to chlorine bleach, but be sure to protect your hands with rubber gloves, even when you use a long-handled brush, because even splashes of bleach can hurt your skin. This is true also for strong commercial preparations for toilet bowl cleaning.
The best way is to get a good commercial rust remover made specifically for porcelain. Be sure to read the directions carefully.
CAUTION: Never combine bleach with toilet bowl cleaners; the mix can release toxic gases.

• If all else fails, gently rub off truly stubborn rust stains with extra-fine steel wool or with wet-dry sandpaper (available at hardware stores).

• Cola that has gone flat can be poured into the toilet bowl. If left to soak for an hour, the drink will clean the bowl.

(Sort of a scary thought, isn't it? Makes you wonder what cola does to your body's plumbing!)

• A quick way to remove a lot of stains in the toilet is to drop in several denture cleaner tablets, let them foam and bubble, scrub and brush, and flush away.

• CAUTION: Chemical toilet bowl cleaners, commercial or homemade, should never be used to clean the bathtub or sink, because the chemicals will etch and ruin their finishes.

Once the glaze finish is removed from sinks and bathtubs, they will stain gray even with normal daily use and be difficult to brighten with ordinary cleaning.

Certain epoxy finishes or reglazing can be applied by professionals or by using finishing kits available at some hardware stores. This is a major project, and prevention is a better idea.

If you haven't been lucky enough to prevent the glaze from being removed from your tub, reglazing is a good alternative. Look in the Yellow Pages under "Bathtub Refinishers" or "Bathtub Reglazers." Be sure to ask to see references, or talk to references, and ask how long they have been in the business and if the people you called were happy with the job. Once this has been done, you must be sure never, ever to use abrasive cleansers on that finish, or it will simply be a waste of your money.

Cleaning the Bathtub

• You can enjoy your bath without leaving a tub ring if you add water-softener bath crystals or bubble bath to the water. If you are out of anything fancy, try a capful of mild liquid dish-washing detergent in the bathwater. Of course, this is if you have no allergies, and this is not preferable for young children.

• Rub away ring-around-the-tub with an old nylon stocking rolled into a ball. Old pantyhose can become a nonscratch scrub pad for cleaning sink and tub. You can also use old skin-cleaning pads once they become too worn and abrasive for your skin.

• A nylon-net ball or pad will scrub away rings without the aid of any cleaner.

• If you have to deal with a stubborn bathtub ring, try covering it with a paste of cream of tartar and hydrogen peroxide. When the paste dries, wipe it off along with the ring.

• To get rid of bathtub rust stains, try rubbing them with a paste of borax powder and lemon juice. If the stain persists, use a dry-cleaning solution. (You will also find commercial preparations for this chore; follow directions exactly.)

• You can clean a rubber or vinyl bathtub mat by tossing it into the washer with bath towels. The terry cloth scrubs the mat, and all come out clean at the same time.

• A quick way to clean the bath mat is to spray it with a foamy spray bathroom cleaner, let it sit a few moments, scrub, and rinse with very hot water.

Shower Cleaning

Shower enclosures are a chore to keep clean. If you can teach the people who live and shower in your house to wipe down the shower walls and glass doors with a rubber window wand wiper or the towel they've just used while they're still standing in the tub, you can stretch the intervals between vigorous, thorough cleanings.

Eventually, some cleaning has to be done, but it can be less of a chore if you use the following tips.

• When the walls need a thorough cleaning, run the shower water at its hottest temperature so the steam will loosen the dirt before you start to scrub on it.

CAUTION: Don't stay in the tub for this.

• To clean in a jiffy, without even getting your hands wet, use a sponge mop dipped into a mixture of one-half cup vinegar, one cup clear ammonia, and one-quarter cup baking soda in one gallon of warm water. (Yes, yes, vinegar, ammonia, baking soda, and aren't they great?)

After cleaning, rinse with clear water.

• Never use harsh abrasive powders or steel-wool pads, because they'll scratch porcelain tile or fiberglass.

• To get mineral deposits off a shower head, remove it, take it apart, and soak in vinegar. Then brush deposits loose with an old toothbrush. Clean the holes by poking them with a wire, pin, toothpick, or ice pick.

• If the shower head cannot be removed, take a plastic sandwich bag, fill it with vinegar, wrap it around the shower head, and attach it tightly with a thick rubber band. Let it sit overnight. Proceed with the cleaning.

• Lemon oil furniture polish will remove water spots on metal frames around shower doors and enclosures.

• Glass shower doors will sparkle again if you clean them once a week with a sponge dipped in white vinegar. This is a good tip; regular cleaning of any part of the bathroom will help you avoid having to use strong chemicals and lots of energy (yours) to clean it.

My favorite way is to spray with pre-wash spray, let it sit a few moments, and simply wipe away with a sponge. Use a handful of nylon net or a plastic scrubby to really get at the grungy stuff, and then rinse it all down the drain.

• You can wash plastic shower curtains in the washer. Wash them with towels to get some automatic scrubbing action.

Put them in the washing machine with one-half cup detergent and one-half cup baking soda, along with two large bath towels.

Add a cup of vinegar to the rinse cycle, then hang the curtains up immediately after washing and let them air dry.

• You can get wrinkles out of the plastic shower curtain and soften it at the same time by tossing it into the dryer with the towels for a few minutes.

A shower curtain doesn't need to go through the whole drying cycle; some will all but melt! Just let it spin for two, three, or four minutes, depending upon the heat of your dryer, then remove it from the dryer and hang immediately.

• When you clean a plastic shower curtain, you can keep it soft and flexible by adding a few drops of mineral oil to the rinse water.

Mirrors

Some people keep full-length mirrors in their bathrooms as reminders to stay on their diets. There's nothing like finding out where all those calories go after they leave your lips. But whatever size mirror you have, a shiny one makes the whole room look clean.

• To make your bathroom mirror sparkle, try polishing it with a cloth dipped in a borax-and-water solution or in denatured alcohol. Wipe dry to shine with a lint-free cloth, newspapers, paper toweling, or an old nylon stocking.

• Rubbing alcohol will wipe away that dull hair spray haze from a mirror.

• This is one of my favorite hints. For a quick swipe, to make the bathroom sparkle, dab a little rubbing alcohol or even vinegar on a facial tissue, wipe the mirror, and it will sparkle and shine.

• Bathroom mirrors won't steam up if you run an inch of cold water in the bathtub before you add the hot water.

• If you need to defog a bathroom mirror in a jiffy, try "spraying" it with hot air from your hand-held dryer.

• To help prevent the mirror from getting foggy, wipe it with an anti-fog product that is sold for automobiles. Or, if you have a medicine cabinet where the mirrors slide over each other, close them so that one mirror is covered while you're taking a shower. Then, when you're ready to use the mirror, simply slide the door back and there's an unfogged mirror to use.

• This glass-cleaning solution is good for cleaning mirrors in any room. Mix two cups water with one cup isopropyl rubbing alcohol (70 percent) and one tablespoon household ammonia. Pour into a clean pump-spray bottle.

Cleaning and Organizing Bedrooms and Living Areas

When you get ready to do a serious deep cleaning of the entire house, you will sabotage your whole effort if you take the clutter from one room and distribute it to the others. What gets picked up should get put where it belongs and, if it doesn't belong anywhere, it should be given to a charity or thrown out.

• Work in one room at a time and don't switch to another until the first room is finished, even if it takes several days. Seeing progress in one room will give you a greater sense of accomplishment than having several half-finished, mostly torn-up rooms.

• If the first room's work has taken most of the day, don't start another when you're already tired. Wait until morning, when you're more likely to be in the mood to clean thoroughly.

• Remember, it's easier to do a little each day. Get rid of papers and junk as they accumulate, and vacuum and dust daily if you can.

• If you clean your living room daily, you'll always have one clean and orderly refuge from clutter. One clean room prevents your feeling overwhelmed by a whole house in need of attention. And, you'll have someplace to sit comfortably if a friend drops over for a coffee-chat break.

Organizing and Cleaning Bedrooms

• Organize your dresser drawers. Shoe boxes that fit inside drawers make great dividers for underwear, stockings, and jewelry. Divide to conquer is the motto for drawer organizing. To organize your closets, see Chapter 7, which deals with cleaning out closets and clothing management.

• Keep a hall tree handy in the bedroom or walk-in closet for airing clothing that doesn't get washed after each wearing. A hall tree is a good "guest closet" too.

• To make your bed easily, attach two safety pins on the underside of the bedspread—one on each side at the end of the mattress to indicate its width. Feel for the pin, and line it up with the edge to save yourself from walking back and forth, from one side of the bed to the other, lining up the spread.

You can line up sheets the same way, except instead of using safety pins, sew a couple of colored stitches on each side. This saves a lot of steps if you have a king-size bed.

• Unless you are one of those sleepers who completely pulls apart the bedding each night or you have a bed partner who does it, you can make your bed before you even get out of it, like I do.

When you're ready to get out of bed, sit in the middle of the bed and pull up the sheets, blanket, spread, and so on, then smooth out any folds, then slide out the side. Then finish off the head of the bed in whatever way you keep it.

If you just use a quilt or coverlet, instead of a bedspread and blanket, and let the pillows show, all you have to do is fold the top of the top sheet over the edge of the quilt before you slide out and the bed is made.

• Having one side of the bed close to a wall is a problem when you're making the bed. If you have a lightweight spread, you can pin weights (nuts and bolts) to the underside of the spread's edge. Then the spread will slide right down into place on the wall side.

• A lace or cut-work tablecloth spread over a colored sheet can be a pretty guest-room spread and a way to store and to get more use from the tablecloth.

• If you have the space in your closet, keeping your bedding in the bedroom where it's used saves you steps at bed-changing time.

• And a way to really save space is to put the bedspread or extra blankets on hangers and hang them at the very back of the closet.

• If you're short on bedding storage space, keep guest-room beds made up and toss a fabric softener sheet or a mildly scented bar of soap under the blanket to keep the linens fresh smelling.

• If you have a daybed with a pull-out twin bed underneath and only one guest, have the guest sleep on the pull-out bed instead of the top one. Then, instead of having to arrange pillows and spreads on the daybed every day, you can just slide the bottom bed into its usual place each morning.

• Store extra pillows on beds and sofas. Cover them with zippered corduroy or other room color coordinating pillowcases.

• If you make your bed with sheets still warm from the dryer, they will "iron" themselves on the bed, and you'll save time by not having to fold them up and put them away.

• Although we've always been taught to rotate sheets and towels in our linen closets to keep them fresh, if you don't live in a damp climate and your house is always air-conditioned or heated, you may not have to do this at all. In fact, it may make more sense to use only one set at a time.

You can just use the same color-coordinated sheets and towels over and over right from the dryer, without ever having to fold and put them away, until they are worn out, and then you can choose a new color scheme without having a closet cluttered with half-worn-out things that don't match your rooms anymore.

This is one of my father's favorite hints. It is his way of solving the how-do-you-fold-the-fitted-sheet problem—he doesn't.

Also, rotating your sets of sheets and towels means that all of these items will last longer but will wear out at the same time. It's really easier on the budget to replace only one set at a time.

General Cleaning

Adopt a routine or a sequence of cleaning steps such as the sequence shown below, which works well for cleaning just about any room in the house. When you use the same routine over and over, it becomes so automatic that you can think about something else while you're doing it. Some people like to "plug in" to their radio or cassette earphones while they clean. Music with a beat helps beat the cleaning blues. Here's a top-to-bottom routine to try.

1. Pick up all papers, magazines, or any other clutter that doesn't have to be there.
2. Dust knickknacks, paintings, lamps, and so on.
3. Dust or polish all wood furniture.
4. Vacuum floors, carpets, and upholstered furniture.
5. Dry mop, sweep, or scrub non-carpeted floors.

6. Do any heavy cleaning chores such as window cleaning, silver/brass polishing, miscellaneous repairs, and so on.
7. Close the door and go on to another room. Closing the door keeps dirt and dust from getting back into clean rooms and gives you the satisfaction of having finished something.
8. If you pick up items that need to go to another part of the house, don't leave that room. Put them outside the door and then remove them all at once. Don't let yourself get sidetracked.

General Cleaning and Repairing Tips

I've tried to arrange these tips in the order of the cleaning routine suggested above, so that the quick-clean tips are first and the deep, serious, grungicide hints follow.

Picking Up Clutter

• Drag around a plastic or paper garbage bag or wastebasket as you clean, so that you won't have far to go to throw away clutter.

• Make up a cleaning kit. Use a box, plastic carrier with a handle, or bucket to tote all of your cleaning supplies around so that you won't be running back and forth for rags, furniture wax, window cleaner, vacuum bags, and so forth.

Knickknacks

• You can wash most knickknacks in less time than it takes to dust them if you swish them in water containing a touch of liquid detergent. Then, rinse and drain on a towel. If you want to make sure every crevice is dry, use a hand-held hair dryer to blow away moisture.

• To wash fragile objects without breaking them, put them on a towel-covered tray in the sink and spray them first with window cleaner and then with water. Let them air dry on a towel.

• To keep your phone clean and germ free, wipe it with an alcohol-soaked paper towel often. Most of us don't think about cleaning a phone, but it does need a wipe every now and then. I know mine does.

Lamps

• Clean lamp shades and see how much more light your lamp will give off. Don't forget to clean the bulb too! You can dust them with a new, soft paintbrush or your vacuum cleaner dusting brush.

• If you need to go beyond dusting, you can wash some lamp shades. Check the instructions that came on their labels. (You did save the labels in your household file, didn't you?)

When lamp shades aren't glued to their frames, gently wash them in the bathtub with warm water and a spray hose. Dry them quickly after washing so the frames won't rust. An electric fan or hair dryer can speed the drying process.

Cleaning Oil Paintings and Frames

Valuable oil paintings should be cleaned by experts. It's too risky to use home remedies on such things. And, according to most experts, it's better to under-clean than overclean (which could severely damage paintings).

The simple inexpensive oil paintings that most of us have in our homes may be cleaned as follows. (You must decide values of paintings to be cleaned at home.)

• The surface of most paintings gathers household dust, which can be removed with a soft brush. Never use a rag or a feather duster. Threads from the rag or feathers can get caught in any tiny lifted areas in the oil paint or cracked ridges, causing damage to the painting. A camel or badger hairbrush is best; use a gentle back-and-forth motion. A vacuum brush attachment is too coarse and will scratch a varnished painting.

• To clean a deeply carved picture frame, use an empty clean, dry, plastic squeeze bottle; pump the bottle like small bellows to blow dust from tiny crevices. (This works when you are cleaning 35-mm slides, too.) Of course, one of my most favorite and the easiest way is to use your hand-held hair dryer on blow, with cold air only.

• To make a tarnished gilt frame gleam again, wipe it with a turpentine-dampened rag. Chipped gilt frames can be repaired with touch-up kits available at some hardware stores.

Dusting and Polishing Wood Furniture

Most of the time we need only to dust furniture with a feather duster or a soft dirt-collecting cloth. Some people wax and oil their furniture regularly. Others wax or oil only when they feel a need to work off excess energy. Many of the tips in this section will help you put a shine on your furniture without ruining most of your fingernails and getting yourself too tired to appreciate the results of your work.

The good news and excuse for not waxing and polishing too often is that using too much oil on furniture eventually darkens it, because dirt and oil form a film on the surface. I once used a commercial furniture cleaner on a very old piece of furniture bought at an auction and was amazed to find very elaborate light fruitwood-colored veneer designs underneath what I thought was a plain, dark walnut finish.

In all cases, when you are planning to wax or oil furniture, remember that the finish on the furniture determines which method you will use. Generally, high luster furniture needs a liquid polish or paste wax, which dries to high shine. Low luster or satin finish furniture needs a greaseless cream polish or wax that protects without shine. Natural oil-finished furniture needs to be reoiled with the type of oil originally used by the manufacturer (or boiled linseed oil). Most manufacturers say it's not good to switch back and forth with different products, using wax one time, oil the next, and some other polish later.

• To dust furniture with a double-barreled approach, dampen two old cotton gloves or socks with furniture polish, slip them on, and then dust with both hands.

• To remove sticky residue that collects on wooden furniture and around the handles of varnished kitchen cupboards, use a good furniture cleaner. You can find one in hardware stores and some larger grocery stores, usually in the furniture refinishing or housewares department.

While you are there, buy some fine (0000) steel wool. Do not use any that is coarser; make sure the package has at least four zeroes. This will remove any residue that the cleaner leaves behind. Be careful to rub the wood very gently, with the grain, and only until the buildup is removed. Don't rub excessively or you will scratch the finish.

After cleaning, apply a good furniture polish and buff to a shine.

• Furniture polish recipe: Here's a tried-and-true recipe for furniture polish that doesn't create an oily/waxy buildup and doesn't put a high, glossy shine on wood, just a nice, deep glow.

Mix together one-third cup vinegar, one-third cup turpentine, and one-third cup boiled linseed oil, which is available at most paint stores. DO NOT attempt to boil your own linseed oil; the oil is highly flammable.

CAUTION: ALWAYS label the container clearly. DO NOT use this polish on plastic or laminated furniture.

To use this polish, moisten a soft cloth with it and rub over your furniture, going back over it with a clean cloth.

• Most water rings on wood tables can be removed easily if you get to them right away. Immediately moisten a cloth, dip it into cigar ashes (some people claim cigarette ashes work well too), and rub the milky spot gently. You can also mix mayonnaise or vegetable oil in with the ashes.

If no one in your house is a smoker (and we sincerely hope they aren't), using mayonnaise or vegetable oil and a dry cloth first just might do the trick.

• Paste shoe polish covers small scratches, marks, or discolorations on furniture, cabinets, or wood paneling. Use dark brown on dark wood, tan on lighter wood. It works like magic and leaves a nice glow.

• If you sprinkle a little cornstarch on furniture after you've polished it, and then rub it to a high gloss, you'll find that the cornstarch absorbs excess oil and leaves a glistening, fingerprint-free surface.

• To avoid leaving fingerprints while polishing furniture, wear cotton gloves. They'll protect your hands from the polish, too.

• If you keep ashtrays in your house, give them a wipe with the cloth you've used for waxing furniture; it makes them easier to clean. Please note that I said, "If you keep ashtrays in your house," because many people have put ashtrays to better use—to hold paper clips, soap, jewelry, or pot plants—because they've quit smoking and have non-smoking homes.

• Got paper stuck to a polished table? Saturate the paper with cooking oil and let it sit awhile, and it will peel right off.

• You can hide mini-scratches on finished wood by rubbing walnut or pecan meat over them.

• Leftover tea makes a good cleaning agent for varnished furniture.

Repairing Furniture

Most of us can do simple repairs on most furniture ourselves. Really valuable antiques are best repaired by professionals. Check with a few of the best antiques stores in your town to find out where they send their work. Ask to see samples of repaired furniture before you release your valuable pieces to a repair shop and then agree beforehand what will be done—repairs, replacement of parts or hardware, reupholstery, refinishing wood, or just cleaning and polishing it. Some people like to totally refinish antique or old pieces, and others feel that the antique value is destroyed when anything beyond serious cleaning and functional repairs is done.

Here are a few tips on repairing the "dings" that show up in our furniture from daily use.

• Dents in wood furniture can be "ironed" out—really, they can. If you have a dent (where wood fibers are not actually cut, just bent), set your electric iron on medium heat and get a damp cloth.

Place the cloth on the dent, then hold the iron on it until the cloth begins to dry. Repeat the process (redampen the cloth each time) until the dent is raised.

• If you have a pesky cabinet or dresser knob that keeps coming loose, dip the screw end into clear fingernail polish or shellac, then return the knob to the hole. When the polish or shellac hardens, the screw will be set and the knob will be tight. (And your aggravation will be gone!)

• When your chair wobbles because one leg is shorter than the others, you can lengthen the short leg by molding a piece of wood putty in the shape of the chair leg tip. After the putty dries, sand and stain it to match the leg and glue it in place. No more wobble-rocking!

• When wooden drawers stick, you can make them glide better if you rub the contact surfaces with a bar of soap or an old candle stub.

Just remember that you've unstuck the drawer the next time you open it; otherwise, you'll pull with your usual "darn this stuck drawer" force and end up with everything dumped on the floor for an unplanned drawer-cleaning session.

• You can tighten loose furniture leg casters by wrapping the caster stems with rubber bands before reinserting them.

• When you are repairing furniture or putting together unassembled new items fitted with dowels, most of the glue gets pushed into the bottom of the hole and the rest of it squishes out of the rim when you insert the dowel into its hole.

This happens because the dowel is exactly the size of the hole, and the result is that the joint may not hold as well as it should. If you cut a few grooves into the dowel, the glue will distribute itself along the dowel surface into the grooves and you'll get a better bond.

• Wicker furniture can be kept from getting wobbly by lightly misting old wicker pieces with water, using a plant mister every now and then. You can tighten wobbly wicker furniture by washing it outdoors (or in the shower if it will fit) with hot, soapy water; then, rinse with a hose and let it air dry. The water treatment will shrink and tighten the wood and cane.

• If you need to dismantle a piece of furniture to repair it, number/label the parts with strips of masking tape so that you can put them all together again.

Use this tip for furniture that disassembles-assembles for moving. It's hard enough to get your life back in order when you move without adding extra confusion to the chaos.

• Here's an old-fashioned but effective way to unwarp a table leaf or other board, using water and hot summer sun. Thoroughly water a sunny, grassy area; place the board concave side down on the wet grass. As the dry side of the board absorbs moisture from the grass, the moist (convex) side will get dried out by the sun and usually, in no more than a day, the board will un-warp itself.

Refinishing Furniture

To see a Cinderella develop from an Ugly Duckling is a very rewarding experience. You can find many new products on the market for deep cleaning and refinishing old, pre-owned (sounds better than "used") furniture nowadays, all of which save time and energy. You can also find excellent-quality unfinished furniture to stain in colors of your choice and to blend in with furniture you already own.

• Keep dust circulation to a minimum by switching off the central heating system in your house before you begin refinishing and varnishing furniture indoors. However, you must always keep your work space well ventilated and with a constant temperature over 70 degrees Fahrenheit. Cooler temperatures prevent finishes and glues from working properly.

• Many furniture strippers and stains will dissolve ordinary rubber gloves; buy heavy-duty gloves to protect your skin and fingernails.

• Wear cloth work/garden gloves when sanding or steel-wooling raw wood to prevent putting your fingerprints on the wood. Oils in your skin can make marks that show up when you wipe on the stain.

• Old socks and cotton knit underwear make great wiping cloths for stain. Inside-out terry sports socks absorb well for wiping off stain, and fuzzy nylon men's crew socks make good applicators for some stains and sealers.

Carpet Care

• When you vacuum, take slow, overlapping strokes (at least seven strokes) to really clean out embedded dirt particles.

• If you have a pet and the resulting problems with fleas in your carpets, your vacuum cleaner is your best ally in the battle against these pests. Always vacuum thoroughly after applying flea killers. Some people toss a few mothballs into the vacuum cleaner bag to kill the bugs that get evicted from their homes in the carpet.

• You can't vacuum well if the bag is full; check the vacuum cleaner bag often. If the bag must be emptied, you can prevent dust clouds from polluting your home if you empty the vacuum cleaner bag into a large plastic garbage bag. Hold the mouth of the bag shut as you dump the dust inside it. If your vacuum cleaner uses disposable bags, keep them handy in your cleaning tote.

• Shedding is common in new carpeting, as loose fibers left over from the manufacturing process rise to the surface. Don't panic!

• Static electricity in some carpet fibers plagues us mostly in the winter months when humidity is low in the home. The commercial anti-static sprays made especially for fabrics and carpets found in supermarkets are effective. Running a humidifier can help. (It's also good for your skin and lungs if very dry air causes you to have dry skin or breathing problems.)

• You can use a steam iron to remove indentations caused by furniture legs. Hold the iron above the indentation, but don't let it touch the carpeting. Let the steam penetrate the area. The fibers should spring back to normal. You may have to repeat the steaming for stubborn dents. Use a brush to fluff up the pile after steaming.

• A quick-fix way to do this is to place a single ice cube in the indentation. As it slowly melts, the moisture will go into the fibers and plump them up.

• It's a good idea to keep drapes closed on sunny days. Overexposure to the sun will fade some carpet fibers.

• Carpeting that has not been tacked down properly will wrinkle, especially on humid summer days. Winter heating removes the extra moisture, so the rug usually lies flat. The only way to eliminate this seasonal wrinkle is to have the carpet restretched.

CARPET STAINS AND REPAIRS

While many of the stain removal tips in Chapter 7, "Clothing Care," can also be used when removing spots and stains from carpets, you need to take a few extra steps when you are working with them.

• After using the appropriate solution for the spot or stain, it's important to rinse the area. With clothing, of course, you can just hold the garment under running water or immerse it. With carpets, after you rinse the area with clear water to remove all detergents or other stain removers, you have to blot up as much of the moisture as you can to prevent rings from forming around the area you worked on.

Here's how: Place an old white towel or wads of white paper towels (use white to prevent any possible color bleeding) over the wet area, then walk around on the towels, reversing them so the dry sides are touching the carpet. Keep doing this until the area feels mostly dry.

Then place another dry white towel on the area and weigh it down (with bricks, a heavy book wrapped in foil or plastic wrap to protect it from moisture, or a stack of magazines) so that it will help draw out any remaining moisture. Leave the weighted towel on the area overnight. In the morning or whenever the carpet is dry, fluff up the nap with your fingers, a brush, or the vacuum cleaner.

• Clean all spills immediately. Set stains will be difficult to remove, especially those from beverages that contain sugar and from pet urine. (See Chapter 7.)

• Mysterious returning spots: A mysterious stain that keeps reappearing could be from an oily substance that was not totally removed or cleaned well. It could also be coming up from the foam or back of the carpet.

Sometimes products used to clean the carpet can be at fault if they leave a sticky film that attracts dirt and lint.

• Bleach spots: You can recolor small bleach spots with this home remedy. Mix food coloring or clothing dye with water to make the correct shade and apply. The color can be reapplied as it fades. Because wet fibers appear darker in color than they really are, you'll have to allow the retouched area to dry before you can tell if the color is a match. Don't toss out the mix; you may have to reapply the color.

• A color crayon can be used in a pinch. Color the spot, then cover with wax paper and iron on low setting. This can be reapplied if it fades.

• Musty-smelling carpets: A musty smell is usually a sign that the carpet or padding is damp. If it cannot be taken outside to dry in the sunlight, dry it with a fan, or if it's a small area, use a hair dryer on a low setting.

• If the odor remains after the carpet is completely dry, there may be mildew on the back. Try sprinkling some baking soda underneath (if the carpet is not tacked down) and on top. Wait a day, then vacuum.

• If you are so unfortunate as to have a carpeted room get flooded, you'll have to remove the foam padding and allow it to dry before you can get the carpet to dry.

If the flooding is very bad, please take the time to remove the entire carpet and all of the padding and allow to dry thoroughly before replacing. If you try to do it halfway, and think you can get away with it naturally drying on the floor, you're asking for trouble, because the backing and the padding will eventually mildew.

• Repairing cigarette burns: Cut out the burned section of fibers. Using cuticle scissors helps. Gather some strands and fuzz from an out-of-the-way spot, and glue them in the hole with fabric glue. Place a piece of wax paper over this repair, put a book on top, and allow it to dry thoroughly for at least 24 hours.

• If the burn is large and deep you may have to call a professional to reweave the area. Burn holes in furniture upholstery can also be rewoven by professionals.

Upholstered Furniture

• To remove cat or dog hair from upholstery, rub a rubber glove over the upholstery; the hair will roll into a neat pile with each glove stroke. You can minimize the amount of shedding by brushing your pets regularly. Some cats love the attention, others protest, but it's worth a try. I even know some cats and dogs that love to be vacuumed!

• Upholstered furniture sold after 1970 usually has a letter code somewhere on its tag that tells which cleaning or spot-removal methods are safe for the fabric.

The code is as follows:

W—Use water and cleaning agents or foam mixed with water.
S—Use no water. Use dry-cleaning solvents.
W-S—Use either water-based or dry-cleaning solvents.
X—Don't use liquid or foam cleaning agents. Soil can be removed by brushing or vacuuming only.

• Upholstered leather furniture should never be cleaned with oils or furniture polishes; these may make the leather sticky. Clean leather chairs or tabletops by rubbing with a lather of warm water and castile or saddle soap. Wipe with a clean cloth and buff dry with a soft cloth.

• Vinyl furniture can be cleaned with a solution of warm water and mild detergent. Rub to loosen soil, rinse, dry with towel. Commercial vinyl cleaners are available and best used for greasy or stubborn stains. Vinyl fabrics can be waxed with milk paste wax such as automobile wax.

• The most-often-asked-about stain to remove from vinyl or leather furniture is ballpoint pen ink. Simply use a cotton swab and dip it in a little rubbing alcohol, then gently dab at the stain. Some people use hair spray on the cotton swab, but you must be careful because that does leave lacquer. After removing the ballpoint ink, wipe with a damp sponge and recondition the leather or vinyl.

Dry-Mopping, Sweeping, Scrubbing, and/or Waxing Non-Carpeted Floors

• To prevent scratching the floor when moving heavy furniture across uncarpeted areas, slip scraps of old carpeting, facedown, under all furniture legs.

• If a newly cleaned floor continues to be sticky or tacky after more than 20 or 30 minutes of drying, or if the polish layer powders, flakes, or scratches easily, it may be due to old polish that was not removed, cleaner residue not well rinsed off, too much polish, or not allowing enough time between polish applications.

The solution is to clean the floor thoroughly, removing all polish, and then to reapply polish according to directions on the container.

• Buildup of soil between polish layers can cause white or light-colored vinyl floors to yellow. Removing all of the polish and starting over can help. Exposure to strong sunlight or being covered with a rug with a rubber backing or furniture also can yellow such floors. Sometimes, such yellowing is permanent.

• In a fix and don't have a dustpan when you're sweeping the floor? Just take a paper plate, cut it in half (and a really easy hint is to moisten the edge), set it on the floor, and there you go—a disposable dustpan.

Wood Floor Care

Hardwood floors are prized for their beauty and durability; if you have them, you are lucky indeed. Generally speaking, water is wood's enemy and should not be used to clean wood floors unless the manufacturer's instructions say it's okay. Normally, wood floors are cleaned with solvents such as turpentine, nontoxic dry-cleaning fluids, or liquid or paste spirit-solvent waxes.

• The best thing you can do for wood floors is to sweep or dry mop as often as possible. The culprit is ground-in dirt, so the more you sweep it, the better it will look.

• Zap your mop with a little spray wax before dusting wood floors and you'll keep them shiny-clean with only a few minutes of effort each day.

• CAUTION: When spraying wax on mops or furniture, don't let wax "puddles" accumulate on the floor. You'll have the equivalent of slippery and dangerous ice patches, which people won't see but which they will find the hard way—by falling on them.

• Very old and dull wood floors may need to be sanded and finished. You can refinish them yourself; many new easy-to-use products are available at hardware stores.

• Never use liquid wax made for vinyl flooring on wood floors. It tends to darken wood. Use paste wax or liquid waxes specifically for wood instead.

• Always read the directions on the wax container. Some products will specify that you have to remove all other finishes first, and you may not be up to that chore. Other products, such as paste waxes, may require machine buffing, and if you don't have a buffer, you'll have to rent one for waxing day.

• Sanding floors by hand causes so much friction that you can get friction burns on your fingertips even through work gloves. Some people have even sanded the skin right off their hands. If you are determined to sand by hand, apply masking tape to all fingertips and put on gloves to save your skin.

• If you get small slivers from steel wool or some types of soft wood in your fingers, instead of poking around in your skin with tweezers, try spreading a film of white school glue over the sliver areas. Let the glue dry, then peel it off. This method works eight out of ten times.

• Don't let sanded wood set any longer than 12 hours before you apply the stain or finish. Raw sanded wood absorbs moisture, which could affect the way it absorbs stain colors and/or the adhesion of the finish.

• Instead of using a rag to apply paste wax to floors when you wax them by hand, slip a glove-style potholder or working glove over your hand to get a better grip and to protect your skin. The gloves are more durable and easier to clean than your skin.

• You can hand buff a floor to a beautiful shine with a pad made by inserting a folded old bath towel into an old nylon stocking. The wax buffs to a shine faster than you'd think could be done by hand. The stocking will get snagged and you'll have to change it frequently, so gather up a bunch of old ones.

• Dancing chair legs (or actually chair feet) often mar hardwood floors. Try applying self-adhesive-backed moleskin to the bottoms of chair legs to help them glide smoothly across the floor without making marks.

• If furniture feet have dented your floors, you may be able to fill the dents with clear nail polish or shellac. Since they are clear, the floor color will show through and the dents will be less noticeable.

(Now remember, this is a Heloise home-style hint, but it sure does work in a pinch and will alleviate some of the aggravation from staring at that dent day after day after day.)

Squeaky Floors

• Whether or not you want to silence a squeaky hardwood floor probably is determined by the ages of your children. While the pitter-patter of little feet added to squeaky boards can drive a parent a bit balmy, such squeaks can be a parenting aid when you have older children. Many teens have inadvertently announced their late-night arrivals with squeaky floorboards.

Here's the tip for whoever will benefit from it: Try sprinkling talcum powder over the "musical areas" for a dry lubricant. Sweep the talc back and forth until it filters down between the cracks and you'll probably get blessedly quiet floorboards.

• If the squeaky wood floor is under tile or carpet, you might be able to eliminate the squeak without removing the floor covering. It's sometimes possible to reset loose boards by pounding the loose nails back into place. Place a block of scrap wood over the squeaky area to protect the flooring and then pound with a hammer.

Care of Vinyl Floors

Vinyl flooring is usually referred to as "resilient flooring," in contrast to "hard-surface" flooring such as wood, stone, concrete, marble, terrazzo, and ceramic tile. Linoleum, asphalt, rubber, and cork flooring is no longer manufactured, but some people still have these materials in their homes. Most of these materials, except wood and cork, can be cleaned with water or mild detergent or household cleaners as described below.

• When floors are only slightly soiled, just sweep or vacuum, then damp-mop with a clean sponge mop and warm water, pressing hard enough to loosen surface dirt.

• When you wet-mop, attack small areas at a time, and be sure to rinse the mop frequently in the bucket of clean water; otherwise you are just smearing dirt around the floor instead of cleaning it up. Change the water when it's dirty, which may be several times for a large room.

• Really dirty floors need to be washed with a no-rinse cleaner or a general-purpose liquid detergent. Flooring manufacturers warn against washing with soap, dish-washing liquid, or gritty powders or cleansers.

• REMEMBER: When you scrub asphalt tile floors with water, wring out the cloth or sponge well to avoid soaking the floor with excess water. Excess water can seep into the seams and loosen the adhesives that hold the flooring. We want to destroy dirt, not our decor.

• Always follow the directions on the no-rinse cleaners. For most of them, you apply them with a sponge mop and just wipe them up.

• When using the detergents recommended for your type of floor, prepare the bucket of detergent and water according to label instructions. Use two buckets: one for detergent solution and one for your rinse water.

Scrub the floor as follows:

1. Dip the sponge mop into the bucket.
2. Don't squeeze or wring the mop out before you spread the cleaning solution over a small area.
3. Wait for a minute for the detergent action to loosen the dirt. The detergent is supposed to work for you, not you for your detergent.
4. Scrub the area with the mop, then wipe up the liquid.
5. Rinse well, being sure not to leave any detergent on the floor. Be sure to change rinse water often.

• Always rinse floors with clean water, even when the directions for the floor cleaner say you don't have to.

Flooring manufacturers tell me that the reason no-wax floors get dull is that they are not rinsed properly after detergents and floor cleaners are used on them, or the incorrect floor cleaner is used on a no-wax floor. It's very important to check with the manufacturer of the no-wax floor that is in your home to be sure you're using the proper cleaning agent, if any agent is to be used at all on it.

If you don't thoroughly rinse no-wax floors, a shine-hiding, sticky film builds up and traps dirt. The more often you wash without rinsing, the more film buildup you get.

• When your floor dries after rinsing and still has a dull film, try mopping again with a solution of one cup or so of white vinegar to a bucket of water. (Yes, I know, where there's Heloise and a bucket of water, there's a cup or so of vinegar. But, believe me, when it comes to shine, vinegar does it.)

• If your highly waxed floor gets dull between washings, mop it with a solution of one cup of fabric softener in one-half pail of water.

• Before you put a new coat of wax on your linoleum or tile floors, you'll need to remove the old wax to get good results for your efforts. If you mop with a solution of three parts of water to one part of rubbing alcohol, the floor will be clean and ready for new wax.

• If you're all fired up to wax your floors and find out that you have no commercial wax, don't quit when you're "on a roll." You can "wax" a floor with a solution of two tablespoons furniture polish and one-half cup vinegar added to a bucket of warm water.

• A long-handled paint roller can be used to apply wax to floors when you don't have an official waxer. Rollers work fast and reach under furniture for you.

• You can hand buff your newly waxed floor and get your muscle-toning exercise at the same time. Just wrap a bath towel around each foot and "skate" around the floor. And of course, be very careful while you're skating so that you don't fall.

• Shoe heel scuff marks on resilient flooring can be removed by rubbing them with a pencil eraser or fine, dry steel wool. Crayon marks come off when rubbed with a damp rag containing toothpaste or silver polish.

• If you drop a raw egg on the floor and don't have an eager dog to clean it up for you, sprinkle the egg glob with salt, let it sit for 12 to 20 minutes, and then sweep it up with a broom.

• You can patch a gouge in resilient flooring if you grate a flooring scrap with a food grater, mix the grated flooring with clear nail polish, and then plug the gouge. This tip is not for dents, just gouges or holes.

Draperies and Blinds

• You can toss most drapes or curtains into the dryer for a few minutes on air setting to remove dust.

• An aerosol spray made for cleaning crystal chandeliers will clean painted metal blinds. With the blinds in a semi-closed position, spray and then wipe off the dirt droplets with paper towels or terry towel rags. Liquid window cleaner and our homemade cleaner will also work, but you'll have to totally wipe each slat instead of just wiping droplets.

Cobwebs and Other Fuzzy Dust

• Vacuum moldings, air-conditioning/heating vents, and corners of walls to get rid of fuzzy dust and any cobwebs that may be on the ceiling.
If your vacuum extensions aren't long enough, you may be able to reach corners with a broom, mop, or fishing pole covered by an old pillowcase, T-shirt, or nylon net.

• Unreachable cobwebs can sometimes be "caught" if you wrap a racquetball or tennis ball in a dust rag and then toss it up into the cobweb corner.

CAUTION: Don't get too enthusiastic when tossing the ball or you'll "score" costly knickknack-breaking rebounds.

Walls and Woodwork

• Dust walls before washing and wash from the bottom up so that drips won't make their marks. Clean small areas at a time, then rinse and dry, before moving to another area.

• Wash most painted surfaces with soap or mild detergent and water, or mild commercial household cleaners.

• You can soften soap waters and rinse waters by adding one tablespoon of borax or a commercial water softener per quart of water.

Wall Coverings

Since there are so many types of wall coverings—paper, plastic, fabric, resin coated or impregnated materials—you need to get the manufacturer's care directions when you have the walls covered.

• If you don't know what your wall covering should be cleaned with, always test cleaners on an inconspicuous place before proceeding. Colors can bleed, papers can come off the wall, and who knows what else can happen if you use the wrong cleaner!

• Most washable coverings can be gently washed with mild detergent and cool water. Work from the bottom up, using as little water as possible. Work on small areas and overlap as you wash. Rinse with clear water and blot dry.

• Many nonwashable wall coverings can be cleaned when rubbed gently with art gum eraser, fresh white bread, or doughy wallpaper cleaners (available at hardware stores). If you use the doughy cleaner, knead and turn it often so that you are using clean surfaces on the wall. (I knew there had to be some good use for white bread.)

• Spot-clean wallpaper before spots set. Blot grease spots with paper towels or facial tissue while you press lightly a warm iron over the towels or tissue.

• A paste of nonflammable dry-cleaning solvent and absorbent powder (fuller's earth, talcum, cornstarch) can be applied to a stain, allowed to dry, then brushed off.

• Crayon can sometimes be sponged off with dry-cleaning solvent. Pencil marks and smudges can sometimes be removed with art gum or pencil erasers. Always rub gently.

• Ink may be removed by bleach, or commercial ink remover may work on wallpaper, but either one may also remove the color of the wallpaper; test first.

Heavy Metal Cleaning

Many ornamental metal objects are lacquered and should not be cleaned with any commercial or homemade cleaners, which may remove the lacquer. Always check the tags of ornamental metal objects to find out how they should be cleaned. After noting what the item is on the tag, store the tag in your household file for reference. Don't depend upon memory.

BRASS AND COPPER

Tarnish can be removed with commercial cleaners or with some of the homemade cleaners listed below. Those made with lemon juice or vinegar will give copper and brass a bright finish, and the oil and rottenstone cleaner will give these metals a soft luster.

• Saturate a sponge or cloth with vinegar or lemon juice, sprinkle salt on the sponge, and then lightly rub, rinse, and dry.

• Rub with a paste made by adding flour to the salt and vinegar or lemon juice, rinse, and dry.

• Make a thin paste from rottenstone (an abrasive powder available at hardware stores) and an oil such as cooking or salad oil. Wipe off excess oil after rubbing, polish with a clean cloth.

• Brass fireplace tools can be buffed with fine emery cloth, which is available at hardware stores.

CHROMIUM

• Most of the time, chromium plating on small appliances, faucet handles, and so forth can be cleaned with sudsy water and buffed dry.

• If suds aren't enough, rub with baking soda that has been sprinkled on a damp sponge or cloth, or wipe with vinegar; buff dry. Use commercial cleaners for really stubborn gunk.

PEWTER

• Rub with a paste made by mixing denatured alcohol and whiting (an abrasive powder available in hardware stores). After the paste dries, wash, rinse, and buff with a soft cloth.

• To get a duller finish on pewter, make a paste with rottenstone and oil, rub, rinse, buff dry.

• Corrosion can be removed by gently rubbing with fine (0000) steel wool dipped in oil.

Decorating Tips

I like to visit people whose knickknacks are personal treasures (which has nothing to do with price) instead of just decorator dust catchers. I have many things in my home that are heirlooms, gifts, or just things that entertain me every time I look at them. For example, I have a butler at my door—a mannequin dressed in full tuxedo. Everyone who visits me has fun "talking" to my "butler."

Not everyone will have a "butler," but we all accumulate certain treasures that we are fond of and that give our homes a personal look rather than a magazine photo layout look.

• To give a room a focal point, group photographs or any other souvenirs and personal collections in one place rather than scattering them about the house. Then you'll have one large, memorable, attractive display.

• If you tend to collect things made from a single specific material—such as shell, brass, wood, copper, porcelain, or whatever—you'll find that when you group your collection, everything will "match" no matter what color, size, or shape it is.

Hang-Ups

• Quilting is an American art, and quilts are as appropriate for wall hangings as European tapestries. Attach wooden rings to a quilt and hang it from a wide, wooden rod.

• Frame anything that appeals to you, such as an old map, family documents (Grandpa's citizenship papers), children's artwork, a nice piece of print paper or fabric, needlework art.

• Oil paintings usually are not matted or covered with glass. Etchings and delicate flower prints are usually covered with glass and put into lightweight frames.

• When preparing to move, as you take down wall hangings and pictures, remove the nails or hooks from the walls at the same time and tape them to the back of each object. Then, when you're ready to rehang them at the new place, you won't need to look for hooks or nails.

• Tabs from aluminum cans make great hangers for lightweight pictures. Drive a nail or tack through the rivet into the picture frame, then bend the tab to the desired shape. This won't hold heavy pictures, but works well on lightweight pictures and wall plaques.

• If you're hanging a picture from a molding but you don't like the looks of the exposed picture wire, substitute nylon fishing line. The transparent nylon is almost invisible and your picture can star on its own.

• Giving an inexpensive, glossy picture the texture of an oil painting is easier than most of us would think. Purchase some nylon net and cut it to overlap the picture; tape the corners to keep the net flat and taut. Brush shellac on lightly, let it set for a couple of seconds, then carefully remove the net and let the picture dry. After it dries, it will have the texture of canvas and look like an oil painting.

• Picture hanging can be frustrating if you simply try to "eyeball" the right spot to put the hook. Some people measure with tape and yardstick and still don't get the picture where they want it. You can place a picture exactly where you want it the first time by following this method.

Cut a sheet of paper to the exact size of the frame. Position the pattern on the picture's back side and pull up taut the picture's hanging wire so that you will see an inverted V. Mark the "V" point on the pattern and poke a hole through that marked point.

After you determine where you'll put the picture, place the pattern on the wall, and use the V point hole to make a pencil mark showing exactly where the nail should go. The picture will hang precisely where you want it.

• If the picture isn't too heavy, another time-saving method is to hold the picture itself by its wire and decide where you want it positioned. Wet a fingertip and press it on the wall to mark the wire's inverted V point. The fingerprint mark will stay wet long enough for you to drive a nail and hook on target.

• Take the guesswork out of arranging several pictures on the wall; do it like a pro. Spread out a large sheet of wrapping paper or several taped-together newspapers on the floor and experiment with frame positions.

When you decide on a pleasing grouping, outline the frames on the paper, tape the paper to the wall, and drive hooks through the paper into the wall. Then remove the paper and hang the pictures.

• Group pictures of similar subjects, colors, frames, or sizes. When putting a grouping over a large piece of furniture such as a sofa, it's usually better to keep the bottom line even. But no rules are permanently nailed to any wall; use an arrangement that pleases you.

• Sometimes a picture that was positioned correctly has a mind of its own and won't hang straight. Give it some gentle guidance by wrapping masking tape around the wire on both sides of the hook so the wire can't slip. Or install parallel nails and hooks a short distance apart: two hooks are better than one for keeping pictures in their places.

• Squares of double-faced tape affixed to the frame's two lower back corners also will keep pictures from roving.

• Don't lose a perfect picture grouping when you repaint a room. If you insert toothpicks in the hook holes and paint right over them, when the paint dries, you can remove the toothpicks and rehang your pictures.

• And a quick, easy way to remember the grouping is to take a photo of your picture arrangement.

• To prevent a plaster wall from crumbling when driving a nail or hook into it, first form an X over the nail spot with two strips of masking tape or transparent tape.

• Make small rooms look larger and brighter by installing mirrors on one wall to create double width with reflections of opposite walls. This works whether you are installing mirror tiles or hanging a mirror collection.

• Hang mirrors to reflect you but not the sun, because some mirror backings are adversely affected by direct sunlight.

• When hanging a mirror with screws that go through mounting holes in the glass, don't tighten the screws all the way. Leave enough play so the mirror won't crack if the wall shifts.

8

6* _ALL-NEW HINTS FROM HELOISE_

Decorating Windows

• Hanging plants can substitute for curtains on windows. (And talk about no-iron, drip-dry!)

• An Indian print bedspread can become an instant drapery. Hang it full width across a window, then pick up a bottom corner to open the "drapery" diagonally across half the window, and secure with a tieback.

• For an airy, summery window, try stretching gauze or chiffon between two dowels, and hang them inside the window frame.

• Glue fabric to cheap window shades, finish the edges with braid or fringe, and you won't need curtains. In bedrooms, an inexpensive way to achieve a coordinated look is to buy extra matching sheets to use as window dressings, table covers, and even as throws over chairs.

If your fabric is rather heavy, the roller springs won't work well and you may have to keep the shade at half mast all the time, so plan the pattern accordingly.

• Colorful printed bed sheets can be made into curtains for any room in the house. They can also be stapled to walls for a fabric "wallpaper" look.

• "Frame" a window with bookshelves, either built-in or freestanding. You can top "store-bought" shelves with a board if they are as tall as the window and thereby add an extra shelf across the top of the window. You'll be adding storage space and avoiding curtain maintenance at the same time.

Wallpaper Decorating Tips

• When you are selecting wallpaper, remember that if it has one or more of the dominant colors already in the room, the wallpaper will tie everything together.

• If you have a large room and want it to appear smaller and cozier, choose a wallpaper with a large, bold pattern. Don't, however, use it in a small room, because bold patterns will "close in on you" and make the room look small and crowded.

• A mural-pattern wallpaper makes a small room appear larger.

• You can raise or lower ceilings with wallpaper. A high ceiling seems lower if the walls are papered with a bold pattern. A low ceiling seems higher if the walls are papered with a small print or a texture.

Extraordinary Decorating with Ordinary Things

• Children's room too small? Add a miniature hammock to a corner in a child's room to make a bed for all those stuffed animals.

• A nonworking fireplace, primed and freshened with paint, makes a cozy niche for an aquarium or flower/plant arrangements.

• Need an instant centerpiece? A branch cut from any blossoming tree or bush makes an unusual centerpiece on a dining or coffee table. Greenery of any kind can be used; just add something appropriate for the season, such as artificial red holly berries or peppers or Easter eggs.

• Just about anything that holds water can be a vase. Display flowers in a crystal ice bucket, fluted champagne glasses, mugs, cocktail pitchers.

• You don't have to throw away a favorite crystal water glass or pitcher when it gets a chipped lip; use it to hold fresh or artificial flowers. Silk flowers can be arranged in favorite containers that don't hold water.

• Buy gourds in the fall at the supermarket. Use them for a month or so in an arrangement, then put them someplace warm and dry for a while. The gourds become very light as they dry, and the colors mute beautifully with age.

• Garlic braids or dry hot peppers threaded on a long string make a kitchen decor cook!

(And the garlic, according to legend, keeps away vampires. I've never seen a vampire in a kitchen that has garlic hanging in it! Of course, I've never seen a vampire in a kitchen without garlic either.)

Storage Space to End Clutter

• Put old bookcases into closets for ready-made shelving. You can paint them to match or leave them as they are.

• Install shelves over the commode in the bathroom to hold towels and miscellaneous bathroom accessories.

• Use pegboards to hang up utility items such as tools, pots and pans, sewing supplies, or anything else that fits on a hook or peg.

• Check out the notions departments of variety stores to find ways of hanging up ironing boards, irons, and other household aids with various "over-the-door" devices.

• Shoe bags can be used in many rooms and not only for shoes. They'll hold sewing supplies, crafts tools, kitchen utensils, and anything else that fits.

• Two nails or pegs can hold brooms, rakes, shovels, and other garden tools on the garage wall so that they are out of tripping range.

• The best tip is to use every nook and cranny in your home for storage—just add a bit of imagination and innovation!

CHAPTER 4

Home Maintenance

M aintenance and making minor repairs prevent major problems and budget-breaking bills.

However, not everyone can fix plumbing or do carpentry and painting, and many people can't do any "fix-it" activity beyond picking up the phone to call in a home service person. And sometimes, having the pros fix what you have broken while trying to fix it yourself costs more than it would have to call for professional service in the first place.

However, many people can do simple repairs, and just about everyone can do preventive maintenance. The maintenance and simple repairs tips in this chapter will help even an "all thumbs" person to make household helpers last longer so that you get your money's worth from them.

Here are two important and very basic tips.

• When you build a house, build on additions, buy an already built one, or rent a house, find out which pipes are gas and which are water; the location of all buried pipes; the location of electrical or other cables; the location of all fuse boxes; which outlets are 220V (for air conditioners and stoves) and which are 110V. If the house is in an area that still has septic tanks, know the location of the tank and its lateral drains.

Knowing these things will prevent the digging up of phone cables when you are landscaping and will help you know when something is wrong. For example, a constant pool of water in one part of the yard could mean a broken pipe or a malfunctioning septic tank.

If you have to hire someone to fix buried plumbing or wiring, think about the extra labor costs for paying a professional person to walk around looking for pipes and connections or guessing at where they ought to be. That time and money is best spent actually fixing whatever is broken.

• Many adult education courses are available through city colleges and school districts to help you learn about home maintenance and automobile repairs. Such courses are useful even if you don't plan to do major projects yourself, because they help you deal with the service people you hire.

Plumbing

• Here's a simple plumbing tip that can save all sorts of mess: Teach everyone in the house where the main cutoff valve is and how to use it, as well as the various sink, toilet, and washer cutoffs so that all family members, housekeepers, and baby-sitters know how to to stop a flood before they are up to their ankles in water.

Drippy and Noisy Faucets

• You don't have to turn faucet handles off until they feel tight. Just turn until the water goes off. Any further turning compresses the gaskets, which will make the faucets leak.

• If you have a drippy faucet disrupting your sleep in the middle of the night, tie a two-foot-long piece of string around the faucet so that the drips can go down the string from the nozzle into the drain without making any noise. If you don't have string, wet a small towel or washcloth and drape or wrap it around the faucet any old way that makes it catch the drips silently.

• If your faucet squeals (a sound as penetrating as a fingernail on a blackboard), the stem's metal threads and the faucet's threads are grinding against each other. Take the handle and stem off, then coat both sets of threads with petroleum jelly, and you won't have goose bumps every time the faucet is turned. And the handle will be easier to turn, too.

• Faucet aerators need cleaning. Unscrew the aerator, take the screen out, and rinse it. If it is totally clogged with mineral deposits and hard water buildup, you can soak the aereator screen in vinegar to remove that, and then put the entire mechanism back together.

Clogged Drains

While it seems that drains get clogged at the most inconvenient times, the fact is that drains warn us ahead of time. The problem is that we tend to ignore a "slow" drain until it's too late. It's so easy to ignore unseen gunk, isn't it? Prevention is the best idea.

• If you have a completely clogged drain, try a "plumber's friend."

• DO NOT use drain cleaners in completely clogged drains; if the plumber's friend doesn't do the job, call the plumber!

• Plungers get better suction if their rubber caps are covered with water. To keep from spattering the walls, yourself, the sink countertop, and just about anything in a radius of five feet when you are "plunging" a small sink, make a tent from a bath towel over your arm, the plunger, and the splatters.

• Some sinks and all tubs have overflow openings. If you plug this opening when you use the plunger, you'll get better suction and force.

• If the plumber's helper doesn't unclog the clog, you can try dislodging it with a straightened wire coat hanger, bent at one end to form a small hook. However, the best advice at this point may be to call a plumber.

• If the drain is only slightly clogged, it can sometimes be cleaned by flushing boiling water down into it. A solution of one pound of washing soda in three gallons of boiling water can be poured down the drain.

• Commercial drain cleaners can also be used. However, commercial drain cleaners should always be used with caution, because some may damage drain pipes and the finish around the drain.

• If you have young children and don't like to keep drain cleaners around the house, buy only the amount of drain cleaner needed to do all of the drains in your house at one session and then put the cleaner in the drains as soon as you get your groceries into the house. By the time you've put them away, you can flush all the cleaner away and throw away the container.

• CAUTION: Always be careful when disposing of containers with chemicals; wrap them so that children and pets can't get at them.

• To help prevent clogged drains, use the following procedure once a month. Make a home-style noncorrosive drain cleaner by mixing one cup baking soda, one cup table salt, and one-quarter cup cream of tartar in a small bowl. Stir thoroughly. Store this cleaner in a clean, covered jar. (You will have 2 ¼ cups of drain cleaner.) CAUTION: Label the container so that this white powder isn't mistaken for food, and don't store it where food is stored.

To use this drain cleaner, you need to pour one-fourth cup of it into a drain, then immediately add one cup of boiling water. Wait 10 seconds, then flush with cold water for at least 20 seconds.

• To keep kitchen and bathroom drains clear of hair and clogged grease, try this weekly: Pour one cup baking soda into the drain, followed by one cup vinegar. As the soda and vinegar foam, flush the drain with very hot water.

• When floor drains, such as those in shower stalls and basements, are clogged and the clog isn't close to the opening, try to unclog the drain with water pressure from a garden hose. With the hose attached to a faucet, feed it into the drain as deeply as it will go; close up the open spaces around the hose by tightly jamming rags into the opening. Then turn on the water full blast for a few minutes.

Plumbing Repairs

• Wrenches can really mess up chrome-plated plumbing fixtures. Wrap the fixture with a double layer of plastic electrical tape before attacking it with tools.

Noisy Pipes

Isn't it awful when your plumbing "sings"? Sometimes it's the water pressure that makes pipes screech and whine and sometimes vibrate and bang against the walls in extreme cases.

• If the water pressure in your house is at or higher than 70 to 80 pounds per square inch, you may have to install a pressure-reducing valve to silence your protesting pipes. To measure the average water pressure in your home, you need to attach a pressure gauge to the cold-water faucet nearest the main shutoff valve. Since you probably don't own such a device, if this problem is annoying enough, you may want to call a plumber to fix it.

Or you can wait until the next time you have a plumbing repair and tell the plumber about the water pressure problem, but say that you want this checked when you make the appointment. "By the way, will you check . . ." is not a good way to get things done. The plumber may have a tight schedule and have only enough time to fix whatever it is you called about in the first place.

• If a noisy water pipe is banging against a wall, try wedging a wood block between the pipe and the wall. If you are handy, you can clamp the pipe to the block for more stability.

Frozen Pipes

Protection of pipes in cold weather is a must, and the amount of protection can range from foam pipe wraps, which you buy in the hardware store, to covering pipes with straw when you live in rural areas. The idea is to protect pipes from the cold wind and temperatures so that they don't burst.

• Some people let faucets dribble to keep the water flowing and less likely to freeze, but in some areas, where water pressure is low, having everyone's water running, even at a dribble, can hamper fire fighting with inadequate water pressure. Find out what is the appropriate way to protect pipes from freezing in your community by calling a county Cooperative Extension Agent or watching for the TV and newspaper stories that are inevitable when a freeze is predicted.

• To thaw a frozen pipe, heat the pipe starting at the tap end. If you start in the middle, steam from melting ice can burst the pipe. Open the tap so that melting ice and steam can run off.

• In a pinch, you can use a hair dryer to thaw frozen pipes.

Toilet Tank and Bowl

If you've ever had a faulty toilet (or septic tank) cause an overflow, it's an experience you'll never forget, despite wanting desperately never to think about it again.

• Don't flush a clogged toilet if there is only a little water in it. Flushing will cause it to overflow. Get out the old plumber's helper, and if there isn't enough water to cover the rubber cup, get water from some other source and pour it over the plunger cup to make the suction better. Some people poke an unbent hanger down the commode, but if you do this, it may scratch the bowl and then the scratches will stain. A real plumber's "snake" from the hardware store is probably better to use. If the plumber's helper or snake don't work, call the plumber. The clog may be farther down into the drain and need to be "rooted" out with a motorized device.

• If you aren't getting enough water from the tank to flush the bowl clean, check the tank's water level. If the water level in the tank isn't within 1 ½ inches of the top of the overflow tube, you need to bend the float arm UP slightly so that more water will be allowed to enter the tank.

• Conserve water by placing a sealed or foil-covered brick in the toilet tank so that less water is needed to activate the flush mechanism. Be sure to place the brick so that it does not interfere with the flushing mechanism.

• You also can place an upright glass jar (quart or pint mayo size will do) into the tank. The jar will remain filled with water when the tank is flushed, saving a pint or quart each flush. The weight of the water will keep the jar in place.

• Many automatic toilet bowl cleaners that you drop into the tank contain strong bleach, which ultimately "eats up" the soft parts of the flush mechanism. Read labels before you buy!

Septic Tanks

• If you live in an area that has septic tanks, you might want to flush down something to keep its chemical activity going. Here's a septic tank activator recipe. Mix two envelopes of active dry yeast with a pound of brown sugar in a large bowl. Add four cups of warm water. Stir until completely blended. Allow the mixture to rest in a warm place for 10 to 20 minutes until foamy and increased in volume. Flush down the toilet. Commercial activators can also be bought at hardware stores.

Water Heaters

• If you live in a hard-water area, you need to drain your water heater monthly to get rid of the mineral deposits that collect on the bottom and that eventually prevent the heater from functioning properly.

Directions should have come with your water heater, or ask the plumber who installed it.

• If you've been away for an extended time, you can prevent possible explosions by opening all hot-water taps for a few minutes after reentering your house to release any possible hydrogen gas that may have built up in the water heater.

Water Purifiers

• If you have a water purification system, change the filters periodically. Follow the recommendations of the manufacturer.

• When you have a purifier with a holding tank, run the tank for several minutes if you've been away so that the tank will be refilled with fresh water.

Using Tools

Hammering Safely

• If you have to pound in a nail at a level that is below your knees, face away from the wall, standing or crouching near the nail. Pound in the nail by hammering toward the rear.

• If a nail is too short to hold, press it through a piece of cardboard or index card. Hold the paper in one hand and the hammer in the other. Tear away the cardboard before you pound the last taps or tap the last pounds, whichever sounds right to you. The cardboard will protect the wall from "hits and misses" too.

• You can also place the nail between the teeth of a comb to hold it while you're hammering.

• Use a nail punch for the final hammer drives to prevent "scars" on the surface from "hits and misses."

• When you have to drive a nail into a crevice, use a nail punch set to get the nail all the way in.

Using Screwdrivers

• Screwdrivers come in different sizes. Using the right size will keep the screw head from being damaged.

• If you make a small hole with a nail first, it is easier to screw in a screw.

• If you soap or wax screw threads, the screw will go in more easily.

Window Repairs

Oh come on, don't say, "I don't do windows." Unless we hire other people to do them we all have to do windows once in a while or we miss all the sunshine. For many of us, doing windows is a major project even if it's just to clean them. Some of the tips below go beyond the mere cleaning level but are simple repairs that can be done with simple tools.

• When the window gets stuck, get a block of wood and place it on the spot before you tap (not pound) the window sash with a hammer. If you hit the sash directly with the hammer, it will dent.

• To remove cracked glass from a window without cutting yourself and having dangerous pieces of glass to clean up, crisscross both sides of the broken pane with many strips of masking tape before you tap it out with a hammer. The tape will hold most of the pieces together safely.

Window Screens

• Repair a small tear in wire screening by pushing the wire strands back into place with an ice pick. If you can't completely close up the hole, sparingly brush clear nail polish or shellac across the remaining opening. After the sealer dries, reapply until the pinhole is invisibly sealed. Blot up any drips of sealer that run down the screen to make this a neat job.

• A clean cut or tear in a window screen can be stitched together if you use a long needle and strong nylon thread, fishing line, or fine wire. As you zigzag-stitch back and forth across the cut, don't pull the thread or wire too tightly, because this will pucker the patch. After you are finished with the mend, apply clear nail polish to keep the thread or wire from pulling loose.

• If the screen has a large hole, cut a patch from a screening scrap of the same type of screening, then zigzag the patch into place. Apply clear nail polish to the stitching to reinforce it.

• You can heat-fuse a patch when you have to repair fiberglass screening. Just lay a fiberglass patch over the tear or hole and carefully run a hot iron around the patch edges. You'll need to put some foil over the screen and patch to keep the iron from touching it directly.

• Aluminum screens tend to pit, but you can prevent this kind of damage if you clean them with kerosene. Just dip a rag in the kerosene and rub both sides of the screen and frames; wipe off excess. This treatment is also a rust inhibitor for older screens.

CAUTION: This is an outside job and kerosene is flammable. DON'T light anything up while you are doing this and do it outdoors, where you'll have plenty of ventilation. ALWAYS work with and store flammables in a cool place. It's best to buy only what you'll need for one job so that you won't have to store it at all.

Repairing Doors

• Take the squeak out of door hinges by lubricating the pin with petroleum jelly. Unlike oil, petroleum jelly won't drip on the floor.

• When you need to polish door hardware (on furniture as well as entryway doors), cut a cardboard shield so that it fits around the metal parts and then hold the shield in place with masking tape while you work on the hardware.

• Sliding door safety: Many people already do this, but it bears repeating. Apply a decal on sliding glass doors at eye level so that nobody will mistake a closed door for an open one. I even have one down at eye level on the special door for my schnauzer.

• People have been known to walk into lightweight screens too, so you might want to put a decal or sew a zigzag of colored yarn on the screen.

• For door locks that seem to stick, try some graphite in the lock before calling the lock repair service. Often that will clear up the problem immediately.

Repairing Walls

Patching Walls

• Quick-patch nail holes in white walls with white toothpaste or with moistened crushed aspirin and push it into the hole.

• After patching nail holes in colored walls, use a dab of watercolor paints if you don't have leftover paint. You'll be amazed at how closely you can match colors with water paint.

• You can also cover over the patch on colored walls by using color-coordinated typewriter correction fluid.

• If you have leftover paint, touch up small spots with cotton swabs instead of a brush. You don't waste paint and you don't have a brush to clean.

• To patch larger holes, use joint compound, available in any hardware store. You can use an upside-down lid or a bathroom plunger for a mini-hod (a hod is a trough used by masons to carry mortar), in which you can mix the compound and hold it while you are doing the repair. Hold on to the lid's knob or the plunger's handle with one hand and trowel away with the other. (When you've finished, make sure you rinse out the lid before any residue hardens.)

• If you add a tablespoon of white vinegar (I know, vinegar again!) to the water when you are mixing patching plaster, the compound won't dry so quickly and you'll be able to work more slowly.

• When you are filling wide cracks in plaster, it's best to fill from the inside out, pressing fresh plaster in with a putty knife or a trowel.

• A beer can opener makes cutting loose plaster out of a wall before patching a large crack a snap. You can use the pointed end of the opener to undercut and widen the opening.

• When a screw hole in the wall has worn grooves, stuff the hole with a cotton ball soaked in white glue, let it dry for 24 hours, and then put the new screw into the hole securely with a screwdriver.

Painting Outside and Inside the House

If you've had the advantage of learning to paint by watching a pro or at least a semi-pro, you can probably paint with a minimum of smears, drips, and mess-ups.

Unfortunately, most of us learn how to paint by trial and error . . . and mostly error. Ultimately we learn how to prepare a surface before we paint, which part or area of anything to paint first, and how to clean up instead of having to throw away our painting clothes and paint equipment. The tips below will help both novices and semi-pro painters to do it all better, more easily, and ultimately more cheaply.

When to Paint

Spring is the ideal time to paint a house's exterior. Do it as soon as the weather turns warm enough, but before the temperature gets too hot. When the heat is blistering, paint dries too quickly and leaves marks where strokes were overlapped.

Spring usually puts us in the mood to redecorate anyway. When flowers start blooming and nature renews itself, we want to make our whole environment fresh and new.

Before you rush out to the paint store, do a little planning so that you'll have some idea about the color you want and the equipment you'll need when you go to the paint store.

Get advice from the salesperson in the paint department. Some paints and varnishes are better applied with man-made bristle brushes and others are better with natural bristles. Edges of brushes are made feathered or blunt, and each bristle tip works best with specific types of paint or varnish. Also, a variety of rollers and paint pads is also available. Using the correct implement to spread the paint will ensure the best results.

Information printed on the paint or varnish can will tell you what sort of applicator to use and give you general instructions about painting. Always check the label to find out if the paint or varnish you are buying is appropriate for the surface you want to cover—wood, stucco, masonry, or metal. Certain paints are better for certain wear areas, such as porch paints for walk-on surfaces, enamels for woodwork, flat for walls, and so forth.

Color Selection

Cosmetic application of paint to your house is like applying eye shadow, blusher, and contour makeup to your face. It hides the bad and accents the good.

• Take a photograph of the outside of your house, then look it over and determine what you don't like about it. Study the photograph to see if your house looks top heavy, small, or dumpy.

• If your house is small and you want it to look larger, paint the trim, walls, and shutters a light color. If you are reroofing, add a light-color roof.

• If your house looks too narrow and tall, paint the upper story a darker shade than the lower story.

• To make a house look less dumpy and awkward, use a dark color on the roof and the side walls. The dark color outlines and limits the shape of the house against the landscape and sky and helps in making it look less chunky or short.

• To help minimize unattractive trim, paint it the same color as the house, and it will be less conspicuous.

Preparing the Surface for Paint

If the surface is properly prepared, your paint job will look better and last longer.

• Water stains on the ceiling: You can't paint over water stains or mildew on walls or ceilings. You'll need to pretreat the spot by either applying a commercial spray product from paint or hardware stores or you can apply shellac, let it dry, and then paint over the area.

• Paint does not adhere well to dirty surfaces. If paint is applied to dirty surfaces it is likely to peel, crack, or blister off the walls. First, scrape off all loose, peeling paint. Then scrub the surface well with a detergent solution and a broom or long-handled brush. Rinse well. You can use a garden hose to wash down exterior walls.

• Mildew is a problem in shady areas on house exteriors. Mildew looks like fuzzy patches of black dirt. If your house has mildew, wash it with a mixture of one quart of bleach to every gallon of non-ammonia detergent solution. After cleaning, let surfaces dry thoroughly before painting. CAUTION: Please be careful with the bleach and don't let it get on something that it could whiten or streak. You might want to drape plastic drop cloths over the shrubbery and flower beds; if you are using bleach, remove any fabric awnings and lawn furniture cushions from the splash areas.

• Be sure to wait for dew to dry before painting. Paint will not bind on a surface that is wet from morning dew or on a prime coat that is not thoroughly dry. And without proper bonding, paint will peel.

• Wrinkling occurs when too much paint is applied or when the paint is too thick. You can correct wrinkling easily by sanding the surface and brushing on paint of a lighter consistency. See the paint can for thinning directions.

• Don't try using a flame to soften alligatored paint. The flame can shoot into a crack and ignite the sheathing.

• It's not always necessary to remove the old paint when you are preparing old wood surfaces for paint. Seal all knots with thinned shellac and sand when dry. If the knot is loose, tighten it with wood caulking. After the caulking has dried, coat the spot with shellac and then sand the area smooth.

• Revolving disc sanders shouldn't be used to remove paint from wood siding, because they tend to gouge the surface.

• When painting the outside of your house, drape newspapers over the tops of doors and then close them. You won't paint the doors shut.

• To avoid marring a paint job when leaning a ladder against clapboard siding, cover the top ends of the ladder with heavy woolen socks. The paint will remain unblemished.

• Windowpanes intimidate even the most ambitious home improvement buffs. Believe me, you can paint the wooden strips around windowpanes without getting paint on the glass and having to endure a pain-in-the-neck cleanup job. Cut newspapers into long one-inch strips, then dip each strip in clear water. Gently pull the strips between your thumb and forefinger to get some of the water out and then stick the strips onto the windowpanes up close to the woodwork.

Because the strips dry out, you can do only two panes at a time, but if you don't have to painstakingly dab at narrow wood strips, you can really lay that paint on fast. Lift the paper strips off after you paint and wipe remaining water off the glass with a paper towel wrapped around the tip of your finger.

• Also, smearing petroleum jelly on the windowpane itself will make it easy to remove any paint that happens to drip onto the glass.

• Or you can use masking tape to tape around the window frame on the glass, but be sure to remove it as soon as the paint dries so that the goo doesn't adhere to the glass.

Using a Ladder Safely

• To safely position a ladder so that it won't fall forward or backward, the distance from the ladder's base to the wall or tree should be one fourth of the ladder's extended length.

• If you are going to work on a ladder in front of a closed door, lock the door so that you won't be knocked over if someone inadvertently tries to open it.

• Paint cans tumbling and splashing around on your kids and pets or anyone beneath your ladder is funny only in cartoons. Here's how to avoid paint showers when kids and pets might just nudge your ladder while you are working.

Securely tack the lid from a two- or three-pound coffee or shortening can to the bucket shelf of your ladder with the rim facing up. After filling the can with as much paint as you think is safe, set it into the plastic lid. The grip will hold well enough to hold the paint can against most wobblings. You can even move the ladder with paint in place if you're reasonably careful. Of course, nothing will help if you and the ladder tip over; better keep the kids and pets out of the way.

Dripless Painting

There is so much information about paint (how to thin it, how to get it off clothing, etc.) on the paint can label that it is really a good idea to keep the can from being covered with drips. That's why you shouldn't wipe your paintbrush against the lip of the paint can. The lip will soon fill up with paint, which will dribble down the side and cover all the information.

• If you stretch a strong rubber band around the can lengthwise and use it to wipe your brush, you'll keep all the drips inside the can, where they belong.

• Or, using an ice pick, punch holes in the rim of the paint can, and the paint will drip through the holes back into the can.

• You can pour as much paint as you'll use into a coffee can or other container. Keep the remainder covered, if you are working outside and want to keep dirt, leaves, and insects out of your main paint supply.

• Painting rain gutters is easy, but down spouts can be tricky. To protect the downspout's interior against rust, drop a string with a weight on it down through the spout and tie a sponge to the string's bottom end. The sponge should be large enough so that it must be compressed to fit inside the spout.

Using plenty of paint, soak the sponge and then pull on the string to squeeze the sponge up through the spout. The paint will spread evenly from bottom to top as the sponge goes up.

Cleaning Up

• As soon as you finish painting, and before paint has a chance to dry and clog the nozzles of spray paint cans, pop the nozzles into a small glass jar and cover them with lacquer thinner.

• You don't have to completely clean up your paint roller, brushes, and pan between coats. After you apply the first coat, store your roller, brushes, edger, and other equipment into the paint tray and then put the whole thing into a plastic bag. Leftover paint and the applicators will stay pliable and fresh until you are ready to start the second coat a few hours later or the next day. Wrapped in foil or plastic, paintbrushes can be stored for a longer period of time.

• If you line your paint tray with a plastic bag before pouring in your paint, cleanup is no chore. After you've finished, you can toss used rags, paper towels, or disposable paint applicators into the tray, then turn the plastic bag clean side out as you remove it from the tray. You'll have messy rags wrapped up and a clean tray.

• You can also press a sheet of aluminum foil onto the tray before pouring the paint into it, and when you're finished, wrap up your paint rags and so on in the foil when you discard it.

• Soaking a new oil paintbrush in linseed oil for a day before it's used will make the brush last longer and easier to clean.

• Also, adding a capful of fabric softener to a quart of water and then soaking the paintbrushes in it will do the same trick.

• If you clean paintbrushes by just poking them into a can of solvent or turpentine and letting them soak, you'll find that the bristles get squash-bent tips. But if you take an empty coffee can with a plastic lid and suspend the brushes from the plastic lid so that the bristles don't rest on the bottom of the can, you'll be able to reuse those brushes.

You need to make two slits in the center of the plastic lid to form an X, then push the brush handle up through the X and replace the lid, which will protect the brushes and prevent the solvent from evaporating.

• If you pour the solvent for cleaning your paintbrushes into a heavy-duty clear plastic bag and then put the brushes into the bag, you can work the solvent into the bristles throughout the plastic without messing up your hands.

• To clean a paint roller, you start by rolling it as dry as possible, first on the newly painted surface and then on several sheets of newspaper. Then remove the roller from its support and clean it with water, solvent, or whatever is suggested for the type of paint you've used.

• You can reuse the paint thinner left over from cleaning brushes. Here's how: Pour paint thinner into an empty coffee can. Then, after you've cleaned your brushes in it, cover the can tightly, put it in a safe place out of the reach of children or pets, and let it rest for several days. Paint from the brushes will settle to the bottom as sediment. Drain off the "clean" thinner into another can and store for reuse.

• After cleaning your brush, give it a final rinse in water containing fabric softener; it will stay soft as new.

• Paste type of paint removers remove paint spots from brick.

• If you get oil-base paint on your work clothes, pour a little turpentine on the spot and rub it with a soft toothbrush. Then wet a bar of body soap and rub this into the spot, brushing gently with a toothbrush. After you have washed the garment with your regular detergent, the spot should be gone.

CAUTION: Turpentine is flammable. ALWAYS do this away from any flames and in a well-ventilated place. (See Chapter 7 for more on removing paint from clothing.)

After the Job Is Over

• If you write the amount, brand, and color of paint you used for a room on the back of a light-switch plate in that room, you'll always have a handy reminder of how much and what kind of paint to buy when you repaint.

Storing Paint

• You can keep paint in an opened can from drying out if you make a pattern from the lid from wax paper. (Don't use plastic wrap.) Lay the wax paper directly on the paint, then put the lid on. The paper really will keep the either oil-base or water-base paints fresh for months! The paper is easy to remove and can be reused if you wish.

• If, for some reason (such as losing the lid), you can't store paint in its original can, you can store it in a gallon-size plastic milk jug.

Be sure to label the jug with a marker, noting the color, number, and store where you bought it. When you need to touch up, shake the jug well, pour a dab or two of paint into a throw-away margarine tub, and touch up the spot.

• If you mark the label on the can with the level of remaining paint before you seal the lid for storage, you'll know how much is left inside without having to open the can the next time you want to use it. You can use a marker or just dab a paint-level mark with your paintbrush.

• If you mark the label with the room in which the paint was used, reordering the paint for touch-ups is easy.

• A partly used can of paint can be stored upside down to keep a "skin" from forming on the paint surface. But, before you turn that can upside down, be sure the lid is tight or you'll not have any paint to store because it will be flowing all over the work surface.

• If you have leftover paint that has lumps or shreds of paint skin, strain it through window screening to delump or unlump it before use.

• Also, to unlump paint, use an old pair of pantyhose stretched across the can.

• If you stir a drop of black paint into it, white paint won't yellow.

Painting Cupboards and Cabinets

• When you're painting cabinets, paint the insides first, then the tops, bottoms, and sides of doors before you paint the door fronts. This keeps you from having to reach over already painted areas and smearing the paint and yourself.

• You won't have drips on drawer fronts if you remove the drawers and paint the fronts when the surface is "faceup."

• It's always best to take off hardware before painting, but if you can't, coat the hardware with petroleum jelly before painting. Paint splats will wipe right off.

• You can wrap doorknobs with aluminum foil or enclose them in plastic sandwich bags to protect them from paint smears.

Spray Painting

Spray painting is quick and there are no brushes to clean, but if you aren't careful, you'll have a worse mess to clean up than a few brushes, rollers, and a tray. To help prevent unsightly spray paint mess in garages, on lawns, in car ports, and in driveways when painting, try the following.

• When spray painting small items, place them inside a large cardboard box. Spray the exposed surfaces, then turn the items to expose other surfaces for painting.

Spray painting in a box helps to eliminate ugly spots on grass or concrete, and it also keeps the paint mist from "attacking" shoes and clothing.

• If you've bought everything for painting but the plastic paint tarps, old plastic tablecloths, plastic shower curtains, and even old draperies or furniture throws make good substitute paint tarps. Fabric won't protect anything from liquid paint spills, but it will protect surfaces from spray paint mist.

• Some people need to protect themselves as much as they need to protect the environment when they spray paint. If you have allergies, you may be bothered by the fumes from spray paints and varnishes. Wear a surgical mask to keep the paint fumes and mist out of your nose, bronchial tubes, and lungs.

This may be a good idea even if you're not allergic to paint. I know people who wear surgical masks when they mow their lawns or spray insecticides in their gardens. I think your health is always more important than appearances or the few dimes it costs you to buy protective masks and goggles.

• Also, this is the perfect time to wear your old glasses, so that when you're painting ceilings, paint doesn't splatter in your eye.

Do's and Don'ts for Home Security

• Don't leave spare keys in the traditional places: in mailboxes, under door-mats, under pot plants, and so forth. Find a secret way of concealing the extra key, such as putting it in a film canister, or a small can, or wrapping it in a wad of foil and then burying it in a special place in the garden where it can easily be dug up when you've forgotten your keys.

• Don't leave notes for repair people or family members on the door where anyone can read that you will be home at a specific time.

• Unless you have an answering machine, adjust your telephone ring to its lowest volume if you plan to be away from home for a day or longer. Prowlers know a home is empty if the phone rings unanswered.

• Use timers to switch lights, radios, and TV sets on and off when you're not at home, so that your house appears to be occupied at all times.

• When you go on a trip, don't cancel your mail and newspapers; you'll just be letting a lot of strangers know you'll be gone and for how long. It's better to have a neighbor take in your mail, newspapers, and any flyers left on your door, so that your house looks occupied.

• If for some reason your plans to be away from home have been publicized, as through announcements of a funeral or wedding, hire a house sitter or have a friend stay in your house while the event is going on. Burglars often use newspaper announcements that tell who will be where and how long to schedule their "working hours."

• A barking dog is the best prowler alarm and burglar deterrent. Even a small yappy dog is an effective announcer of people presence.

• Have a locksmith reset all of the lock tumblers when you move into a new house, or buy new locks. Nobody knows how many sets of keys are with how many people!

• If you don't already have them, install double cylinder locks that need to be opened with a key from the inside and outside. Then, if a thief breaks a pane of glass in your door to get in, he's still have to fiddle around with a lock instead of just a knob.

• When door hinges are set on the outside of your house, all a burglar has to do is knock out the pins from the hinges and the door will come off for easy entry. It's best to reset hinges inside.

• Burglars can easily break glass panels set beside doors and then reach around to open the door from the inside. If you have such doors, put up a grille over the panel to fortify them. Use double-cylinder locks to prevent thieves from breaking in.

• Burglar-proof your glass patio doors by buying adjustable safety bars at hardware stores or by cutting a pipe, metal bar, or broom handle exactly to the measurement of the inside bottom track of the door so that you can wedge it in on the track when you want to bar the door.

• If your sliding door is installed so that you can't drop a broom handle in, simply drill a hole through both sliding doors and then insert a bolt or a nail to keep the doors from sliding.

• If you think that someone can enter your house through your attached garage, a C clamp can provide extra security. If your garage door lifts on a track, the door cannot be opened if you tighten the C clamp on the track next to the roller.

• Prowlers can't tell that you are gone because your car is not in your garage if you cover your garage windows with a frost plastic decorative paper or spray with a can of frost.

Fire Safety

Here are some do's and don'ts to protect your home from fire.

• This is the number one, most important, tip: Never spend more than 30 seconds fighting a fire. If the fire can't be extinguished, warn others and get out of the house. Go to a neighbor's house to phone the fire department.

• Hold family fire drills on a regular basis and make sure that everyone knows what to do in case of fire. Make double sure that everyone can actually get out of the house according to the plans you have made.

• Have a designated meeting place where all family members will congregate for a "head count" to make sure everyone did get out of the house.

• Keep combustible materials away from the furnace, which can give off flames or sparks at times, and keep them away from all pilot lights, such as on the hot water heater.

• Don't keep lawn mowers that contain gasoline in unventilated rooms with hot-water heaters. Here in Texas, where I live, we have one or two explosions/fires each year because of the intense heat that builds up in such dangerous conditions.

• Don't run extension cords under the rugs. They can wear, fray, bend to expose wire, be bitten by pets, and then short out to cause a fire. The U.S. Consumer Product Safety Commission has been conducting a study of the causes of appliance cord failures, because such failures result annually in about 5,500 home fires, 70 deaths, and more than 200 injuries. Check your appliance cords and extension cords for the beginning signs of wear, then get them repaired or replace them before they are totally worn. Your life is worth more than any repair bill or extension cord cost.

• Buy a fire extinguisher and make sure to check its effectiveness date regularly. Also, keep baking soda on hand for extinguishing small emergency kitchen fires.

• Don't install a gas cooktop near windows where curtains can blow into the flames or where wind could extinguish the cooking flames. If you already have such an installation, keep that window closed, don't have curtains over the stove, or vent the drafts by installing draft guards, which you can buy in hardware stores or through some catalogs.

• Install smoke detectors in your home with just a screwdriver and the set of instructions that comes in the box.

In fact, install smoke detectors on each floor of your home, usually in the hallway near each separate sleeping area.

• Don't mount a smoke detector too close to areas such as the kitchen, where smoke and steam from cooking will activate the alarm; in a bathroom, where shower steam may activate it; or in the garage, where combustion products from the car's engine can set it off.

When you buy your smoke detectors, you will get instructions for proper placement and for checking the batteries to make sure they are still working. CAUTION: If the batteries are dead, you are not protected.

• More people are overcome by smoke and inhalation of chemicals produced by burning textiles and other parts of the building than are burned by fire. If you have to go down a smoke-filled hall, crawl on the floor and put a wet cloth over your nose and mouth to serve as a filter.

• If you are in a room and suspect there is fire outside it because of smoke or an actual alarm, touch the door before opening it. If it is hot, DON'T open it. The fire is likely to rush—more likely, explode—into the room before you can get the door closed again.

Heat rises, so the top of the door will warm up first. If the door feels cool but you see smoke curling in at the bottom, the area on the other side is filled to the floor with smoke, and you must find another way out. Smoke rises and fills a room or a hallway from the top down. If you are on the first floor, get out through the window and don't worry about breaking it or pushing out the screen. If you have to break a window, put a blanket over yourself or find a way to protect yourself from cuts.

• The universal signal to fire fighters when you are in a multi-story building is to hang a sheet out of a window to say, "Somebody's in here; come get me."

• CAUTION: Before you open any windows, if you are in a hotel or apartment, take wet sheets, blankets, towels, and stuff them around the door. Opening the windows can cause the heat and smoke from the hall to explode into the room.

Washing Windows and Large Objects

Windows

Sometimes, when you think it's foggy outside, it's really grime on your windows. Eventually it will get so bad you can't use the excuse that you are trying to filter out the sun's rays to keep your furniture from fading.

• My best window-washing hint is that when you dry windows, dry them on the outside from right to left, and on the inside, dry with the strokes up and down. That way, if there's a streak, you can tell whether it's on the inside or the outside of the window.

• Second, the best and cheapest thing to use when drying windows is newspapers. You don't need to use paper towels or cloths that have lint on them. There seems to be something in the printer's ink that makes windows shine and sparkle, and it hasn't cost you an extra penny.

• Always wash and dry windows on an average day, not on an extremely hot, sunny day, because the washing solution will dry too quickly and you'll end up with lots of streaks.

Your House

• Try hosing down your house. You won't get the windows perfectly clean, but you will get some of the daily dust off and the bonus is that you'll get a lot of cobwebs off the rest of the house. Do this on a hot day in your swimsuit and cool off at the same time. Get the children into the act and you'll end up with a day the whole family remembers! (Let the children use water pistols and you control the hose—claim parent privilege!)

• If you have textured aluminum siding on your house, the texture will gather dirt, but this accumulation is easily removed by attaching a car-washing brush to your hose and just brush rinsing the house about every six months or so, depending upon how much rain and dust your climate abuses your house with. You don't really need any soap or detergent. Water will usually do the job.

Polishing Large Appliances

• You can wax large appliances with appliance or car wax to make them shine. Wax will "erase" fine line scratches nicely if you are selling the appliance.

Car Washing and Maintenance

• Dirt, pollen, bird droppings, road gunk, and salt (in winter climates) accumulate on our cars and make them look years older. Not removing the mess ultimately damages the paint surface, and even if you don't care about how your car usually looks, the dealer will certainly care when you try to trade it in for a new model.

• After you wash your car at home, wipe down the car with old terry towels instead of just letting it dry. The chlorine in city water will leave droplet marks if you don't towel dry your car.

• The pros use soaps on cars with zero pH factor. The pH factor is the amount of acidity or alkalinity in a solution: high pH signifies high acid; low pH signifies a very alkaline solution. Both are bad for your car finish.

• Detergents are not the best cleaning agent for a car. If you use detergent to wash your car, mix only a small amount in a large bucket.

• Use only clean rags on your car. It takes only a bit of grit to scratch a line across the finish. Use plastic or nylon net scrubbers to get stuck-on soil off the car. Terry cloth is better than chamois for washing and good for drying too.

• A good heavy-duty paste wax will last six months or more and will give the finish better protection than liquid waxes, as a rule.

• If you don't have a sealed battery, check to make sure your battery has water in it; water evaporates especially fast during intense summer heat. Water is cheap, a new battery is not!

• If the battery terminals are heavily corroded, the quickest and easiest way to solve the problem is to pour a can or bottle of carbonated soft drink over them; it will eat away all the corrosion.

• Or, you can mix one or two tablespoons baking soda with water and pour over battery terminals, and again, it will bubble away the corrosion.

• After removing the connection to the terminal, and cleaning it well, rub a little petroleum jelly around the post and the inside of the terminal, and then reattach. This will help prevent the corrosion, which is the major cause of not being able to recharge the battery.

• Carry duct tape in your car for emergencies. You can patch belts and make many minor repairs with it that will last long enough to get to a garage and help.

Garages

• An unpainted garage door can swell and warp and then be hard to open. Let the door dry out when you have dry weather for a few days, and then paint all surfaces, including the edges, to seal the wood so that it won't absorb moisture.

• If you have an automatic garage door opener, you may find that your garage door mysteriously opens and closes when you haven't meant it to. It's possible that someone else has an opener set on the same frequency as yours. If you can't reset the frequency or have it done, be sure to unplug the opener mechanism when you are at home, especially at night, or when you are on vacation to ensure keeping your garage door closed.

Parking Your Car in the Garage

Even if you know that your new car is the same size or just an inch or so wider or longer than your old one, parking it in the garage is a test of your depth perception. Here are a few tips on parking without nicking or denting either car or garage.

• Paint bright or luminous stripes, or stick on reflector or brightly colored tape on the rear garage wall to help you aim the car down the center.

• Stick reflector tape on anything that seems to be in your way at night, if you don't have good lighting in the garage.

• If knowing when you should stop is a problem, hang a ball on a string from the garage ceiling so that it touches the windshield at about eye level when you have the car in the right place. If you hang the ball in the center of your parking space, you can use it for a centering guide as well as a stop sign. Bright colors and a piece of reflector tape will help you see your guide.

• Old inner tubes cut in pieces can be used to pad anything that you tend to brush against with your car or touch when you open the car door, such as support studs, framing, or even the nearest walls. Other padding materials include carpet scraps, old rubber mats, and foam rubber.

• If you like to back into the garage, an old tire hung at bumper height can be a wall-protecting, dent-preventing stopper.

Greasy Garage Floors

• Grease and oil spots are unsightly in a garage, but the real problem is that people step in them and bring the gunk into the house. An old cookie sheet or cake pan filled with cat litter or sand and placed at the drip site will collect leaking grease or oil. If you don't have cat litter or sand handy, use a piece of corrugated cardboard to fit the cookie sheet and change it as necessary.

• Staple heavy-duty aluminum foil to a piece of corrugated cardboard for a disposable drip pad.

• Clean up oil and grease spots by applying paint thinner, then covering them with cat litter, dry cement, or sand, and letting the absorbant remain on the spot overnight. Sweep up the absorbent material and repeat the process if you have to.

• Other absorbent materials include baking soda and cornmeal. Just sprinkle on and sweep off, repeating the process until you've got a clean-enough garage floor.

• If the absorbents don't work, try dousing the spot with full-strength laundry bleach and wiping up the excess with rags or paper towels. CAUTION: Wear protective gloves when you're using bleach or other strong chemicals.

• If you still can't get rid of the stain and it bothers you, paint a wide black stripe the width of the space between your car tires and use the stripe as a centering aid.

Storing Things in the Garage

Garages tend to get dumped in, and stuff just accumulates in them. In climates where people don't have basements, garages have to serve as combination basement/garage storage areas, and you really can get an accumulation of jumbled-up "junque." ("Junque" is plain old junk you don't admit to being junk.)

• If you're handy, you can use up all that air space in the top half of your garage by building storage shelves on side and back walls. If you're not, peg boards and ready-made shelving are for you.

• Save floor space by hanging garden tools, sports gear, bikes (on special heavy-duty hooks for that purpose), or anything else that will hang up.

• If you're not afraid that your family will overload them, you can install deep shelves in the back end of the garage so that your car hood will be under them.

• Lay a platform or shelving across ceiling joists in the garage, on which to store seldom used or seasonal items, such as storm windows and window screens.

• Take a tip from your city's parking lots. Paint "parking area" lines on the garage floor to designate spaces for bikes, the lawn mower, or other large objects, so that these "targets" have their own spaces and you'll be less likely to hit them with the car when you're pulling into the garage. (Isn't it annoying to have to get out of the car to move a bike or lawn mower a couple of inches so that you can drive in? Especially if you've had a bad day!)

The Final Word on Maintenance

Take time to relax and to enjoy the people in your life. You only get one chance at savoring each day. Once the day is over, it's over. Don't miss opportunities!

I get a lot of letters from women who feel guilty about not having homes as spotless as their mothers had. I tell them that nobody ever died from a little bit of dust. Most of us just don't have the same life-styles our mothers had, and we don't have the time to keep house as they did.

I've never heard a eulogy in which the person was praised for having a perfectly clean house, car, office, whatever. People are remembered for a sense of humor, kindness to others, community service, and other achievements that affect the well-being of others.

CHAPTER **5**

Plants and Yard Care

House Plants

T his is my favorite subject. I'm a whiz at growing avocado plants. Some of mine are so tall they touch the ceiling. They're really beautiful and so much fun to grow.

Have you ever thought about making an indoor garden of plants from fruits and vegetables bought at your local food market? The advantage is that you have the fun and satisfaction of seeing things grow without putting out a lot of money. And, if pits and seeds don't grow, not to worry, they were free!

Planting Pits and Seeds

• Usually, I allow three to four days for the pit or seed to dry. Plant it in three parts potting soil and one part vermiculite—fat, rounded end down at least an inch into the soil.

Place in a window (but not in harsh sunlight); a plant light also works well. Be sure to keep the soil damp but not soaked. You should see the beginning of the sprouts in three to four weeks. I always plant several seeds, since some won't sprout.

• Start avocado plants by putting three toothpicks into the seed at about the middle. (If the seed were the earth, you'd put toothpicks at its equator.) Put water in a glass and put the avocado fat side down into the glass. The toothpicks will hold it up so the water level is covering only half the seed. Be sure to change the water often, as it tends to get algae.

It doesn't take long for it to sprout. When there are enough roots, put it into the soil mixture described above.

I'm especially proud of one of my avocado trees. It's seven years old and twelve feet high. It grows in my home beautifully.

• Mango seeds are easily grown. Lay each pit flat on top of potting soil, then push it down into the soil. Keep it damp and somewhere where it will remain warm. These take about a month to germinate. They will sprout a root and then the seedling.

• Date palms grow nicely too. Start with unpasteurized dates. Plant the pits and keep the pot moist and warm. Wait (as usual). Date pits, like most palm seeds, are slow to germinate. So be patient.

• To grow a coconut palm you need an unhusked coconut. Place it on top of sandy soil in a wide-diameter pot. Keep the pot warm, damp, and in good light. The shoot will emerge from one end of the husk. It usually takes about three years to grow a three-foot tree.

• You could add a finishing touch to your indoor garden by sprouting fresh unroasted coffee beans. Roasted beans won't germinate. I've had some very good luck, but be prepared for some failures, because coffee beans are a bit temperamental. Do you suppose it's too much caffeine?

A Medicinal Plant

The aloe vera plant is pretty and practical because it's excellent first aid for minor burns. Aloe vera jelly soothes the pain and aids healing. Apply the jellylike fluid in the lance-shaped leaves immediately to minor dry burns, scalds, and cuts and scrapes.

Just pick a leaf, break it open, and squeeze on the jelly. Each leaf contains quite a lot of fluid, so when the break in the leaf looks dry, just peel back the outer skin of the leaf and you'll get more fluid. A bad burn may require several applications. Serious burns should be seen by a physician as soon as possible.

Keep a plant in the kitchen, where most burns occur, or by the back door for those painful sunburns.

Plant Cuttings

Some plants will root in water, but it's obvious that water is not a plant's natural domain. In fact, roots that form under water have a different structure than roots formed in soil, so, when a water-started cutting is planted, it has to grow a whole new set of roots. It's better to start cuttings in soil.

• Here's a simple home method.

Place one to two inches of a very light potting soil and vermiculite in the bottom of a "zipper"-closing plastic sandwich or food storage bag. Moisten it thoroughly, but pour off any excess water.

Snip small, actively growing cuttings with a sharp knife or shears, cutting at an angle. Wet the cut ends and dip them into root hormone (available at nurseries and other places that sell plants). Trim off any leaves that cover the lower one to two inches of the cuttings and plant the tip into the soil.

Inflate the bag by sealing it almost across the top, then blow into the bag as you complete the seal. This keeps the plastic from touching the leaves.

Leave the bag in partial light, not full sun, until the cuttings have rooted. This may take from three days to three weeks, depending on the plant. Check to be sure the soil stays moist.

• You can put larger clippings in a pot filled with vermiculite and potting soil. Do the same as above, clip stems and wet the end, then dip into root hormone and put into soil.

Watering Your Plants

• If you own a freshwater fish tank, instead of throwing out the water when cleaning, use it to water the plants. It's a great fertilizer.

• If you have opened bottles of club soda left over, feed the contents to your house plants or outdoor plants. Flat soda is beneficial to green, growing things because of all the minerals in it.

• Cool the water left over from cooking spaghetti or potatoes and use to water your plants. They love the starch.

• After you boil eggs, use the cooled water on your house plants. Egg water is packed with growth-stimulating minerals. Diluted plain Jane coffee (no sugar or cream) is my Heloise home fertilizer, too.

• Melted snow contains minerals that make it good for watering your plants.

• If your house's rain gutters have a spout, you can collect rainwater for your plants by putting a large plastic garbage can under the drain spout. (I have a friend who used to use rainwater as a final rinse for her hair; she said it made her hair soft and shiny, though I haven't tested this hint.)

• Put your plant watering can under the shower before you step in. The first spray is enough for a dozen plants, and helps conserve water. Some people may think this is a silly hint, but I live in central Texas, where conserving water is a serious responsibility, especially if we are having a long, dry spell in the summer.

• Save the rinse water from dish-washing if you wash and rinse dishes by hand. Mist plants with it, as the soap film kills some pests such as mites and scale. This occasional misting won't hurt most plants (except for African violets).

• Use an old knitting needle or a pencil to test when your house plants need watering. If the needle or pencil eraser inserted into the soil comes out dry, get out your watering can.

• Group plants together rather than scattering them sparsely. When clustered, they create their own moist environment.

• During cold weather months, a room filled with house plants will benefit from the moisture provided by a portable vaporizer. So will you; vaporizers keep the air from getting so dry that some carpets produce almost enough electricity to light up the room, or so it seems. Isn't it unpleasant when your clothes cling to your body, every person you touch is "shocking," and worst of all, your skin feels like parchment and looks worse from winter dryness?

Watering Plants When You're on Vacation

• If you're planning a short vacation, try this. Put a big bucket of water in the bathtub and place the plants around it. Cut string in lengths long enough so that you can put one end into the soil and have enough string to reach from the plant to the water and down to the bottom of the bucket. The plants will "sip" enough water through the string to survive while you're gone.

Drainage Tips

• Every plant container should have drainage holes. If you're using a recycled one such as a plastic food tub, be sure to make holes. Trapped water causes root rot.

• Cracked walnut shells, broken pieces of clay pot, marbles, stones, or fruit pits can be used to provide drainage at the bottom of a house plant pot.

• For a lightweight drainage layer in the bottom of a hanging planter, use pieces of foam packing material.

• Set small potted plants on pebble trays filled with water. The moisture from pebble trays cuts down the plant's transpiration loss and you save water. This is especially true of African violets.

• Slip shower caps over the bottoms of hanging planters to catch the light drips when watering and remove after an hour or so.

Plant Pest Control

• A garlic clove planted beside your house plant will keep many types of pests away from it.

• When people take house plants outside for extra sun and then return them to their places indoors, they sometimes unwittingly bring bugs indoors too.

If you want to take plants outdoors, keep them isolated from other house plants for three to four weeks after you bring them back in. If you detect bugs on the plants, wipe the stems and leaves with a mild soap-and-water solution.

• If you think there may be root-damaging worms in the soil of your potted plants, place a slice of raw potato on the surface of each. The worms will crawl out to get at the potatoes, and you can capture and destroy them.

• When one of your house plants appears "sick," attach a pest strip, then cover the plant for a few days with a plastic bag. Keep the soil moist and don't seal the bag; it should fall loosely around the pot. Keep out of the sunlight.

By the time you remove the bag, the plant should have perked up nicely, because all of the pests will be on the strip.

• You can do a bug check by giving your plants a good soaking in the shower. The water will force many plant invaders to the top, because they'll be trying to escape drowning (a fate too good for such evil varmints) and you'll be able to see what's living beneath the soil surface. I once discovered that one of my ailing plants had millipedes in it.

I was glad that it was the only plant I'd put into the tub that day. The millipedes could have scurried over to healthy plants. Having lots of legs sure makes them move fast! Anyhow, knowing that it was millipedes made it easy for me to choose an insecticide to kill them. I'm happy to report that the millipede-infested palm tree got well and is still alive three feet and four years later.

• To get rid of plant lice on African violets, you'll need hair spray and a plastic bag big enough to hold the potted violet. Spray the hair spray into the plastic bag (never on the plant), then put the plant into the plastic bag, twist or tie it shut, and let the plant stay in the bag for a day.

TLC (Tender, Loving Care) for Plants

Home-style remedies:

• Unless they are fed regularly with fertilizer, potted plants, whether indoors or outdoors, can develop nutrient deficiencies they might not get if they were growing in an outdoor bed. The cure is commercial plant food, used according to directions.

• An ailing house plant can be treated with a tablespoon of castor oil dribbled on its soil, followed by a thorough watering.

• To make plant leaves shine, swab only the tops with a soft cloth dipped in glycerine. Unlike other gloss-producing substances, glycerine won't collect dust.

• Just like people, plants last longer if you don't let them go to seed. As blossoms begin to fade, it's best to cut them off, and that's where the plant-people analogy ends, because there's nothing to cut off with people. You just love them anyway, faded or not.

• If you pinch the tiny new shoots at the growing points, you'll encourage branching, which produces more growth for flowering. While most plants benefit from pinching, never pinch back palms; it's fatal to them.

Indoor Vegetable Gardens

If you have the space, you can grow vegetables indoors in artificial light.

• Lettuce does especially well when grown under fluorescent lights. Plant your lettuce garden in the basement, the attic, or anywhere the temperature stays between 65 and 70 degrees Fahrenheit during the day, and drops about ten degrees at night.

• Here's a novel but effective way to grow parsley in your kitchen or on your sun porch: Slice sponges in half and sprinkle them with parsley seeds. Arrange the sponges on dishes in a sunny location, keep them moist, and watch that parsley grow.

• Here's how you can grow your own sprouts in the kitchen.

Alfalfa and some other types of sprouts for your salads will grow on sponges just like the parsley will. The seeds are sold at health food and many upscale grocery stores.

Old jars, especially those from large-size instant tea, make good kitchen counter sprout growers. Use brown-tinted jars for mung beans (bean sprouts) and clear jars for other sprouts. (Mung bean seeds should be grown without sunlight to prevent them from producing green bean sprouts.)

Punch enough holes into the lids with a nail to allow you to drain the sprouts while the lid is on; it functions as a strainer. You can also make a strainer lid from the rims of two-piece canning jar lids and screening or cheesecloth. The cheesecloth, of course, is not reusable.

• Now, here's how you grow sprouts in jars.

Put in about an inch or so of mung bean, alfalfa, wheat, or whatever seeds into the bottom of the jar and let the seeds soak, covered with water, overnight or over a day, if you start in the morning.

Drain the soaking water. Allow the seeds to settle on the side of the jar; keep the jar on its side as the sprouts grow. Then irrigate the seeds/sprouts every day by pouring water on them and then draining them with the strainer lid on.

Let the sprouts grow until they are a size you like, then irrigate them one more time, drain, and put them into the refrigerator to stop growth, still in their jars, which can of course, stand upright.

• I have found that it's better to stop bean sprouts from growing more than two or three inches because they get leaves and too-long roots beyond that length. I stop most sprouts from growing when they show their first hints of wanting to leaf out.

• To get rid of the seed husks, especially on bean sprouts, before eating them, you can put them in a bowl or strainer and blast them with cold water at the greatest pressure you can get from your faucet. Then put the sprouts in a bowl filled with water, and swish them around so that most of the remaining hulls will float to the top or sink.

You can pick every single hull off if you want to, but I usually get bored with the process after the wash and dip and just leave the few remaining hulls in with the sprouts, which can then be eaten raw in salads or in sandwiches or, in the case of bean sprouts, used in Oriental dishes. Wheat and alfalfa sprouts are often baked in health breads. Once you get used to having fresh sprouts, you won't think growing them is an extra-effort chore at all.

Storing Garden Pesticides

Things that kill household and garden pests can also kill people. Always be careful with pesticides and ALWAYS keep them out of children's and pets' reach. Families with small children or people who live in neighborhoods with small children would probably be wise to store all poisonous chemicals in a padlocked cabinet or footlocker that is clearly marked POISON or DANGER.

• Manufacturers of pesticides are required to use signal words to call attention to how toxic certain products are to people. The signal words are:

DANGER—This means highly toxic. A taste to a teaspoonful can kill the average person.
WARNING—This means moderately toxic. A teaspoonful to a tablespoonful will kill the average person.
CAUTION—This means low toxicity; the product is comparatively danger free. It will take an ounce to more than a pint to kill the average person.

• The symptoms of pesticide poisoning include headache, giddiness, blurred vision, nausea, confusion, and diarrhea. If you have any of these symptoms after being around pesticides, see your physician and take along a container of the pesticide so that the physician can find out what chemicals are in it and treat you accordingly.

• When you use pesticides, carefully read the label twice to be sure that you use it on the pests it's recommended for and know what precautions to take when using it.

• Wear protective clothing and wash with soap and water after using pesticides. Don't smoke, eat, or drink until you have washed up.

• Never mix pesticides in an unventilated area, and don't use them on windy days. Keep children and pets away when you are treating an area and for a reasonable period of time afterward. Always read the prescribed times on the container.

• ALWAYS keep pesticides in their original containers. If the container is damaged and you have to put the pesticide in another container, don't use food, beverage, or medicine containers that might be mistaken for edibles. Mark containers clearly with DANGER and POISON in red, enclosing any labels that identify the contents.

• Clean up all spills from leaky containers. Put paper-bagged pesticides into heavy plastic bags for safer storage.

• When you dispose of pesticide containers, wrap them securely before putting them into a garbage can, where curious animals might get at them. Empty containers usually have some residual powders from the pesticide, which could harm anyone who gets in contact with the container.

• It's better to buy smaller amounts that get used up quickly and don't leave you with so many pesticides on your storage shelves.

Outside the House

Digging into Gardening

• The soil depends upon where you live, and different parts of a locale can have different soil conditions. If you are having topsoil trucked in, buy it only from a reputable garden firm; otherwise you'll be trucking in weeds or weed seeds in the soil that will make your garden life miserable for years to come.

• You can use an old window screen to sift topsoil before putting it into flower beds, but it would be difficult to sift the topsoil for an entire yard.

• If you want to keep your fingernails clean but think that using garden gloves is clumsy, before you go out to dig in the dirt, dig your nails into a bar of soap, or coat their undersides with nail whitening pencil. Your nails will wash clean easily.

• Before you start applying fertilizer to the soil, it's best to have a soil test so that you'll know what to add. You don't want to spend a lot of money on fertilizers that you don't need, and worse yet, if you don't know whether your soil is alkaline or acidic, you may actually add the wrong chemicals and make your soil less suitable for planting.

• Also, in many parts of the country, the soil has so much heavy clay in it that sand must be mixed with the soil to lighten it if anything is to grow well. In other parts of the country you need to mix sand and humus/compost in with the soil before planting.

• When you test your soil, you need to take at least a coffee can filled with soil to a local nursery or send the soil sample to your local county Cooperative Extension Service. To get directions on how to do this, look in the telephone book's section for United States Government, Agriculture, Department of— Extension Service and Home Economics Agents. You can label the container with an address label to make sure it stays properly identified.

Getting Gardening Help

The U.S. Department of Agriculture has booklets that will give you information about your area's gardening conditions, planting according to season, and just general good information. You can also get help with diseased plants from the USDA county extension horticulturists.

• A neighborhood garden center can be another resource. Neighborhood centers may have the advantage over large garden suppliers, because they often are aware of your particular neighborhood's gardening conditions and can help you select plants and control plant diseases.

• If you have just moved into a neighborhood, walk around to see just what grows well in the shady and sunny parts of your neighbors' yards before you go out to buy plants.

• If your city has a botanical center, it too can be a learning experience for you, because most centers will have displays of what grows locally as well as more exotic plants.

• Local county agents and gardening experts often write newspaper gardening columns, which can be good resources for information on planting and maintaining a garden, whether you grow flowers, fruits and vegetables, or just trees and grass.

• Local county Extension agents are more than happy to help you with any questions regarding gardening, landscaping, soil content, and so forth. Use your tax dollars, and give the agent a call.

Shrubs and Other Plants

• You can have fruit trees in a small yard. Plant dwarf fruit trees as a hedge or train them to grow against a trellis, wall, or fence. To make a fence from dwarf fruit trees, plant them only two feet apart and prune them three to four times during the summer. (The technical gardening name for such a fence is *espalier;* after pruning, such trees look like a main stem with many branch-arms going off to the sides.) Check with your nursery for your area's dwarf fruit tree varieties suitable for this use.

• Berry bushes also make good "edible" shrubs and hedges.

• Grass needs sun. If you don't plan to prune trees or shrubs to let the sun shine through, you'll have to plant ground cover plants under them, such as ivy, jasmine, or whatever is usually used for ground cover in your area.

• When you are planting bedding plants or ground cover plants, plant them close together to discourage and smother weeds that might want to poke through.

• You can also discourage weeds in flower beds by covering the soil with bark, compost, leaves, or whatever is usually used for mulch in your area. Mulch not only discourages weeds, it keeps the soil moist and decomposes as organic matter to enrich the soil. Leaves are free mulch!

Composting

Compost is a combination of manure, leaves, shredded grass clippings, and newspapers, which means it's one of the best recycling ideas around, especially when you consider the problems many cities are having as they use up available landfill sites!

It can also contain other organic matter, such as bark, humus, and peat moss. Soil can be added to help break down the compost materials. In some parts of the country, people can use organic garbage (fruit and vegetable peels, melon rinds, coffee grounds, and so forth) in their compost piles, but in other parts of the country, such as where I live, such organic matter tends to attract nematodes to the soil, thereby harming the plants. Consult local gardening resources for information on how best to garden in your area.

• You can use compost in its various stages to smother weeds and to conserve soil moisture and moderate its temperature. You don't have to wait until it's all decomposed.

• When you apply compost to your garden, you shouldn't pile it up near plant stems or tree trunks. If you do, stems and trunks may rot.

• Compost piles need to be turned frequently to keep them moist.

• Collect the bags of leaves and grass clippings and stacks of newspapers that your neighbors set out for trash pickup and then work these materials into the compost pile. This is recycling and saving money on fertilizer at the same time!

• You don't need a leaf shredder to shred compost materials if you have a motor-powered garden tiller. You can make a pile of leaves one or two feet high, and then run the power tiller through the pile to shred up the material so that it will compost more quickly.

• A power tiller helps you to mix compost into the soil before planting flower or vegetable beds; in some cities, such relatively expensive gardening aids can be rented.

Garden Beds

• If you don't have much space for a garden, organizing plants according to size lets you grow both flowers and veggies in the same bed. You can plant beans with sweet peas and tomatoes behind marigolds, put peppers in with petunias, and otherwise combine nature's bounty.

• Marigolds tend to repel mosquitoes, so they'll make your gardening more comfortable as well as pretty if you use them as a border around the garden plot.

• If you plant onions as a border around your garden, harvest the green ones to "thin" the row, then allow the remaining onions to mature to full-sized ones.

• Garlic can also be a border plant. Harvest the garlic chives for your salad by snipping off the green spikes; more will grow back.

• If you can, try to plant tall-growing plants on the north and northeast side of your garden so that, as they grow, they won't shade the rest of the bed.

• If you're planting a vegetable garden in the city or on a small lot, try to avoid shade from buildings and large trees. Large trees take soil nutrients and moisture away from your garden, besides blocking the sun. Remember that a tree's root system can reach way beyond the span of its branches.

• Veggies need at least six hours of direct sun each day, sometimes as much as eight to ten hours, so if you try to grow tomatoes, peppers, or eggplant in the shade, you'll get nice green shrubs but nothing to eat.

Planting an Herb Garden

• Here's my favorite tip for planting an herb garden: The best place to plant herbs is as close to your kitchen door as possible. Use pots and containers if that helps you grow them more conveniently to where you'll use them. If you have to walk through mud or other plants to get to the herbs, the chances are you won't use them at all, because it will be just too much mess and trouble.

• If you want to get the most pleasure from an herb garden, plant the herbs where they can be touched, picked, or brushed by people walking past them, because herbs don't release their fragrances until they are brushed or bruised.

• Thyme, marjoram, and parsley grow only a few inches high, so position them as borders where they won't be overshadowed by the other plants.

• Coriander, tarragon, and dill grow to about two feet high or more. These plants can be the center of a walk-around herb garden plot or be at the rear of a plot that is against a fence or wall. If you have shorter plants in front, you can easily reach the tall ones.

• If you grow rosemary and bay leaves in clay pots buried just beneath the surface of your garden's soil, you can easily move them indoors when the weather turns cold so that they will continue to provide flavor year-round. What a treat!

• Some herbs will really spread and try to take over an herb garden. Perennials like wild marjoram, tarragon, and mint will take up more space each season if you don't tell them where to stop. If you confine their roots with a buried section of stovepipe, they'll stay where you want them to.

• To get the best flavor from herbs, cut them just before they flower, when their oils are at peak. When cutting for storage, the best time to cut them is at mid-morning on a sunny day.

• Store them by freezing, drying, or in oil or vinegar. Use the oil and vinegar as preseasoned cooking ingredients.

• If you have refrigerator space, home-dried herbs, fruits, and vegetables keep better stored there.

• Some seasons, tomato plants go crazy and produce so much that you can't even give enough of them away. A food dryer can reduce buckets of tomatoes to quarts. Dried tomatoes can be crumpled and added with your dried herbs to flavor stews and soups, and they'll take much less space than canned or frozen ones.

Planting from Seeds

• When you're planting seeds in rows, use a broom handle to form the trenches. Place the broom handle on the line where you want the row, then step on it until it makes a groove about one-fourth inch deep in the soil and you'll have a straight trench with uniform depth.

• Some very tiny seeds need only be pressed into the soil surface. Check the seed packet for directions. When sowing such fine seeds on the surface of seedling trays, sift a light layer of sand or flour (use a strainer) over the soil surface so that you can see where the seeds are. The sand or flour also will keep the seeds undisturbed and from sticking to whatever you use to tamp them down.

• If you need to plant each seed in a separate hole, use a pencil, pen, or chopstick to poke holes in the soil, and mark it at the depth the seed needs to be planted so that the depths of the seeds are uniform.

• Here's a rule of green thumb for seeds: They need to be covered (sprinkled, not packed) with soil up to four times their smallest diameter. The next step is to moisten the soil, but not with a deluge or you'll wash the seeds away.

• When you are growing your own bedding plants, you can speed up seed germination by placing the seed trays on top of your refrigerator, where the temperature of 72 to 75 degrees Fahrenheit will encourage speedy growth. Or, place them on top of a TV set that is being used all day or on a dryer that is being used and cover lightly with a paper towel or light towel so that no draft disturbs the seeds.

• Always use fresh potting soil for starting your seeds and wash your hands between handling outdoor and indoor plants to prevent spreading plant diseases.

• When you are handling tiny seedlings to transplant them from trays to ground, don't pick them up by the stems. Stems are fragile and will break. Instead, let the plant fall out of the little plastic seedling tray into one hand; sometimes you need to gently squeeze the bottom of the little plastic tray and then transfer the plant to your other hand so that you can cup your palm and hold the plant by its roots. These baby plants need TLC.

• If you keep unused seeds in their packets and then put the packets in plastic bags, stored in the refrigerator, many of them will keep for years. If any don't keep, you won't have wasted any money because you'd have thrown out unused seeds anyhow!

Growing Fruits and Vegetables

• If you save bedding trays from season to season to use for sprouting your own seeds, wash them thoroughly before planting seeds so that your new crop will be free of plant diseases.

• You can use plastic-foam egg cartons for sprouting seeds. Just poke a small drain hole in the bottom of each cup and fill them with soil. Use the lid as a tray beneath this homemade planter. You'll be recycling the egg cartons for one more use before they're discarded.

• Sprout seeds or grow strawberries in an old gutter spout filled with soil. You can attach the spout to a fence if you are using it to grow strawberries or other short-rooted plants. Hanging plants from a fence solves the lack-of-sun problem in some yards and keeps weeds from getting in with the real plants.

• Corn takes up too much space in a small garden, but if you grow it in a washtub filled with soil, you can use your other garden space more productively. You'll get better results if you grow a small variety and, since it's not in the ground, you'll have to water it more often.

• Many herbs, flowers, and vegetables grow well in whiskey barrels, washtubs, and other containers, but remember that when you grow anything in a container, it needs to be fertilized and watered more often than plants grown in the ground. Don't forget to make drain holes in the bottom of the container that you are using.

• If you just don't know where some perennials (those that come back every year) will do well in your garden's shady and sunny areas, try planting them in containers so that you can move them around until you find the places where they'll have best growing conditions. Once you find out which beds they are happiest in, you can put them in the ground.

• You can also use movable containers when you are planning flower beds of perennials. Arrange the containers where you think you'll want those plants, and if they look right for that spot after they are fully grown and in bloom, you'll know where to plant them when it's time to put them into the ground.

Getting Rid of Plant Pests Without Strong Insecticides

A National Gardening Association survey published in the summer of 1988 revealed that insects "bugged" 33 percent of the gardens of people in the survey.

• For a healthy spring and summer garden, thoroughly clean out all garden junk in the fall. Get rid of vines, stalks, stems, or rotted fruits and vegetables.

• Pesty aphids, mealy bugs, cabbage worms, spider mites, and young scale can be removed from plants with a strong jet of water from your garden hose. You may not have to spray with pesticides.

• Chives resist both plant pests and virus diseases and can help the rest of your garden to do the same if you give it a "drink" of chive tea. Steep about one-half cup finely chopped chive leaves in one pint of boiling water (enough to cover the leaves). Let steep for 15 minutes and cool, then spray on your plants as a preventive treatment.

• Horseradish planted near potatoes will keep potato beetles away.

• Onions planted next to beets and carrots will keep bugs away.

• Planting basil near tomatoes keeps worms and flies away. Besides, it will be convenient when it's salad-picking time.

• Aphids and red spider mites will stay away if you use a rhubarb spray made by pouring two pints of boiling water over a pound of chopped rhubarb leaves. Let the mixture steep overnight; strain and add a tablespoon of detergent to the rhubarb "tea," then spray on vegetable plants. I knew there was a good use for rhubarb leaves!

CAUTION: Rhubarb leaves contain poisonous oxalic acid. DO NOT spray within a week of harvesting and keep children and pets away.

• When you first notice that insect pests are munching on your plants, you can either pick them or their eggs off by hand or brush them off into a jar coated with detergent.

• A mixture of one-half cup mild liquid dish-washing detergent to a pint of water can be used to spray both sides of plant leaves to kill insects. Wait an hour, then spray or hose down with clear water.

Lawn Care

The kind of lawn you plant—seed, plugs, sod—depends upon the growing conditions in your yard.

• When you lay sod, you'll get a smoother look if you stagger the joints of the rows of sod strips the way bricks are laid.

• Even the best-laid plans—and lawns—of gardeners and lawn layers produce some weeds. If you pull weeds in the early spring before the weeds have had a chance to flower and reseed themselves, you'll have a better chance of getting rid of those pesky things. Also, weeds grow faster than real grass, so if you have lots of them, you'll have to mow more often in the heat of summer.

• When you use chemical weed killers on your lawn and have children or pets playing on it, be especially cautious and read the labels. Many of these chemicals are extremely toxic. Some directions say that the chemicals for weed or flea killing must be allowed to dry or that some waiting period should be observed before children and pets can be allowed to play on the lawn again. Don't take any chances.

• In hot weather, it's usually better to set your lawn mower blades higher so that the longer grass shades and protects the roots.

• Your lawn still needs you in the fall. This is the best time to rake out summer's debris (clippings, dead leaves, etc.), which if allowed to remain on (and in) the lawn will keep water and air from the roots.

• Fall is the time to feed your lawn before winter's break from the growing season. Usually, people wait until leaves begin to fall and then apply a nitrogen-rich fertilizer. After applying fertilizer (with a spreader borrowed from a garden center if you don't own one) you need to give the soil a good soaking, down to a depth of three or four inches.

• You don't have to have a hole in your lawn beneath your roof's drain spout. Just put a large flat stone or garden step-stone beneath the drain spout, and rainwater will spread out instead of eroding the topsoil.

• One way to avoid all lawn care is to plant different kinds of ivy as ground cover instead of grass. You may have to cut it back once in a while, but you can give your mower to someone else and then sit on your patio and enjoy life.

Watering

Conserving water and making trees and plants resistant to drought conditions is common practice were I live, and recurring drought conditions in other parts of the country show that the need for water conservation and defensive gardening is important throughout the United States.

• Your garden needs its watering early in the morning so that leaves will dry quickly in the sun. When leaves stay wet all night after evening watering, spore and fungus diseases may get established.

• Because many plant diseases are encouraged by wet leaves, it's better to water toward the soil instead of at the leaves. However, don't cause a deluge that washes the soil away from the plant; water gently.

• If you don't want to stand and direct the hose to a specific area in your flower bed or to water certain shrubs or trees, bend a coat hanger into a V to hold the hose; you can poke the straightened-out hook end of the hanger into the ground.

• If you have potted plants on high ledges or hanging too high to reach, tie a bamboo cane (fishing pole) with twisties or string to the hose so that the cane and hose together are a rigid wand that reaches high up to the plants. Put an adjustable spray on the end of the hose so you don't wash away soil when you water the plants.

• When you water plants, soak the soil thoroughly when watering. A light sprinkling can cause roots to come to the surface and then get baked to death by the sun. The idea is to get roots to go down deep where they won't be subjected to summer heat.

• Many gardeners in hot climates actually train their plants (especially vegetables like tomatoes, squash, broccoli) to go deeply for water. Instead of watering directly on the plant, they make or buy soaker systems—hoses or pipes with holes in them that are placed between rows of plants or in garden beds and lawns, which keep water on the ground and prevent evaporation.

• You can easily make an inexpensive irrigation system by digging "watering holes" beside plants and between rows. Here's how it's done:

1. At the time of planting, dig holes about a foot deep, a foot or so from each plant or between plants.
2. Then, insert into the holes 32-ounce juice cans with tops and bottoms removed or similarly sized plastic pots (the kind larger bedding plants and house plants come in) with the bottoms cut out.

The cans or pots form walls that keep the holes from collapsing when you fill them with water from a hose. Watering this way soaks the ground beneath the plants and draws the roots downward.

• Special tubes for watering trees are available in garden stores that attach to the hose so that water is directed beneath the surface, thereby drawing roots downward, where they are protected.

• If the heat has wilted your potted patio plants (Say "potted patio plants" fast, three times in a row!), you can revive them by standing the pot in a watertight tray filled with moist gravel so that the humidity from the tray will perk up the plant. Mist the plant well with a mister, but be sure it's not in direct sunlight or this will only add to the wilted condition of the plant.

• If your potted plant is so totally dry that the roots and potting soil have pulled away from the pot sides, immerse the plant in its pot in water that is at least one inch above the top of the pot rim. Let the plant stay in the water for about 20 minutes until the bubbles stop rising to the surface and the roots and soil have absorbed enough water to swell up and fill the pot as before. Then remove and allow the plant to drain.

Gardening Equipment

• Long-handled garden tools can be stored in a metal garbage can. (Plastic garbage cans will work only if they are heavy enough not to tip over when the tools are inside.) Attach S hooks to the rim of the can for hanging smaller tools. Then you can tote the whole can to wherever you are working and have your tools handy.

• To store your garden hose, wrap the hose around a sturdy wooden coat hanger and hang it on a hook in the garage.

• Spring a leak? You can repair small holes or cracks in a rubber garden hose with rubber patches and adhesive tape.

1. Sand the surface around the hole lightly with fine sandpaper and sand the surface of the rubber patch, which you can cut from an old tube.
2. Apply contact cement to both sanded surfaces and wait until the cement is dry to the touch.
3. Press the patch over the hole very firmly and then wrap the patched area with rubber or vinyl electrical tape or duct tape. If you don't want to worry about repairing the hose, turn it into a soaker hose. Use an ice pick to punch holes along the length of the garden hose.

• Quick-patch small leaks in plastic hoses by just barely touching them with the tip of a hot ice pick. The idea is to melt the plastic so it self-seals the holes.

• Safety tip for sawing wood: When you use a chain saw, cut only wood that is smaller than the length of the guide bar; otherwise you are likely to have the saw kick back and be hard to control when the saw nose is buried in wood.

Garden Walls and Fences

• If you're having trouble with the neighborhood cats (or your own) using your well-worked vegetable garden soil as a comfy litter box and your baby plants as nap sites, try enclosing the beds with 4- to 5-foot wire fencing (sold in rolls at hardware stores) supported by steel fence posts. The posts need no cement and are just driven into the ground and have places on which to hook the fencing wire. While it's not really decorative, this type of fence is too flimsy for cats to leap up on and will keep cats out of your garden plot. (It's strong enough only for bird perching.)

• You can keep "varmints" and other animals from walking along wooden horizontal-slat fences by nailing carpet tacking strips on the top edge. (These strips are wood, about an inch wide, and have tiny carpet tacks pointed upward so that they hold carpeting in place when it's installed over wood floors.) The tacks are not big or sharp enough to actually hurt the animal, but they do make walking along the fence unpleasant enough to make the animals stay away.

• To paint wire or chain link fences or decorative ironwork quickly and without wasting spray paint, use a sponge to wipe on paint. This job will go very quickly if you have two people doing it. With one on either side of the fence, you dab sponges together and will paint both sides of the fence at one time without wasting paint. Rubber gloves are a must to protect your hands.

Stepping Stones, Walkways, Driveways

• Make your own "Hollywood Walk of the Stars," whether it's a cement sidewalk or a series of poured cement stepping stones: Have family members put their handprints, names, birth dates, or some other important dates in wet cement. We did just this when we built our home, and have names, initials, and date firmly etched in cement for posterity.

• If you use carpet remnants and strips of old carpet between garden rows, you won't have to step in mud when you pick your veggies and flowers. Either buy cheap remnants and pieces or use discarded old carpet for a "garden walkway."

• Old carpet can be used also for a greenhouse floor.

• If you have small cracks in your blacktop driveway, you can patch them with sand and liquid blacktop sealer. Fill the crack partway with sand and then pour the sealer into the crack. The sand will absorb the sealer, and you can repeat the process until the crack is filled and the surface is smooth.

Snow Shoveling and Ice Removal

• Before using your snow shovel, coat the front and back heavily with paste wax, and the snow will slide off fast and easy. The plus is that you won't be banging your shovel on the walk or driveway and bending the edge. If the snowfall catches you without paste wax, use an old candle or some canning wax—any wax works.

• Instead of trying to lift heavy, wet snow, move it with a metal garden rake—teeth up or teeth down—and you'll spare your back and arms a lot of lifting.

• A lightweight aluminum snow shovel is a good dustpan when you're cleaning off the patio or car port, and you can shovel leaves against the curb to clean gutters in front of your house, too.

• If you store some sand, rock salt, melting crystals, or any of the commercial products used to melt ice and snow in clean, dry plastic milk jugs, it's much easier to dispense the ice melters where you want them to be. Keep a jug handy beside the front or back door and in your car in case you get "iced in" one day.

• When you need to unstick a car from packed snow or ice, you can get traction if you keep a couple of coffee cans in the car filled with any kind of grit, such as cat litter, sand, small gravel.

• In a pinch you may even be able to get some traction for your auto tires from old bath towels, carpet scraps, or blankets stashed away in your trunk. Just place the towels behind or in front of the two driving wheels, depending upon whether you are going forward or backing up.

Outdoor Lighting

• If you live in a cold climate, you can avoid replacing burned-out hard-to-reach lightbulbs in the bitter cold if you replace them each year at end of the fall season and before the cold winds blow. You probably won't need to climb those ladders, trees, or poles until spring. If the bulbs you've removed are still good, save them for indoors or warm-weather outdoor use.

• Moisture often makes bulbs in outdoor fixtures stick when you try to remove them. Bulbs will unscrew more easily if you rub a light coat of petroleum jelly on their threads before you insert them. This also works on inside light fixtures that have a tendency to rust, as in damp basements or garages.

• Dim outdoor lighting in your yard or campsite brightens up if you place shiny, reflecting aluminum foil behind the lamp/light. If you need to enhance a flashlight's glow, wrap a collar of foil on the lighted end.

Swimming Pools

Few activities are as refreshing in the summer as jumping into a cool pool or sitting in spa bubbles, if your pool has this feature. Pools, unfortunately, do require maintenance, even if the newer ones are easier to care for than older models.

• You can have a pool in a small or narrow yard. Lap pools are popular in cities, where land is too expensive for expansive yards. A lap pool need be only about four feet deep, about four feet wide, and as long as you can get it. Often a lap pool's cement will be colored black or dark green, and when it's not being used for exercise swimming, it serves as a reflecting pool for nearby garden beds or other landscaping.

Pool Safety

• Always keep a rope, life ring, and/or your long-handled skimming net or pool brooms near the pool and in easy reach so that they can be used as a rescue pole in case a swimmer needs help.

• Take a tip from the public pools: Install a floating rope that shows where the deep part of your pool begins.

• Not all pool covers are safety devices that support weight, and small children and animals can drown even in a shallow puddle that forms in a pool cover. Don't take a chance.

• Children always need adult supervision when using a pool. Don't leave a child alone even for a moment to run into the house, whether it's to answer the phone or the front door. All it takes is a few seconds for a tragedy to happen.

• Swimming and first-aid/CPR lessons should be a must when a family installs a pool.

• Make family rules about how many and which children can be guests at the pool. To ensure the safety of all guests, you have the right and the obligation to ban those who won't follow your safety rules.

• The chemicals used to clean and sanitize pool water can be harmful when improperly used or stored. If mixed with other chemicals or elements, pool chemicals can cause explosions and fires.

• As with all chemicals, store out of the reach of children and in their original containers. Make sure that lids are tightly closed and do not stack different chemicals on top of one another.

• Never mix two chemicals together, and use a clean scoop for each chemical to avoid combining material from old and new containers.

• NEVER add chemicals to the water if swimmers are in the pool. And allow for the correct amount of time after adding chemicals for anyone to swim.

• Replace your test kit each year.

• Follow all safety rules regarding handling electrical switches, wires, and other equipment around water (including a portable phone).

• Never replace bulbs in underwater lights yourself; get an expert to do this.

Keeping the Pool Clean

• Have a foot rinse-off dishpan or tub near the pool to keep grass clippings and dirt out of the pool.

• This may be the biggest thing ever made from Heloise nylon net: If you sew, you can make a nylon net pool cover by sewing together strips of the net so that you can completely cover the pool. Hold this cover in place with gallon plastic jugs along the side of the pool filled with sand or water. If you have an above-the-ground pool, the cover can be clipped to the pool sides with spring clothespins. The advantage of nylon net is that it's so light, even with leaves on it, one person can handle it. This is an ideal, inexpensive way to make a cover for a hot tub/spa.

NOTE OF CAUTION: This pool cover is NOT a safety device and should not be considered to be such a thing. It WILL NOT SUPPORT THE WEIGHT of even a small child or animal. It is only a method of keeping leaves and bugs out of the pool.

Mowing the Grass Near the Pool

• It seems obvious, but if you're a new pool owner, you may not think of this: If you don't have a grass catcher on your lawn mower, be sure to "shoot" the cut grass away from the pool instead of into it, and, of course, vacuum the pool after or during, not before, a mowing session.

Pool Cleaning

• If you have an automatic pool vacuum sweeper, the kind that rolls around the bottom and sides all by itself, you'll find that an old knee-high stocking or pantyhose leg can be held on with a rubber band to serve as a disposable "vacuum cleaner bag" or liner for the mesh bag that comes with this wonderful pool aid. A few runs in the stocking won't matter, and the bonus is that you don't have to untangle bugs and bits of things from the vacuum bag mesh—just throw the whole thing out!

Keeping the House Clean and Your Sanity When You Have a Pool

If you install your pool as your house is being built, you can make provisions for clothes changing and bathroom going so that you don't have a parade of wet people through the house.

If you've added a pool to an existing home, you'll have to make some rules about drippy-wet traveling in the house or you'll begin to wonder why you ever wanted a pool.

• A small tent can be a temporary changing room during pool parties.

• A small garden "shack," such as those that come in kits, can be a pool house, and if you are willing to deal with it, you can install a camper's toilet in the garden shack.

• Make a path to the bathroom with inexpensive runner rugs and insist that all swimmers use it. Call it the "Yellow Brick Road" and yourself the "Wizard of Oz" or use some other catchy name to make this rule more acceptable.

• Have an outdoor hanging place (rack, clothesline, fence, lawn chair) for wet towels and bathing suits. If you have a large family or many swimmers, you can't keep up with washing so many towels each day. Even putting all the wet things in the dryer gets tedious by mid-summer.

Wading Pools for Small Children

• Molded pools and slides can be very slippery, but little feet can pitter and patter safely if you install bathtub appliqués or bathtub mats with suction cups at strategic places, such as the bottom of the pool and the step before the slide (a half of a mat may serve here, so you can install the other half in the foot rinse-off tub beside the pool).

• If the wading pool will fit into your child's sandbox, installing it inside the sandbox not only prevents a pool-size section of dead grass in your lawn where you've put the pool, but the sandbox seats on the sides are also pool seats.

• Put a stool or lawn chair beside your child's wading pool and soak your tired, aching feet while you supervise the play.

• At the end of the season, you can wash small, lightweight inflatable plastic pools in the washer—with some towels, just like you wash a shower curtain. If you wish, you can take it out before the spin cycle and just hang it on the line to dry.

Other Uses for Small Plastic Wading Pools

• Small children can sit in a small (empty of course!) plastic wading pool when they snack in front of the television set—no spills or goo on the carpet to clean up!

• A hard plastic wading pool with a pad on the bottom can be a handy playpen or bassinet for a very small baby, with supervision. (Especially at Grandma's house! It can be kept under a bed when baby's not visiting.)

• Since they are so easy to slide under a bed, outgrown rigid plastic wading pools can be used for toy bins, storage of craft items, plastic-bagged out-of-season clothing, or anything else that's lightweight and will fit under the bed.

Taking care of house plants or spending time in the yard and garden can not only provide beautiful scenery, but, for many people, me included, great pleasure from pruning, watering, and fussing. The results can be beautiful and eye-appealing, and many times the free plants you get from your cuttings can really add to the appearance of your yard or living area. If you just don't have a green thumb and can't be bothered with the care and feeding of another living thing, look around for some real-life-looking artificial plants. No fuss, no watering, no repotting, and when you get tired of them, just toss them in the garbage without guilt.

CHAPTER 6

Children

I'm just now experiencing motherhood as a stepmother to a thirteen-year-old boy. Like any other parent, I'm learning a lot.

Babies

They look so fragile—little fisted hands flailing about . . . tiny slit-eyes that open to stare in wonder at lights and moving things . . . wobbly, disproportionately large, bald or tousled-hair heads on too-frail necks. . . .

And their faces get so very red when they cry.

When it's your first baby, crying is scary because you are absolutely sure you must have done something wrong to cause it. That first night home ALONE with a new baby (and you feel alone no matter how many people are around to help you) is the scariest of all.

If you live through that first night, and generations of parents have survived it, you'll realize that your baby cries because the poor little thing can't talk.

Once you can tell a fuss cry from a hunger or discomfort cry, you are officially a parent. Baby tending becomes easier because you feel competent.

You'll also feel more competent if you aren't exhausted. Use your hospital or birthing center stay to rest. When you come home, focus on people, not the house; the dust will wait for you—use your energy to enjoy your baby and to share this pleasure with other people in your family.

If you are breast-feeding, you have the perfect excuse not to bother with household matters. You need your energy to feed and enjoy your baby. Babies grow up faster than you'll ever know. These moments won't happen again. Savor every single one.

If you're not breast-feeding, the advice is the same, except that other people can also feed the baby and more actively enjoy those precious first months in baby's life.

Feeding time, no matter who does it or how it's done, is a time to nourish souls as well as bodies. The person feeding the baby enjoys the cuddlings as much as the baby.

Make sure you have a comfortable chair and a place to put your feet up when you feed the baby. Always use feeding time to relax yourself. Babies are smart little creatures who seem to sense tenseness, and then respond with tension of their own. (If you don't believe this, next time you're on an airplane or in a restaurant listening to a crying baby, check out the person carrying that baby. More often than not, the tenser the carrier, the more fretful the baby.)

For most parents, first babies are the most awesome because that's when they are the most inexperienced, but all babies are wonders, and you can enjoy all of them more if you prepare for them.

Bringing Baby Home

• Hang a DO NOT DISTURB or BABY'S SLEEPING or MOM'S RESTING sign on your front door, warning solicitors and others that to ring your doorbell is a "no-no."

• If you own an answering machine, use it. Set the answering machine to answer any incoming calls on the first ring so as not to wake you or the baby during rest periods.

• An answering machine can also be a wonderful announcement maker. Record a message including the baby's time and date of birth, weight, length, and name, as well as "We are napping now and will call you back later."

• A new twist to the old passing out of cigars by proud fathers is to pass out pens with "It's a Girl" or "It's a Boy" printed on them. These make great keepsakes for loved ones and friends alike. Also, they can be given to women friends and nonsmokers.

Feeding Baby

• If you are bottle-feeding, always write the time and date that you opened the container of liquid formula (whether it is ready-to-feed or concentrate) on the can. For easy dating, keep a permanent black marker in a kitchen drawer or on the pantry shelf where you store the formula or even tied to a string attached to a drawer pull so it won't mysteriously walk out of the kitchen, for easy dating. Most formula should be used only up to 48 hours after opening (except for the powder form). This can be especially important when baby first comes home and is on a demand feeding schedule.

• If you stand them in a soft drink carton, those wobbly baby bottles won't tip over in the refrigerator.

• Try highlighting the ounce markers on baby's bottle with nail polish or a waterproof marker; you'll be able to read them in a dimly lit room and know if baby's at "burping time" and has consumed the usual amount for a feeding.

• Regulate the flow through the nipple by tightening the bottle collar for a slower flow and loosening the collar for a faster flow. Remember that too fast a flow might make some babies gulp their liquids and result in too many uncomfortable air bubbles in their tiny tummies.

• You can enlarge the holes in baby bottle nipples if you boil them for about five minutes, then allow to cool for about three minutes with toothpicks lodged in the holes. Or use a sterilized needle to enlarge the holes. If the opening is too large, just reboil the nipple and it will close up.

• If you store bottle nipples in a cool, dry place, they will last longer.

• An occasional brushing with a salt solution prevents baby bottle nipples from deteriorating.

• Whether or not you should heat baby's bottle in the microwave oven is controversial. Some authorities say that you should never warm a bottle in a microwave oven; the formula may be too hot, even though the bottle itself is cool to the touch. Also, excessive heat destroys vitamins.

• An old-fashioned yet safe way to heat a bottle is to put it in a pan or bowl and run hot tap water over it until the temperature is just right.

• If you warm baby's bottle in the microwave oven, here's how: To warm an eight-ounce bottle in a microwave oven, remove the nipple and put on high power for 10 to 25 seconds if the milk is at room temperature and for 25 to 45 seconds if it's cold from the refrigerator. Individual microwave ovens work differently, so times vary. Shake the bottle to mix well.

• CAUTION: Whatever way you heat the bottle, always shake the bottle after heating to mix well, and make it a habit to always test a few drops on the inside of your wrist to feel the temperature just before feeding baby.

• Some parents like to keep extra formula in the refrigerator to add to a too-warm bottle. You can also cool a too-hot bottle by placing it in a pan and running cold water over it for about 45 seconds; then, always retest.

• A baby fed in as upright a position as possible is less likely to suffer from trapped air bubbles. This position enables that stubborn bubble at the bottom of the stomach to rise more easily when baby is burped.

• It's not always necessary to pound baby's back to get those burps. Often massaging baby's back will bring up burps more gently.

• Some babies will burp as soon as they are placed on your shoulder or on their stomachs on your lap. Since many babies spit up when they burp, place a clean cloth diaper, towel, or other designated burp cloth on your shoulder or lap when feeding baby.

• One of the more effective ways of burping a baby is to have the baby seated on your lap and leaning forward supported by your hand, while you stroke or pat baby's back with your other hand. If your baby tends to spit up, hold a diaper under his chin with your supporting hand. This method works better with babies that are a month old or so, when their heads aren't totally wobbly.

• To rid the bottles of sour milk smell, fill them with warm water and add a teaspoon of baking soda. Shake well and let stand overnight. The next morning wash and sterilize as usual.

• You can boil the bottle nipples in a glass jar of water in your microwave oven. A teaspoonful of vinegar in the water will prevent any hard water deposits in the jar.

• Using bottle straws will help formula flow evenly no matter what position the bottle is in.

• When the time comes, baby can be weaned gradually from the bottle by letting him drink directly from the familiar container, but with the nipple removed or replaced by a soda straw.

Breast-Feeding

If you have decided to breast-feed, the main rule of thumb is to be comfortable and relaxed during feeding. Pick a favorite chair or area of your home and set up a feeding area with all the necessities you may need.

• A cushioned rocker, armchair, or sofa with low arms will help to make you comfortable while nursing.

• There is no rule that says you can't catch up on your reading while you are breast-feeding. If you are a tense person, reading may actually be relaxing and help you go with the flow, so to speak. Remember, being comfortable and relaxed is important for your flow of milk.

• If baby falls asleep while nursing at breast or bottle, take a tip from Mama Cat. No, I don't mean that you're supposed to lick the baby! But, if you gently stroke baby, especially on the cheeks and chin, you'll activate the baby's natural suckling mechanism so that feeding continues.

• Leakage of milk from the breasts can be absorbed by nursing pads, but even these will become soaked occasionally. To prepare yourself for such an occurrence in public, wear printed tops as much as possible. The stains from leakage will be less visible than if you are wearing a solid color. Also, print tops don't show baby-carrying wrinkles as much as solid colors do.

• If you run out of nursing pads, cut circles from one of baby's disposable diapers or panty liners to substitute for them.

• To ensure privacy when nursing away from home, place the baby on the lower corner of a receiving blanket instead of the middle as usual. Take the top triangular part of the blanket and place it over your shoulder when placing the baby to your breast. Baby won't smother and you can avoid the stares and curiosity of onlookers. You can also pin a small patch of self-gripping tape to the shoulder seam of your clothing, and sew a similar patch to the top corner of the "nursing" blanket for added security and privacy.

• While shopping in your local mall or clothing store, ask an attendant if you can use one of the dressing rooms to feed your baby privately and comfortably. It's more pleasant than the rest room.

Giving Baby Solid Foods

• Never feed baby directly from a jar that you intend to put back into the refrigerator half full. The enzymes in baby's saliva will be carried to the inside of the jar on the baby's spoon and will cause a breakdown of the food after feeding.

• Use an egg poacher to heat baby's food all at the same time. Each compartment will hold a different food item, and cleanup is easy.

• If you make your own baby food, you need to cover the blender blades with at least one inch of food to get lump-free baby puree.

• Blocks of baby food can be frozen in an ice cube tray, so you'll have variety in feedings without spoilage or waste. (Two cubes generally makes one three-ounce serving.)

• When a baby food jar lid just won't screw off, punch a small hole in the lid to break the vacuum seal, and the lid will twist right off.

• You can use cleaned, used baby food jars for many things, including a small, wet, traveling washcloth. Of course a plastic self-sealing bag works well too.

• Many babies fret when they are put to bed because the sheets are cold. If you put a heating pad in the crib or bassinet while baby is feeding, the bed will be as comfortably warm as your arms were, and baby may not even notice being returned to bed. And a quick way to warm sheets for baby and adult alike is to use your hand-held hair dryer.

• When traveling, take along a premixed feeding of one half dry cereal and one half powdered formula in a container. When you stop for lunch or dinner, just add hot water or formula, and the baby's food is heated and ready to eat. Add jar fruit or vegetables if desired. No waste, no fuss.

• If you are traveling cross-country, you may want to select a brand of bottled (non-fizz) water and then use it consistently for your baby's drinking or for mixing with powdered fruit, and so forth. Some babies are sensitive to the different mineral compositions of water in different locales and might have digestive disturbances from the changes. Check with your pediatrician.

• When baby proves to be a finicky eater, put his favorite food or fruit on the front part of the baby spoon and the dreaded vegetable/meat to the back.

When the fruit goes in, so does the vegetable/meat without the fuss. Sometimes they catch on to this trick a little too easily, but it's worth a try.

• Keep a felt-tipped marker handy to mark on the jar lid the date it was opened. This will ensure that baby eats only freshly opened foods. You will find that it takes no time at all for jars of foods to accumulate in the refrigerator, especially if you like to feed your baby a variety each day.

• If you use instant baby food, move the colored plastic lid to the bottom of the unopened can (thus exposing the lift tab), and you can easily tell which one is opened and which is not.

• When baby is ready for table foods, use a nut grinder to grind up table foods if you don't have a baby food mill.

• You can make your own baby foods by selecting fresh fruits and vegetables and steaming and pureeing them. Refrigerate or freeze small portions in covered ice cube trays; when frozen, pop out and put in a freezer-safe bag and clearly mark.

• Introduce new foods when the child is very hungry and therefore not too discerning about what it eats. As in all things you do with children, the "teachable moment" is the best time for any activity. It is always easier and more pleasant to lead and guide children; pushing them always takes more energy and gets more resistance. (If you don't believe this, ask any experienced parent, especially one who has survived teenhood!)

Feeding Toddlers and Young Children

• Awkward little fingers can hold on to a drinking cup more easily if you wrap several wide rubber bands or strips of tape around it.

• Finger foods are the key to self-feeding when toddlers get into "Me do it myself." When a toddler is learning to self-feed, sliced hot dogs, cooked carrots, potato hunks, or the non-fat oven-bake French fries found in the freezer section of the supermarket can be eaten by hand while you spoon-feed other foods. Finger foods can be put directly on the high chair tray; it eliminates the distraction of a plate.

• When you have picky eaters and children who don't have hearty appetites, think small. Make little meatloaves in muffin tins instead of serving a big slice; cut sandwiches into fourths; make "silver dollar"–size pancakes; cut fruit into slices or squares.

• Serve different bits of food in muffin tin compartments to make mealtime more interesting. One compartment will even hold a small drinking cup. Serving with a muffin tin is especially useful when a child is sick in bed.

• Try edible containers: An ice-cream cone will hold tuna, egg salad, cottage cheese, or yogurt.

• Serve messy sandwich salad fillings in pita bread, or cut pockets into unsliced buns to hold the fillings. Soft, sliced bread will fold over most fillings.

• Sloppy Joes will be less sloppy if you serve them this way: Cut a quarter-inch-thick layer from the top of an unsliced hamburger bun. Scoop out just enough bread to leave a "bowl" with "walls" to hold the sloppy Joe, then put the lid back on.

• Make breakfast more interesting with a cereal parfait: use one-half cup vanilla or fruited yogurt, 1 1/3 cup dry cereal, and about a third of a sliced banana or equivalent with other soft fruit, such strawberries or peaches. Layer half of the yogurt, then the cereal, the remaining yogurt, and then top with fruit. Gosh, this even sounds good and healthy for adults.

Or make a breakfast banana split by peeling and splitting a banana and putting it into a dish for splits or a flat bowl; then sprinkle it with about a cup of dry cereal, and top with about a half-cup vanilla or fruit yogurt; garnish with a bit more of the dry cereal or some strawberries or grapes.

These aren't just for kids' breakfasts; have one yourself!

• Here's a recipe that's full of good stuff and could be a terrific snack or even a breakfast bread: Mix together two slightly beaten eggs, one-half cup chunky peanut butter, one-fourth cup honey, two-thirds cup nonfat dry milk powder; then add three cups dry cereal (I've not tested this with flakes, just "pebbles" type of cereals). Spread into a greased eight-inch pan. Bake for 20 minutes at 325 degrees Fahrenheit. Cool before serving and cut into six bars. The bars can be wrapped individually and stored in the fridge. For more flavor, you can spread these with jelly just before eating.

High Chair Helps

• Some babies are born wigglers. You can keep an overactive child's high chair from tipping by latching the chair to a wall with a childproof hook and eye.

• Tie a small child to the high chair with a large dish towel folded diagonally so that the bias part goes across the child's chest and the points are tied behind the chair back.

• NEVER leave a small child alone in a high chair, whether tied/belted in or not. Either is dangerous.

• If your baby keeps sliding down the seat of his high chair, place nonabrasive bathtub appliqués or a rubber sink or tub mat on the seat area of the chair. Baby's bottom will stay put.

• Try attaching a rubber-suction soap holder to baby's plate or bowl to keep it stuck to the tray when baby goes through that "drop and throw" stage.

• Attaching a towel bar to the back of a high chair will give you a nifty place to hang baby's bib and a washcloth, or even a half roll of paper towels.

• For quick cleanups when the high chair is a mess, and once baby self-feeds it will really be a mess, put it in the shower with a warm-water spray for a few minutes. Turn water off and wipe down, give it a quick rinse, and towel dry, and the high chair will look brand-new. (I would not suggest this for a wooden high chair.) I know one bachelor father who routinely takes the metal high chair to the car wash with him on Saturdays.

• If you spread a large plastic garbage bag, plastic tablecloth, or paint drop cloth beneath the high chair, you'll save a lot of floor cleaning and wiping.

The alternative is to have a perpetually hungry dog hovering under the chair. You may have to give the dog a bath if baby plays "Feed the doggie" and food lands on the dog instead of the floor, but no system is perfect!

Bath Time

Bath time can be a nice experience for both you and your baby. Just remember, one day without a bath is not a disgrace. If you skip a day because you are just too exhausted, nobody will come marching into your home and demand to erase your name from baby's birth certificate.

• Bath time shouldn't be a shock treatment. Always use warm body-temperature water, tested by dipping your elbow or wrist into it (your hands are used to greater temperature variances than your arm).

• Make sure the hot-water temperature on your hot-water heater is set at 120 degrees Fahrenheit or lower when you have small children in the house to prevent possible scalding during bath time. Again, always test baby's bath water first with your elbow as a safety precaution.

• Most babies hate having rough washcloths dragged across their faces. Make an envelope from the washcloth by folding it over your hand. With your hand wrapped in the washcloth, gently wipe baby's face with S motions. Many mothers prefer to wipe each of baby's eyes with a separate large cotton ball or at least one eye with each corner of the washcloth to prevent spreading bacteria from one eye to the other, if any might be present.

• Bath time is a good time to massage baby; the touch of your hands is important to an infant's emotional development. Besides, rubbing a soapy baby is fun; they smile and giggle and make you feel like you are one heck of a good parent.

• To keep soap or shampoo out of an infant's eyes, gently rub petroleum jelly on the eyelids and eyebrows. The jelly will make the shampoo run sideways rather than downward.

• An inexpensive plastic infant seat, with metal legs and cushions removed, will fit nicely into a sink or portable tub, providing a secure seat for baby.

When bathing baby in the sink, make sure the faucet is completely out of the way. Babies have a way of grabbing and clutching things.

• A soapy baby won't be as slippery in the tub or sink if you line the tub with a towel or cloth diaper and if you wear a soft, cotton glove on one hand.

• You'll keep yourself dry even when baby splashes if you clip a towel around your neck like a bib. The bonus is that you have the towel ready to wrap around baby when the bath is finished.

• When baby graduates to the bathtub, put the metal legs back on the plastic infant seat and you will have a non-slip bath seat until baby can safely sit alone in a bathtub of water.

• Setting a clean plastic clothes basket in the tub will help you hold onto a small child during bath time. Put the basket into the tub, add water, and put the child into the basket.

• Non-slip cutouts on the bottom of your tub will give your toddler better footing in the bath and will give you better footing when you shower in the tub.

• If you let your toddler wear a small diving mask or eye goggles, bath time is fun, and you can rinse those shampoo suds off without tears!

• When toddlers reach the stage when they want to wash themselves, stuff an inside-out terry sock with small chunks of soap and fasten the open end or put soap pieces into a slit sponge. The toddler can scrub away without losing a slippery bar of soap in the bathwater, where it can be stepped on. Or, use a clean nylon stocking or the bottom part of a pair of pantyhose and drop a small soap sliver or two in, tie in knots, and give this to the baby to scrub with and to hold on to and play with.

• If you put baby powder into your hand before you apply it instead of just sprinkling it, it won't get into baby's face, and if you are powdering a toddler who is standing up, you won't get powder all over the bathroom.

Baby's Laundry

Did you ever imagine that one sweet little bundle could dirty so much laundry? Well, they can, and it won't get to be any less in the years to come.

• Cloth diapers can become a laundry problem if you neglect to rinse them, thus letting stains set in. Wash only about 18 diapers at a time, because overloading will not allow the diapers to get thoroughly clean. Wash diapers in hot, soapy water. You may add bleach if necessary daily or every two to three washings to remove stubborn stains. When using bleach, run diapers through a second, final rinse, adding one-half cup of vinegar to the water to be sure there is no soap or bleach residue left in the diapers. Note: Using fabric softener too often will cause the diapers to be less absorbent.

• When clothes are stained with formula and stains are left to set, they become permanent. No amount of bleach or magic formula will remove them. This is why it is very important to try to remove the stain as soon as possible.

• To remove formula and other stains from baby's clothing, soak the clothes in an all-fabric bleach (also called non-chlorine bleach) that contains enzymes. Look for it on the shelves where laundry products are sold. Follow the directions on the back label for amounts to use. Use this type of all-fabric bleach on a daily basis and you will find the laundry will be cleaner. But always rinse well, so the bleach doesn't remain in baby's clothing.

• Diapers will be soft if you soak them as soon as you remove them in a solution of borax and water according to the directions on the box (about a handful or so of borax to a diaper pail of cold water). Always rinse off feces in the toilet bowl before soaking.

Soaked diapers (and milk-stained undershirts that have been soaking in borax water with them) can be dumped into the washer after you pour off any excess water from the pail into the toilet bowl. You don't have to wring out or even touch the diapers, the washer will do that for you.

Put the washer through a cold rinse cycle with a bit more borax, then wash through the heavy-duty cycle in the hottest water available with a mild detergent or soap.

With some washers, you need to add a second complete rinse to get all of the detergent out; some washers can be programmed for a second-rinse cycle. Most of the time you won't need fabric softener with this system and will have absorbent and odorless diapers.

• Using a diaper liner will help cut down on stains. You can purchase them or make your own, using soft, washable, and reusable material cut to fit. Or, for disposable diaper liners, cut to size handy disposable dishcloths.

• Keep an unwrapped bar of soap handy near baby's changing table. It makes a great pin cushion and the soap helps the pins slide easily through the cloth diaper.

• Disposable diapers have almost replaced washing diapers for people who can afford them. Of course, washing or worrying about getting them clean is not a problem with disposables, so I am all for them. The only drawback that I have heard about is that sometimes, one will have tabs that don't stick. You can use such a diaper if you secure it with duct or masking tape.

• The new diaper wipe cloths are wonderful as well. No more stacks of dirty, wet washcloths to deal with each day.

• Turn the baby wipes container upside down when not using to keep the top wipes moist. Store new containers of wipes this way too.

Little Tips for Little People Care

• When giving baby medicine, place the nipple part from baby's bottle in baby's mouth and administer the medicine with an eye dropper into the nipple. The medicine goes down easily as baby tries to nurse the nipple.

• Cut those scratchy tiny fingernails while baby is sleeping. You'll find blunt-end safety scissors at drugstores to make baby manicures easy.

• Hang blankets on a skirt hanger in the closet to save drawer space.

• Save labels from the baby food jars and diapers for special offers that will save you time, money, and energy when caring for baby.

• When baby outgrows the crib and starts sleeping in a bed, slide the crib mattress under the bed so at bedtime it can be pulled out to protect the child from any falls.

• Some children will roll back to the center of the bed if you place pillows or blanket rolls on the sides of the bed to serve as bumper guards.

In a Pinch

• If you're away from home and find you have no bathtub for baby, put a small plastic mesh laundry basket with holes in an adult-size bathtub. Place baby inside and wash away.

• If you run out of sheets for baby's bassinet, use standard-size pillowcases.

• For a bib, take a small child's old T-shirt and cut up the back, leaving the arm holes and neck opening intact. Slip over baby's head.

• Or use spring clothespins or those elastic clips that hold ironing board covers on the ironing board to fasten a washcloth or hand towel to baby's shirt for a quickie bib.

• Or use a sweater guard to hold a washcloth for a makeshift bib.

Teething Pain

• When your child is teething, soothe the pain and give him vitamin C with frozen orange sections. Baby will love both the coolness and the sweet taste. Frozen bananas are good too.

• Other teething biscuit substitutes are hardened bread, biscuits, or bagels.

• When some babies are teething they get so fretful that you may need a topical anesthetic for their gums if you or baby are to get any sleep. Check with your pediatrician before using such preparations, even if they are available without prescription.

Keeping Kids Safe

Safety for Kids' Sake

Accidents are the number one health hazard for all children. They kill more children than the five leading fatal diseases combined.

Falls, suffocation, poisonings, drownings, and burns cause more deaths to infants from birth to 12 months than all diseases combined. More than one-third of childhood deaths between the ages of 1 and 14 are caused by accidents.

And, in addition to being the greatest single cause of death of children under 15, accidents are the leading cause of permanent or temporary disabilities in children over 1 year old.

Three basic safety rules for infants are:

1. Never underestimate how fast babies develop physically and mentally; they can literally learn new tricks and movements while your back is turned.
2. Always expect the unexpected.
3. Never leave a baby alone unconfined by crib or playpen unless he or she is asleep, and in a confined, safe area.

Toy Safety

Babies are accustomed to receiving pleasure with their mouths. They examine new things with their mouths as much as with their eyes. This is a natural thing to do, and until the baby or toddler is old enough to understand "no" and actually understand why putting things in the mouth is a "no," adults must always be on guard against children swallowing small objects.

Even some 4-year-olds will swallow small objects, and many young children will poke small objects into their noses or ears for no reason other than to see if they will fit. Hospital emergency room personnel will testify to this!

Children need protection from their curiosity and natural tendencies. One mother told me that you can't trust a child under 18 to follow safety rules, and she's not sure if you can trust one over 18 either, because that's when the rules really get complicated.

• Toys should be too large to swallow, too tough to break, and have no sharp or hard edges.

• When a choking child can't clear the obstruction by himself, try putting his head facedown over your lap and gently pounding on his back. Get help by calling your local emergency number if this doesn't work.

• Very small infants enjoy watching and listening. A mobile firmly fastened above the crib will entertain a baby and stimulate development and response. All mobiles must be well out of baby's reach when he begins to grasp at things, which can occur when you least expect it.

• You can hang rattles, bells, music boxes, and other toys above or near the crib, but be sure baby can't grab them or strangle on the strings from which they are suspended.

• Teach other children in the family about baby's needs and make sure they understand which of their toys can and cannot be shared with baby.

• Show other children in the family how to hand a toy to baby; many a baby has been accidentally clouted with toys from siblings who were "only trying to be nice."

Poisonous Plants

That philodendron you chose so carefully for your low-light den, that hyacinth plant you bought to put spring into your living room, or the rhododendron and daffodils you planted just outside your front door could poison your child.

Third on the list of most-common human poisoning substances, plants poison thousands of children every year, and not all of the poisonous plants are out in the country or in forests; many are in our homes and backyards. Here are some plant protection tips.

• Curious children will taste almost anything and must be taught not to pick and eat anything, no matter how familiar it looks, without showing it to you first.

• It goes without saying that you have to watch creeping babies or toddlers like the proverbial hawk because they are the ones most likely to put things in their mouths. It's their natural tendency to do so as part of their "examining new things" process.

• You can get information about poisonous plants in books, from the Poison Control Center, and from your local county Cooperative Extension Agent, who will be familiar with plants that grow in your area.

• Check the tags on plants before you buy them; most tags show common names and scientific names. If you have very young children, it seems to me that it's simpler not to have such plants around. "Out of reach" is relative; who knows when a child will become a climber? If you have older children, they should be instructed not to taste.

• The two most dangerous common plants are certain types of mushrooms and oleander. Other common indoor and outdoor poisonous plants include:
   Poison Hemlock
   Stinkweed (all parts, especially the seeds)
   Hyacinth (the bulb)
   Wisteria (pods)
   Have the Poison Control Center number at hand. The best thing is to tape it directly on the phone or program it into a programmable phone.

• Keep syrup of ipecac (an emetic) in your medicine cabinet, but know when to use it. Vomiting may not always be the best solution to getting rid of something a child has swallowed. Get a good first-aid book; most drugstores have them, and frequently chain stores give away free pamphlets on first aid. Don't wait until you have an emergency to read the book or pamphlet; be prepared. The Boy Scout motto is a good one.

General Safety Tips

One of the best child safety laws to be passed in many states in the past few years is one that deals with disposing and storing used refrigerators and freezers. It's just so unfortunate that it took nationally publicized suffocations of children in discarded refrigerators to get people aware of this terrible danger. Always remove the doors of refrigerators that are not being used. Some people turn the fridge door-side to the wall, but I'm not sure that this is effective. The appliance could be moved for whatever reason and left available to the first child playing hide-and-seek.

• ALWAYS keep these items out of the reach of small children: matches, guns, knives, cosmetics, plants, bulbs, seeds, insecticides, all household chemicals, medicines, and breakable objects such as glass or china. Young children can't distinguish real guns from toys, edibles from non-edibles, and they will taste and touch just about anything out of curiosity. Most of us realize how important it is to keep things out of children's reach, but sometimes we get careless and it only takes a minute for a child to light up a match or lighter, cut a finger, or swallow a pretty pill.

• Remove the plastic spray nozzle from old aerosol cans when you discard them to prevent children from finding the cans and spraying chemicals into their own or others' eyes.

• Buy electric socket guards to keep little fingers, especially little drool-wet fingers, out of the sockets.

• You can buy plastic cupboard door guards, or if you have very young children, you can just roll up a magazine or newspaper and stuff it tightly through the cupboard hardware to make the cupboards stay securely shut. Another way is to use a bicycle lock to hook through the handles or even around knobs to keep little ones from opening doors and drawers.

• Identify your child's bicycle and your child at the same time. Either tape securely to the handlebars an index card showing name, address, and phone number or put that information on the bike with printed tape. With so many things to identify, buying a tape maker is a good investment. You could even color code each child's possessions.

Safety When Kids Help Around the House

A recent survey in the *Working Mother* magazine revealed that, in helping around the house, 8-year-olds are operating microwave ovens and vacuum cleaners and 11- to 12-year-olds are using clothes washers and dryers.
When children help:

• Instruct them on proper use of appliances and what to do in emergencies. Why not write out the instructions, maybe even take photos of the steps, and tape them above the washer or where the vacuum is stored, at eye level for the children?

• If children are allowed to cook, buy them cookbooks aimed specifically at children so that they can easily understand the directions.

• Teach children kitchen safety. So often we develop automatic safety habits and forget that novice cooks need to be instructed in such matters as using pot holders and cutting boards, in knife safety, and in what to do in case of burns.

Special Children's Care

Caring for a Sick Child

• Check out your drugstore's baby department. Many inexpensive medicine nipples and plastic spoons are available for medicine giving that don't dribble like a teaspoon and measure medicine more accurately too.

• ALWAYS give all of the medicine prescribed by the doctor, even after the child is feeling better. It's possible to feel better before all the "bugs" are out of the child's system. Old medicine leftovers should not be given to children (or taken by adults either), because chemical changes take place when medicines age that make them useless or even harmful.

• Keep a "barf" bag, bucket, or bowl under the bathroom sink or in some other convenient place. It can be placed bedside when sick children feel nauseated.

• If you have a child who tends to get carsick, a plastic bag inside a paper sack is a good emergency "barf bag." It's even more handy to have a few airline "accident bags" on hand if you are a frequent flyer and have access to them. These airline accident bags come in very handy for disposing of disposable diapers.

• Can't look into a child's throat? Try using a small lollipop for a tongue depressor. Sing the "ahh" with your child to get cooperation. Tell a young child you are trying to see the insides of her toes; she'll open her mouth to laugh.

• Many children balk at swallowing vitamins or other pills and tablets. If you can't get liquid forms, bury the pill in applesauce and see the pill go down the hatch! You may have to crush some tablets before mixing them with applesauce or other fruit puree.

• Sick-in-bed munchkins get bored even when they don't feel particularly energetic. Gather up books, coloring and drawing supplies, small toys, and games and then wrap them and label them with the time of day or order in which they can be opened. Your child will have something more fun to look forward to than just another spoonful of medicine.

• Read to a sick child. It's so hard to set aside reading time for children when TV is so distracting. Reading makes being sick an opportunity instead of just an unpleasant happening.

• Use an adjustable ironing board as a bedside sick table; it can be used to serve meals on—simply adjust the height to fit the little person. Also, to make it easier on the attendant adult, rather than running back and forth to serve food and drink, why not set up a little refreshment center? An ice bucket filled with ice, two or three bottles of fruit juice, a few plastic cups, and a plastic pitcher of water so that the bed-bound child can at least help himself to a glass of ice water or fruit juice whenever wanted.

Getting Dressed

• Trace paper patterns of clothing that already fits properly, and you can buy your child clothing without taking her along to the store.

• Zippers and snaps are easier to use than buttons when you are dressing a toddler. Anything that pulls on with elastic is even better.

• Putting shoes on a wiggly toddler is a test of stamina for both parent and child . . . unless you trap the child in a high chair so his little self stays put!

• Choosing what to wear gives children practice in decision making and encourages them to get dressed by themselves. But don't say, "What do you want to wear?" or you'll have a kid in swim trunks when you want to go to church. With very young or rebellious children, it's better to say, "Do you want to wear the blue shirt or the yellow one?" The child gets to make a decision, and you don't have to pretend you never saw that child before when you both appear in public.

• It's so basic that few people think about it: If you want your children to hang up their clothes, make sure they can reach the hanging place! The same goes for brushing teeth and combing hair; put the mirror where a child can see it!

• If you sew your children's clothing, it won't have labels to indicate which is the back and which is the front of the garment. Sew in a piece of ribbon or trim or decorative stitchery to indicate the back of garments. You can use matching tapes, ribbons, trim, or thread on garments that are to be worn together so that your child will match instead of mix.

• Mark one shoe with tape, marker, or whatever so that your child can tell the right from the left. Or mark the insides of each shoe.

• Keep shoelaces tied by dampening them before tying.

• The knees of jeans will last longer if you put iron-on patches inside the knees when they are new.

• You can make a "suddenly grown" child's winter jacket last to the end of the season by adding knitted cuffs to the jacket sleeves. Either buy ready-made knitted cuffs of matching or complementary colors at notion counters or use the ribbed ends of tube socks. As a bonus, the cuffs keep out cold air.

• Mitten clasps can hold more than mittens. They can hold a towel around a child's neck for an emergency apron or bib and they can be clipped to overall straps to keep them from slipping off tiny shoulders.

• Another way to keep those overall or skirt shoulder straps in place is to sew self-grip tabs where the straps cross.

• Fix that scuff hole in your child's rubber boots by using an inner tube repair kit from the hardware store.

• Identify your child's snow boots with colored tape or any other marking so that you will see the same boots you bought for that child come home every day. That boot pile at school has lots of similar boots, and most kids just grab and shove them on!

• If your child has a constant "slip of the tongue"—in his shoes, that is—cut two tiny parallel slits in the shoe's tongue, then pull the laces through the slots to tie as usual; the tongue won't slip down out of place. You can do this to adult sneakers too, if they don't already have tongue slits.

Having Fun with Children

Too often we spend so much time feeding and keeping children clean and safe that we forget to play with them. Children can be fun, they really can, and they grow up so fast—faster than we can keep track of. We don't want to be the kind of parent who pays attention to the children only when we tell them it's time to do something or when they need discipline . . . we don't want to be, but it's easy to slip into such a pattern unless you set aside time for play.

Working mothers are the ones who get the most "guilt trips," because they sometimes think that if they stayed home to bake cookies and be there with their children 24 hours a day, they'd have perfect children. They forget that children whose mothers stay at home can get into trouble at school or home too. Many studies have come out to show that just being at home with children doesn't always mean that you are spending time with them.

The term *latch-key children* adds to the guilt that working mothers feel. I wish we could come up with another, less grim-sounding name for these children. To me, they are "HUGS Kids"—"Heloise's Up-and-coming Go-getter Super Kids." I think they deserve hugs for learning to be independent and for being important family members and helpers. And, I think parents who teach their HUGS Kids to be self-sufficient deserve hugs too. Perhaps the bumper sticker that says "Have you hugged your kid today?" should be changed to "Have you hugged each other today?" Then, nobody would have a totally bad day, no matter what went wrong at work or at school. (Yes, kids have bad days too.)

Birthday Parties

When they have birthday parties for very young children, many parents make a rule that the number of guests equals the child's age. Huge numbers of toddlers or preschoolers often cause so much confusion that nobody has a good time, and until a child is three or more, the birthday celebration is mostly for the parents and relatives anyhow.

• Write the name, address, and time of the party in bright Magic Marker on balloons. Your invitation won't get tossed out before it's read, and the guest will have fun just anticipating the party.

• Action is the name of the game at a birthday party. Give everybody something to do. Let the guests decorate their own place mats and paper plates. Give each guest non-toxic felt-tip markers and cover the party table with shelf paper so the little artists will have plenty of room for their creativity. Even some older children will enjoy this.

• Very young children are seldom good losers, and a birthday party should be a happy occasion, not a series of tearful wails. Play games that let everyone play and win some sort of prize.

• If you have an undecorated frosted birthday cake ready and a big dish of sugar cookies, the birthday child can decorate the cake with jelly beans, candies, chocolate bits, and so on, and the rest of the kids can decorate the cookies, using instant frosting.

• If you poke each birthday candle into a small marshmallow, wax won't drip onto the frosting and discolor it.

• Have birthday cupcakes for very young children so that everyone has a candle to blow out. They are more easily eaten by small fry than cake slices anyway.

• Go to the max with easy cake eating. Make cupcakes in flat-bottomed ice-cream cones.

Fill the cones two-thirds full with batter and bake according to the timing for cupcakes. You can use different flavors of cake batter and colored cones, if you wish. Frost and/or decorate as usual.

• In a hurry with cupcakes for children's parties or school food donations? Place a marshmallow on top of cupcakes for a few minutes before they are to come out of the oven and they will be instantly frosted.

• Kindergarteners can make their own party hats if you provide old wallpaper samples, gift wrap, or newspaper comics, scissors, yarn for the ties, newspaper for making streamers, and a stapler. CAUTION: Supervise stapler use by small children; tiny fingers can fit under the stapler.

Playing with Kids

• Toddler artists love to squish and squeeze play clay into wondrous shapes. Here's a recipe you can mix up yourself: Mix in a plastic container that can be tightly sealed two cups of flour, one cup of salt, and just enough water to make the mixture rubbery and soft. Keep sealed to prevent drying out.

• You can make your own fingerpaints too. Mix one-fourth cup of cornstarch with 2 cups of cold water and boil the mixture till it thickens. Pour mixture into suitable-size containers and add harmless food coloring.

• Here's a recipe for fingerpaint or decorative play plaster: Mix two cups of soap flakes and two cups of liquid laundry starch in a large bowl. Blend with a wire whisk or an electric beater set at high speed until the mixture has the consistency of whipped cream. To color, add four to six drops of food coloring and beat the mixture again. Mix a fresh batch for each play period.

• For no apparent reason, paint containers and brush-dipping jars for water-coloring spill over when used by children. It's some sort of rule. You can avoid too many spills by cutting an opening in a sponge to fit the container and inserting it into the sponge, which will prevent tipping and absorb dribbles.

• Wrap crayons several times with masking tape, and enthusiastic little fingers won't snap them in two when creating colorful designs.

• Metal flip-top bandage containers hold crayons just like the original boxes did.

• Preserve the freshness of colors in valuable kid art by spraying the master-pieces with hair spray.

• When the princess or the prince needs crown jewels, make necklaces from dry macaroni (elbow, stars, whatever has holes) that has been dipped in water with a few drops of liquid food colors, drained, and dried. String with dental floss and a fat needle such as a needlepoint needle, which also has a larger hole for threading.

• You can make potato necklaces that end up looking like costume jewelry if you cut up potatoes into irregularly shaped pieces (the more angles the better) about one inch thick. Thread the potato pieces on dental floss, as with macaroni necklaces, so they are about twice as long as you want them to be. Allow them to dry in a food dehydrator, in the sun, just in a warm garage, anywhere where they can hang undisturbed for about a week, depending upon how humid your climate is. Each "bead" will dry to about half its original size, and the irregular shapes will become even more irregular. Knot the floss, spray paint (flat or enamel finish) the necklaces any color or use wood colored paint, and you have costume jewelry nobody will ever recognize as potatoes. (These turn out to be so attractive your children may want you to wear one to church, so be careful what you have them make.)

• Glue noodles of different shapes and sizes on the outside of orange juice cans, and leave them natural or spray paint them for pencil holder gifts children can make for adults.

• Toddlers have very short attention spans and lots of energy. They like to keep moving. Empty boxes are fun for them to sit in, push around, or pull.

• Toddlers love to pull things. Attach a string or rope to empty shoe boxes (one or two), a plastic or metal measuring cup, paper cup, paper towel tube, spool, wooden spoon, or anything else that can be tied up and pulled without making a noise that will drive you to aspirin.

• Make a "tunnel" by taking the ends out of a large cardboard box from the grocery store. Let an older child decorate the outside of the tunnel with crayons or paints, or by pasting paper shapes and comics to the "walls."

• Toddlers like to put things into other things. Give them a set of plastic measuring cups to stack and fit. Cut a hole in the top of an old shoe box big enough to allow the toddler to insert wooden spools, cardboard shapes, measuring spoons, or anything else that's safe to play with. The shoe box is fun because the toddler can take the lid off and be intrigued at what's found inside, then empty the stuff and start all over again.

It seems as though some of the favorite toys are those that are made from things at home, so just let your imagination run wild—it doesn't take much money.

Traveling with Children

The late humorist Robert Benchley has been quoted as saying that there are two ways to travel, "first class and with children."

Granted you can't take children everywhere, but it is possible to travel with children with a little bit of class, if you plan ahead.

General Tips for Traveling with Children

• Take some time to be alone with your children if you are at a large gathering of the clan so that you can talk about what is going on and who all those people are.

• Try taking along a tape recorder, and everyone gets to be a recording star. You can even make up new words to old songs and play them for grandparents when you arrive.

• Play such scenery games as finding or counting different state license plates, animals, vegetables, minerals, people—possibly in alphabetical order.

• Play mind games such as rhyming words, opposite-meaning words, and so on.

• Slates and magic slates are great substitutes for paper and pencils. An educational and always available game to play is count pennies, nickels, dimes, and quarters. But be careful—their little minds are very sharp, and you may not end up with any loose change.

• Read books. Bring along a picture album or pictures of people the children will be seeing and tell them who the people are and something about them. (Be careful—children often develop super memories when you make off-the-cuff remarks about Uncle Bob's frugal ways, Aunt Bessie's bad pies, or Cousin Hal's tippling.)

WHEN TRAVELING BY CAR

• Try to take rest stops every two hours or every 100 miles and try to have picnic lunches or light, nutritious snacks of fruit, raw veggies, or cheese and crackers.

• Pack surprise toys, pillows, blankets, clothing changes, and "wipes" or damp washcloths in plastic bags.

• Pack litter bags and have children take turns at "car litter patrol."

• When traveling by car, think about hanging a plastic shoe bag over the back of the front seat so the children can put all of their toys, loose games, and so on in the pockets. Or use a metal or plastic container with a lid to hold crayons, coloring books, and so forth; the children can use it as a lap tray too.

WHEN TRAVELING BY AIR

• When traveling by air, ask for a bulkhead seat so that you have more leg space for children.

• Ask for help from the flight attendants if you need it. Often they have coloring books, cards, and pilot's wings to give to children, which make the trip extra fun for kids.

• Relieve ear pressure on airplane takeoff and landing by having children suck on something (pacifier, bottle, hard candy, chewing gum) or have the children yawn or laugh with their mouths open to relieve the pressure.

Hiring Someone for Child Care in Your Home

Whether the sitter is being hired so that you can have a night out with your husband or friend or is being hired for daily child care while you are working, the person you hire must make your husband, yourself, and your children feel comfortable and secure.

• Check all references carefully. Call previous employers to find out exactly how well the sitter cared for other children.

• When you interview the sitter, don't be afraid to ask test questions such as "What do you do when the baby keeps crying or won't go to sleep?" You need to find out if the sitter's philosophy of child care is compatible with yours.

• For long-term daily child care, agree upon a trial period. Don't make permanent commitments until you are sure that the sitter and child are compatible.

• One of the worst guilt trips parents get is when their children cry when left behind with a sitter. Remember that at certain ages children are more apt to cry than at others. The game of peek-a-boo teaches very young children that when people disappear, they will return. Getting children ready to be left behind is an extended peek-a-boo game. You leave them for longer and longer periods until they can be left painlessly (for you and the child).

Also, you have to accept the fact that at some ages and stages children are more likely to object when left behind.

Here are some tips on conditioning children and leaving without agony.

- If the children are part of your leaving routine, they will be more likely to accept it. Have them help you find your coat or purse, have them help you carry something to the car; even make it a game of pushing you out the door.

- Arrange for the sitter to provide some distraction from your leaving, such as "Let's read a story" or getting out the crayons, blocks, games, or whatever.

- Exchange a big hug and kiss and say that when you touch the kiss-place, you will think about that child, and tell the child to think about Mom or Dad when touching the cheek or nose where you planted that big goodbye kiss.

- If nothing works and you are sure that the sitter is not an ogre, have a talk with the children (but not just as you are leaving) and ask them what would make leaving less upsetting. Most of the time, children just want to know that their feelings are important. Also, if their ideas are used, they have to prove that the ideas are valid.

- Call when you are going to be late so that everyone knows and nobody panics.

Dealing with Older Children

It's tough finding the right supervision for a child who is too old for a sitter and too young to stay alone.

Most child care experts say that children younger than 9 or 10 shouldn't be left alone on a regular basis, no matter how self-sufficient they seem to be. It's important to find some sort of supervised activity either at school or in community programs or with a home sitter. If you must leave older children alone, here are some ways to keep your children safe.

- Teach children what to do in case of emergencies such as injuries, fire, or crime. Rehearse first-aid methods, hold family fire drills, and always teach children not to open the door to strangers and not to let anyone who phones know that they are alone. Rehearse phone conversations with strangers and calling for emergency help with your children so that they know exactly what to say.

Use an answering machine and instruct the child to only pick up the phone and talk when it's someone he knows (parent, grandmother, relative, etc.).

- If more than one child is to be home without adult supervision, be sure to assign each child a responsibility and set up some structure for what activities will be allowed so that the children won't squabble.

• Make sure that children know the consequences of fighting, and follow through on whatever you and they agree will be the consequences. If you have two children who just can't get along, and this is not all that unusual, you'll just have to get a sitter.

• The best solution to problems is communication. Talk to your children about being left alone and find out what they think will make things better. Most children respond better to rules they have helped to formulate.

• Have a message center or leave cassette tapes with information on what the children are to do in your absence. Remind them of scout meetings, appointments, who will pick them up if they are going somewhere by car, and most important, which chores they can do to help the family and to help get supper on the table earlier.

• Many children feel better if you have a regular time for calling home to check if all is well. Some early teens may protest your calling, even when they really want you to call, because they think they should pretend to be totally self-sufficient.

• ALWAYS leave a phone number for where you can be reached.

• Consider a pet. A child who is greeted by an enthusiastic dog or an affectionate cat won't be lonely. Caring for the pet makes the child feel important and needed, and helps develop a sense of responsibility.

A child who is busily taking care of a pet—feeding, brushing, walking it—doesn't have time to be afraid of those "lions, tigers, and bears" that lurk between the walls and in the attics and basements of houses, waiting to scare little children!

Also, even a small, yappy dog will frighten away would-be intruders, imagined or real, and is definitely a better companion than the TV set or a battery-operated robot.

Allowances

My mail tells me that most parents do give their children allowances and that getting children to earn their allowances can become a family fuss.

• If you just can't afford to give the allowance your child asks for, try showing what happens to your checkbook balance after you pay bills. Few children realize what the cost of living is until shown in black (ink) and white or, in some cases, red (ink) and white.

• Children should make their own decisions on how the money is spent after they pay for fixed expenses; the child's birthday or when school starts or ends could be good times to make a yearly reassessment of how much money the child needs.

• Decide when the money will be paid. Weekly for very young children, biweekly or monthly for older teens. Payday should be on a specific day. Maybe on a parent's payday?

• Allowances should not be withheld as a form of punishment, nor should the child be given extra money between allowances.

• Chores are part of family living, and the child has to contribute to the family welfare. Each child should have some responsibilities, according to age and ability, and should not receive payment for doing what is expected of him. Adults don't get paid for brushing their teeth, dressing themselves, and making their own beds; it's part of daily living.

Grandparenting

Kids love to be read to by grandparents. This tip has been in my column and so well received that it bears repeating in this book. Grandparents (and parents too!) can read books and record them on cassette tapes for mailing to far-away grandchildren. Such phrases as "Turn the page" and "Rewind the tape" can be inserted at the proper times. The tapes can be mailed along with the books.

Hearing grandparents' voices helps erase some of the miles between them and their grandchildren in our very mobile society. Besides, it's fun for everyone!

• And, while that tape recorder is still plugged in, how about making a taped letter to Grandma or Grandpa?

• If you have a video camera and VCR, you can make videos and exchange them too. Everybody can be a TV star! (See more on taping in Chapter 10, "Rec-Tech.")

Families Are Forever

Perhaps the best way to close this chapter is to admit that we never really have enough time in the day to do everything, but it's important to set aside time to do the important things.

Family is an important thing. Friends come and go, jobs can give you burnout, money gets spent, and things get broken. Family lasts forever if you put your heart and soul into it, and take time to enjoy it, rather than just tend to serious matters. When you are rearing children, you only go down each road once with each child; enjoy the scenery and the company.

Working parents' time away from home doesn't have to split the family; it can hold the family together if each person in the family feels important to the well-being of everyone else.

Loving and caring are the keys, even when children are called "latch-key children" or, as I suggested earlier in this chapter, "HUGS Kids."

Hugs for everyone!

CHAPTER 7

Clothing Care

Sometimes I like to imagine what it was like to live in the biblical Garden of Eden, where all you had to do was toss away one set of fig leaves and pick another. Not only was clothing free, it was "one size fits all," and there were no colors to match, no crooked seams, no missing buttons, no stuck zippers, and, best of all, no cluttered closets or overflowing laundry baskets.

Nowadays, the price of quality and style is high. "One size fits all" usually means the garment fits almost nobody. Dye lots are such that even those of us who aren't colorblind have trouble making matches; even shades of black and white vex us. Fabrics are water-repellent, spot-resistant, breathable, washable, and, with the emphasis on "naturals," ironable. True "wash and wear" is rare.

You almost need to carry around a dictionary so that when you read labels, you know if you are capable of caring for that suit, dress, shirt, or blouse. We all have a few clothing items that should be declared as dependents on our income tax forms because they cost us so much in dry cleaning. And it isn't just women's clothing. Many men's shirts are so hard to iron the only way to get them really right is to send them to the laundry.

By the way, do you know why it usually costs more to have women's blouses/shirts laundered than men's? It's because men's shirts are standard shapes; they can be pressed quickly on a form. Women's blouses are of so many different designs that most have to be hand finished, which takes more time and, of course, costs more money.

There's a ray of sunshine in the men's/women's clothing enigma though. A few "better" (translated "more expensive") stores have begun to offer free hemming on higher-priced women's suit skirts, just as men's trousers have been hemmed as an automatic service with a sale. By no means are there enough of these stores, but a few are beginning to get enlightened. Unfortunately, some stores are becoming totally unenlightened and are charging men as well as women for hemming.

Frankly, I've always thought that hemming men's trousers is more difficult than hemming women's skirts; it might make more sense to charge for hemming pants and to do skirts for free. Women's skirt hems are shortened the same amount, front and back. Trousers are usually a bit longer (about one-fourth inch) in the back than in front and need to "break" a bit in the front. Just turning up a couple of inches on the bottom doesn't do it, especially since pant legs aren't usually straight up and down from hip to edge.

But this is not a chapter written to crusade for free hemming service; it's about clothing care. Taking care of your clothing means taking some time to read care labels, following the care instructions on those labels, and organizing your closets so that you don't have "pre-crushed" clothing everytime you want to get dressed.

Stain Removal

I think everyone has one blouse, shirt, dress, and so on, that seems to attract stains whenever it's worn. For some reason, when that bad-luck garment is worn, all ballpoint pens seem to be gooey and nonretractable, all chairs have strange stain makers deposited on them no matter where you sit, and, when you wear these spot grabbers to a restaurant, suddenly all waiters have accidents, all soup spoons have holes in them, and you're sure to fall victim to "flying lettuce" or "hyperactive noodles."

Naturally, the "flying lettuce" will have a vinegar and oil dressing and the "hyperactive noodles" will have a tomato sauce so that they will splat a superstain upon your hapless spot grabber. But then, who told you life would be stainless?

There is hope! Our friends at the International Fabricare Institute have sent me the following tips for the care and removal of stains from clothing, and I've found others that work. Here's some first aid for stain removal.

• Spills and stains should be treated immediately. The longer a spot remains, the more difficult it will be to remove.

• Blot up spills with clean, white, absorbent materials (towels, napkins, tissues, etc.).

• Do not overwet. Use small amounts of liquid and blot frequently. Always blot; do not rub or brush.

• Work from the outer edge of the spot toward the center to prevent rings.

• Remove a solid buildup of materials with a tablespoon, spatula, or edge of a dull knife.

• If you take your clothing to a dry cleaner, be sure to call attention to spots and stains, so that they can be pre-spotted. It helps if you can remember the cause of the stain, because the dry cleaner can more easily determine the appropriate remover to use.

• Never iron over a stain. The heat from the iron will set the stain, thus making it almost impossible to remove. A stained article shouldn't be placed in the dryer either.

• Always let your antiperspirant or deodorant dry completely before you get dressed. White stains will appear on clothing if it isn't allowed to dry completely and may permanently damage the material. (See "Pesky Stains," below, on how to remove this stain.)

• There are stains I call "mystery stains." They just appear after the clothing is washed, usually as brown or yellow spots.

These stains are most likely caused by any beverage that contains sugar, such as coffee, fruit juice, and tea. They are relatively easy to remove when they are fresh but become more difficult to remove as they age. They are almost impossible to remove when they have completely set.

• If the clothing is washable, spray the stain with a pre-wash stain remover spray, then wash it using a mild detergent. Repeat the process if the stain still remains.

• Never store clothing away unless it is clean. Although it looks clean, it still needs to be washed so mystery stains won't appear later.

Pesky Stains

• Baby formula: If formula stains are not removed after washing with detergent and bleach try this. Pour lemon juice on the stain and place it in the sunshine for as long as it takes. Sometimes it will work in as little as 15 minutes. If it doesn't get the stain completely out, repeat the process.

Or try this. For white, bleachable articles, place the following ingredients in an enamel, plastic, or stainless-steel container (no aluminum): one gallon hot water, one cup dishwasher detergent, and one-fourth cup liquid chlorine bleach; stir until dissolved. Put in the stained garments and let them soak for about 15 to 30 minutes. Rinse and wash as usual.

• Ballpoint pen ink: Pre-wash sprays will work on some ink stains, and I have found that aerosol hair spray works well too. Place some paper towels underneath the stain. Use some aerosol hair spray on a cloth and then keep blotting the stain and turn the cloth to clean the area until all the ink comes up and wash as usual.

Fingernail polish remover will remove ballpoint pen ink, but be sure it is safe for the fabric. (Test it on a part of the garment that isn't normally seen, such as a shirt or blouse tail.)

• Blood: Although blood stains are difficult to remove unless you get to them immediately, I have found that unseasoned meat tenderizer works well on fresh stains. Rinse with cold water first, then pour on some meat tenderizer. Let it stay on the stain for a few minutes and then wash the clothing as usual.

Try washing the stained article with a detergent containing enzymes, found on the supermarket shelf with all other detergents or bleaches. Enzyme detergents won't damage colored fabrics and work best on wine, coffee, tea, chocolate, and dairy stains.

You can also bleach the stained article with 3.5 percent hydrogen peroxide, but use caution, as this may bleach color also. Wash and rinse the article with cool water.

• Candle wax: Using the dull edge of a knife, scrape off as much of the hardened wax as possible. Place paper towels on either side of the wax-stained area of the fabric and iron on a low to medium setting; the wax will absorb into the towels. Change the towels often, as they become soiled.

If any stain remains, apply liquid detergent and water, and then rinse or wash as usual. Dry-cleaning fluid may be necessary to remove any dye from the wax.

• Catsup or chili sauce: Blot up as much of the stain as you can using a white cloth and cold water. Use an enzyme detergent as a pre-soak and launder as usual.

Hydrogen peroxide can be used on bleach-safe fabrics. Rinse with cold water after bleaching.

• Chewing gum: Apply an ice cube to the gum to harden it or place the garment in the freezer. Then scrape the gum off with the dull edge of a knife or spoon until all the gum is removed. Apply an enzyme detergent as a pre-wash spray to the back of the stain, rub in well, and wash as usual.

• Chocolate: Soak the garment for 30 minutes in cold water. Rub some detergent into the stain while still wet. Bleach will remove it, but use only with colorfast clothing.

• Cleaning-fluid rings: Sometimes these can be steamed out if the garment is held over a teakettle. CAUTION: Steam can burn; put the garment, not your hands, over the steam spout.

• Cosmetics: A bar of soap does a great job. Wet the stain and rub the soap into it. If the stain remains, use regular liquid detergent. Gently work it into the stain and then wash the garment as usual.

• Fingermarks on felt: Try rubbing the fingermarks with the finest sandpaper you can find. Rub gently with the felt's nap until the marks don't show.

• Fruit juices: Soak for about 30 minutes in cold water. Rub some detergent into the stain while it's still wet. Wash as usual. If this treatment doesn't work, apply hydrogen peroxide if the garment is bleach-safe, then rinse well.

• School glue: For school glue, apply some water and blot. Mix one teaspoon of a colorless, mild detergent or dish-washing liquid in a cup of lukewarm water and apply to the stain. Rinse with water and blot until dry.

• Grass: Apply an enzyme detergent and blot. Rinse with water or mix one tablespoon of clear household ammonia with one-half cup of water and apply to stain, then blot and rinse. Or mix one-third cup of white vinegar with two-thirds cup of water. Apply to stain and blot until dry. Wash as usual.

If the material is white and bleach-safe, use bleach according to bottle directions.

• Grease: A quick remedy for grease stains that occur when cooking is to apply some talcum powder or cornstarch to the stain. Apply just enough to cover the grease. You'll see the powder get thick as the grease is absorbed. Wipe it off and put fresh powder on, let stand awhile, and wipe it off again.

Place the stain facedown on paper towels and go over the back with full-strength liquid detergent or dry-cleaning solvent (don't mix these), using a clean, white cloth. Mechanics' hand cleaner may also be used to remove the spot. Launder as usual.

• Iron rust: Moisten the stain with water, apply lemon juice, and then rinse. You may have to repeat the treatment several times to get the stain out. CAUTION: It may be wise to test lemon juice on an inconspicuous place on the garment to make sure it won't bleach certain colors. Of course, if you can't wear the garment with the rust stain, it probably doesn't matter if it gets a bleach spot!

• Lipstick: Before washing, treat the stain with a pre-wash spray or rubbing alcohol and blot the spot with a clean, white cloth or paper towel. Keep applying the spray, always using a clean section on the cloth, or change the paper towel when you blot the spot.

You can also try wetting the article, then rubbing the stain with a bar of face soap. Wash as usual.

• Margarine or butter: Mix one teaspoonful of a colorless, mild detergent or dish-washing liquid in a cup of lukewarm water. Apply to stain and blot until dry. Mix one-third cup white vinegar with two-thirds cups of water; blot. Rinse with water and blot until dry. If all else fails, apply some dry-cleaning solvent and blot. Launder as usual.

• Mildew: Apply white vinegar or salt and lemon juice to the garment to kill the mildew. Then place the clothing in the sun. Wash as usual.

Bleach will kill mildew; follow directions on the bleach bottle.

• Milk: Soak article in warm water, using an enzyme detergent as a pre-soak product.

• Oil-base paint: A bit of turpentine or paint thinner can remove this if the fabric is color-safe; rinse well. Be sure to follow directions on the can of turpentine or thinner.

Rub with a detergent paste and wash as usual.

• Water-base paint: You will need to get to this stain as soon as possible; after this has set it cannot be removed.

Rinse the stain well in warm water and wash as usual.

• Perspiration: The International Fabricare Institute says that applying a large amount of deodorant and using cold "hard" water (high mineral, low alkaline water) when washing the garment can cause this problem.

Many deodorants and antiperspirants contain aluminum salts. When combined with laundry detergent and cold water, the salts cannot be easily dissolved and therefore remain on the fabric.

Before washing the garment, rinse the area with plain water, then wash with the rest of your laundry in either warm or hot water with good suds.

To remove fresh perspiration stains, apply diluted ammonia to the stains and rinse with water.

For old stains, try applying white vinegar and rinse with water.

• Scorch marks: Moisten the fabric, then place it in the sun. You may have to remoisten it several times. Persistent marks can be bleached with hydrogen peroxide if the fabric is bleach-safe; then rinse well.

• Pet urine stains on carpet: You'll get the best result if you get to the stain immediately.

Blot up as much liquid as possible with absorbent white paper towels. You will need to change the towels often, until no more moisture comes from the carpeting. Sponge a little white distilled vinegar on the stain to neutralize the urine. The vinegar also helps to stop discoloration of the carpet.

Blot the vinegar right away so it doesn't go through the carpet backing. Rinse by dabbing with water. Then mix two tablespoons of mild liquid dish-washing detergent to one cup of water. Apply this sparingly. Blot up any excess.

The final cleaning step is to rinse the stained area with clear water to remove all the detergent. Then, blot up as much of the wetness you can.

Place an old white towel over the wet area, then walk around on the towel. As it gets wet, change to a dry part of the towel. Keep doing this until the area seems pretty dry.

Place a dry towel over the area and weight it down. The towel will absorb any leftover moisture from the carpet and make it dry more quickly. Leave the towel on overnight. When it's dry in the morning, fluff up the carpet nap with your fingers.

• Urine stains on mattresses: Blot up as much as possible if the stain is still wet. Use upholstery shampoo on the stain and rub the spot from its outer edge to its center to avoid making it any larger. Spray with a dry fabric air freshener to prevent a musty or urine odor. If possible, put the mattress out in the sunshine to help air it. Note: Urine stains may cause permanent dye removal from fibers.

• Water on velvet: Hold the fabric over steam spouting from a teakettle for a few minutes; then shake off steam moisture until the garment is dry; then brush up the nap.

• Wine: First, blot up or rinse all liquid. Many have had luck pouring club soda on the stain, then rinsing in cool water. Many times the dye from wine is difficult to remove and sometimes impossible.

Try this: Mix one teaspoonful of a colorless, mild detergent or dish-washing liquid in a cup of lukewarm water; blot. Then mix one-third cup of white vinegar with two-thirds cup of water; blot. Then mix one tablespoon of clear household ammonia with one-half cup of water. Rinse thoroughly with water and blot until dry.

After treating the stain, launder as usual.

Laundry Tips

Following these simple guidelines will give you much brighter washes, even the first time.

You should know that not always getting bright-as-new clothing is not necessarily your fault. Manufacturers of white goods sometimes add brighteners to white fabric that wash out, partially with the first wash. This is especially true of cotton-synthetic blends. When the brightener washes out, a slight graying sometimes results.

• To get white clothing whitest, always use the hottest water safe for the fabric. If you have to use hard water, add water softener along with the detergent to increase the detergent's efficiency.

• If bleach is necessary, for maximum effectiveness add it after the load has washed for about five minutes. Never wash colored clothes with white ones, because color can easily transfer to the whites.

• Spot-treating and scrubbing the bottoms of socks, collars, and so on, before washing is always a good idea. An inexpensive way to scrub out stains is to wrap a bar of soap in nylon net, bunch it around the bar so it's rough, then tie a knot in the net or secure it with rubber bands.

• When you buy a new washing machine and are getting acquainted with unfamiliar automatic cycle changes, watch the dial closely to see where the last rinse cycle starts. Mark that spot with an arrow-shaped triangle of masking tape or red nail polish. This is the place you'll add your fabric softener. (Naturally, this is for machines without automatic softener dispensers.) Thereafter only a quick look at the dial will tell you if it is time to add softener. Mark each cycle (normal, permanent press, and gentle) the same way.

Do not overuse fabric softener, particularly on toweling. The overuse of fabric softener will cause the towels not to be absorbent.

• If your clothes come out wrinkled from the dryer, it may be that you are overloading the dryer and not allowing the clothes to tumble freely. So just wet a washcloth, hand towel, or whatever, wring it out well, and put it in the dryer with the clothes.

Let the clothes spin awhile longer, and they will be just as wrinkle free as can be.

• To remove dust and freshen drapes, valances, and quilts, put them into the dryer, turn the heat control to "air fluff," and add a fabric softener sheet.

They come out wrinkle-free and fresh-smelling.

• In the spring, save the lint you removed from the filter. Put it outside and watch the birds pick it up to use as nesting material. They'll have the softest nests in town!

• If you own a cat, be careful to check inside your dryer before you turn it on. Many a tabby, seeking a nice warm place to nap, has taken a spin in the dryer, with disastrous results. When you're in a hurry, you don't always check before you toss in a load and start the machine.

So, be careful. It's a good idea to close the dryer door in between taking clothes out and putting clothes into it. You won't have to change the light bulb so often either!

Putting Away the Laundry

• Save sorting and folding time by folding socks together as you take them out of the dryer or off the line.

The rest of the laundry seems to get folded faster, since there's no pile of socks to deal with.

• When folding clothes after washing and drying them, put fresh laundry under the existing stack (sheets, towels, handkerchiefs, underwear, etc.), so they will be rotated and the same ones won't be used all the time. Or place the fresh sheets on top and always grab off the bottom of the stack.

• Save space in a small linen closet by folding the towels, then rolling them.

• For a fresh scent, open bars of soap and put them between the sheets and towels in your linen closet and in your dresser drawers. Not only do the linens and clothes smell good, the soap lasts longer because it hardens.

• Used fabric softener sheets will also prevent musty smells wherever you store clothing or linen. Do not allow them to come in contact with silk.

• When children or adults in a household wear nearly the same size and/or have matching outfits, it's hard to tell which clothes belong to whom.

You can use a laundry pen to initial clothing in an inconspicuous place. Or, if there are several children whose clothing is unsortable, clothing can be color-coded. Assign a different color to each child and mark each one's clothing accordingly. A stitch of thread or dot of permanent ink marker in the child's assigned color on the neck or waist seam of undergarments and on the toe seam of socks ensures matching instead of mixing.

• Have your family help with the laundry. Tape-record detailed sorting instructions as well as instructions on using the washer and dryer. They won't be able to use the time-worn excuse that they didn't know what to do. Or write down clear instructions of how to do these steps, from sorting, to washing, to drying, to folding/hanging, and tack or tape this up in the laundry room.

Trouble-Shooting Washers

These hints may save you a costly service call if your washer or dryer doesn't work. Sometimes it's as simple as a circuit breaker that has tripped, a loose plug, or a blown fuse.

Before you call the service agent, check the following:

1. Some washers will turn off automatically if the clothes aren't balanced. Rearrange them and push the button to start again.
2. There's a button under the lid of the washing machine that stops the machine action when the lid is raised. Check to see if the lid is closed tightly.

3. Is there a kink in any of the hoses or has the drain hose become disconnected from the machine?
4. Are the water faucets turned on?
5. Is the selector button pushed in all the way?
6. Is the plug connected? Has a fuse blown?

• To get rid of the residue left by detergents and minerals in hard water areas, fill the machine with hot water and pour in one quart of vinegar. (Yes, I know, vinegar again!) Run the machine through the entire cycle. The residue should vanish. Do this only occasionally, as overuse of vinegar can possibly hurt the inside of your washing machine.

Trouble-Shooting Dryers

Lint buildup will cause your dryer to take much longer to dry the clothing. Not only can this buildup damage the machine, but it will cost more money in electricity or gas to dry your clothes, and there is also the possibility of fire if the dryer overheats.

Here are a few tips for cleaning the filter.

• Use an old sponge-type fabric softener sheet to wipe off all the lint.

• A comb, hair-pick, pen, or pencil will remove the lint from the filter.

• Appliance service agents say that even though you "clean" the lint filter often to remove all the fuzz, a fine film forms on the filter that keeps air from circulating properly. You need to wash the filter with liquid dish-washing soap, a stiff brush, and warm water every so often. Let the water run through to remove every particle of lint.

• Here are some other trouble-shooting tips for your dryer:

1. Check the outside vent to make sure nothing is clogging it.
2. If it's a gas dryer, is the striker working properly and is the pilot light on?
3. Is the door closing tightly?
4. Has a fuse blown?

Laundromats

Here are some ideas to lighten your load if you do your wash in the Laundromat.

• Wear an apron or smock with two pockets, one for quarters and one for dimes. You can also buy a carpenter's apron at a hardware store and keep it always stocked with things you need at the Laundromat, such as change, sealable bags of detergent, tissues, and maybe a small box of raisins and a toy if you have to take children with you. Or use a heavy plastic self-sealing bag to carry laundry change in.

• Liquid detergent in the large containers is cheaper but not easy to carry. Save syrup or dish detergent bottles with the push-pull tops and use them—one for laundry detergent and the other for fabric softener.

• Powdered detergent can be pre-measured into reusable margarine tubs or sealable plastic bags so that you don't have to tote a heavy, giant-economy box of detergent with your laundry. Plastic rinsed-out yogurt cups work perfectly.

• An easy way to identify the washer and dryer you're using is to put a brightly colored magnet on it. It not only helps you, but others will know it's being used.

• Purchase three laundry baskets or bags; then, sort your clothes before washing. Or sort as you finish wearing them if you have the space. Put permanent press in one, white clothing in one, and colored clothing in the other.

When your family takes something off, they can learn to drop things directly into the proper basket. It's a great time saver, and you'll be teaching your children how to do their own laundry when they go away to school.

I'll bet the freshmen in any college can be identified by their pink socks, dyed by washing with "mixed loads." This tip, of course, helps whether you use the Laundromat or wash at home.

Several Ironing Tips

You can eliminate or at least make some garments easier to iron if you avoid overloading your dryer and if you avoid putting heavy items (large towels, sweatshirts, and jeans) in with much lighter items (made from nylon or polyester, or faux silk). Why crush one garment with another when enough air fluffing will save you energy?

Here are a few tips to remove starch buildup on your iron.

• Run your iron over a washcloth saturated with white vinegar. Place the cloth on a flat surface and run the warm iron over it several times, pressing gently. You'll see all the brown goop come off.

Now run the iron over a clean, damp cloth, to wipe off any remaining starch so that it will not mark the next garment you iron.

The secret is to clean the bottom of the iron frequently so that it doesn't get a major starch buildup.

• One way to clean a steel iron is to rub a small piece of very fine (0000) steel wool gently over the bottom of the iron.

CAUTION: Never use steel wool on a non-stick iron.

Wipe off the bottom of the iron with a clean, wet cloth and dry it well.

Turn the iron on a low setting and place a piece of wax paper on the ironing board. Run the iron over the wax paper several times. Then run the iron over an old towel or piece of cloth to remove any traces of wax. Your iron will be smooth and slick on the bottom.

• Remove the gunky buildup on a non-stick surface by spraying pre-wash spray onto a washcloth; then follow the above procedure.

• To keep your iron from clogging, use distilled water and drain it after each use. Distilled water prevents mineral buildup, the major cause of clogged irons.

• You'll find many excellent iron cleaners on the market that will remove any buildup on the bottom of an iron.

• If the manufacturer's care instructions don't advise against it, you can use white vinegar to clean the inside of your iron.

Fill the iron with vinegar. Let it steam for about five minutes, then let it rest a while. Empty the vinegar and rinse the iron well with water. Then heat it and run the bottom back and forth across a damp washcloth before using it to prevent mineral stains on your clothing.

• Iron detailed parts first so that you don't crush the rest of the garment getting at them after you have finished.

• I like to use sprays; I'm not sure if anyone mixes starch anymore, because it's so time consuming. You can choose a "fabric finish" spray to renew the "hand" or "body" of a garment or a "spray starch" to give a garment more body and stiffness.

• Some people sprinkle garments to dampen them before ironing, but if you use fabric finish, it dampens the garment and adds body at the same time.

• If you've sprinkled garments and then don't finish ironing them all in one spree, you can freeze or refrigerate the clothing in a plastic bag until you can iron again. If you just let damp clothing lie around, it will mildew or smell musty.

• Most of the time, blends of polyester and cotton will come out of the dryer either ready to wear or needing only a touch-up. Don't overload the dryer, and dry clothing of similar weight in each load. For example, if you wash a bunch of heavy towels in with cotton-polyester blouses or dress shirts and then dump the whole load into the dryer, the towels will smash up the shirts and require a longer drying time for the whole load, which ultimately means you'll have more creases to iron than if you put just the shirts and blouse into one dryer load and the towels in another.

Some of the crushed-look cottons really shouldn't be ironed or, at the most, should just be touched up with a steam iron. And whether or not you iron such things as jeans is a matter of taste and energy.

• Iron dark-colored fabrics and damp silks inside out or use a pressing cloth to prevent shine. Commercial press cloths are very good, but you can also use a cotton handkerchief or a linen dish towel if you don't have a commercial cloth.

• Iron embroidered areas from the inside. For extra depth, place them, embroidered side down, on a terry towel or soft (flour-sack fabric), folded dish towel for ironing.

• When ironing long dresses, large tablecloths, curtains, and so on, it's best to put a sheet on the floor under the ironing board so you don't dust the floor and iron at the same time. (I know it saves time to do two things at once, but this isn't one of those times when it's a good idea.) And don't forget to use the large, squared end of the ironing board for ironing these things.

• Use the temperature guide on your iron to determine which temperature goes with which fabrics. Since iron temperatures vary, test the iron on an inconspicuous spot when you are touching up delicate fabric that might melt from too much heat. Follow the temperature guide on the label or hang tag, too; that's what it's for!

• Dresses and blouses with puffy sleeves can be ironing headaches. A simple homemade sleeve roll can be made from a roll of toilet tissue covered with foil, then with terry cloth or any fabric that will withstand the heat of an iron.

• A half-used roll of paper towels, covered as suggested above, can also be used as a sleeve roll.

• A small pressing board to fit inside a pant leg, or whatever, can be made from an empty cardboard tube that fabric stores use to roll bolts of material on. Most stores throw them away, so you'll be able to pick one up. Pad it, then cover it with any desired fabric. This board can even be used as a seam board for pressing straight seams. Just stand it on its side by the sewing machine for easy access.

• A variety of pressing hams (firmly stuffed ham-shaped ironing aids especially useful for blouse/shirt and jacket shoulders and sleeve tops) and sleeve boards can be bought in sewing centers and variety stores to help you iron those parts of garments that don't lie flat on the ironing board.

Ironing Travel Hints

After a generation of drip-dry and no-iron, we've gone back to natural fabrics and, even if some of them are supposed to look "naturally crushed," many still need at least a touch-up. Here are a few travel tips, however, for when you don't have an iron handy.

• Many creases will hang out of garments if you hang them in the bathroom while someone is taking a hot shower; shower steam is a terrific travel "iron."

• I've also used a hot light bulb to "iron" garments in a hotel room.

Ironing is one of those household chores that can be delegated to teens and other members of the family, who can, at the very least, iron their own clothing and, at best, be kind to their parents and iron a few extras. Here's how to push the ol' iron over the clothes to make them wearable.

How to Iron a Shirt or Blouse

1. First iron the back of the collar, then the front of the collar. Some people like to iron the underside of the button and the button-hole facing next; some omit this step entirely.
   Some collars are cut so that they will curve around the neck smoothly. Iron these from their point toward the center, stopping short when the fabric shows a fold. While the collar is still warm, you can fold it along the seamed fold line where the collar and neck facing meet, and wrap it around your waist to curve it.
2. Iron the back and front of cuffs (also, pocket tabs if there are any; these should be unbuttoned).

3. Iron the backs and fronts of sleeves.

Some garments shouldn't have the crease that forms when you flatten the sleeve from underarm seam to shoulder line to iron it. You can buy a sleeve board to insert into the sleeve when you iron it.

4. Iron the shoulder parts—the yolk across the back, and the front yolk, if there is one.

With some garments and some ironing boards, you can do the whole shoulder area without moving the shirt, which is good. Wasted motions take up time that can be spent doing other things. When I was first learning to iron, I used to try different ways of arranging things on the ironing board so that I could iron as fast as possible. That tells you how much I like ironing, doesn't it?

5. Iron the two front sides or the front if it's one piece.

If the front parts are ironed before the back, the spray is less likely to dry out on one side while you do the back and cause one side of the front to look better than the other. The back isn't as important as the front.

6. Iron the back.

If the back has a pleat and it's important to you to have this pleat ironed, you can line up the pleat folds with the shirttail, and give them a good hard press, dampening them well and pressing dry the first time you wash the shirt. Often the lines will stay in the fabric through many launderings and be a guide for future ironings.

How to Iron a Skirt

1. Iron pocket flaps or facings, the undersides of button and button-hole facings (if the skirt opens down one side), and with certain machine-stitched hems, especially on heavy cotton or denim, iron the hem from the inside after spraying it with fabric finish to flatten it. This keeps the hem from rolling up.

2. Iron the body of the skirt.

3. Iron the waistband and, if needed, press the tops of pleats on a pleated skirt. If you are so unfortunate as to own a totally pleated skirt, you can line up the pleats and stick a non-rust straight pin at the hemline and into the ironing board to hold the pleats in place. (Bet you're sorry you bought it! And to make matters worse, dry cleaners charge by the pleat to press such garments!) And now you know why.

• If you have a gathered dirndl skirt and a bit of a "pooched out" tummy, lightly flatten the gathered areas when you iron the waistband so that they won't add more mid-section bulk.

How to Iron Pants

1. Iron pocket facings.

2. Insert the ironing board into the pants, one leg at a time, ironing the entire pant top and as far down on the leg as the ironing board will go.

3. To iron the pant-leg bottoms and put in the crease at the same time, match each pant leg seam to seam, and lay the pants across the ironing board. Tuck the pant leg closest to you under your chin so that you can work on the other leg without having the pants fall to the floor.

Starting at the hem, match the seams and iron sections until you have ironed the inside of the pant leg as far as the crotch. Turn the pants over, tuck the ironed leg under your chin, and repeat.

After both inside legs are ironed, the pants will lie flat across the ironing board so that you can iron the outsides of the legs.

• When pants have pleats at the top, the front crease needs to go from hem to the major pleat. If you use the system above, this usually happens automatically. Then all you have to do is insert the ironing board into each pant leg to touch up about an iron's width of the pleat.

• Some people like to do all this with the pants lying the length of the ironing board. It works if you have short-legged people in the house or a very long ironing board.

Ironing Boards

• If you find that you have to press hard or go over sections of clothing many times to get them ironed properly, you may need a new ironing board pad. Most of the time, we replace the cover only. We forget that we eventually iron the padding flat---too flat to be a cushion when we iron.

• You can put a piece of heavy-duty foil under the ironing board cover and over the pad so that heat is reflected to the undersides of garments, and then ironing is faster. Many of the silicone-type ironing board covers accomplish the same heat reflection.

Dry Cleaning

Professional dry cleaning is much more than just cleaning. It includes different operations performed by skilled people aimed at returning your wardrobe to that like-new appearance.

• Don't store clothing that needs dry cleaning. Any soil or stain left on a garment too long is sometimes impossible to remove without damaging the fabric. This is why it is very important to point out any stains to your dry cleaner when taking the garment in. This includes any that are light in color or invisible (soft drinks or white wine, for example). The heat from the drying process of dry cleaning can turn such stains brown or yellow.

• Frequent dry cleaning prolongs the life of a garment. Not only do stains set with age, making the garment unwearable, but ground-in dirt and soil act as an abrasive (like sandpaper), causing rapid wear of the fibers, and they can attract moths to wool garments.

• Protect your garments from perfumes and colognes, as well as deodorants and antiperspirants, by applying these items before dressing and allowing them to dry. Garments made of delicate fabrics, such as silk, can be seriously damaged by perfumes and hair sprays.

Remember, a good professional dry cleaner is the next most important thing to a good hairdresser. Be honest with them when you take in your garments and point out any stains; tell them anything that you have tried to use to remove the stain before bringing it in. They can work their miracle only if you help them. Many stains are impossible to remove regardless of what is attempted. So please remember that your dry cleaner is only human too.

Quick Clothing Repairs

• In an emergency, if your skirt hem becomes unstitched at an inconvenient time, don't be afraid to use the tried-and-true stapler. Staple from inside out to avoid snagging your stockings.

• Transparent or masking tape will hold on some fabrics. At least until you can get home to change.

• If you are near an iron, fusible tape will work to hold some fabrics. Fabric glue (sold at sewing centers) will work on others. Always test iron-on fusible tape or fabric glue on a seam to be sure you don't totally ruin the garment you're trying to quick-mend. They may "bleed through" on certain fabrics.

• The best way to mend holes in knit shirts is to iron lightweight fusible interfacing onto the wrong side of the shirt.

• Buttons with shanks can be pinned on with safety pins until you have time to sew them.

• When you need a heavy-duty repair for buttons that keep coming off certain garments, sew them on with thin nylon fishing line or dental floss. You have to cut it with scissors to remove the buttons. Hunting, work, and children's clothes and coats seem to be the chief offenders in the button-popping world.

• To extend a skirt waistband in an emergency, loop two rubber bands through the buttonhole (the official encyclopedia name for the loop knot that works here is "cow hitch," but somehow that sounds depressing when you find yourself in this situation!); next, loop the rubber bands over the button.

• If you sew, and want to make a more permanent waistband extender, take a piece of one-inch-wide elastic the length you need to extend the waistband. Sew a button on one end and put a buttonhole on the other. Put the button into the waistband buttonhole and put the elastic buttonhole over the skirt button.

Of course, if you use either of these extenders, you'll have to wear an overblouse. Also, you'll have to decide if you want to buy all new clothes or get rid of those extra waistline inches!

• Bargain garments can be personalized by replacing buttons or by adding trims and appliqués. Appliqués and trims can also hide small permanent stains or burn holes.

• If a burn hole is very small and the fabric texture allows, you can hide a burn hole by cutting a tiny piece of fabric from the seam allowance and gluing it in place (place a small piece of lighter-weight fabric underneath as backing), using fabric glue, fusible tape, or iron-on mending tape placed under the mend with stick-on side up. These mends won't hold well or have a satisfactory appearance with all fabrics, but are worth a try if you don't want to have the hole professionally mended. (With some fabric textures, frayed threads from the seam allowance can be glued instead of a small piece of fabric.)

Sewing

Sewing your own clothes enables you to be your own designer and save money at the same time. Knowing how to sew children's clothes is especially kind to a family budget.

Although I don't have the time to sew much, I appreciate the creativity that goes into making clothes and gifts and decorating homes with custom drapes, curtains, and upholstery. I've known people who have used their sewing talents to achieve rewarding and lucrative careers. There are plenty of non-sewing people around who are more than happy to pay for custom-fitted clothing and alterations.

Here are some sewing tips I think you can use, whether or not you make garments "from scratch."

• The whole skirt hem doesn't have to fall when one hemming thread breaks. When you're rehemming a skirt, knot the thread every few inches. The knots prevent the hem from opening up entirely if the thread breaks.

• Use transparent nylon thread for your sewing machine. You never have to change colors. It takes on the color of the material being used and is a much stronger thread.

• If you're sewing patches on your child's school or scout uniform pocket, slip a piece of cardboard into the pocket to keep from sewing the pocket to the shirt.

To position the patch properly, put it in place and then staple before sewing or use fabric glue to glue the patch in place; let glue dry and then sew it on.

Threading the sewing machine needle can be a challenge for some of us. Try these tips.

• Dampen the end of the thread with a bit of starch when you thread your sewing machine.

• Place a small piece of white paper behind the needle for better visibility. It works like a charm.

• For a fast spool change on your sewing machine (sometimes you want to change a color or type of thread), break the thread close to the spool already on the machine, then tie on the new color with a square knot and change the spools.

Gently pull the thread through all the tension stations and through the eye of your needle, and you're ready to continue sewing.

• One way to thread the bobbin without having to rethread the needle is to pull enough thread through the needle to start the bobbin, and place the bobbin on the bobbin-winding shaft. Then loosen the wheel and fill the bobbin as you normally would.

When the bobbin is full, remove it, tighten the wheel, and you're ready to start again. Be sure to adjust the thread tension on your machine so the thread does not break, both before and after filling the bobbin.

Using Patterns

Here are some hints for sewing clothes from patterns.

• Press the pattern before pinning it to the material. The pieces will lie flat on the material and give a much truer cut than when they are wrinkled from the pattern envelope.

• Lay the pattern out flat and measure it between seam lines. Compare your measurements to those of the pattern.

Check the following measurements: Length of body from waist to neck (bodice length), front and back; width of upper back from top of armhole seam; width across shoulder blades; armhole depth; sleeve length; width across abdomen; and skirt length. For pants, length of each leg and measurements of crotch.

• In order to avoid mistakes when altering a pattern, always make a duplicate of the pattern on a brown paper sack or newspaper and make alterations on this. Then mark the pattern itself.

• If you sew, you know that turning collars and cuffs properly is the key to a professional look. When turning the points of collars and cuffs, trim the seam close to the point as usual, then turn the collar right side out.

Thread a needle and make a rather large knot so it won't pull through the point. Place your needle as close as possible to the stitching of the collar point (place the needle on the interfaced side, being careful not to catch any material on either side).

Pull the thread through, and zip! A beautiful pointed collar. Cut the thread off the needle, close to the point of the collar. You will have no more "rounded" shirt collar points.

• When sewing, you'll have no more mess on the floor if you tape a plastic kitchen-size trash bag to the side of the sewing machine. As you cut and snip, drop the scraps into the bag. Cleanup is automatic.

• When sewing at the machine, use a magnet to pick up spilled pins and needles off the floor. You need to keep pins and needles away from children and pets for safety's sake, and using a magnet is so much less painful than "finding them" with your toes if you like to walk around the house shoeless.

• Use the dusting attachment on your vacuum cleaner to suck the lint and fuzz out of your sewing machine. (Remove the spool of thread, bobbin, and face plate first.)

It's amazing how much accumulates out of sight and can build up between working parts on your machine until the lint is like layers of felt.

• When you're ready to go shopping for parts for your sewing machine, write the name and model number on a small piece of paper and immediately put it in your wallet.

It's a waste of time to go shopping for a new belt, needles, or bobbins if you can't tell the clerk the name or model of the machine.

Storing Sewing Supplies

Organizing your sewing supplies really saves time, and, if you can find things quickly and easily, even mending can become less tedious. Here are some storing tips.

• After you have cut all the pieces out of a pattern, place them, the instructions, and all notions needed for that particular project in a plastic grocery bag that has handles. Drawstring hotel laundry bags are good storage bags too.

You can either hang each project on a hanger or lay it flat until you have time to complete the sewing. It's great if you tend to cut several projects at a time.

• You can store sewing machine bobbins in an empty prescription bottle that has been thoroughly washed. Colors are easy to find when the bobbins are stacked and kept together.

• To keep decorative lace and rickrack together, keep a plastic bag filled with empty thread spools with your sewing supplies. When you purchase lace or trimming, take it out of its package and wrap it around an empty spool, then secure it with a straight pin. You may also keep the trim on the original cards and then put leftovers on the empty spools. In either case, all the trimmings remain tangle free and ready to use on any outfit.

• A fishing-tackle box is the perfect organizer for storing sewing notions. It has compartments of different sizes, and the arrangement of the compartments is very suitable for scissors, needle threaders, buttons, and much, much more.

• To keep your spools of thread in view, drive headless nails at an angle into a peg board or on the right size of board for your needs.

Hang the board over your sewing machine and you will be able to select the color needed quickly and easily, without having to hunt for it.

• Use a bar of soap as a pin cushion. Keep the wrapper on and put the pins and needles in. Not only does it hold a lot of needles, but it makes them slide easily into fabric.

• Make your own travel mending kit. Wrap the small amounts of different-color threads left over from various sewing projects around a small, folded paper or a piece of cardboard. Add a needle threader and a small pair of scissors and you have your own travel sewing kit.

Closets

Closet cleaning may be a chore, but sometimes organizing one part of your life (in this case, it's your wardrobe) can lead to getting organized in other parts of your life.

If you don't believe me, think about the times when you are surrounded by the most household clutter. Is it when you feel as if the sun is shining just for you and the world is yours to dance on? Or is it when you feel as if the world is spinning so far out of orbit that you have lost your footing and are flying off into an outer space black hole?

The point is that when you feel in charge of your life and that everything is going your way, you can control clutter in your home and the rest of your life instead of having the clutter sneak up and control you.

Closet Cleaning

• Try to get rid of clothing that hasn't been worn in at least a year or two. I know we all say, "I'll wear that someday," and then we put it back into the closet to hang around for several more years.

• Start by taking all of your clothes out of the closet. (This is a good time to paint or clean the inside of the closet. It's also a good time to sew on loose buttons and do other repairs on clothes you want to keep.) As you put your clothes back into the closet, decide what you really want and really will wear again. Be ruthless. If you want to save the outfit you were wearing when you met that special person in your life, it's okay to be sentimental, but don't get carried away.

• Try this adaptation of the "A, B, and C" method of time management: Make three piles of clothing, A, B, C. The A clothing will definitely be kept. The B clothing might be kept. C clothing hasn't been worn for a year or so, for whatever reason, and won't go back into the closet. After putting the A pile back into the closet, go through the B pile again. If necessary, redivide the B items into A's and C's. Put the second group of A's back into your closet and make a mental note to yourself that these were almost discards. (The next time you clean your closets, if these same items are B's, they should immediately go into the C's for discarding.) Put all the C's together in large plastic bags and donate them to a non-profit group.

Donate Your Discards

• Knowing that your discards have value to somebody makes it easier to be objective when you sort the "Keeps" from the "Keep Nots." You will be helping yourself and somebody else at the same time. Battered women's shelters across the country, for example, always need women's and children's clothing, bedding, and towels, because their clients often come in with only the clothes they are wearing and obviously can't go home to get their possessions. This is where everything I "go through" is taken.

Pre-owned clothing is used by different organizations in different ways, depending upon its condition. Some organizations sell wearable clothing as fund-raising; others distribute it to needy people. Some organizations shred nonrepairable, nonwearable clothing, then sell it by the pound to rag dealers.

• Call the organization that will receive your discards to find out what it will do with them. Often, if an item is not sold during its allotted "rack life" of six weeks or so, donated items are passed on to individuals who use clothing and household items to help the homeless and others in need.

Many organizations, such as the St. Vincent de Paul Society and several other church and veterans' groups, operate thrift shops that use your donations to fund their operating costs and charitable causes. Some national organizations, such as the Salvation Army and Goodwill Industries, will repair donated items before resale, thus providing jobs for various people, including handicapped people. Such organizations will accept just about any kind of discards.

• Clothing that is too frayed and worn to be wearable can be given to groups that raise funds by selling to rag dealers.

There is no point in cleaning wearable clothing that is going to end up as rags. Conversely, it is not fair to give "almost rags" to a group that tries to maintain a presentable shop of nice, serviceable clothing. That's why it's best to call before you donate used clothing and other items. The bonus is you may find out that the organization will pick up items in your neighborhood. If the system is that you leave your donations on the porch to be picked up when the truck goes down your street, remember to clearly label what is to be picked up, with the name of the organization, or you may end up unintentionally donating lawn furniture, and so forth, that you wanted to keep!

Ending Closet Clutter

Need more hang-ups in your closets?

• Buy 18 inches of quarter-inch brass chain. Put one sturdy wood or metal hanger through the second or third link and hang it from the closet rod. Let the remainder of the chain dangle and put other hangers through the links as desired.

This is an excellent way to hang blouses, skirts, and children's clothes. You also can hang a chain in a soft garment bag so you get to use the wasted space at the bottom. Or just suspend a chain from the ceiling of your closet.

• Plastic milk crates sold in most department and variety stores can be stacked on their sides to form shelves or used to hold various items such as sweaters, shoes, and handbags, and then stacked on each other or on shelves in closets. When they're on shelves, you can just pull them out as you would drawers.

• Hang blouses and shirts in the closet according to color. Then when you're in a hurry, you can find what you need to match whatever you're wearing. And you may find, as a dear friend of mine did, that she had over thirty navy blue blouses because that was her favorite color. So now when she goes to shop, if she reaches for navy blue she closes her eyes and sees the vision of her closet and goes to another color.

• This hint helps young children who are learning to dress themselves and adults who are color-blind.

Put matching pants, shirts, socks, and even the underwear (for children) on one hanger. Getting dressed then becomes a matter of grabbing a clothing "ensemble" from the closet and putting it on. No more kids in "clown" outfits; no more beige shirts with gray suits and brown socks.

Children have parents to make "ensembles" for them. Color-blind adults need to get help from somebody who cares. Adult clothing could be numbered with laundry pens for identification and sorting, too. For example: Everything that goes with the blue suit is 1, the brown ensemble is 2, gray is 3, and so on. Of course, it's necessary to write up an index so that you don't forget and mix a 2 with a 3!

• This is a great idea for organizing children's dresser drawers. Put matching clothing in large zipper-type plastic bags and put them in the drawers. Children feel grown up selecting their own clothing, and it will all match.

• In regard to children's dresser drawers, you can help children and the sitter by labeling each drawer's front. Note the articles in each on an index card or stick-on note paper. It will save time and also a mess, since they won't have to dig through every drawer.

Storing Infrequently Worn or Seasonal Garments

• Wedding gown: After cleaning, wrap in unbleached muslin or acid-free white tissue paper, then wrap in blue tissue paper and store in a sealed box in a cool, dry place. It can last for many, many years and generations.

• Those under-the-bed boxes that are often on sale at variety stores are really convenient for storing your out-of-season clothing. They're out of the way, but still easy enough to get to when needed.

• Storing clothing in plastic garbage cans keeps it clean, off the menu of munching moths, and out of your way in your crowded closet. Lay the garbage can on its side. Start with your skirts. Roll them vertically, hem to the waistband, until you have a long, thin roll. Place the hem against the bottom of the can. If the waistband extends out of the can, that's all right.

Next fold blazers, lining side out, and roll them. Place hem side down on top of skirts. Continue with vests, slacks, dresses (fold from waist and roll).

By putting all hem ends down, the wider top portion of the can allows more room for bulk like shoulder padding in blazers. When the can is filled, stand it up and fold over skirt tops.

Place an inventory list on top of the clothes; drop in a few mothballs; if you want to, put the lid on; then seal. Store the can at the back of your closet until you need the contents again. If you store this can in an attic or dry basement, be sure to label it so that it doesn't accidentally get pitched out. You want to see your clothes again. Or place a round piece of plywood over the top of the trash can, throw a pretty tablecloth over it, and have a corner table.

It may sound unbelievable, but I got 17 skirts, 7 blazers, 4 vests, and 11 sweaters in one 30-gallon can.

- Don't ever store furs, leather, or leather-type garments in plastic bags; they need to breathe. If you need to keep them from gathering dust, cover them with old cotton pillowcases or sheets. You can also buy special "breathing" bags in notions departments for furs and leather; considering the price of such garments, a few dollars more for the proper storage bag doesn't seem like extravagance.

- Closets need to breathe too. To prevent musty odors in them, be sure they are well ventilated. Open the windows in the bedroom and open the closet doors a few hours each day.

- And NEVER put dirty clothes back into the closet. Not only will they cause odors and attract fabric-damaging insects, they won't be fresh and clean when you want them to be.

If you must hang a jacket back in the closet after wearing it and it may not be as fresh as you would like but it's still clean, turn the jacket inside out and hang it on a hanger outside the closet to allow it to breathe before putting it back into the closet.

- Always store your clothing out of direct sunlight and strong artificial light. Some of the brighter-colored fabrics and many silks can oxidize and fade.

Clothes Shopping

- Be sure to clean your closets before your next shopping trip so that you know what you have and won't buy things you don't need.

- Avoid emergency shopping whenever you can. It's a lot easier to select a special party dress or good suit that makes you look terrific if you aren't shopping for a party or job interview that's (Gasp!) tonight or tomorrow! And that's the best time to find the best bargains.

- Buy quality. Well-made clothing will fit, look, and wear better than poorly constructed clothing. Expect to pay for quality construction, but don't assume that all expensive clothing is carefully constructed. In moderate and more expensive clothing, check the following:

1. Seams should be flat and smooth. If the seams show signs of puckering when a garment is bought, they will only get worse after wear and laundering.
2. Patterns should be matched well at seams, collar, and armholes.
3. Buttonholes should be properly reinforced; buttons should be in proportion to the buttonholes and design of the garment.

4. Top stitching should be even; threads should not pull or pucker.
5. Shirt/blouse collars or cuffs that have stiff fusible interfacings should have the interfacings smoothly fused to the fabric. If they appear to be improperly fused in a new garment, they may pucker when the garment is washed, and no matter how you struggle to iron the collar or cuffs, they'll still look rumpled.
6. Trim should be sewn on properly and be of materials compatible with the garment. For example, nylon lace on a cotton blouse will surely melt at the heat you'll use to iron the cotton part of the blouse, but may be compatible with most polyester blouse fabrics. Trim such as beading should be sewn on instead of glued; glued trims don't stand up well to repeated washing or dry cleaning.
7. Check the care label to make sure that the garment can be cleaned by a process you can afford. With a few exceptions, clothing is required by the Federal Trade Commission to contain a permanent label with the care instructions. Manufacturers are required to specify only one care procedure, even when several are safe, and to warn consumers when certain garments will be damaged by certain cleaning methods.
8. Take special note of instructions for lined garments. Lining and garment fabrics may be incompatible. The result is that while the outside of the garment may be washable, the nondetachable lining must be dry cleaned.
9. Sizes vary. It's important to remember that different manufacturers and designers use different size standards. It's possible to wear size 8 or 10 in one label and still need size 12 in another label. On one particular shopping day I went from one store wearing a size 4 and 6 to three stores down, where I couldn't squeeze into even a 12. Let me tell you what that did for my psyche.

   Sometimes this inconsistency in size standards makes you feel as if you have to go home and weigh yourself to make sure you haven't gained a size. Wouldn't it be wonderful if all the manufacturers would get together and decide upon standard size charts for men's, women's and children's clothing? I would think that the time saved by not having so many gifts returned to stores would make it worthwhile.
10. Check for motion. When trying on the garment, walk around and sit down in the clothing to be sure you can move and sit comfortably in it.
11. Consider when and how often you'll wear the garment. Fabrics should be compatible with your use of the garment. Obviously, fragile fabrics are better suited to special-occasion wear than they are for everyday workaday wear and the resulting frequent laundering or cleaning. Remember, very soft or loosely woven fabrics have a tendency to pill or ball up easily if subjected to a lot of friction, such as sit-fidgeting on that office chair. Certain fabrics (like rayon) lose their pleats quickly. Pleated fabrics can be expensive to dry clean, since most cleaners have cost-per-pleat rates. Lightweight wools and jerseys keep their shape and need little ironing. They make good traveling clothes.

• When you buy new clothes, note a description of the garment on the label and then save the tags in a file, envelope, shoe box, whatever, so that you can refer to them when you need to launder or dry-clean the garments.

• When shopping for a particular garment to match something that is in your closet, don't take a chance on guessing what color is right. Snip a very tiny piece of fabric from an inside seam and carry this with you to find a perfect match.

• When you are looking at a very expensive garment or even an inexpensive one, figure it on a cost-per-wearing basis. If you are going to buy the perfect smashing black dress, blue blazer, or winter coat, if you wear the garment for 4 to 5 years and wear it 10 to 20 times in a season, even if it's a very expensive garment, the cost per wearing breaks down to less than $10 per wearing to even $5 per wearing. However, if you are buying a nice little shell or tee to wear with shorts in the summertime and are going to wear it only three times or so, it isn't worth spending more than $50 dollars on.

Personal Tips

Organizing Yourself

• Most of the well-organized people I know make lists. They use calendars, notebooks, bulletin boards, whatever works to keep track of the things they need to do. Writing it all down means never having to say, "I'm sorry, I forgot."

• Keep a small 3″ × 5″ memo book in your purse or pocket and write down whatever you need to remember. For example, if someone at a meeting asks you a question, you can call back with the answer if you have written the question and the person's phone number in the notebook. You can scribble the names of people you have just met or bits of information you might need in the future into the notebook, and then you won't forget names and facts.

Label these notebooks with the dates they were carried, such as June–December 1988, and then keep them so that you'll have all sorts of phone numbers and information handy when you need it.

• Spiral spelling test notebooks sold in school supplies sections are good for "To-Do" lists. They are about half the width of a secretary's notebook and are lined and numbered. If you have access to a heavy-duty paper cutter, you can cut a secretary's notebook in half lengthwise to make a To-Do list notebook.

• Instead of a memo book, you can buy a spiral pack of 3" × 5" index cards and use it like the memo book, but the advantage is that you can remove the cards from the spiral pack and file them in an index card file box.

• Believe me, if you have trouble remembering the names of people you meet at business functions, the little memo book is a wonderful aid. Writing down any information puts it more firmly into your brain's file cabinet, and if your brain is not recording that day, you can look up your notes anytime. I've even taken out my notebook in the rest room and written down the names of the people seated at my lunch table so that they will get engraved on a brain cell somewhere in my head.

• When you are given business cards at various functions, write down on the back of the card the function and the date and any other tips that identify the owner of the business card. Otherwise, you end up with a pile of business cards in a desk drawer that don't mean a thing to you.

• Keep track of birthdays and anniversaries by writing into your calendar all the important days at the beginning of the year. Then don't forget to check it at the beginning and middle of each month to make sure you'll get the card or gift bought in time.

• Some people buy greeting cards and address them in bunches every four months or so, then put the pack of cards into their bill-paying organizers (the accordion fold envelopes that have space for each month) so they are ready to go at the beginning of the month when the bills are paid. It's probably better to mail greetings early than not at all.

• One problem with paper is that you can accumulate so much of it that eventually you are buried in an avalanche of the stuff. Try to handle everything only once. Read your junk mail if it seems appealing, then throw it out. Read your bills and put them into whatever system you have for paying them. Read personal letters and answer them, or put them where they will get answered on your letter writing day.

• If you are constantly losing things right there in your own house, you have accumulated too much space-hogging, closet-cramming, shelf-sagging, aggravation-causing plain old and usually useless stuff. On a day when you are in a good mood to organize (or a bad mood that makes you want to throw things out), start tossing useless stuff into the trash or give it away to charity or anyone you know that might have a use for it. This applies to excess paper, books, magazines, clothing, whatever is your personal compulsion to collect.

Letter Writing

• If you don't have a postal scale and think your letter weighs more than one ounce, here's a "Rube Goldberg" scale to weigh envelopes that really works.
   Balance a one-foot ruler on a pencil, in the middle, at the six-inch mark. Place the letter on the ruler, centered at nine inches, and a stack of five quarters (which weighs one ounce) centered at three inches. The quarters side will stay down if the letter is lighter than an ounce.

• You can write letters in secretary's notebooks whenever you are waiting someplace, such as at the beauty or barber shop, the doctor's office, in the car when you pick up children, and so forth. A tablet makes lap writing easy, and the people who care about you don't care if you have fancy stationery. When you are occupied, the waiting time seem shorter, and besides, you've used time that would otherwise be wasted. (Unless, of course, you're reading a good book—then the waiting time is never wasted!)

• If you do a lot of letter writing, you can keep track of who owes whom a letter if you make a list of those to whom you frequently write. Then, note the date you've received a letter from a person in black ink and the date you answered the letter in red ink. You can tell at a glance if you owe a letter.

• Use a highlighter pen to mark the parts of a letter that you need to answer or comment on.

• When you receive a letter, address an envelope to the sender immediately and put some stationery in it. Then you can take the envelope with you to places where you'll have waiting and letter writing time. Also, having the envelope stamped and addressed removes that stumbling block to writing for some people.

• Keep envelopes addressed to people you write to frequently so that you can insert newspaper clippings and cartoons that you think will interest that person. Then, when you are ready to write a letter, you'll have the clippings where they belong, ready to go.

• If you don't have time to write more than a short note, the clippings will show that at least you are often thinking about the recipient of your note.

• If your family is scattered throughout the country, put together a family newspaper, with each member contributing at least one article to it. Have one person in charge of gathering the information and getting it copied. Saving these newspapers in a scrapbook can provide a family history for generations to come.

• The newspaper could be compiled at Thanksgiving time, with everyone writing what they are thankful for in the past year, and then mailed so each member receives a copy at Christmas time to reflect upon as the new year approaches.

• If you and your siblings are all too involved with children, church, PTA, and work, keep a diary and send the information to each other at year's end. Knowing you are taking care of your letter writing at the same time is good incentive for keeping a diary, which is also a nice, sentimental family history. If you have a computer, keeping a diary on disk and making printouts is easy.

• Instead of writing, send pictures to small children, cut out of magazines and newspapers or hand drawn even if they are stick people.

• Don't forget to write children's names and addresses down when sending off for freebies or refunds. Children love to receive free things like that. Who doesn't?

Bill Paying

• Since paying your bills on time gets you lower rates, or at least avoids penalties for overdue payments, you need to have a bill paying system.
    Some people pay their bills as soon as they arrive; others pay on the first and fifteenth of the month.
    Some people throw their bills into a drawer and forget about them entirely. These people are called "the defendant" when they are summoned to small claims court!

• Keep track of when bills are to be paid by noting due days on a monthly or yearly calendar.

• One way to keep track of bills is to fill a three-ring notebook with pocket folders. Each month place all bills and receipts in designated pockets (car, insurance, house payments, utilities) and write the check number on the bill it was written for. You can also note interest paid, all income, and payments on the pocket folders so that at the end of the year at tax time you have all the information handy. After you have paid your taxes, you can tie up the notebook, clearly marked with what is inside and the year on it, and store it in a safe place.

• Another system would be to keep all unpaid bills in one folder, along with a list of each bill, the due date, and amount. As each bill is paid, it gets crossed off the list; the receipts, marked with check numbers and any other important information, are filed in folders designated for specific categories, such as utilities, house payments, and car.

• If you enter the phone number of the billing company into your check register, it will be handy if you have to call about a payment problem.

• Don't put messages on the outside of envelopes. Many businesses open envelopes with automated systems, so if you write messages on the outside of envelopes, they are not likely to be seen. Put messages on the bill or a separate piece of paper. Write address changes in bold letters or highlight them.

• Since automated envelope opening systems process as many as 40 or 45 letters per minute, coins or cash can actually fly out of the envelopes as they go through the opening machines. If you must send coins or cash through the mail, tape coins on the bill or a piece of paper with proper identification and write on the bill how much cash you have enclosed. Checks or money orders are, of course, much safer.

• When you send checks through the mail and wrap them in blank paper, it may slow up processing in automated systems. It's assumed that there is correspondence in the envelope, and therefore it is sent to a place other than where checks and bills go.

• If someone else is paying a bill for you, using their personal check, be sure YOUR name and account number are included for proper crediting.

• When you mail order or pay magazine subscriptions, put your code number, found on the mailing label, usually above your name, on your check for added identification.

• If your system is to do all of your letter writing, bill paying, and mail ordering in one session, you can make sure all the envelopes that need checks get them if you fold the sealing flap backward against the front of the envelope and write the required amount of money, if any, on the inside of the flap. Then, when you are finished, you can easily sort the envelopes and see which ones need checks and for how much.

• Make photocopies of all your credit cards. Put one copy in a safe place, such as a bank safety deposit box, keep one at home, and take one with you when you travel for quick reference in case you lose your wallet or have it stolen. (Obviously, you shouldn't keep the copy in your wallet!) Keeping a photocopy of all your credit cards and their numbers in your desk drawer is handy for catalog phone ordering and other bill paying.

I'm so organized I even have one of my major credit card numbers memorized, which means that I don't have to go searching for it when I find something in a mail-order catalog with an 800 number!

Keeping Yourself Healthy

Few of us can afford a personal live-in health counselor, and Mother usually gives up after you leave home, so here's a section designed to remind you that you need to take care of yourself.

Exercising

• Pick an activity and a time of day that suits you and your schedule so that you won't be tempted to skip your sessions.

• Don't exercise strenuously in hot, humid weather or within two hours after eating, because heat and digestion make heavy demands on your circulatory system. Combining these demands with exercise can be too much of an overload on your body.

• Don't wear rubberized or plastic clothing; these garments interfere with perspiration evaporation and can make your body temperature rise to dangerous levels.

• Generally, you should wear lighter clothes than the temperature would usually indicate, because exercise makes body heat. Wear light-colored clothing to reflect sun rays in the summer and dark clothing in winter.

• Warm-up and cool-down need to be a part of your exercise program so that your body gradually adjusts to starting and stopping activities.

Warm-up can be 5 to 10 minutes of walking, slow jogging, knee lifts, arm circles, or trunk rotations.

Cool-down can be 5 to 10 minutes of slow walking or low-level exercise combined with stretching.

• Walk instead of drive whenever you can. Walk up steps instead of taking the elevator. Park your car at the edge of the lot so that you will have a greater distance to walk to your destination.

• Get a dog and walk it. You can't ignore a dog that desperately needs to explore the neighborhood and inspect its trees and fire hydrants.

• Get a custom program designed by a personal trainer, join an exercise group, or get involved with a spa, community center, or YMCA or YWCA. If you develop an exercise program that you really like, you are less likely to get bored and quit.

• If you use exercise video tapes and find that jogging in place on your floor jars your joints too much, try doing the jogging phases of the tape on a mini-trampoline. A small, sturdy mini-trampoline can cost under $50, and they are often on sale. Or try low-impact aerobics.

• A medium-size adult who doesn't want to diet needs to walk more than 30 miles to burn up 3,500 calories (the equivalent of one pound of fat). If you walk one mile every day for 30 days, and don't eat any more or less food than you do in your regular diet, you can burn up one pound of fat.

• If you want to gain weight, you need to consume 100 calories a day beyond what your body needs, and then you will gain about 10 pounds in a year. However, if you want to take those 10 pounds off and keep them off, 30 minutes of moderate exercise daily will do the trick.

• Remember that exercise builds muscle tissue, which weighs more than fat, so if you are involved in a regular exercise program, your scale may not be the best way to determine if you are "fat." The ratio of body fat to muscle is the determining factor. Are your clothes tight or loose?

• When you are dieting, don't totally deny yourself the pleasure of eating your favorite foods. Just eat less of them and learn to view them as occasional treats instead of tempting, forbidden delicacies.

Eating Right

Eating right, according to the U.S. Departments of Agriculture and Health and Human Services, means eating a variety of foods; eating enough starch and fiber; drinking alcoholic beverages in moderation; maintaining your desirable weight; avoiding too much fat, saturated fat, and cholesterol; avoiding too much sugar; and avoiding too much sodium.

Here's some "food for thought" if you are planning to adopt healthier eating patterns.

• A healthy diet will include 20 to 30 grams of dietary fiber, have only 30 percent of its calories in fat, and contain a variety of vitamin- and mineral-rich fruits and vegetables.

• The typical American diet contains about 40 percent fat, despite the warning that a diet of 30 percent (or less) is healthier. It is sad that 540,000 people die each year in this country from cardiovascular disease, including heart attacks and strokes.

Cholesterol in Our Diets

The newest studies by the National Heart, Lung and Blood Institute say that cholesterol levels of 200 or below are desirable. People whose levels are 200 to 239 are considered borderline and require annual testing. People whose levels are 240 or more are considered high risk, and about 40 million Americans are in this category.

• The best way to reduce your cholesterol level is to reduce the animal fat in your diet. Meat, poultry, seafood, and dairy products contain cholesterol. Although there is no cholesterol in vegetables, fruits, cereals, and grains, these foods can contain certain saturated fats that stimulate the liver to produce cholesterol. Coconut, palm, and palm kernel oils have the same effect on your cholesterol level as animal fat and should be avoided. Read labels on packaged foods carefully to learn the fat source and content of products. You will be amazed!

• The American Heart Association recommends 300 mg (milligrams) a day as a healthy cholesterol intake.

Here's how to read labels according the Food and Drug Administration's food labeling regulations for defining cholesterol levels in food:

"Cholesterol Free" means one serving contains less than 2 mg of cholesterol.

"Low Cholesterol" means one serving contains less than 20 mg.

"Reduced Cholesterol" means one serving has at least 75 percent less cholesterol than the food it is replacing.

• Here are five ways to avoid excess fat, saturated, fats and cholesterol in your diet:

1. When choosing your protein sources, eat lean meat, fish, poultry, and dry beans and peas.
2. Trim the fat from meat and take the skin off poultry. Don't add fatty sauces.
3. Go easy on eating egg yolks and organ meats, and when you go to the dairy case, buy skim or low-fat milk and milk products.
4. Avoid fats and oils, especially those high in saturated fat, such as butter, cream, lard, hydrogenated (solid) shortenings and margarines, and foods with palm and coconut oils.
5. Get into the habit of broiling, baking, or boiling instead of frying, and limit fatty foods, such as those which are breaded and deep-fried.

A few simple changes like using skim milk instead of cream in your coffee or using a half of a pat of butter or margarine instead of a full pat are enough to make a difference in your diet. It only takes a little thought to eat as well as you can and help improve your life.

Quality Protein Combinations

Animal proteins are considered "high-quality proteins" and are readily available to the body when eaten. Plant protein sources are considered "lower-quality" proteins, because certain amino acids are either missing or not in sufficient quantities for the body's use. However, when high-quality protein foods are teamed with lower-quality protein foods, the foods are usable in the body. When you are following a vegetarian diet or combining lower- and high-quality proteins, you need to eat the food combinations at the same time so that the foods work as a team in the body.

• If you are combining animal proteins with grains, eat one of the following: a beef taco, milk with breakfast cereal, cheese pizza, a cheese sandwich, meat with Oriental vegetables and rice, milk with rice pudding, tuna with rice casserole, cheese with macaroni.

• If you are combining animal proteins with legumes, eat cheese with bean stew, chili con carne with beans, ham with split-pea soup.

• If you are combining animal proteins with seeds, eat meat with Oriental vegetables and nuts.

• If you follow a vegetarian diet (one with no animal proteins), you can get usable protein in your diet if you combine plant proteins with legumes and grains or legumes with seeds.

• Some combinations of plant proteins with legumes and grains are: baked beans with brown bread, blackeye peas with rice, beans with tortilla or cornbread (one of my favorites!), beans with barley soup, lima beans with corn (succotash), beans with pasta, peanut butter sandwich, refried beans with rice.

Salt

We need sodium in our diets for various body functions, but having certain medical problems such as cardiovascular disease, edema (swelling), hypertension, and kidney disease usually brings on a doctor's recommendation to lower salt intake. Here's how to read labels according the U.S. Food and Drug Administration's food labeling regulations:

"Sodium Free" means one serving has less than 5 mg of sodium.

"Very Low Sodium" means one serving has less than 35 mg of sodium.

"Low Sodium" means one serving has less than 140 mg of sodium.

"Reduced Sodium" means one serving has at least 75 percent less sodium than the food being replaced by this product.

• To decrease the amount of salt/sodium in your diet:

Flavor foods with herbs, spices, lemon juice.
Use garlic and onion powders instead of garlic and onion salts.

• "Heloisey"-style hints to help you reduce your salt intake:

1. Remove the salt shaker from the table.
2. Switch the tops on the salt shaker and the pepper shaker.
3. Combine half sodium substitute (i.e., salt substitute) and half salt.

Sugar

• To avoid eating too much sugar, eat fresh fruits or fruits processed with light or no syrup instead of "heavy" syrup, and avoid soft drinks, candies, cakes, and cookies.

• Sugar has many different names, but by any name the ingredient is the same—sugar. Some of sugar's aliases are sucrose, glucose, maltose, dextrose, lactose, fructose, syrup, and honey. Whether it's raw sugar, brown sugar, or white sugar, it's still sugar.

Keeping these names in mind, read the labels carefully; you will be absolutely shocked that some of the products you thought were all natural, with no sugar, actually do contain some form of sugar.

Fiber

• If you are on a weight-control or weight-loss diet, remember that starches and fiber have about half as many calories as fats, and fiber makes you feel full. High-fiber foods can also help reduce constipation, diverticular diseases, and some types of "irritable bowel syndrome."

Beverages

• Alcoholic beverages are high in calories but low in nutrition. To lose weight, try cutting out all alcohol for a month or two—you may be surprised at your weight loss.

• The National Institute on Alcohol Abuse and Alcoholism warns pregnant women not to use alcohol, because it can cause problems in pregnancy and birth defects in babies.

• NEVER DRINK AND DRIVE!

If You Need to Lose Weight

• Before eating anything, ask yourself if you really want it.

• Keep a food diary.

• Plan and set up a time schedule for meals and snacks.

• Buy a calorie book and record the calories in everything eaten.

• Measure all foods to check portion sizes.

• Drink at least one glass of water before eating. (If you are bored with water, add a slice of lemon, lime, or orange to it, or buy mineral waters as a treat.)

• Use smaller plates so smaller portions look larger. (This is especially true at buffets, where we tend to load up to fill the plate instead of taking just what we normally eat.)

• Divide servings in half, so you can have a second meal.

• Keep lower-calorie foods, like fruit and vegetables, for snacks in the most visible place in your fridge.

• Keep on hand only foods that require some preparation to make snacking a chore.

• Arrange home activities so that you don't pass through the kitchen so often.

• Find non-food ways to reward yourself. (New clothes when you get to a smaller size. A movie or other entertainment instead of an ice-cream cone.)

• Clear the table after each course.

• Throw leftover food away, give it away, or freeze it immediately. (This is especially helpful when you have a party and the leftovers are both extremely tempting and extremely high in calories!)

• Decide what you will order at the restaurant before you enter. (If you planned to order soup and salad, don't go batty when you see a "special" that will quadruple your calorie intake plans.)

• Share a serving with someone else. (Some restaurant pasta entrees are so large they serve two anyhow! Sometimes the pasta appetizer is enough for a meal.)

• Cook with a toothpick in your mouth. (But don't forget you have it there and then eat it! You need fiber, but not such large, pointy pieces!)

• Chew each bite thoroughly before swallowing. (Some people like to count bites and chew each bite a certain number of times.)

• Eat foods high in fiber. They require more chewing and make you feel fuller.

• Most sources say that you are considered "mildly obese" if you are a man with 25 percent body fat or a woman with 30 percent body fat, and are 20 to 40 percent over your ideal weight. For example, a medium-frame 5'4" woman, whose ideal eight is 127 to 141 pounds (according to the 1983 Metropolitan Height and Weight Tables), would be mildly obese if she were 25 to 55 pounds over that weight. Such a person can be treated for obesity by lay persons trained in weight control.

You are considered "moderately obese" if you are 40 to 100 percent over your ideal weight. That same 5'4" woman would be moderately obese if she were 56 to 140 pounds over her ideal weight. Such a person needs treatment by health professionals, and the treatment should include behavior modification, diet, and physical activity.

You are considered "severely obese" if you are more than 100 percent above your ideal weight. A severely obese 5'4" woman could weigh more than 140 pounds above her ideal weight. She should be under the care of a health professional, because medical complications almost always occur in such advanced obesity.

Your Skin

Dermatologists have been telling us for years that tanning causes skin cancer and wrinkles. They say that skin cancer cases have increased 1,200 percent since the 1930s, when tanning came into fashion.

In my *Heloise's Beauty Book,* I wrote that not all the "leathernecks" are in the U.S. Marine Corps; many of them are on the golf course and other places where necks get exposed to the sun regularly.

Here are a few kitchen remedies for skin conditions.

• Lemon juice is a safe skin bleach; apply to hands, elbows, knees, and so on, and leave it on for about 15 minutes. Wash and apply your favorite lotion.

• My favorite facial is the Heloise Honey Facial:

After I clean and steam my face, I apply honey and then leave it on for two or three minutes until it's sticky (some people like to leave it on for 10 minutes). Then I press in and snap out my fingers on my face—but gently! I always avoid the areas around my eyes, because that skin is more sensitive than the rest of the face. I remove the honey with a warm, wet towel or washcloth.

Honey cleans out pores, so they seem to shrink and you can more easily get blackheads out.

• Steaming your face before beginning a facial is a tip you'll get from most cosmetologists. But you don't need to rush out and buy a steamer. (A doctor told me that steamers tend to harbor bacteria and mold spores, so when you are steaming, you are also inhaling bacteria and mold spores—not a good idea, to say the least!)

Just pour hot water into a basin, tent a towel over your head, then hold your face over the water for about five minutes. You can also dip a washcloth into hot water and apply it to your face, dipping and redipping for about five minutes.

• You can use the washcloth technique while you are soaking in the tub. You can also give yourself a facial while you are soaking in the tub.

• Moisturize your skin after treatments. Moisturizers don't actually add anything to your skin; they trap the moisture in it so that it doesn't dry out, plumping up the skin cells.

The two heavy-duty, industrial-strength moisturizers are petroleum jelly and lanolin, and you'll find them in most commercial moisturizers. Other moisturizers are mineral oil, urea, stearic or lactic acid, and squalene (from shark liver oil). Urea, lactic acid, and squalene are also found in human skin and sweat. Lanolin is a very good moisturizing oil, but many dermatologists warn acne-prone people to avoid lanolin because it can cause blemishes to break out.

(And we all know when skin blemishes erupt: three minutes before your first date with someone you've drooled over for eons, on your wedding day, whenever you have an appointment with a professional photographer, and need I add more? Skin really is a mirror of our health and emotions.)

• Generally, you care for your skin by:

1. Cleaning it properly according to whether it's dry, oily, or combination skin.
2. Removing dead skin cells with washcloths, puffs, or scrubs.
3. Applying moisturizers immediately after washing to keep surface moisture from evaporating.
4. Replenishing moisture throughout the day. (I like to spritz my skin frequently with mineral water during the day.) I also wear sunscreen at all times to protect my skin from harmful rays.

• If your hands and feet get very dry and chapped, before bedtime apply olive oil or petroleum jelly, put on cotton gloves or socks for your feet, and your hands and feet will soften and be soothed overnight.

• If you have sore, red, rough, blemished, irritated skin, or if you notice any change in a mole or freckle or other skin condition changes, see a dermatologist.

If You Still Smoke

If you smoke, the U.S. Surgeon General, the American Cancer Society, the American Heart Association, the American Lung Association, and umpteen other health associations, plus the people who love you and Heloise all recommend that you quit.

• According to statistics, the number of smokers is declining overall. But the same statistics show that women are not giving up as easily. Most women are afraid to quit smoking because they are afraid that they will gain weight.

When you consider the way smoking causes wrinkles and all the wrinkle creams women buy, you'd think that women would want to quit more than they do. If you don't believe that smokers are more wrinkled, just look at someone who's over 40 and who's been smoking for 20 or more years and compare that person's face with a non-smoker's face.

As this is being written, the U.S. Surgeon General, C. Everett Koop, has declared that nicotine is as addicting as cocaine and heroin, and that most smokers kick the habit five times before they actually succeed. But you can't succeed at all if you don't try. Give yourself a break; break the habit.

Here are some tips from various sources to help you.

• You don't have to gain weight when you quit smoking. Try cutting 100 calories from your diet daily and exercising enough to burn about 50 calories. The exercise will help you feel less tense too.

• Many people crave sweets when they quit smoking. Try using artificial sweeteners and, to feel full, eat high-fiber breads and cereals.

• Talk to your doctor about prescribing nicotine gum. It's been very effective when follow-up care and behavior modification techniques are used.

• Pharmaceutical companies are researching slow-release adhesive patches, aerosol inhalers, nasal sprays, and other medications, such as antidepressants, to help ease smokers' withdrawal symptoms. The drug companies estimate that 85 percent of the 50 million smokers in this country want to quit but that it will be several years before their researched products will get to the market-place.

• Hypnosis, according to some researchers, works about 15 percent of the time. Acupuncture has not been very effective, the research shows.

• Medical sources estimate that only about 25 percent of people can stop smoking without a program. The people who are most likely to quit and stay off tobacco are those who are quitting for themselves (to avoid health consequences, to save money), and those who are most likely to fail are those who are trying to please someone else or are personality types who must have instant results. You gotta want to do it! And you gotta keep at it!

• The American Cancer Society has a stop-smoking program that has helped many smokers to quit. The society is listed in the phone book. A call to them could be the most important call you ever make.

Having a Healthy Smile—Dental Health

• Brush and floss thoroughly at least once daily and after meals when you can.

• To make sure you are brushing and flossing properly, you can buy disclosing tablets at the drugstore. Chew these tablets after you brush, then rinse and spit out the excess. The plaque (gooey bacteria-laden substance that sticks to your teeth) that you have missed with your toothbrush will be bright red. This color isn't permanent, it's just a harmless vegetable dye. Brush again to remove the stain. Using disclosing tablets is especially effective with children when you are teaching them how to get into all the corners of the mouth.

• Here are the signs of tooth decay that should send you rushing to your dentist:

1. If a tooth is sensitive to heat, cold, and sweets.
2. If chewing causes pain.
3. If there is swelling or drainage at or below the gum line.
4. If you see a brown spot on a tooth.
5. If you have pain in the mouth or sinus trouble that doesn't go away.

• Tooth decay isn't the only way you lose permanent teeth. Did you know that three out of four people older than 35 have periodontal disease? Gum disease causes 70 percent of all tooth loss. And the real shocker is that more than half of all Americans older than age 18 have at least the early stages of gum disease; even 5- and 6-year-olds have it!

Here are the warning signs of periodontal (gum) disease:

1. Bleeding gums—if your gums bleed when you brush your teeth, it's not normal; you should see a dentist even if you don't feel pain.
2. Gums that are red, swollen, or tender.
3. Gums that have pulled away from the teeth.
4. Pus coming out from between the teeth and gums if you press your gums.
5. Loose or separating permanent teeth.
6. Your teeth fit together differently when you bite.
7. Your partial dentures or other dental appliances don't fit as they did previously.
8. Bad breath.

• Orthodontics isn't just for children anymore; adults can get their teeth straightened too, in many cases, and the old "metal mouth" look isn't always mandatory. Some people can have braces attached to the backs of the teeth.

Those Sneezy, Wheezy Days with Allergies

Those of us who suffer from allergies are the darlings of the advertising world. We consume antihistamines and decongestants, and nobody knows how many forests have been destroyed to produce the paper pulp for our nose tissues.

Here are some helps for allergy sufferers.

• See a doctor. Your allergist has a whole new battery of tests and medications to help you. Using some of the new inhalants before going where the pollen is will help a lot, and some of the new antihistamines, available by prescription, won't make you drowsy.

• Get rid of the allergens when you can. Cut your grass before it goes to pollination and seed; wear a mask when you mow the lawn to keep from inhaling the dust and pollen the mower is throwing into the air; find out when your town's peak pollen times are and stay indoors during those times; shower and shampoo immediately after working or playing outdoors to get pollen off your skin and out of your hair.

• When bedding is hung outside to air, pollen flying around in the air gets on it and is brought indoors with it to irritate you when you try to sleep in that "fresh" bed. Use a clothes dryer instead of hanging clothes and bedding outside.

• Often, people find out that they are allergic to feathers when they have a chance to sleep away from home on polyester-filled or foam rubber pillows.

• It's not uncommon to be allergic to dust mites, which live in carpets and furniture. Dry air (winter heat and summer air-conditioning) controls these mites.

• Occasionally, allergy-prone people will get some relief if the air-conditioning is not colder than 70 degrees.

• If you are sensitive to molds, you may be aggravating your allergies when you turn on your car air conditioner. Many car air conditioners are contaminated with mold spores, and most of them blast out at you when you turn on the air conditioner. If you run the air conditioner with the vent closed and your car windows open for a short time (better with you out of the car), you may get relief. You can have your air conditioner cleaned out at some car dealers and service centers.

• If you are allergic to molds, say goodbye to "real house plants," because molds grow in their soil and on their pots. If you replace your real plants with fake silk ones, don't forget to dust them, because you may be allergic to dust too.

• It's better to vacuum up dust and pollen and all the other stuff floating around and landing on the furniture if you have allergy sufferers in the house. A feather duster just throws the dust someplace else, where the poor allergy person can breathe it in just as well as if it were still on the tops of furniture!

• Yes, you can be allergic to pet dander, and yes, pets bring pollen into the house on their fur, but, like other animal lovers, I don't want to even think about getting rid of pets!

(However, if you have someone living in the house who becomes seriously ill with asthma or has other serious allergy problems from animals, you may have to consider that sad possibility.)

• If you have skin allergies, work with your allergist to find out if it's fabrics, metals (in jewelry), plants, or whatever, and then eliminate whatever you can. I know lots of people who are allergic to fabrics that contain even small percentages of wool, linen, or ramie, and many dyes can also irritate the allergy-prone skin.

The Eyes Have It

• Never share eye makeup and don't try on other people's glasses. These are ways to transmit eye diseases and infections. Some cosmetologists even say you should use a fresh cotton ball for each eye when you are removing eye makeup to avoid transferring bacteria from one eye to the other.

• Remove eye makeup by patting cleanser on closed eyelids and lashes; wipe lightly with a damp, natural sponge or soft cotton. Some of the new waterproof mascaras will come off with soap and water. You can remove eye makeup with mineral oil, petroleum jelly, or baby oil, all of which are less expensive than commercial preparations.

• Remember that nail polish ingredients can irritate eyes. When you are putting yourself together, wait until your nail polish is completely dry before you start on your face.

• Soothe tired eyes by covering them with two cold slices of cucumber or cold used tea bags while you take a 15-minute rest.

Sunglasses

So much is written about the need to protect your eyes from ultraviolet radiation that most of us know we need to protect our eyes. Eye doctors say that just about everybody needs protection in the summertime, and people who work outdoors may need protection no matter what season it is.

• Lenses should be labeled to say they meet American National Standards Institute Z80.3 standard, which means they block 95 percent of the radiation.

• Polarizing lenses cut the sun's glare, but some people find them distracting because they let you see stress patterns in some types of glass.

• Photochromic lenses darken in sunlight and lighten indoors, and although this is convenient, they may not clear completely indoors—a problem for people who have weak vision and need extra light.

• Here's a quick test for nonprescription sunglasses:

Hold the glasses at arm's length and look through them at both vertical and horizontal straight lines in the distance, such as window frames or the edges of a door.
Slowly move the lens back and forth across the line. If the line distorts, don't buy the glasses.
Also check for evenly applied color. If the lenses are darker at the top and shaded so that they are lighter at the bottom, be sure the shading is gradual.

Eyeglasses

• Getting tinted lenses in your glasses can cover a multitude of "sins," not to mention wrinkles.

• You can clean glass lenses with a drop of vinegar (Yes, vinegar again!), but don't use it on plastic lenses. Most glass or plastic lenses will come clean if you clean them with warm water and dry them with a lint-free cloth. Many instructions for glasses say not to use tissue on plastic lenses, because it causes fine scratches.

• Scratched eyeglass lenses are annoying. Try making a creamy paste of talcum powder and water in a small dish. Then rub the paste gently on both sides of the lenses and wipe it off. The talc will polish tiny scratches without making new ones.

• Avoid scratches by never putting your glasses down on their lenses. Either keep them in their case or set them so that they rest upside down on the glasses frame.

• If you are one of those unlucky souls who can't find your glasses without your glasses, try taping an eyeglass case to your nightstand or table beside your bed or wherever you take off your glasses, and get into the habit of putting them into it. Or nail a holder to the wall. I know people who have stepped on their glasses trying to find them, and I can't think of anything more inconvenient than broken glasses, can you?

Contact Lenses

Contact lenses are wonderful inventions, but a lot of my mail is about losing and finding them. It's almost as if contact lenses were made to be lost! Paying the extra money for lens insurance when you first buy your contact lenses can be a real money saver if you're the kind who loses them often.

Here are some tips that may work for hard and soft contact lens wearers.

• Try using a small spice or herb jar with a perforated plastic lid to wash lenses so that when you drain the water out, it goes through the perforations and the lenses do not. You can rinse in the same type of container. No more lenses down the drain.

• Put a towel or washcloth in the sink before you start to clean your lenses so that they don't get washed away.

• If your lens goes down the drain, you might be able to rescue it by wrapping absorbent cotton around the end of a long-handled screwdriver, wooden spoon, and so on, and then poking it as far down the drain as it will go. You might get lucky and the lens might stick to the cotton.

• If you drop a lens on the floor or on furniture, try covering the end of your vacuum cleaner nozzle with nylon net or pantyhose. You may be able to vacuum it up.

• Sometimes, if you shine a flashlight around where you think you dropped the lens, it will reflect the light and that tiny sparkle will guide you to your lens. You'll get better reflection sometimes if you place the flashlight on the floor and roll it instead of aiming the light at the floor from a standing position.

Choosing the Right Type of Contact Lense

• If you are very athletic, need extremely sharp vision for your job, do a lot of camping and traveling, and if you must have good vision the moment you wake up, extended-wear lenses may be for you. However, don't be overly optimistic about them. When the maximum time is given for keeping them in between cleanings, it means just that—maximum. You may have to remove your extended-wear lenses more often than the standard time. Ask your doctor for advice and then follow it to avoid irritation, infections, and damage to your precious eyes.

• In addition to the cost, your vision problem, lens prescription, life-style, and personality determine the type of contact lenses right for you. For example, impatient people do better with soft lenses, because they have the shortest adaptation period. Careful, reliable people will be able to deal with the extra care and frequent office visits required with extended-wear lenses.

Talk to your optometrist about the many different types of lenses before you make a choice.

The Taco Test for Determining If Lenses Are Backward

• When putting in your soft contact lens and it is on your index finger, you can make sure the lens isn't backward by bringing the edges together.
If the folded lens looks like a taco, you're holding it the right way. If it flares outward or looks like a bow tie, the lens is turned inside out.

Make Yourself Comfortable

Several of these tips are from the Arthritis Foundation and are designed to help those who suffer from this painful disease, but they can be used by any comfort seeker.

• Take the soft (pink or gray) foam rubber "tube" off a curler and put it on a pencil or pen for comfortable writing. This is such a good tip you may want to buy some curlers just for the foam, even if you never use them on your hair. They can also be put on nail files, toothbrushes, mascara wands, and eye pencils.

• Lengths of soft foam rubber insulator tubes normally used to cover outdoor pipes in the winter can be wrapped around rake, broom, mop, and vacuum cleaner handles and then held on with rubber bands or duct tape to make them easier to hold. These tubes are usually dark gray, in about four-foot lengths, and sold in hardware stores. They are slit for easy wrapping and can be cut with ordinary scissors.

• Put an adhesive bandage over the place rubbed by your scissors when you cut heavy fabric before it gets red and you get a blister.

• Tape a small piece of soft foam rubber on any finger or spot that gets abused, such as your thumb if you type a lot at a typewriter or computer.

• Save your fingernails and your temper—use a "church key" type of can opener to pry lids or poke holes in cardboard boxes.

• Quick-mend a split or torn fingernail with a drop of fast-drying glue. It'll hold until the damaged part of your fingernail grows out. If you need to strengthen the tear, glue on torn bits of white tissue paper—a smaller piece covered by a larger piece—and then file the paper to conform to your nail after the glue dries. Polish if you want to cover the mend.

• Hair tangled? Mix up some creme rinse in a "spritz bottle" and spritz those snarls before trying to comb them out.

• If you have arthritis or other hand problems, buy a plastic handle made for spray paint cans at the hardware store and use it on other household spray cans, such as cleaners, furniture polish, fabric finish, or hair spray.

• Wrapping wide rubber bands around doorknobs will give you a better grip on them. They can also be wrapped around jar lids for easier opening.

• Wrap duct or masking tape around a paring knife handle until it's fat enough for a good grip.

• No shaving cream? Don't scrape your skin; substitute crème rinse or shampoo. Apply them to wet skin.

• If you can't bend over to reach your legs when you are shaving them, tape your razor to a wooden dowel long enough to suit your needs.

• If you have to wear a soft cervical collar after a neck injury, you can keep it cleaner by wrapping it in knee-high stockings (or a pantyhose leg); they won't interfere with the self-gripping tape closure like a silk scarf will. And, since stockings come in different colors, you can coordinate them with what you wear.

Also, you can decorate the collar even more with a pin or silk flower. Anyone who's ever worn one for a long time knows how dreary you begin to feel, and decorating the collar actually lifts your spirits a bit.

First Aid for Poisoning

With so many chemical compounds stored in our homes, the danger of poisoning is very real, because many of them can have serious poisonous effects if they are consumed or inhaled, or if they come in contact with your skin.

Syrup of Ipecac and Epsom Salts

It's a good idea to keep syrup of ipecac, to induce vomiting, and epsom salts, which has laxative action, in your medicine cabinet for emergencies.

CAUTION: You shouldn't use either one unless you first check with the Poison Control Center or your doctor, because different poisons are dealt with differently. ALWAYS follow the directions given you for use of poison remedies.

The Poison Control Center Number

• If you have a programmable phone, put the Poison Control Center's number into it, and color the button red with a felt-tip marker.

• If you don't, put the number on a label and stick it on your phone. Each region has a different Poison Control number. Your region's Poison Control Center number may be listed inside the phone book cover or may be listed in the white or Yellow Pages. You can also get your region's toll-free number by calling the information number: 1-800-555-1212. Get the number today; don't wait until you have an emergency and are either sick or in a state of panic!

Teach children where the Poison Control Center phone number is and show them how to dial the number. Be sure to explain to them that it is not a game.

Common Potentially Poisonous Household Products

Here's a list of some common household products and the poisoning symptoms they can produce.

1. Cleaning products
   Ammonia, bleach, dish-washer soap, disinfectants, drain cleaners, toilet bowl cleaners—irritation or chemical burns in mouth and esophagus.
   Furniture polish—coughing, sleepiness.
   Laundry detergents and soaps—vomiting and/or diarrhea.

2. Garden and garage products
   Antifreeze—coma, blindness, convulsions, drunkenness.
   Fertilizers—vomiting or diarrhea.
   Gasoline, kerosene, turpentine, paint thinner, solvents, thinners, degreasers, charcoal lighter fluid—coughing, coma, burning irritation.
   Insecticides—headache, increased body secretions, vomiting, diarrhea, convulsions.
3. Personal products
   Nail polish remover—irritation and dryness inside mouth and esophagus.
   Perfumes, aftershaves, mouthwashes (if drunk), rubbing alcohol—incoordination, depression, coma, convulsions.
   Shampoo, soap, lotions—vomiting and/or diarrhea.

• Your medicine chest contains many wonderful health aids, but if taken to excess, your medicines can become poisons. Here are just a few of the common medicines and the poisoning symptoms they produce:

   Antibiotics—allergic reactions, such as swelling, skin eruptions, breathing difficulties, shock.
   Antihistamines—hallucinations, agitation, convulsions, coma, fever, depression.
   Aspirin—fast breathing, ringing in ears, shock, sweating, fever, convulsions.
   Camphor—convulsions, excitement, feeling warm, coma.
   Cold preparations—hyperactivity, convulsions, coma.
   Iron and vitamins with iron—bloody vomiting and diarrhea, shock, coma.
   Oil of wintergreen—fast breathing, ringing in ears, shock, sweating, fever, convulsions.
   Sleeping pills—convulsions, respiratory depression, coma.
   Urine test tablets—chemical burns inside the mouth, throat, esophagus.

• ALWAYS KEEP ALL OF THE ABOVE SUBSTANCES AWAY FROM CHILDREN OR PETS. DISPOSE OF THEM SO THAT CHILDREN AND PETS CAN'T GET AT THEM WHEN THEY ARE IN THE GARBAGE.

• Never take medicine in the dark. Always turn on the light and read the container's label to avoid taking the wrong medicine or a poison by mistake!

• Dispose of old medicines by flushing them down the toilet.

CHAPTER 9

Working Couples

Working Couples

Something happened on our way from the 1960s to the 1990s. The percentage of women in the work force rose from 35.7 percent in 1960 to 55.8 percent in 1987.

By the 1970s the majority of wives were working outside the home either part time or full time, and the census figures of those years showed that only 7 percent of American families had a father who brought home the bacon, a mother who stayed home to fry it, two school-aged children who ate it, and a dog named Rover who got the leftovers.

Now, as we nudge the 1990s with another generation, many women don't expect to get married and live happily ever after by wearing an apron all day and baking pies, unless they are chefs in restaurants. Many men don't expect to be the only one in the family to bring home the "baco chips." (High-cholesterol fat/bacon is out, soy-protein "baco" substitute is in!) With or without children, the two-income family has become as "normal" as the "Leave It to Beaver" Cleaver family was in the 1950s.

Certainly the refrigerator door, bulletin board, or whatever is used as a message center is the core of a working couple's relationship, especially if their hours don't coincide. Keeping track of where everybody is becomes even more complicated when the couple has children.

Whether they are "yours, mine, or ours," according to many reports children are being nurtured by both parents instead of spending most of their time with their mothers.

When both people in a marriage travel in their work, they almost need to make appointments with each other to discuss important matters and just to make the kind of small talk that binds people together.

I know about this problem firsthand. I travel a lot, giving speeches and promoting my Heloise books and column, which is in five hundred newspapers. I have to keep in touch with my editors and readers so that I can produce a column with information they can relate to. I can't get a real feeling for what is going on with people across the country if I stay in my office. Reading my mail, of course, is a major contact with readers, but seeing them in person is very important.

In the middle of all this, I am a wife and a stepmother, which means I have to keep some sort of balance between my work and my personal life. My husband, David, also travels in his work, which means we have to make time so that all three of us can be together.

Taking Self Time

Like the other women in the United States who perform this double juggling act, I have to set priorities and then rearrange them every now and then. And, like the other jugglers, sometimes I have to let certain chores go so that I can have time with the people I love, and sometimes I have to allow for self time so that I can recharge my personal batteries and keep my enthusiasm going for everything I do.

One of my favorite ways of celebrating self time is to just take a day off, and, if possible, lounge around in bed catching up on my reading, watching TV, or whatever helps me escape. I even fix my meals on a tray and eat them in bed, as if I've been served by a personal maid and butler. Since I schedule this self time, I don't feel guilty about taking it. People who make lists can put self time on the list and then check it off just like the other completed "tasks."

Also, I don't think such self time is only for women; men need it too. Perhaps couples could trade off weekend self days, taking turns being the maid/butler for each other.

Or why not take selves time, and both take the day off together? And, if you don't want to lounge around, remember that not all vacations need to be out of town; anyone can play tourist wherever they live.

Dining In and Out but on the Run

Cooking from scratch was a matter of pride in Grandmother's day, but now even Grandmother takes shortcuts. A stroll through the supermarket shows you the many meals that need only be reheated or have one ingredient (such as meat or fish) added, and in 20 minutes you have dinner. I wonder if the idea of adding the chicken or shrimp (or whatever) was developed to keep us from feeling guilty about thawing or opening a can of something for dinner without adding any personal touch to it.

Eating Out

Here are a few tips on eating out that may help you lower your bill.

• To get a reservation at a very popular restaurant, try calling late in the day or shortly before you want to leave the house to see if there have been any cancellations or no-shows.

(Of course, if there haven't been any, you'll be looking for a place to eat without a reservation and will have to go to a less popular restaurant.)

• Ask the waiter if you and your companion can split a course. If the answer is no, decline to order it. But much of the time, rather than lose money, the waiter will probably agree.

• Consider going out to lunch instead of out to dinner. Often, lunch costs as much as 50 percent less. The portions are smaller, but with so many restaurants serving such large portions anyway, eating lunch out just means not having to ask for a "people bag."

• When you're eating out, here's one way to confirm restaurant coffee freshness: If cream swirls up brown, you have a freshly brewed cup of coffee; if it swirls up gray, the coffee has been on the burner too long. (I guess that if you don't put cream in your coffee, you probably can't confirm what your taste buds are telling you.)

• Does computing 15 percent for a tip tax your brain's math department? It's easier to do in small bites. Use your mental math to take 10 percent of the bill, then add one-half of that 10 percent for a total of 15 percent. For example: If your bill is $17 and some change, figure 10 percent of $17 is $1.70; then add half of that amount (.65) for a 15 percent tip of $2.35. Then, you can round the tip out to $2.50 if you wish. Or buy a "tip card," available in greeting card shops and some bookstores.

Eating at Home

Eating at home is still the least expensive way, and so many new products are on the market that in some cases cooking at home is "fast food."

To add to speedy preparation, the new foods are microwaveable and in single five-ounce portions for those who eat alone or for those who eat with people who don't share their tastes for certain foods. Single portions mean never having to eat someone else's favorite vegetable!

• Single-portion frozen desserts are diet aids. You can't have seconds because there aren't any, unless you like to eat piesickles!

• If you live alone and think it's too much trouble and mess to cook for one, consider cooking for yourself and a neighbor, as in "I'll make the casserole if you make the salad, and let's have dinner together." Couples can do the same, especially when you and your friends want to eat out but can't afford to do so. Potluck dinners aren't only for church get-togethers! Eating at someone else's house is eating out!

A Place to Live

An apartment lease is one of those standard-form legal documents that people may not read carefully enough to know the difference between landlord's and tenant's rights, which causes all sorts of trouble later on if terms of the lease are violated by either one.

• Most leases are drawn up by landlords, so if you are the tenant, remember whose side the lawyer was on. READ CAREFULLY! If you are the landlord, make sure your rules are in the lease.

• In addition to paying the first and last months' rents, you will be asked to pay a security deposit. Be sure to read what that deposit will cover. Nail holes in the wall may be a reason for not returning that security deposit.

• The lease will tell which repairs are made by the landlord and which by the tenant. If you are the tenant, keep all receipts for repairs or cleaning (such as carpet cleaning) in case you need them in small claims court for getting your security deposit back.

• Find out what a "clean" condition actually is, according to your lease, and when you move in, make note of all existing damage, soil, or stains.

• Take photos of furniture and carpeting when you move into a furnished apartment in case you need to show how worn they were when you moved in. Or even ask your landlord or apartment manager to stand in the photo with you. If you are the landlord, photos will show how new the furnishing were when the tenant moved in. Include a sign or newspaper with a date to prove when the photos were taken.

• Landlords and tenants need to agree on certain provisions, usually found in the lease's fine print and often not read by novice apartment renters. Here are some of them: Restrictions on children, pets, using an apartment for a home office, appropriate dress in the lobby/common areas, cooking on balconies, pot plants on windowsills, radio/TV antennas, storage and parking areas, the landlord's right to enter the apartment with or without notice whether or not the tenant is home, any additional services provided by the landlord, and, finally, conditions for eviction and terminating the lease.

• If you need to move before your lease is up, find out if the landlord will let you find another tenant to fill the apartment so that you won't be responsible for rent payments. Permission to sublet from the landlord does not release you from legal obligations to the landlord under the lease.

• You need permission to sublet if you want to rent part of your apartment to another person, or you can have the new person sign the original lease as an additional tenant, with the landlord's permission.

• If you are the landlord, be sure to tell your insurance agent if the apartment is furnished or unfurnished and then figure the additional insurance for a furnished apartment into the rent.

• If you are renting a furnished vacation cottage or home, you should store valuables and take photos of each room, major appliance or furniture pieces, and the exterior of the house, in case you have to make insurance claims because of damage or theft.

Money Matters

Because two-income families have more money to spend, they have a greater need to know how to manage their money. Standards of living tend to rise with income, so "rich" is relative. You go from having enough money for your "needs" to having enough money for your "wants."

Many couples get into financial trouble. This is especially true of couples who, instead of shared financial communication, have "his money" and "her money" arrangements, and don't ever get around to talking about how much "total money" they have.

Managing the Budget

• Money management experts believe that each partner should have some money that is separate from the family account that can be spent without mutual discussion and agreement.

• Couples planning to have a baby and have the wife stay home for a period of time to care for the baby might want to live on the husband's salary and save the wife's income as a nest egg for the extra expenses they'll have because of the baby.

Saving Tips

• If you have trouble saving, use payroll savings plans so that a certain amount of money gets saved with each paycheck.

• Make savings a fixed part of your budget instead of something you do with leftover money (there is no such thing for many people). Save a fixed amount, whether it's $20 or $200 per month, and put this money in an interest-bearing account so that compounded interest will make the account grow.

• Check out the different accounts offered by your bank to find out how much interest your savings will earn. Often you'll need to maintain a minimum balance of $500 to $2,500 or more to earn interest. Be realistic about the minimum balance that you can maintain.

Setting Up a Home Office

When you set up a home office, designing it to suit the one who uses it most of the time makes sense. If both "heads of household" work at home, it may be better to have "separate but equal" home offices if you have the space. Keeping a desk is such a personal thing that few people can share one. And it's always the messy ones who marry the neatophiles, isn't it? Although my main office is at one end of our house and David used to share an office off of that, he decided he needed his own space, because he said my secretaries' chatter was driving him crazy.

Finding Office Space

• Look around for nooks and crannies that will serve as an office if you don't have a separate room to use.

• If you don't have a separate room, do you have space for a fold-up, built-in desk so that you can confine your work and cover it up when you want to protect it from curious children and leaping cats?

• You can easily hide a corner-office mess from view with a three-panel screen.

• The dining-room table is a favorite working place because of the large working surface of the table. If your dining room isn't in the mainstream of traffic and if you seldom use it, the dining room may be a good office, but metal filing cabinets probably won't enhance its decor, and so you won't be able to keep everything you need in the same place.

Home Office Hours

• If you work at home in a home office, you have to develop a work schedule, even if it's a flexible one. It's too easy to procrastinate when you are your own boss and can take all the coffee breaks you want because the pot is there in the kitchen.

• Get a DO NOT DISTURB sign and have a place to hang it in your office; then make sure the rest of the family knows what it means. It's hard for a family to grasp the idea that someone who is still in the home is actually at a job, especially if that someone is Mom! Believe me, I know; I still haven't explained this to Zinfandel, the schnauzer, or Sheba, the keeshond. They just can't believe that I am really working.

Tax Breaks for Home Business Offices

According to a recent survey by the New York consulting firm of Link Resources, more than 11 million women are working from their homes with full- or part-time businesses.

• If you run your own business from your home, the IRS allows deductions only if you use your office exclusively and regularly for business, whether it's just a desk, a room, or a whole floor. The details can be found in IRS small business information booklets. Call your local IRS office to obtain them.

• Here's an important tip for people who use home office deductions: These deductions can become a liability if you are required to pay capital-gains tax on a fraction of the profit of a home sale equal to the proportion of household expenses you've deducted from your taxes. To avoid this, you need to convert the office back to personal use before the year of your house sale.

• Another important tip: Home-office deductions may flag your tax return for an audit, so it's best to consult a tax professional, keep extremely careful records, and follow the law to the letter.

Office Furniture and Equipment

• If you like the large surface of a dining-room table and have an extra room for an office, there's no rule that says only a desk can be a desk! A dining-room table from a used furniture store, with or without leaves, can be a desk. Remember when you used to study in the library at those large tables? You can have that atmosphere too. Just make sure your chair is the proper height for your desk/table.

• A prefinished hollow-core door mounted on two file cabinets, sawhorses, or concrete blocks can be a desk. You might need to use self-gripping fabric strips or dots or double-sided carpet tape to keep the door from sliding on metal file cabinets.

• Don't forget the old student bookcase of boards and brick stacks. You can buy prefinished boards for your brick-and-board bookshelves.

• Multicolored plastic "milk crates" can be used for files. You can even color-code what you store with these. Depending upon the casualness of your home decor, these crates can be part of the decoration because of their colors, or they can be stacked in a closet. Small plastic baskets from variety stores can hold "in" and "out" stuff.

• Use fiberboard cubes for bookcases and files, and to support a door/desk. These cubes, usually sold unassembled, are often on sale at hardware stores. When you paint fiberboard, you need to brush on a base coat. If you try to spray paint a first coat on fiberboard, you'll find that it absorbs paint like a sponge. It will take so many cans of paint to get a nice finish that you will wish you had bought a ready-made bookcase (or whatever) instead of trying to "do it yourself."

• These cubes also hold long-play record albums and are very sturdy when stacked on their sides.

• When you are selecting a chair to go with your desk, match the seat height to the desk for your comfort. If you will be spending long hours at the desk, your legs shouldn't dangle. If you know you are going to be spending a lot of time sitting on this chair at your desk or work station, it might just be worth the investment to buy a very good adjustable chair. It will save you many aches and pains in the long run.

• For comfort, the table for a typewriter or computer keyboard needs to be three to four inches lower than standard desk height. If you don't have a typing table or computer furniture of the ideal height, adjust your chair accordingly.

Personal Computers

Perhaps computers are the most prominent of the new hi-tech electronics in United States homes and offices. Adults who didn't learn about computers in school have been pushed into the computer age by their jobs. Many adults learn about computers from their children, who view them as ordinary classroom equipment, on the same level with the pencils and Big Chief tablets their parents used in "the olden days."

Computers are really a blessing for columnists like me who have lots of irons in the fire, or documents in memory, if we're going to speak "computerese" in this chapter.

The "Hints from Heloise" column is produced on computers and word processors, and my secretaries—Kelly Moravits, Ruth Rozelle, and Joyce Buffolino—and I marvel at how fast we can get our work out now. I don't know how we managed without them.

All the information used in my columns is checked and edited by me and by my staff and editors. Computers enable us to send copy via modem to each other and then to discuss the columns on the phone or on the modem "chat" mode within minutes. What used to take weeks takes only days, and sometimes only hours.

As with all new technology, there's a lot of information that's not in the manuals, many of which are hard to understand unless you have a doctorate in computer sciences (and maybe not then!).

General Computer Use Tips

A lot is learned by trial and error.

• For example, in my office, we learned that, if several people will be turning a computer on and off, a note on exactly how to do this should be taped on the computer or near it. We almost had a service call because we thought one of the computers was not working. Actually, someone had turned off the monitor and computer by using the individual switches instead of the power surge protector's main switch the way the person who usually works on that computer turns it off; then someone else saw the red button lighted up and switched off the power surge protector. The next morning, when the power surge protector was switched on, nothing happened.

We "entered" the instruction "use the power surge protector switch only" into the "memory" and then put notes by all the computers just in case somebody's brain got a "delete" command.

• We've also learned that when many people are working on the same document, it's hard to keep track of who has done what and when. That's why we put messages at the top of each document to serve as a history of that document, listing the different document names it has had, dates, and to whom it was sent by modem. The person working on the document notes the date she worked on it and a short description of what she did—just a phrase or word, nothing elaborate. I always note the date when I have seen and done the final editing of the material. This way, we all know what's going on and if the document we call up on the computer is the most recent one.

You can find commands in your software to mark the first page of notes so that it doesn't get printed when you print the document.

You can call up this information from your computer, but it's a time-saver if you can see everything you need to know about the previous work on a document when you call it up.

• Here's a hint on saving computer repairs from my computer consultant, David Kantor: It is better for your computer circuits to be turned on and left on for the day than turned on and off many times. Each time you turn on your computer you have a surge of power going through it, he explains, so the fewer turn-ons the better.

• If you need to leave your computer for a break, leave it on but dim the screen to black or turn off your monitor, because leaving documents on your screen for long periods of time can actually burn impressions into your screen.

Power Surge Protectors

• My researcher, Marcy Meffert, learned from a very expensive experience and from my computer consultant, David Kantor, that unless the bar of outlets into which you plug your computer equipment actually has "Power Surge Protector" printed right on it, it is really just a heavy-duty, multiple-outlet fancy extension cord. One stormy day in New Orleans, a power surge occurred while she was starting up her floppy disk-drive computer, and it badly (and expensively) damaged the disk drive. (She no longer boots up computers during storms, even with the power surge protector.)

• Many computer owners use computers in older homes in newly renovated city neighborhoods. If you are one of these people, you may want to have the power company check your main power lines. Often older homes (about 50 years old and more) have had numerous additions and changes in the electrical systems while retaining the same power lines run to the house when it was new and have had to supply only electricity for lightbulbs and MAYBE a refrigerator. The drain of microwave ovens, freezers, and other modern technology, including a computer, may be too much for such inadequate lines. The resulting frequent power surges and power outages can damage your computer or disk drives if they occur when you are using your computer.

• You may want to run a separate line for your computer if you have it on most of the day or night. Marcy, who lives in an older home, had numerous and very expensive problems with her computer and disk drives until she had new lines (more than twice the thickness of the old ones) installed by the power company to her fuse box; ultimately she had a separate line installed for her computer.

Transporting Disks

• My computer consultant says that although airport X rays and security gates may not damage your computer disks, it is safer NOT to let them go through the security system, because they CAN be damaged. Ask the attendant to hold the computer disks while you and your baggage go through security.

• Heat can damage disks. The temperature of the air in an automobile can be oven hot when the sun's rays beam in on car windows. Floppy disks kept in a car can warp or suffer other types of damage. You can help your disks keep cool by putting the disk caddy into an insulated box, such as a soft-drink cooler, while you are transporting them or by leaving them in the car for short periods. It's probably better if you just don't ever leave them in the car in the summer or in very warm climates.

• Store disks away from light and such heat sources as windowsills, hot desk lamps, and heating/cooling vents.

• Although some people put labels and indexing information on disk jackets, it's really more efficient to put the labels on the disks in case they get mixed up. Just remember never to write with ballpoint pen on a labeled disk, because it may damage the disk; use felt-tip markers.

Working, Writing, Editing, Saving, Moving Copy Around

• I have learned that keeping your fingers low to the keys with the palms of your hands almost touching the base of the keyboard makes typing faster, but everyone has to experiment to find the best way.

• Sometimes moving papers from one side of the computer to the other is all it takes to break the monotony and relieve neck strain of long hours at the computer.

• I like to use a clip stand to hold printed copy beside the computer.

• Having a telephone beside your computer is a must even if you don't have a modem; I have my phone on the wall beside my work station to keep it out of my way. With the phone beside the computer, I can phone various institutes and agencies to get information and then type it right into the computer as I get it. Also, I can call up documents when conferring with my editors so that I've got the copy we're discussing right there before me, where I can add notes and changes right away.

• Try keeping self-stick notes beside your computer so that you can stick them on the side of the monitor or nearby wall to remind you of copy changes, new names of documents, things to do, and anything else that pops up while you're working and don't want to interrupt your train of thought.

• Marcy found that because her new keyboard was more sensitive than the one on her first computer, she sometimes tapped the "enter" key accidentally whenever she was deleting to clean out her files and thereby deleted whatever document was listed first in the index.

Her previous work was on floppy disks only, so when she'd see the file delete, she'd forget about her new hard disk "bak" file and practically fall to the floor in a sobbing heap thinking she'd deleted hours of work. Now, to prevent panic, she keeps a fake document titled "1AAAA" in her files. All "1AAAA" says is "This is a fake document." If she accidentally deletes "1AAAA," she keeps her cool. Using the number 1 and four A's ensures the fake document of being first in the index.

• When you move paragraphs or sections around in a document, usually you save them by moving them to a glossary or under a certain document name on the disk and then call them up to insert them where you want them.

Most of the time, you will never need to see these document parts again and they will just clutter up your indexes and have to be "killed" or erased at some point.

• Here's a timesaving tip on how to avoid this clutter: If you always save temporary document parts under a certain name, such as "graph" or "thing" or another name that's never given to other documents you want to save, the computer will overwrite the previous document part saved under those names and you won't have lots of useless little bits and pieces taking up disk space and confusing you when you call up the index.

• When using certain software, you can delete parts of documents and save them elsewhere on the disk. The command to the computer is to delete from the cursor to the last word of the section you want to delete.

Since the last word of the section you are deleting and saving may have been used elsewhere in the document or in that section, the computer may delete to the wrong place. However, if you type your name at the end of the section to be deleted, you can tell the computer to delete as far as "Zelda" or "Helmut," which are words not likely to be used elsewhere in the text.

• To avoid having to read through all sorts of documents on the "doc" menu of a hard disk computer when she calls up whatever she's working on, Marcy usually considers any "doc" file document that has been worked on and sent to its destination as "finished" and "filed out of sight," so she deletes it from the "doc file." It's still on the "bak file" of her hard disk if she needs it for reference or rewriting.

• Like anyone else who is prudent, cautious, and scared to death losing hours of work (AGAIN!), each of us has learned to back up on a floppy disk any document that has been worked on during the day or has been designated as "finished," as an extra precaution.

• When working on floppy disk drive computers, you can provide back-up copies by making two copies of each document, each on a separate disk, just in case the "microchip monsters" decide to zap your circuits or damage the disk.

• Save time looking up small segments of miscellaneous information from your index by creating a "trivia" or "misc" file. Giving each small segment a separate index name soon clutters your index, and usually you forget what the names represent and waste time calling each one up to find out what it says.

• When you are typing in a correction, put in the correction before you delete even a single word, so if your mind hasn't "saved" the information, it's not gone to that big glossary in the sky (or wherever such info goes), never to be retrieved again.

Buying a Computer

• Get a company that services what it sells, offers training programs, has a good track record in your area, and has experienced consultants to help you select your software and hardware.

• With computers, you think about software first. You don't buy equipment and then find out what it can do. If you are familiar with certain softwares and know which ones you want to use, be certain the computer (or less expensive "clone" of a brand-name computer) that you select will operate the software that meets your needs.

This sounds elementary, but many people walk into shops, buy any Brand X computer, and then find that it doesn't do what they want it to do. For example, it's possible to bank by personal computer via modem, but you need a computer that has software enabling you to do such things.

• Some people may need only a word processor instead of a computer; others may want to do desktop publishing, which can't be done on all computers or with all printers. Still others may need desktop models that can fold up into a drawer, closet, or briefcase each day.

• If you have to keep your computer tucked away on shelves inside an armoire or closet instead of on a desk or table, you'll want one that has a lap keyboard so that you don't have to move all of your equipment out each time you need to use it.

• Make a list of what you want to do with your computer and printer, and where you'll use it, so the store consultant can help you make the best selection; and, like when you are making medical care decisions, get a second or third opinion. Read computer magazines if you can understand them.

Learning How to Use It and Getting Rid of Computer Phobia

• My best tip for getting rid of computer phobia is to play some games on your computer. Once you see that you can touch every one of the keys without creating a disaster or losing everything that's in it, you'll be more comfortable doing actual work on a computer.

• If you really are so certain that you'll lose your work, practice double caution for peace of mind: Make duplicate disks and always keep one of them out of the computer while you are working. You can't add or delete on a disk that's not even in a disk drive. You can also stick the little protector tabs that come with disks on the notch of your duplicate disk so that the "file" is "locked up."

• Computer training is available at many computer stores, and you can often hire a consultant to give you one-on-one lessons for an hourly rate. To get the most for your money when you hire such a consultant, schedule the training session for a time when you won't have any interruptions from telephones or visitors. Read the manual BEFORE the lessons and practice a few simple steps so that you'll know what questions to ask once you are "on the meter" and paying for time.

• Adult education classes are offered at many colleges and universities, but find out if the classes will work with the brand of computer you have bought, or sign up for an introductory course before you buy.

• Many large cities have computer clubs, some of which have sub-clubs for different computer brands. Club members train each other and share tips.

Dealing with the Glare of Computer Screens

• Tinted lenses in your eyeglasses can reduce glare. Use brown tints to reduce the glare of green text and blue-tinted lenses for amber text.

(If you have untinted plastic lenses, you can get them tinted to suit your computer needs. Also, you may be able to get the tint in your eyeglasses changed. See your optometry shop for advice on your type of lenses.)

• If your home office includes a computer, place the computer so that the screen is not getting a glare from windows or lights. You can buy glare-reducing screens for some computer monitors, and if you can't get a screen for your specific model, measure the screen, buy a glare-reducing screen that will cover the monitor's screen, and attach it with stick-on self-gripping fabric tape or dots.

Computing in Comfort

See the home office section in this chapter and then get tips from other computer owners on how they set up their equipment.

• Some work station arrangements cause people who wear bifocals to have to tilt their heads at an angle that allows them to read computer screens through the bottoms of their lenses, a position that's a real pain in the neck.

The solution is to get plain reading glasses made up with the prescription of the "bifocal bottoms." If you find optical chain specials of "Buy one, get one free" or reduced prices on second pairs of glasses, make that second pair your computer glasses.

• If your chair is a bit too high and/or your legs are a bit too short:

A phone book makes a good footstool, and the bonus is that you always know where it is!

Try wearing wooden clogs, wedgies, or some other thick-soled shoes when you work at the computer. You can "raise the floor" from one-half to one or more inches with shoes, and sometimes that's all you need! If you like to walk around barefoot or in socks for comfort, you can keep your "computer shoes" under the desk or worktable, ready for slipping your feet into when you sit down to work.

• Give yourself a break—literally. Take a break from your computer every now and then to walk around, stretch your legs, unkink your muscles, and refocus your eyes. Not only will you feel better, your work will go more smoothly if you don't push yourself into "lock" positions.

(It helps if you have a dog that just has to have a walk every few hours. Then you'll not only get a walk but some fresh air at the same time! The bonus is that you can tell the dog all about your work and get positive feedback every time.)

Speaking Computerese

It helps to know the language when you are in a foreign land, and for most of us the computer is a foreign territory. Here's a mini-dictionary of a few of the most basic terms to help you with the language of computer use.

BAUD: A baud is like "miles per hour" on your car. It's a measure of how fast data go through a port. A modem's measure is "baud rate," which means the higher the rate, the faster the information is transmitted.

CPU: Central Processing Unit, which means it's the computer without keyboard or monitor.

DATA BASE: This is really the "files"—the stored information. The categories in this file are called "fields," such as last names, phone numbers, address categories.

DOS: Disk operating system—this is the computer's "brain," and without a DOS you just have some silicon chips in a box.

DISKS: These are your computer "file cabinets."

Floppy disks: Not really floppy at all, these square 5¼" or 3½" diskettes have replaced the magnetic tape used with the first computers for data storage.

Hard disk: A hard disk can hold nearly 28 times as much data as one 5¼" floppy disk. Unlike floppy disks, which are inserted and removed from disk drives, the hard disk stays inside your computer.

MODEM: The name comes from what used to be an acronym for "modulator-demodulator," and what it really does is to let your computer talk to another computer via the phone lines.

MONOCHROME: A single-color monitor, mostly amber or green. A monitor that is like a color television set is an RGB monitor (red, green, blue monitor).

MOUSE: A type of "pencil" or "pointer" that lets you draw and edit on the screens of some computers.

PC: Stands for "personal computer," and it's a generic name, even if it was started by a well-known computer maker.

PC COMPATIBLE: Because IBM has been considered the standard computer, software designers made software that would run on IBM PCs, and this software is called PC compatible.

PORT: A computer name for "connection." You plug your printer into the appropriate "port."

Parallel port, serial port: A parallel port sends information through the cable by ranks, while a serial port sends it in a single file. Frankly, most of us aren't concerned about HOW information is sent. We only care about IF it's being sent. However, it's nice to know what your repair person is talking about if this term is used.

RAM and ROM: RAM means "random-access memory" and is the part of the computer's memory that YOU can use, as opposed to ROM, which is the "read-only memory" part of the computer's memory, which the COMPUTER uses to do its work.

SOFTWARE: These are the programs that are used by you and your computer to do whatever it is you bought the computer for. Without them, you might as well not have a computer at all.

SPREAD-SHEET PROGRAM: Helps you to put numbers together.

WORD PROCESSOR: This is the "typewriter" part of the computer, which helps you edit, move information around inside the document, and in some cases check spelling.

Computers as Household Helpers

You can make all sorts of forms to help you keep records easily. Here are just a few.

• Make a shopping list "form" that enables you (and everyone else in your house) to check off items you need, and magnetize it to your refrigerator door. You'll have a shopping list made out and ready to go when you are. Leave some blank lines to add seldom-bought items.

• Print a form on business envelopes to keep track of your trip expenses. (If you open the flaps of the envelopes, the envelopes will ride piggy-back on each other on the printer roller.) Take the envelope along with you on the trip and put all receipts in it, and then you'll be organized when you sit down to add it all up.

Here's a sample of what to print on your envelope.

Trip to: .... Date: ....
Purpose: ....
Expenses .... $ ....
Amount reimbursed .... $ ....
Amount to be declared on income tax as gain/loss .... $ ....

• Make a form to keep track of your calories or food units when your doctor or dietician gives you a diet.

• Special software advertised in health/nutrition magazines is available by mail that enables you to plan a diet for nutrition and calories. Such softwares have the calorie, fiber, fat, and nutritional content for as many as 1,500 different foods, and some even include analysis of fast foods from national restaurant chains so that you can calculate what you eat out as well as what you eat in.

• The repeat function used in making diet charts is also useful if you want to add short (just a paragraph or two), newsy notes to a mail-out like Christmas cards or birth announcements. Just fill a page with duplications of your short note, perhaps with a dotted line at the end of each duplication to serve as a cutting guide, and print. Cut the note strips apart and tuck one in each envelope.

• If you put your favorite recipes into the computer, all you have to do is print them out when someone asks you for them or if you are taking them to a potluck supper where recipes are requested.

• Collectors can make forms to use for recording dates of purchase, prices, appraisals, and any other information about the things they add to their collections.

• Menu forms and To-Do forms for entertaining and other "remembering" can be printed on computers.

• Letters to family members can be done on the computer. Just do a segment of general news and then add a personal message to each person receiving the letter at the top.

Note: If you always add the personal message at the top, you won't forget to change the name after "Dear ———."

• Here's a tip on a sticky subject: Computer games are fun for the whole family, but if you make a rule about no sticky foods being eaten while "playing computer," you won't have to clean off your computer after every family session. Liquid of any kind is a no-no!

Printers

• Some printers use either film or nylon ribbons. Since the film ribbons, which print more clearly and one time only, are more expensive than nylon ribbons, which print until you replace them, it saves money to use the nylon ribbons for first drafts and family letters and to use the more expensive film ribbons for final copies of reports and documents.

• You can also save older nylon ribbons and use them for first drafts and letters. Then, use new ribbons for final copies and other documents.

• A tractor feed, optional on some printers, helps to keep the paper from becoming slanted when you are printing long documents. If you don't have a tractor feed and if the weight of the printed pages drags on the paper feeder, making the pages of a long document crooked, it'll help to tear off your document every 20 or so pages.

• One of the problems with new technology is that we tend to look for complex solutions to simple problems.

For example, Marcy's printer feed appeared to be shredding the continuous-roll paper edges. After wasting time checking out the feed mechanism, she looked into the paper box itself, where she found tufts of cat hair. It seems that her paper-box-loving cat, Hexe, was sneaking into her office at night and nesting in the paper.

Now she guards it from cat attacks by putting it on a small stool that, with the added paper box height, just barely fits under the printer's table. Hexe still lurks around the stool but can't get into the box.

CHAPTER 10

Rec-Tech: Television, Stereos, Cameras, and More

Today's Technology

Hi-tech has flipped our switches all over the country.

Even people who were around before the automatic pop-up toaster are using programmable microwave ovens and VCRs, and even some of our coffeepots have computer memories.

Let's face it, the American love for doing it fast has spurred hi-tech development onward to the point where half the homes in the United States have VCRs so that people can tape and view movies instead of merely watching TV. Hi-tech electronics is here to stay, and if we use it efficiently, it will help us instead of making our lives more complicated.

General Tips

• I know it's been said before, but it can't be said too often. Always keep the instruction books that come with your audio and video equipment in your household appliances file.

Each camera, and tape, record, and compact disc player has its own operating instructions, and whatever you did before and even some of the tips in this chapter may not work with your present equipment. Also, your booklets provide information about model and parts numbers when you need repairs, and have instructions for preparing the equipment for moving.

• If you don't understand the directions in the booklet that comes with your equipment, call the help phone number, which should be printed somewhere in the booklet, or call information (1-800-555-1212) to find out if the manufacturer has a toll-free consumer help number.

• Always keep all your equipment—cameras, tapes, records, and compact discs—away from direct sunlight, heat, and humidity. Never cover ventilation slots while the equipment is in use; trapped heat causes serious damage.

• Deliberate misuse can void the warranties of electronic equipment.

• Sometimes you can make substitute covers for your VCR and some other types of electronic equipment from various plastic bags, plastic by the yard, or, in some cases, a rectangular plastic dishpan. But most of the time, the covers sold for these appliances will fit better and do a better job of protecting the equipment from dust and moisture.

CAUTION: Always remove protective covers when using any electronic equipment to prevent heat damage!

• Before you make a service call for any electronic equipment that malfunctions, always check all switches, control knobs, and connections to make sure they are properly set. Seems obvious, but sometimes we get so wrapped up in what we are doing that we forget to the check the obvious and to perform all of the start-up steps.

• Always have any electronic equipment that has been dropped or exposed to water or moisture checked by a professional to ensure against electric shock or fire hazards.

• The Electronic Industries Association says plugging electronic equipment into a voltage surge suppressor is a good idea, because it will protect such rec-tech appliances as your VCR from power line surges. However, it doesn't protect against direct lightning strikes.

• When you have any electronic device repaired, have the service technician verify that the manufacturer's specified replacement parts have been used. Use of proper replacements prevents fire, shock, or other hazards. Also, ask the service technician to perform all safety checks noted in the service manual when the repair is completed.

• If you keep a service history on your equipment either in a notebook or on index cards, it will help you remember if and when you've cleaned your video or audiotape heads, the last time you had the stylus checked by an audio equipment dealer, when you've had any of your equipment professionally serviced, and so forth.

At the top of the page or note card, write the name of the equipment, the model and serial numbers, and installation or purchase date. Then record the dates you've cleaned it yourself or had it professionally serviced.

Make notes on professional services that include who did it, the type of service or repair, its cost, and your comments, such as "had to wait a week for parts, too expensive, find other service person."

If you cleaned the equipment yourself, note what cleaners you used, how you used them, and if you had any problems. Also note when you changed batteries and fuses.

Such maintenance records need not be elaborate, just short comments that will save you money in the long run and keep your equipment at its best performance.

• Here's a good shopping tip:

Sometimes, two heads are better than one. If you have a friend who is as confused about hi-tech equipment as you are, try researching together. One person could shop around gathering information from store brochures and sales people, and the other could gather consumer information magazines and other publications. Then, together, you can make a plus and minus chart of the benefits of different brands and help each other figure out what to buy.

You might even talk a salesperson into discounts, since you are buying two sets instead of one—asking for discounts is always worth a try, and you'd be surprised how often you'll get them. Think of the discount you'd get if your whole exercise class was buying!

Television

• Fuzzy television pictures don't always mean that something is wrong with your set. Before you call the service shop—and don't think this is silly—try cleaning your screen. And don't be too shocked at how much dirt a screen can collect! Wipe the screen with a damp, soft, clean cloth and then let it air dry.

• CAUTION: Never apply liquid or aerosol cleaners on the screen, and unplug the set before any cleaning.

• If you have a projection television set, do not touch or attempt to clean the screen; you may damage it beyond repair. Call a service professional.

• High winds or birds landing hard on an outdoor antenna can put it out of line. If you notice a change in reception, check to see if your antenna is bent or turned, or if its lead-in wires are worn or corroded. Installation and repairs of outdoor antennas should always be done by professionals.

• If a picture is bad on just one channel or if you get no picture at all on one channel, read your instruction book to see if your set has an Automatic Frequency Control (AFC) switch on the back. If so, turn that switch off. If the picture improves, readjust the fine tuning until you get a good picture. Be sure to turn the switch on again when you change channels!

• You can get interference (static noises and lines) from too many electrical appliances plugged into one outlet, a CB radio in the neighborhood, a nearby high-voltage tower, or, in some cases, from placing a VCR on top or beneath your TV even if there's a wood shelf in between.

• Projection TV sets often have a darker picture than your regular set. You may have to darken the room a bit to get better contrast.

• Does your TV schedule disappear? Punch a hole at the top, loop a string through the hole, then tape the other end of the string to the TV set each Sunday when the new schedule comes out.

• When you look through your weekly TV schedule, use a highlighter pen to mark the shows you want to see during the week so that you won't miss them.

Home Satellite Television

• Urban-area satellite dishes get more interference than rural ones. If you get interference, call the phone company to find out if you are between any phone relay stations. Television transmitters, Air Force radar facilities, and amateur radio transmitters may also cause interference. To minimize interference, you'll need upgraded and special equipment, such as a feed horn designed to minimize interference.

• Protect the dish from weather by installing it away from prevailing winds or providing some other sort of windbreak. If you decide to protect the dish by installing it in a pit, provide adequate drainage.

Video Cassettes and Recorders

• Never stack video tapes, TV schedule booklets, or anything else on the recorder. "Insulating" your recorder with stacked stuff keeps all the heat it generates inside and will ultimately cause deterioration and a service call. Your recorder and cable box need "breathing space" to keep their cool.

• Here are the four things to think about when buying a video tape recorder and some tips for enjoying it.

1. If all you use a video recorder for is playing rented movies, the most basic equipment is fine.
2. If you like to record TV shows for future viewing, look for models that are easy to set up ahead of time for automatic taping.
3. If you record a lot of programs and want to cut out the commercials, remote control is a must, and most models come with it now.
4. If you have invested in expensive video-cam equipment, you'll need a more elaborate type of recorder that allows you to edit and dub tapes.

• Many video shops have special prices for mid-week rentals, and mid-week is when you're more likely to get popular movies.

• Remember to reset the video tape machine clock if you've had a power outage.

• When taping a show, set the "on" time for five minutes earlier than the show's start time and five minutes past the show's scheduled end to make sure you don't miss anything.

• Identify the shows you've taped to save by clipping out the review from your newspaper's TV guide and then tape it onto the video tape cassette or its jacket with the clear plastic tape (¾" covers a review) that you can write on, and you'll know what the film/show is about and who starred in it.

These reviews fit nicely on the tape/jacket side, and if you are taping a series or several shows on one tape, you can usually get three to four reviews in a row on the wide edge. It doesn't matter if the transparent tape overlaps; you can write short notes or numbers on the tape if you need to identify parts 1, 2, 3.

- To avoid taping over a show that someone wanted to watch, stick self-stick notes on the tape jacket to record the date, show, and names of the people who want to watch it. As each watcher is finished, the name is checked off; the last watcher removes the note, which signals to everyone else in the house that the tape is free for recording again.

- To avoid taping over a "keeper" tape, use the "lockout tab" that's on all video tapes. When you remove the tab, the VCR is automatically "locked out" from recording on the tape. If you change your mind and decide not to keep the tape, you can put a small piece of adhesive tape over the lockout hole and record on it again.

- Have a family plan for keeping the remote control mechanism in a specific place; otherwise it will always be so "remote" that nobody can find it.

- Take a tip from fast-food restaurants, which keep their cash registers clean by covering them with plastic: Put your remote control mechanism into a zippered plastic bag, and the TV munchers can press all the buttons without making them icky.

- If you don't have a remote control mechanism with your older recorder, but have cable, you can rent remote control for cable.

- If you have an old-style plug-in remote control mechanism, tie bits of brightly colored ribbon on various places of the cord so people won't trip on it and dislodge it from the recorder.

- If you are an enthusiastic videophile and took a lot of home movies or collected movies before you bought a VCR, a tele-cine adapter, sold at many electronics stores, lets let you convert home movies or film slides to videotape. Commercial film companies can also do it.

- Many recorders allow you to record your favorite programs even if you are gone for a week. When you are learning how to program your VCR, do some practice programming to make sure you have mastered your VCR's system. Practicing when mistakes won't matter prevents losing the shows you want because of incorrect settings.

- Check the TV listings at the beginning of the week, set your VCR to tape the shows you want taped, and then let the VCR remember the taping sessions that are so easy to forget.

• Use a highlighter pen to mark the programs in your TV schedule so you can see at a glance what you've chosen to tape.

Videotape Care

• Keep videotapes away from any heat source to prolong tape life and preserve recorded material.

• Store recorded videotapes vertically to protect them from dust and dampness.

• Tapes should be fast-forwarded and rewound at least once a year.

• Always take up tape slack before playing. Wind the cassette hub with your finger until it's tight. You can run new tapes on fast forward before using to remove any slack unevenness.

• Never take tapes from cool to warm places just before playing them. If moisture condenses on the tape, it will stick to the video head.

• Beware: A tape left on top of a TV set can be erased when the TV is turned on due to the TV set's magnetic field. (Computer diskettes stored near telephones can lose information stored on them, because phones contain magnets too!)

Caring for Your VCR

• Many unnecessary service calls are made because of bad connections. If your VCR is connected to a defective cable converter box (which is, in turn, connected to the TV set), the VCR won't record properly even if it plays prerecorded tapes. Try connecting the VCR directly to the TV set. If it works properly, you'll know to call the cable company instead of your VCR repair service.
   Tape heads get clogged by oxide particles that chip or flake off from tapes. You can prevent clogging by using quality tapes (labeled "high grade" or "super high grade"), which don't shed oxide easily. Discard tapes after about 100 hours of use, and clean tape heads regularly.

• If the picture is distorted or has tiny white flecks, the tape heads may need cleaning. Use the head cleaning system suggested by your VCR instruction book or the one below.

• If you use a commercial tape head cleaner tape, please follow the directions explicitly. Run the tape for only 10 to 15 seconds or whatever the exact time prescribed on that specific tape. Longer is not better. It will only tend to gum up the tape heads more.

Portable VCRs/Camcorders

• These wonderful rec-tech devices should never be left in intense heat. When used outdoors, they should never be pointed directly at a bright light source. Bright lights can burn pick-up tubes in cameras that have them. Direct light can damage the CCD (charge couple device) in cameras that have them.

• Clean the lens with a soft cloth or brush, and keep the cover on when the camcorder's not in use.

• To protect your camcorder, check out the rain and thermal covers available from equipment stores. If you use your camcorder in cold weather, a thermal cover will protect it for operating at less than 32 degrees Fahrenheit and from condensation when you take it indoors from the cold.

• Keep a plastic bag in your equipment bag so that you can protect your camcorder from moisture damage when it rains.

• Never travel with a portable VCR that's not protected from shock and moisture by a hard case or custom-fitted shock bag. Also, let the camera get adjusted to extreme changes in temperature before you try to operate it.

Here are some trouble-shooting tips.

• Color balance: Check for adequate lighting and proper setting on the color temperature correction switch. Also check to see if the white balance needs adjusting.

• Color rendition: Check scene lighting, if color temperature correction switch is set properly, if color control knob needs adjusting, if the color setting on the TV set or monitor needs adjusting.

• If the fade switch is on, the VCR won't pause immediately when the trigger is squeezed.

Videotaping Tips

• Many of the cassette-taping tips can be useful for videotaping. You can voice your comments and descriptions on the newer video recorders so you don't have "silent movies." In that same vein, when you are videotaping family events, remember that the idea is to film moving people even if you have them standing together. You can use a still camera for "picket fences" of family members frozen in position.

• Like TV reporters, talk while you film with your camrecorder. Record your "Gee whiz!" feelings instead of just descriptions and straight information. If you record impressions "on site," you won't sound like a dull travelogue later and will better capture those special moments.

• Use your camcorder to film antiques and family treasures. Describe them while you are filming them, as someone shows all sides and the manufacturer's marks on the bottom and, if they are gadgets, demonstrates how they work. Add any anecdotes about the treasures.

• Film a party and have guests tell their favorite jokes. Then, years later, you can decide if the jokes are still funny. Or each guest tells a favorite guest-of-honor story.

• Treat your taping sessions as if you were making a TV documentary:

Start your party filming with pre-party cooking and other preparations; finish with the cleanup.
Start wedding films by showing the bride putting her makeup and veil on. If available, you could start a wedding film with some footage of the bride and groom that led to this important occasion. Have the camcorder scan the bridal pictures of the newspaper's wedding and engagement announcements page, leading to the announcement of the engagement or wedding.
Show the "locknut A's" being joined to "toggle bolt Z's" when a child's bike is being assembled and then show the child learning to ride it.
Film a few scenes of the pool's construction and then show your family enjoying the new pool.

• You can also have fun using your imagination and newspaper headlines or book jackets for titles, even if they are only semi-appropriate. For example, *A Tale of Two Cities* or *Europe on $5 a Day* could be the title for your vacation trip film. "Hurricane Gilbert Leaves Path of Destruction" could be the title preceding your after-party shots or a film of children playing after they've totally emptied a toy box. *The Joy of Cooking* could be the title preceding a barbecue scene. "Classified" cut from the want-ad section could be the title for just about any tape.

Audio Cassette Tapes

• Store tapes in their protective plastic cases to prevent dust buildup and damage to the tape surface.

• Cassette tapes should be kept tightly wound. If a tape gets loose, you can tighten it by inserting your finger or a wooden pencil into one of the holes and then turning the hub.

• Try not to touch the tape surface itself when a tape gets unwound, because you can scratch it and lose parts of the recording.

• Tape players need cleaning and demagnetizing occasionally (about every 10 to 30 hours of play) to help eliminate noise on the tapes and maintain the output levels. You can buy tape cleaning and demagnetizing kits.

Here's what they do: The cleaner removes oxides that come off the back of the tape and adhere to the tape heads, capstans, and pinch rollers of your player.

(You can use concentrated isopropyl alcohol and a cotton swab too, but avoid using rubbing alcohol, which could damage the pinch rollers.)

As always, read the manufacturer's instructions for care of your player; they'll tell you which fluids to use.

• When you demagnetize your tape machine, be certain that all recorded tapes are at least one foot away from the player to avoid erasures. The demagnetizer removes residual magnetism from the player. It can also erase parts of the tape. In fact, to avoid accidental erasures, you shouldn't store tapes near any magnetic source, including speakers and television sets.

• One of my resources says that all prerecorded cassettes manufactured after 1984, whether higher-quality chromium dioxide (CrO_2) or standard (ferric), will automatically play back on the "normal" setting (if your deck has an automatic sensing device). If you have manual settings, use "normal" for all post-1984 prerecorded cassettes for optimum playback. Modern technology enables us to play tapes without making all sorts of adjustments.

• Not many people have the seven-inch reel-to-reel type of audiotapes, but collectors of these tapes often find that the old labels and boxes in which they are stored are worn, not to mention covered with notations about what's on the tapes.

If you stick adhesive-backed shelf paper (with simple patterns or solid colors) on the boxes so that you wrap the sticky paper around the front, the hinged part, and the back of the boxes, you not only cover the boxes and make them look nice, you reinforce the hinges. Then you can play the tapes to make sure what's on them and properly label the boxes so that you can index them.

Storing Audio Cassette Tapes

• Audio cassette tapes are about the size of an index card, so if you're lucky enough to find old library card files at antiques or "junque" shops, you'll have a handy, dust-free storage case for audio tapes.

• The "cubby holes" of antique desks can hold tapes and your portable tape recorder too.

• You'll have a handle on carry-out audiotapes if you store audiotapes in a plastic tote (the kind sold to carry household items and cleaners).

• The three- or four-section plastic divided silverware trays usually used in kitchen drawers can be used as a cassette tape tray. And, if you have space, the tray can be put into a drawer and kept clean.

• Computer disk files will hold two rows of cassette tapes if they're standing sideways. Buy them at discount or on sale. They come in various sizes, so you can keep the different types of music and tapes separated for easy finding.

Putting It on Tape

Cassette-Taping Tips

• Take a tip from store-bought tapes: Do mark your tapes with "Side A" or "Side 1" if what you have recorded continues from one side to the other. That way you'll know exactly where the material you taped is located. Add also the date, name, and subject or time span of the information (if you are taping the history of your family as remembered by one of the grand old members!).
  Here are some tips for things you'll have fun taping.

• Living histories: Tape the history of your family at reunions, using the family's patriarchs and matriarchs as speakers. Other generations will thank you.

• Take a portable recorder and two-hour tape to the nursery to record baby's first cries, and then add baby's coos and gurgles, first words and expressions. As your child gets older, record favorite nursery rhymes and songs. You can even record short conversations in which you ask questions and the child answers. Older children can enjoy being "stars" when they record, "This is Betsy, I'm six today, and my favorite color is purple. . . ." With an introduction, you'll automatically be identifying the tape. It's important to record dates, occasions, and baby's name in writing as well as verbally on tape. (Years later all of the children in the same family may sound the same, and you won't know which child said what!) These are keepsakes and "sharesakes," because you can save tapes for yourself and children and also copy them for grandparents who live far away.

• Birthday parties: Tape the "Happy Birthday to You" each year, with a few of the comments at the end from the birthday person (adult or child). You may also want to have the guests record their names and some other pertinent facts.

• Surprises: If you are surprising someone at the office for a special occasion, arrange for someone to tape the "honored" person's reactions. Then give the honoree the tape as a remembrance.

• Grandma books: Have Grandma or Grandpa tape children's books, telling children the page numbers and when to turn the page. With so many families living apart, anything that keeps up awareness is very valuable.

• Letters: Tape (on cassette or videotape) letters from friends, family, or children to grandparents or to people who are blind or visually impaired.

• You can cassette- or video-tape a message to someone who is just too ill to read a letter and add some music or a stand-up TV comic's act from television to spice up your "letter." Don't make it too funny if your friend is recovering from surgery and might pop a few stitches!

• Taped "round-robin" letters can be passed around among friends so that everyone can keep in touch. Each person who receives the tape can add a message and mail it to the next person on the list, which is sent along with the tape. The tape can make a full cycle if each person on the list will be honor-bound to mail it onward.

A second tape can be added if the first is full, and once each person has had the chance to hear everyone on the list, you can start all over again, recording over the first tape, or save for history.

• Tape carefully chosen music or a collection of favorite artists as a gift "concert" for a relative or friend.

• Instead of a letter, tape your favorite music and send it to a friend or relative with a note that says, "Here's what I've been listening to lately. I'll trade it for a tape of your favorites."

• Notes: I've seen many tourists cassette-taping their impressions of what they see on their trips. It's easier than writing notes, and some of the microcassette sets are so small and light they are actually more convenient than a notebook! In foreign countries you can tape the accents, and in many cities here and abroad you can tape street musicians too, for your memory bank.

(Don't forget that you may be expected to tip musicians and, if you are taking pictures or making tapes in third-world countries, you are expected to tip children with coins or gifts such as balloons or candy and some adults with a certain amount. If you are on a guided tour, ask the tour guide what is appropriate.)

• Carry padded envelopes and mail your tapes home if you accumulate too many.

• When you are studying a foreign language, try taping verb conjugations or other exercises. Then you can play the tapes in the car (if they don't put you to sleep) or anywhere else when you need those rote-memory study sessions.

• To make a self quiz on tape when studying for tests: First record questions, then leave a pause of 10 to 20 seconds, and then record the answer. When the tape is played, the recorder becomes the tutor, since there is time to answer the questions after each one, and then the correct answer is given by the tutor-tape.

• You don't have to miss your favorite radio shows if you're gone. If your radio and tape recorder permit it, set them up on a timer so that you can tape radio shows as conveniently as you tape TV shows with your VCR.

• Books on tape make long car trips seem short. You can even "read" those classics you've always wanted to read but never had the time for. Taped books cost about the same as hard-cover books, and you can trade tapes the way you trade novels. Taped books are often on sale at bookstores. Many main-branch libraries have books on tape to borrow too, so you don't have to buy them.

• You can substitute books on tape for music when you wear a headset and catch up on your reading while you jog or walk or just relax in your backyard.

Musical Notes

Compact Discs

Music lovers love compact discs. Even if you have a "tin ear," you know how wonderful the sound is. But these discs are expensive and need care.

• After playing your compact discs, return them to their protective plastic cases. Scratches affect the sound. Be especially protective of the unlabeled side, which is the one the laser reads. Handle your CDs only by the center and edges.

• The correction system of a good player will handle scratches, so you may hear a note indistinctly or hear a split second of "mush" instead of the "tick, tick" that you hear when regular records are scratched.

• Your player will ignore some dust. However, when grease or skin oils from handling fill the tiny pits in compact discs, the laser can become "confused" and reflect the wrong way, which can result in garbled sound.

• To clean a CD, it's best to just wipe it with a dry, soft, lint-free cloth. You can rinse it under running cool water and blot dry with a lint-free towel. When you wipe your CD, always do it in a straight line from the center to the edge. Never clean CDs with solvent or abrasive cleansers. Some sources say that you can use ethyl alcohol as a solvent if necessary, but most say commercial cleaning kits are the safest way to clean CDs.

• Most of the time, the player's error-correction circuits compensate for defective discs, but really bad defects will cause a clicking noise or cause the player to mistrack the disc.

• Occasionally, a disc will have an uneven coating of aluminum, which causes poor reflectance. You can detect poor reflectance by holding a CD up to the light and looking for a mottled or unevenly mirrored surface.

• You can copy CDs onto cassettes for your car, but you may find that very quiet musical passages can be lost and very loud passages may be more than your tape or cassette player can handle.

• See the section below about playing CDs in cars.

• CAUTION: Compact discs are made of polycarbonate plastic, and while it's not easy to warp them, they will soften at 220 degrees Fahrenheit. When you have CD discs in your car, protect them from the sun's heat. The sun will warp them if you leave them on the dashboard or seat.

• Although CDs are considered to be virtually indestructible, they should always be stored away from heat and dust and handled as instructed above to prevent scratches and fingerprints. As this book is being written, there is disagreement among the experts about the life of compact discs. Some are saying they have a life expectancy of eight years, certainly disappointing to collectors. A British firm's research indicates that the shiny reflective layer beneath the disc's surface is made from a substance that chemically self-destructs, making the layer cloudy. Cloudiness makes the laser beam bounce back, spoiling your music. Some firms are considering changing the substance used in manufacturing the reflective layer.

• Although they are only about 4¾" in diameter, and therefore take less storage space than regular records, many of the storage tips for records will be suitable for CDs. If you've invested in many discs, it's probably better to buy commercially made storage cases especially designed to protect them.

• If you carry around your CDs in a portable case (to play in your car or elsewhere), don't tempt thieves by identifying the case's contents with labels.

• Portable cases should fit under a car seat, protect the discs from shock, and have secure handles. Some portable cases have a lift-out plastic liner that can be used for home storage.

Compact Disc Players

• Although a compact disc player doesn't have a stylus, and claims are made that it can be bumped without damage, avoid jolting the compact disc player anyway. Jolts may put the laser off track. One of the main differences between more and less expensive players is that the more expensive players are better able to cope with vibrations and shocks. They are not indestructible!

• Don't turn up the volume as soon as you start up your CD player. It can send a blast of clipped and distorted sound through your audio system, which, in turn, can damage the speakers' tweeters.

• The first thing to check if your player doesn't play when you start up is the disc loading slot or door containing the beam. All CD players are designed so that the lasers won't operate until the slots or doors are properly closed.

• Don't panic if your CD goes off for no reason that you can see. A spark generated by touching your player after walking across a carpet may be the culprit that shut it off. If this happens to you, turn the player off, wait about 30 seconds, then turn the power back on. All should be in order.

• With an adapter, portable CD players can be plugged into a car cigarette lighter and played through a car sound system or cassette player. Foam-padded automotive shock absorber brackets designed especially for CD players and sold at CD dealers will solve the problem of bumpy roads jarring the player.

Record Players/Turntables

• Place your record player or turntable in a stable location to avoid having the stylus bounce and scratch the record surface.

• To get the best sound, cover only one of two opposing surfaces in your "music listening room" with sound-absorbing materials. For example, if you have a carpeted floor, don't use acoustic tiles on the ceiling. If you drape a window, don't drape the opposite wall. Remember that glass reflects sound and upholstered surfaces absorb it.

• When setting up your stereo system, make sure you have followed the instructions for tone arm weight and pitch adjustment to ensure proper playing of your records and to avoid unnecessary damage to them.

• Don't expect your stylus or needle to play on forever. Check the manufacturer's directions for play life. A diamond stylus is good for about 1,000 hours of play. If you don't know how long you've had your stylus, take it to an equipment store to have it checked for wear.

• Some systems allow you to change the stylus yourself. However, if you have a service technician check your stylus for wear, you can, at the same time, have the stylus force adjusted and the tone arm balanced. Keeping the stylus and tone arm in best condition protects your record collection and therefore saves you money in the long run.

• The stylus can collect dust, and commercial stylus cleaners are available in electronics stores.

• CAUTION: Never touch a stylus with your fingers, because even the lightest touch can break or misalign it. If you are dusting a stylus, always brush from back to front, never from front to back or side to side.

• Keep your turntable covered when it's not in use. If the turntable is dusty, you'll get fuzzy, garbled sound. Clean the turntable with a damp, lint-free cloth.

• Before getting your turntable serviced when it's not working properly, check the fuses. You can check and replace fuses yourself with some systems, and instructions for doing so are in the manufacturer's instruction book.

• CAUTION: Always unplug the system before checking or replacing any parts. And never use wrenches or pliers to tighten connections—use fingers only! And, the rule is: If it doesn't fit, don't force it, because you are either doing something wrong or you have poor-quality parts.

• Children often lose the adapters that you need for playing 45-RPM records on their players. If you stick a spool (the kind that holds 325 yards of thread) on the record player post, you'll have an adapter that isn't so easily lost.

Records

• When you buy records, take off the plastic skin wrap and then always store your records in their protective inner sleeve and jacket in a vertical position. If you have a large collection, you may want to store records in categories (jazz, classical, pop) and/or alphabetically by artist's name or album/song titles.
  Some handy record/album storage bins include:

1. The fiberboard cubes available at most large hardware stores, which can be painted to coordinate with the room or, in the case of students, in school colors. Heavy and stackable, these cubes can be "built" into a sturdy place for a turntable and other sound equipment.
2. Plastic milk cartons have become popular for storing and moving records. If you have small children toddling about your house, you can tie straps made from wide elastic across the openings of these crates. You can still get the records out without too much trouble and baby will be discouraged from damaging your record collection.

• Help very young children to learn how to take care of their records. In large print, mark a letter of the alphabet on the upper right-hand corner of the jacket and then the same letter on each side of the record that goes into this jacket. You'll be teaching "ABCs" and neatness at the same time to your preschoolers.

• When the jackets of 45-RPM records get too shabby to protect the records, put the records (and the jackets too, if they are collector records) into a small, zippered plastic bag and they'll stay dust-free. The plus is that you can still read the labels through the plastic bags.

• Children's 45-RPM records can also be stored on an empty, solid deodorizer plastic cartridge. Just pull the top up and off and "spindle" the 45s.

• When you are moving records yourself, you can place a thin foam rubber sheet between albums to prevent damage from bumps and jarring.

• When you pack your possessions into your car, never put your records where the sun will shine on them, even if your car is air-conditioned. Sun shining through the car window can be warm enough to damage records.

• Sometimes warped records can be "unwarped" to a more playable condition if you place the record on a warm, flat surface such as the television set or top of the fridge and then weigh it down with heavy books. Leave the record undisturbed for several days. While this won't work for all records, it's certainly worth a try, because the warped record is useless anyhow.

• If a record is permanently warped beyond use and cannot be salvaged, you can put it over an appropriately sized cake pan or any metal form which is sized so that you get the "border" width you want, and then "bake" it in an oven at 350 degrees Fahrenheit for two or three minutes. You get a cute ruffled tray for holding spice bottles in the kitchen and many other things. You can also melt records over clay flowerpots and then, if you put some waterproof tape (duct tape, layered) over the hole, you'll have a "pot plant saucer" that adds black accents to your pot plant collection.

(If you don't normally do crafts, this is one that's fun, because it doesn't require equipment or cleanup. Also, if it doesn't turn out the size you want, you haven't lost anything, because the record was useless anyhow.)

• If your records have been dampened somehow and have become mildewed, try washing them as follows:

1. Holding the record by the edges, rinse both sides under a stream of cold tap water. After rinsing the record well and while it's still wet, squirt a small amount of mild liquid detergent on your wet fingertips. Rub around the record gently, being certain to rub with grooves and not across them. (No bar soap, just mild liquid detergent, please!)
2. Rinse well, still holding the record by its edges, and give it a few shakes to get most of the water off.

3. Set the record on edge in a safe place to dry. Never use a terry towel or other lint-producing fabric to dry records. Instead, get a cloth sold just for wiping records.

• If you really treasure your records, wear white cotton gloves while handling and cleaning them to prevent leaving smudges, fingerprints, and dust that can damage the records and the stylus.

• To clean records so that they play well and long, use a kit available where sound equipment is sold, which contains an applicator brush and anti-static cleaning fluid. The fluid removes residue and restores anti-static properties to your records. The fluid can also cut down on friction and thereby lengthen your records' life, because it provides lubrication between the stylus and record grooves.

• You can "poof" away dirt and dust from your records with a clean plastic squeeze bottle from eye or nose drops. But be sure it is carefully cleaned and totally dry.

Speakers

With more television shows broadcasting in stereo, speakers are becoming as important to viewing pleasure as they are to listening pleasure.

• You can use an adapter to get stereo sound from an older stereo-adaptable TV set (check model numbers with your dealer). With a non-stereo-adaptable TV set, you'll need a service technician to convert to stereo if your model permits it.

• Most manufacturers say that lower-priced speakers sound better if located off the floor and away from corners. "Ear level" will give the best sound from lower-priced speakers.

• Higher-priced speakers radiate more of their energy to the rear or sides and bounce more of their sound off the walls, producing more of a stereo effect than conventional speakers.

• You can get theaterlike "surround sound" by hooking a surround sound device to your stereo TV set and VCR, tape deck, or CD and spacing four speakers around the room. If the surround sound device is used with non-stereo TV sets or VCRs, it simulates stereo effects.

• When you are buying speakers, make sure that each speaker in the pair sounds the same. Different-sounding speakers could indicate defects or damage. Also, make sure you can return or exchange the speakers if they don't sound right in your "listening room" at home.

Headsets and Stereo Headphones

Headsets make jogging and walking more pleasant and prevent people from inflicting their musical tastes upon others, but CAUTION: Don't play your headphones so loud that you don't hear oncoming traffic. It is illegal in many areas to wear a headset while operating any kind of motorized vehicle.

• Even open-air type of headsets, which are designed to let you hear outside sounds, may be turned up too high to allow hearing them and be a threat to your safety.

• Continuous extended playing of headsets at high volume can damage your ears. If you have a ringing in your ears, either reduce the volume or stop using headsets.

• Whether you are buying a headset or a set of stereo headphones, comfort is the priority. If you can (perhaps by borrowing from a friend), try wearing the model for a half hour or so to comfort-test it. Just putting a set on for a few minutes won't tell you much. If you can't test it for an extended time, find out about the dealer's return/exchange policies.

• Another reason to try out stereo headphones is that if you are new to their use, you may not like the superstereo effect they give to music. Violins sounding as if they are coming in from the far right and music recorded with multiple microphones and other supersound techniques can be very uncomfortable to some people.

• Most stereo headphones come with cords ranging from 7 to about 14 feet. If you need a longer cord than that, get an extension cord from an audio shop. (If you've bought an electrostatic model that uses non-standard cords, you'll need to lengthen the wires to the adapter.) Some newer models are cordless and work well up to about 50 feet away from the source.

• If you like to hear music or watch TV until you fall asleep, you can buy headphones that turn off themselves and the TV set after you nod off.

Audio-Video Furniture

• Check that the wiring holes are where you need them and are convenient for organizing your equipment. Otherwise, you'll be drilling holes for wiring!

• Many antique armoires can be converted into audio-video centers, with the advantage that, in addition to being fine furniture, the armoire doors can be closed to keep dust out when they're not being used.

CAUTION: When you plan audio-video centers, always make certain that the equipment is well ventilated to prevent overheating when in use.

• Don't operate electronic equipment placed on beds or carpet; such soft surfaces can prevent ventilation at the bottom and cause overheating.

When the TV Tube Plays Its Last Picture Show

• One of my readers wrote that her family inserted an aquarium into their old TV cabinet and now watch fish instead of television shows, which, in the case of some shows, may be a whole lot more entertaining!

• Large console chests are often very good pieces of furniture, and too often a seriously burned-out television set can't be repaired, nor can the works be replaced so that they fit properly into the chest. After removing the works, plywood that can be stained, good-quality see-through plexiglass, or stained glass can be inserted into the television tube opening. Then the top can be removed and then replaced so that it's hinged from the back. The console can then be used to store blankets, toys, out-of-season clothing, or any other bulky and not-too-often-used items, such as punch bowls, chafing dishes, or large serving trays.

Where you keep the converted console chest depends upon the room decor and how well your project turned out.

If the console is not too tall, the top can be padded and upholstered, placed in a hall, and used as a bench and for boot and shoe storage.

Recycling is always a good idea, and if you can enjoy being creative, it's an even better idea. It saves money for you and saves the environment for all of us.

Cameras

• There are so many cameras with so many different operating procedures that I can't begin to give tips in this book, but here's one that will save you a trip to the repair shop: If your 35-mm camera won't click and the shutter seems to jam, you may not have a broken camera. Get new batteries! Camera batteries run the whole camera, not just the flash mechanism. (I thought I'd gotten sand in the camera at the beach and sand was jamming the shutter!)

• Take the batteries out when you aren't using your camera (or battery-operated cassette recorder) and they will last longer. A small amount of "juice" is being drained from the batteries as long as they are in place.

• In damp climates, or if you've taken your camera to a damp place, such as the beach, the battery connection point can corrode. You are less likely to have this problem if you remove batteries as a matter of habit when you store your camera for a couple of weeks. If you've been at the beach or fishing, you might want to dab the battery section off with a cotton-tipped swab to dry the area and clean out dirt/sand specks.

• Since most pocket cameras are made to focus with your right eye, vision problems in that eye can also cause picture-taking problems for some people. But, if you turn the camera upside down, you can use your left eye for focusing. The camera and film don't care if the up side is down or vice-versa.

• Here's a tip for you if you've ever "taken pictures" when there isn't any film in the camera. If you put a twistie on the camera strap when you put film into the camera and always remove it when you take film out, you'll always know when your 35-mm camera is "on empty" and you won't miss important photo shots.

• If you are taking instant camera pictures at a special occasion such as a shower or wedding, why not put the pictures into an album (the kind that has lift-up plastic covered pages) and then present the album to the honoree as a remembrance at the end of the party. Honeymooners would enjoy taking the album along so that they can see their wedding pictures before the official ones arrive from the photographer.

• When you move into a furnished apartment, take photos of furniture and carpeting so that you can show how worn they were when you moved in. If you are the landlord, photos will show how new the furnishings were when the tenant moved in. Include a sign with a date to prove when the photos were taken.

• If you own a furnished vacation cottage or home and rent it out, you should store valuables and take photos of each room, major appliance, or furniture piece, and the exterior of the house in case you have to make insurance claims because of damage or theft.

(The above two tips can also be used with your camcorder.)

- Save 35-mm film containers to use as mini-storage for all sorts of things, such as: spices for camping cookery, pill bottles (always label pills), paper clip holders in your purse or briefcase, and many other tiny things.

Carrying Around Audio/Video Equipment

- A backpack may be more useful and comfortable for carrying all your cameras, film, and tapes than some of the traditional bags made for that purpose.

- Lose your camera case? A small padded and zippered cassette tape case with a handle will hold many types of cameras, along with extra film, and cushion it when it's in your suitcase or on the overhead rack of a tour bus. Cassette tape carriers can also cushion cassette players safely in your carry-on bag.

- You can pad a camera case for traveling safely by gluing foam rubber to its inside surfaces.

- A cosmetic bag will hold extra film and a small camera, and the advantage of having the film and camera in a case is that you can quickly take the case out of your carry-on bags and hand it to the security attendant to hold while your bags are X-rayed and you go through the security gate.

- Stick an address label on your camera and each film container so that if you do lose these items, a finder can return them to you.

- Put lens caps in your pocket, camera case, or in some special place each time you take them off, or buy them two at a time, because they'll get lost. Or get a camera that has the lens cap attached with a cord.

- If you do a lot of photography, invest in a photographer's vest available in catalogs and specialty clothing stores, such as outfitter stores. These multi-pocketed canvas vests are useful for fishing, camping, scout troop leading, and a variety of other activities that require you to keep track of bits and pieces. They are sturdy, washable, and sized generally enough to be shared by family members.

- When you are going fishing, don't miss that great fish picture. Take your camera along, but protect it from water by sealing it in a plastic bag and then putting the bagged camera into a coffee can with a lid.

- In hot weather, your car can get to 100 degrees-plus temperatures very easily. Protect your camera and film by keeping them in an insulated foam cooler if you have to leave them in the car. The plus is that potential thieves won't see an expensive, attractive camera, just a cheap, unattractive cooler, and so they aren't as likely to be tempted to break into your car. (Although it's always best to lock things in your trunk, some trucks and hatchbacks don't have good hiding places for valuables.)

• Electronic television video game cartridges fit nicely into eight-track tape carrying cases. Store them free from dust and protected from damage and then tote them to friend's house when you want to.

• Computer disk games that you have copied yourself and that have written instructions as well as disks can be stored and carried around in pocketed loose-leaf paper holders that children usually use for different subjects in school. The printed information sheets are hole-punched and fitted on the grommets, and the disks are stored in the pockets. You can use different colors for each game and, if you feel artistic, draw appropriate pictures on the front of the folder.

Rec-Tech Information Source

Many of the electronic equipment tips in this chapter came from the Electronic Industries Association, Consumer Electronics Group, which offers free care, maintenance, and safety pamphlets from its "Consumers Should Know" series to those who send a stamped, self-addressed envelope to the association.

To request pamphlets, state the subject (television, compact discs, audio products) or pamphlet name when you write and include a No. 10 stamped, self-addressed envelope. A separate envelope is needed for each pamphlet. The address is: Electronic Industries Association (HH), 2001 Eye Street, N.W., Washington, D.C. 20006. You can call to get information on pamphlet subjects and for the names of various pamphlets. The phone number is 202-457-4900.

• Your public library also has numerous books to help you research before you buy.

Help Tech

Answering Machines

We take these machines for granted, but the tapes do wear out and you may be missing your messages due to malfunctions. Most machines have a setting that allows you to check your outgoing message periodically to see if it's working properly.

• Remember that when you replace the tape that receives messages, you need to replace it with a tape made for answering machines. Most regular cassette tapes have a lead segment at the beginning that doesn't record anything. If you put an ordinary tape into an answering machine, you'll miss parts of or most of the first message on the machine. Answering machine tapes have no "empty" lead space and will record immediately.

• These mechanical secretaries need to be cleaned with a head cleaner for audio cassette recorders to keep on taking your messages. See the manual for how often.

• Don't think that the only time you can use an answering machine is when you are out. Teach yourself to let the phone ring and the machine answer when you are busy doing something that just can't be interrupted, when you are taking a nap break, and when you're in the garden, pool, or tub. It may take you awhile to get comfortable doing this; however, you will be amazed at how many times it's simply a wrong number or a salesman.

If you turn up the volume, you can hear the message being given on your machine and then decide if you need to call back immediately.

• If you have a new baby, put a message on the machine that gives the baby's weight and other vital statistics, then say that you and the baby are napping and you'll call back later.

• Use your message for other good news announcements too. Not all messages have to be straightforward and businesslike.

• Some messages can actually be messages, such as "Kevin or Barbara, call Kim at 211-9333 after six P.M. Friday."

• Play background music while you record your message and, if you like humor, try some of the prerecorded messages or tape conversations from humor albums, TV shows, comics' monologues, and so forth. At Halloween you could put horror sounds from scare records on your tape; at Christmas, it could be a carol; Valentine's Day, a silly but short love poem. If you aren't inspired by holidays, let your imagination entertain you and your callers. We've even had Zinfandel, our talking miniature schnauzer, bark a message to our callers.

• Give an alternative number that the caller can use to reach you if there is one.

• Don't ever have your message say that nobody's home; let a prospective burglar guess.

• If you've been having too many telephone sales calls or calls from anyone else that you don't want to talk to, let your machine answer all calls, and then return important calls immediately.

• If you are having a series of obscene or just annoying callers, it's better not to put your name or any other identification on the machine. Just say, "Leave your message at the beep and I'll call you back" until the harassing calls stop. Don't return calls to any name or number that you don't recognize. Most of the time, the caller will hang up. If not, you have a record of what was said if you report the call. Look in your phone book for instructions on what to do about annoying or harassing calls. And don't hesitate to call your local phone company for help with this problem.

Telephone Installation

Installing your own phones with modular plugs and jacks means that you have to know the dos and don'ts. Here are a few from the Electronic Industries Association.

• Don't ever attempt to install telephone wiring if you wear a pacemaker.

• If you take the phone off the hook when you're working on it, you'll reduce the possibility of small electrical shock if the phone rings.

• Don't place phone wire in any conduit or outlet box that contains electrical wiring or water pipes.

• Never place a telephone jack where it would let a person use the phone in the bathtub, shower, swimming pool, or anywhere else near water.

• Four-conductor telephone station wire used for house wiring is very low voltage, so you can safely hide it under carpets, between walls, over basement ceiling joists, up and around doors and windows.

• But don't run any wire through places where it will be damp, excessively hot, pulled out by mistake, or subjected to abrasion. (Worn wires can cause interference.)

Cordless Phones

Most tests show that even though the newer models are much improved over the old ones, these phones don't really deliver the sound quality of regular phones. However, they are useful if you are involved in some outdoor activity and are expecting a call that you don't want the machine to answer.

• Expect a certain amount of "false ringing" with these phones; it comes with the territory.

• Also coming with the territory (literally, with the area in which you live) is a certain amount of interference from power lines and metal (plumbing, chain-link fences, sliding doors, screened porches). Even positioning your body between the base and handset can reduce the calling range.

• Although most models allow use of only one FCC channel, it's really better to spend the money for a multi-channel phone. If your neighbor happens to have a cordless phone on the same channel, you'll suffer party-line syndrome—one phone owner can't call out if the other is on the phone, and you can listen to each other's conversations.

Multi-Function Phones

Use your imagination with the functions of these fun phones.

• What a time-saver programmable phones are! Not only can you program frequently called numbers of friends, relatives, businesses, and emergency aid numbers, you can program pizza delivery, weather, time, and any other useful numbers.

• Speaker phones work better for group phone calls than having several people get on different extensions, which may weaken the signal and make hearing each other difficult. Also, everyone gets to hear what the person on the other end of the line said, so he or she won't have to keep repeating, "I'm fine, thank you" or "It's [snowing, raining, steaming hot, horribly cold] here."

• When using a speaker phone with lots of people, it helps if you say, "It's Jane" or "This is Bob" before you start to talk, so the people on the other end of the line don't have to keep asking, "Who said that?"

• Phones with redial or busy-dial functions will help you win radio phone-in prizes, because it's faster to punch one button than to dial or punch a whole phone number's worth of buttons when you're trying to get through on a very busy line or be the first caller.

• Being able to punch only one button also helps if you are trying to voice your opinion on radio and TV phone-in talk shows, which have super-busy lines.

• When you have any problems with these phones, the first thing to check is if the batteries need replacement—something we didn't need to think about with old-style phones. Some booklets recommend changing batteries every six months or so without waiting for any malfunctions.

Car Phones

Working moms, people who work out of their cars and/or drive deserted roads, and others who need to be contacted at any time are buying car phones in increasing numbers. If you are planning to buy one, here are some of the features you should consider.

• A glass-mounted antenna, which allows the signals to be picked up without having a hole drilled into the car body.

• Easy-to-use controls. Most of these phones have controls on the back of the handset.

• Memory and speed dialing; it avoids a lot of button pushing, which is safer. However, you really should pull over to the side of the road and stop when you are using a car phone if it's possible. Dialing and driving don't mix!

• A speaker and microphone will let you have your hands free for driving and let others in the car participate in the conversation, just as a home phone with a speaker does.

• A portable unit allows you to connect to a battery pack so that you can walk away with the phone and still use it when necessary. And you can remove it from the car so that it won't tempt thieves.

• Call timers are available to help you keep the toll costs down by keeping calls shorter.

Intercom Systems

Although the best system is one installed when a house is built, you can buy equipment to install yourself. Simple systems can be made up of just two speakers and wires that get plugged into an outlet.

Intercoms are safety devices that let you know who's at the front or back door and if you should open it, as well as energy savers, eliminating the need to walk up and down stairs, to and from the garage, or from room to room when you need to talk to someone.

• Use an intercom system in baby's or younger children's rooms, so you know when they are waking up, coughing too much, or, in the case of older children, playing instead of going to sleep. Simple two-speaker setups that are relatively inexpensive can be used to listen in on baby when you don't want the expense of installing a full house system.

• When you are listening to a room with a simple two-speaker intercom, remember to turn up the volume of the "eavesdropping" speaker and turn down the volume of the "listener's" speaker.

TV Shopping Channels and Offers

Being able to order things from TV shopping channels is one of the best help techs for people who just don't have the time to wander through malls or who can't get out to shop. However, it takes some consumer knowledge to shop wisely when a product or item pops up on the screen and tempts you to phone in your credit card number.

Here are some "need-to-knows" about shopping for just about any product, but especially when you are buying from TV shopping shows and special TV offers on merchandise that you can't actually examine hands-on.

• Know the company's refund and cancellation policy.

• Know who pays for shipping charges if merchandise is returned and who is responsible for shipping insurance. What is the company's policy for lost or damaged items?

• Will the company have the right to substitute comparable goods and is there a warranty or guarantee available?

• How long is the shipping time? How do the prices compare with local stores, catalogs, and other local sources?

• As in catalog shopping, keep a record of your order, especially the date you placed it, and the method and amount of payment, including taxes, and shipping and handling costs.

• And, here's a word for the wise shopper: Watch for consumer stories or columns about TV offers and catalog shopping services to find out if any products have been investigated for postal fraud or misrepresentation. The latter is especially a problem, with many weight-loss or medical "miracle" products sold on TV.

• You can find out if complaints have been made about local companies and products and can make complaints by calling or writing your local Better Business Bureau. Check up on nationally sold products and companies by writing or calling the Federal Trade Commission, Complaints and Inquiries, Sixth and M Avenue, N.W., Washington, D.C. 20580. Phone: 202-326-2418.

The Postal Inspector investigates if the United States mail has been used to defraud the public (chain letters, false billing, undelivered merchandise). Write to your Regional Chief Inspector, U.S. Postal Service, if you think you have been the victim of such frauds. You can get the address from your local main post office. The Regional Chief Inspector uses consumer complaints as a basis for investigations.

Comfort Tech

Air-Conditioning

One wonders how people survived in hot climates before air-conditioning made comfort and life as we know it now possible. How our ancestors must have sweltered!

• Since air-conditioning utility costs can be 50 percent of your utility bill in a hot climate, you should choose your air-conditioning system wisely. Buy neither too big nor too small a system. Here's how the Department of Energy says you should calculate to determine air conditioner sizes:

Find out the square footage to be cooled. An air conditioner usually needs 20 Btu for each square foot of living space.

If a room is 20 feet long by 15 feet wide, calculate $15 \times 20 \times 20$ (Btu) = 6,000. The room needs an air conditioner with a 6,000-Btu capacity. Buy a unit within 5 percent of this capacity. (Calculating Btu capacity for central units also has to take a home's individual needs, such as ceiling heights, floor plans, and number of stories, into consideration. Sometimes, more than one central unit is needed in a home.)

• The Btu can be lowered if you have the benefit of trees and shrubs to cool the house; using heat-producing appliances will increase Btu needs.

• Energy efficiency is probably the most important consideration when you are buying an air conditioner, and all air conditioners have yellow "Energy Guide" labels that show their efficiency ratings. Units with a "9" or more are very efficient.

Here are some tips from CARIERS (Conservation Renewable Energy Inquiry and Referral Service) on keeping down those utility bills when you're air-conditioning for comfort in the summer.

• Set the fan speed on high, except in very humid weather. In humid weather, set the speed low. Although you'll get less cooling, more moisture will be taken from the air and this will make you feel cooler.

• When you first turn on the air conditioner, it won't cool faster if you set the thermostat lower than the temperature you want. It will cool to a lower temperature and therefore waste energy and increase your utility bill. Set the temperature that you want and let the thermostat do its job.

• Keeping filters clean can cut your utility bill by 5 to 15 percent. Check filters monthly and clean or replace them as needed.

• If you have acquired a long-haired pet, you'll be surprised at how quickly your filter becomes full of hair! You may have to check it more than once monthly. My service technician told me that if a dirty filter allows pet hairs to get to the AC heating unit's coils, the damage caused is considered "lack of maintenance" and may not be covered by home-owner's appliance insurance. Not keeping the filters clean could be expensive!

• If you place heat-producing appliances near the thermostat, it becomes "confused" and runs longer than necessary.

• The fan motor on outside air conditioners is hard to get at when you try to oil it. Here's how to do it without taking off the cover:

Straighten a wire coat hanger, touch one end to the oil hole, raise the other end, and drip oil onto the wire; the oil will flow down nicely to the oil hole.
(Use this method for any hard-to-get-at oiling place.)

• Most central air-conditioning and heat pump units are placed a distance from the outside wall of your house to help muffle the fan's noise, which means the unit may be deprived of shade from the building. Heat from summer sun increases air-conditioning energy use by about 5 percent. In winter, sun exposure increases the unit's heating capacity.

It's generally recommended that you provide some sort of portable shade for the unit that can be removed in the winter, such as a collapsible lath-covered frame made from two-by-two laths or an awning if the unit is close enough to brace the awning on the house. Awnings can also shade window air-conditioning units in the summertime.

Programmable Thermostats

• If you are gone most of the day, you can save utility bills by using programmable thermostats that will automatically adjust the temperature according to a set of instructions you preset. If your heating needs vary through the day—for example, if you want heat when you wake up, but prefer to save heating bills by keeping your apartment or home cool at night and during the day when you're at work, these thermostats can be a perfect solution. They are sold at electric supply stores and some hardware stores.

Ceiling Fans

There's no question that ceiling fans make air-conditioning and heating units work more efficiently and economically.

• Ceiling fans aren't just for summer cooling. They are especially useful for blowing heat down from cathedral-style ceilings in the winter.

• If you are installing a ceiling fan in a high hallway or in a room with a cathedral ceiling, a remote-control fan can be more convenient, since you won't have to reach for different chains and pulls.

• If you bought ceiling fans when they first became popular and had old-style motors that required regular oiling, you may find that buying new fans is less expensive than repairing your old ones.

Humidifiers

The relative humidity ratio is always given as a percentage at a given temperature. The ideal indoor comfort range, according to my sources, is 40 percent relative humidity with 68 to 70 degrees Fahrenheit, plus or minus 5 percent relative humidity.

• Humidifiers (either freestanding units or those that can be attached to a furnace) prevent electric static in cold climates, your furniture's joints from drying out and getting loose, and your home fabrics from getting brittle and wearing out sooner. They also make your house plants happy. People with respiratory difficulties can benefit from adding moisture to the air, and even people who are normally healthy can get sore throats from too-dry environments.

Also, in cold weather, you feel colder in a dry room; humidifiers generally save about 15 percent of fuel costs in the winter.

• Here's how to test your home or office to find out if the humidity ratio is adequate (and comfortable):

1. Take a glass of water and place three regular-size ice cubes in it.
2. Let it sit, and within five minutes, if your room has adequate moisture in the air, you'll find plenty of condensation—beads of water—forming on the outside of the glass.

If the condensation doesn't happen within 5 to 15 minutes, the room needs humidification.

Of course, if you have static electricity when metal objects are touched and have frequent sore throats and dry skin, you don't need a test for humidity ratios.

• When you are deciding where to put a humidifier, consider that bathrooms and kitchens produce a certain amount of moisture in the air. Therefore it's best to locate a humidifier in an area that's not too close to these rooms.

• In a two-story house, you can put the humidifier at the bottom of a stairwell, but it's really better to have one unit for each floor.

• If you place your humidifier in front of or near a wall heater or radiator, their heat and air movement will increase evaporation.

• Maintenance includes replacement of worn pads, belts, plates, and orifices for solenoid valves, plus cleaners recommended by the manufacturer's manual that dissolve mineral deposits and lime, mold, and algae. Keeping your humidifier clean prevents musty odors, not to mention the possibility of spreading the mold and algae, which can really play havoc with allergies.

Dehumidifiers

In some climates and some tightly constructed homes, high humidity is a problem, especially when many showers, wet towels, drying clothing, cooking, floor washing, and ground moisture add to the situation. Mildewed shoes in closets, musty smells throughout the house, and general physical discomfort for the people in the house are symptoms of too much moisture.

Attic fans can replace warm, moist air with cool, dry outside air, and mechanical dehumidifiers recirculate room air and reduce the relative humidity.

Here are some features to look for when choosing a mechanical dehumidifier.

• An adjustable thermostat regulates the on and off cycles that maintain the selected humidity conditions.

• Exposed air-drying coils let you clean the unit easily and keep it at peak performance, with resulting lower operating costs.

• Catch buckets need to hold at least 10 quarts of water and should be easy to remove and empty without spilling. (Dehumidifiers work by drawing moist air over refrigerated coils. When the air hits the cold surface, moisture condenses and drips off into the collection bucket or to a drain hose connected to a drip tray.)

• An automatic water overflow control shuts the unit off when the water bucket is full to prevent spills.

• Recessed wheels increase stability and mobility. Two recessed wheels are usually enough.

• Maintenance includes cleaning dust and dirt from the refrigeration coils, condenser, and fan units, and, of course, emptying the catch bucket.

Heaters

Room heaters help if you are trying to save energy costs by practicing "zone heating." In zone heating, you close off unused rooms' registers or heating vents, or shut off the furnace and heat only used rooms with room heaters.

• Although room heaters are not as efficient as furnace heat, in some houses room heaters can heat one or two rooms at less expense than a big heater.

• Portable heaters use 110 volts. When selecting a portable heater, you need to check the wattage, because the rule of thumb is that you need one watt per cubic foot of air volume in the room.

Electric Blankets

• Never layer bedding over an electric blanket while it's on. You can cause the wiring to overheat to the point of catching fire.

• If you need a king-size electric blanket and find twin-size ones on sale at a good price, you can tack the edges together and make your own dual-controlled king-size blanket at a cost much less than that of a king-size one.

• If you have a Hollywood-style bed (without a footboard), the electric blanket cord tends to stick out from the foot of the bed and catch your ankle when you are making the bed. Try attaching a cup hook to the underside of the box spring, with the open part of the hook pointing toward the head of the bed. Thread the cord through the hook, and the cord will stay out of your sight and way.

• You can take an electric blanket to a professional cleaner when it needs freshening, or you can launder it yourself, if so indicated on the care label, as follows:

1. First disconnect the electric control and machine wash in warm water with mild detergent. But note that long wash or spin cycles may damage the blanket.
2. When the machine is filled with water, let it agitate a bit so the detergent dissolves if you use powdered detergent, then put the blanket into the water and let it wash three or four minutes at the most.
3. After the water drains, follow with a short spin cycle. Rinse again and spin briefly again so that only part of the water is removed. Press the remaining water out with your hands.
4. Line dry over two parallel lines. Machine drying can damage the wiring.

• NEVER run an electric blanket through a coin-operated dry-cleaning machine; the solvent can damage wiring and cause electric shock when the blanket is used.

• If your electric blanket is old and you don't trust the wiring anymore, you don't have to throw out the blanket. Just snip at the ends of the wires at the head and foot of the blanket and pull out the wires. You'll have a spare blanket at no cost. You can also use the blanket as a filler in a hand-sewn quilt or coverlet.

CHAPTER 11

Pets

It's no secret that I love animals. As this book is being written, three dogs—Zinfandel, the miniature schnauzer; Sheba, the keeshond; Willie, the Brittany—and three birds—Rocky the Military Macaw and Fussy and Doley, male cockatiels—are sharing my home and my life. I have also had ferrets named Fanny the Ferret and Fred the Ferret.

I can't imagine life without pets, and from my mail I know that many people share my feelings about them and enjoy reading about my pets when I write about them in my newspaper and *Good Housekeeping* magazine columns. I get frequent requests for my schnauzer Zinfandel's "autograph" and photo.

Choosing a Pet

When you decide to get a dog or cat, remember that cute little puppies and kittens really do grow up. Some little balls of fur become very large dogs who need fenced-in yards to roam in and long exercise walks. Others become feisty tomcats that annoy neighbors and even their owners with their fighting and spraying if they aren't neutered.

• Find out how big the breed of dog you choose will be when mature. If you live in a house with a big, fenced-in yard, you can have any dog or pet you choose that is allowed by your city's zoning laws. But if you live in a small apartment, you may want to choose small, quiet pets that don't need as much "elbow" or tail-wagging space.

• Add up the costs of pet ownership before you get one. Pets need immunizations and grooming in addition to food, water, love, and attention. Animals that will not be bred need to be spayed or neutered.

• Make getting a pet a family decision so that everyone feels a sense of responsibility for the pet's care.

• Pets can't be given as gifts the way stuffed animals are given. The experts say that choosing your own pet helps to establish a binding relationship with the animal.

• Children younger than three should never be given any kind of small animal as a pet. Many a puppy, kitten, chick, or gerbil has unintentionally been "loved" (translate that as "mauled") to death by a child that really didn't know any better.

• When you're ready to begin looking, don't forget your local animal shelter. It's sad to think about the numbers of stray animals that have to be euthanatized because nobody wants them.

According to the Humane Society of the United States, an estimated 15 to 18 million animals enter shelters each year, and the Cornell University College of Veterinary Medicine estimates that 13 million shelter animals must be destroyed annually—an average of one animal every three seconds. About one-fourth of these animals are purebreds, so it's not just mutts that people abandon or "throw away."

And my personal theory is that most pets that you adopt from a shelter or who adopt you, as Sheeba, our keeshond, did, seem to know that they are lucky and turn out to be very faithful and lovable animals.

I guess, speaking as one animal lover to another (and you must be one if you are reading this chapter), my best Heloise advice is: If you can't properly care for a pet, don't get one. And if you don't plan to breed your pet, have it spayed or neutered.

General Pet First-Aid and Health Tips

• If you can't afford a private veterinarian, call your local Humane Society to find clinics with less expensive services for neutering, spaying, and immunizations.

• It's a misconception that female animals need to have a litter before spaying and that spayed or neutered animals automatically get fat and lazy. Ask your vet!

• Don't ever leave your pet in a car unattended. You may think that it's not hot when it's only 85 degrees and you're parked in the shade, but even with the windows slightly opened, in less than 30 minutes the temperature inside the car can get as high as 120 degrees, causing heat stroke and possibly death. Please, when you go out, leave your pet home!

• Protect kittens and puppies from their own curiosity. Prevent them from licking electric connections that could electrocute them; from falling into swimming pools, where they can drown; from chewing and swallowing dangerous small objects or eating poisonous plants, such as Dieffenbachia, mistletoe berries, and poinsettia.

• Safeguard pets at night. Cats allowed to roam at night and even dogs trained to heel without being on a leash should wear reflective collars or have reflective tape stuck to their collars to alert motorists.

• When you need pet health advice, see a veterinarian, not a pet store owner, who is in business to sell animals and pet food and isn't likely to know much about nutrition, disease, and pet problems.

• Find a veterinarian by asking your friends for recommendations and then have your pet examined once or twice a year and given immunizations, as the vet suggests. As with people, health problems should be found and treated before they become serious.

• If the vet you choose doesn't have time to talk to you and answer your questions, find one who does.

• Remember that after the initial series of immunizations, booster shots are needed annually.

• Warm weather decreases animals' appetites. The heat may cause some dogs to be less active, and therefore they will eat less. Kittens shouldn't be allowed to fast too long; give them frequent, small feedings on hot days.

• Many animals actually like to graze on grass. It's okay for your dog or cat to eat grass; it's their version of salad.

• Worming medications are dangerous if improperly used. Medicate your animals only with prescription medicines from your veterinarian. And, by the way, worms aren't caused by eating candy, nor can they be cured by feeding your dog garlic.

• Since animals can't talk, you have to be a detective to find out if they are in pain. Some symptoms of pain are lameness, stiff neck, reluctance to get up or lie down, and/or tense abdominal muscles. See the vet!

• Keep puppies away from other dogs' droppings. Infected feces transmit a serious disease called parvovirus, which kills 75 percent of puppies under five months of age who get it. Older dogs are more or less immune. All dogs should be vaccinated to prevent this disease.

• If your dog is nauseated, take away all food and water for 24 hours but give the dog small amounts of water to prevent dehydration by providing ice cubes to lick.

• A dog that can't urinate should be taken to a vet at once. It could die of uremia if it doesn't urinate for 24 hours.

• A dog that shows the signs of shock should be kept warm. His position shouldn't be shifted too suddenly, because sudden movements can cause the shock to go into an irreversible stage.

• Prevent dogs from straining with impacted feces by adding a teaspoon of cooking oil to each food serving. The oil will also put a shine in the dog's fur.

• When the vet requests a stool sample from your dog, try not to include any soil in the sample. Dirt can contain harmless soil worms that may confuse the examiner. A clean margarine tub and a plastic spoon will help you scoop up and transport the sample for the vet.

• To give liquid medications to a frisky, objecting dog, avoid a mess by putting the dog into the bathtub at medication time.

• To pill a dog, insert the pill into its mouth, then close the mouth quickly and tap his nose with your finger or gently blow on the pet's face. This causes the dog to lick and then swallow.

- Stroking a dog's throat will make it swallow a pill.

- You can bury pills in cream cheese, peanut butter, cheese, or liverwurst—whatever your dog thinks is a treat.

- Heartworm pills (which are scored for breaking into quarters) can be broken in four pieces and placed on top of your dog's dry food or poked into canned food if your dog doesn't think these pills are a treat.

- Cats and lap-size dogs can be wrapped and held securely in a towel before pills are popped into their mouths. Towel wrapping also works well if you have to apply ointments to eyes or ears of small pets.

- Pet "pillers," which look like a long, thin syringe with a rubber holder at the end, can be used to poke pills down animals' throats. Again, stroking the throat hastens swallowing after the pill is inserted.

- When you start giving a dog heartworm pills, handle the pill as you do his other treats. Have him do a trick for it and then give him the heartworm pill as a reward. (Just the opposite of the way you medicate children, who should never be taught that medicine is "candy.")

- If all else fails when you are trying to pill a pet, just open the pet's mouth and put the pill way back to the throat, close the mouth, rub the throat, and, if necessary, cover the pet's snout. It will usually swallow the pill with this method.

When we started giving Zinfandel and Sheba their heartworm pills every day, we made it appear as if the pills were a treat, covered with peanut butter for Sheba and a little butter for Zinfandel. They both have to speak for their goodies and now they demand them every morning.

Pet Dental Care

According to veterinarians, 90 percent of all cats and dogs suffer from some type of dental disease by the age of six years.

While pets have good natural defenses against tooth decay, plaque and tartar build up after years of soft food diets. Crisp foods and leather chew sticks help, but they don't clean teeth at the gum line, where tartar and plaque buildup encourage the growth of bacteria that can lead to generalized infection, even heart disease.

For your pet's sake, prevent periodontal disease. Here are the symptoms that should tell you your pet needs to see a veterinarian about dental problems:

1. Persistent bad breath.
2. Tartar formation (creamy-brown spots on teeth).
3. Inflamed gum line.
4. Bleeding or receding gums.
5. Loose, infected, or missing teeth.

A veterinarian will treat periodontal disease by cleaning your pet's teeth to remove tartar and plaque. The veterinarian will then recommend regular brushing, along with periodic checkups.

Fleas

To give you an idea about the magnitude of the flea problem: One female flea can create 800 virtually indestructible eggs in her lifetime, and under good conditions 10 fleas can produce a quarter of a million new fleas within 30 days. And the reason you can't just slap one when you see it is that fleas can accelerate 50 times faster than the space shuttle!

In some parts of the country, "flea season" is a torture for animals and humans. Animals can develop "hot spots" (irritated skin patches that are actually hot to the touch and that are rendered hairless by the animals' efforts to bite the fleas), and humans, too, suffer from itchy bites.

• Vacuum floors, rugs, and furniture at least weekly to collect fleas and their eggs, being especially careful to vacuum in dark corners and crevices. Toss a couple of mothballs into your vacuum cleaner bag to kill the fleas as you pick them up and then throw out the bag.

• CAUTION: When you spray commercial insecticides indoors and out it's imperative to follow directions for the particular brand you use. Some directions say that your pet should not be allowed to walk on carpets or grass sprayed with insecticide until the chemicals are dry. Allowing pets to romp on some wet insecticides could poison them.

• To avoid skin irritations from too-potent flea collars, air out the collar for several days before putting it on your dog or cat. But air the collar where it's safe from people and pets!

• Excessive amounts of flea powder in a pet's coat can be licked off and may make your pet ill. Brush off all excess flea powder within 30 minutes after it's applied to prevent your dog or cat from ingesting the residue.

• Don't use flea preparations formulated for dogs on cats. Cats lick/groom themselves more than dogs do, and cat formulas take that into account when the chemical strengths are determined. Many preparations available at your veterinarian are safe for both dogs and cats. Get advice from your vet!

• If you have a cat or small dog that really resists being powdered or sprayed for fleas, powder or spray a bath towel and then wrap the animal in the towel, holding it wrapped for about 15 minutes so the chemicals can work.

• If you have a water-hating cat or a dog too large to dip for fleas and ticks, thoroughly wet the animal's coat, and then spray the dip (mixed in proportions according to directions) onto the pet with a spray bottle.

• Shampooing your dog more than every 10 to 14 days can dry out its skin. If your flea shampoo and dip aren't effective for the entire interval between bath and dip, you'll need to use sprays or powder in between shampoos.

• It's better to let your pet dry naturally after being dipped. Towel drying will remove some of the dip.

• Flea and tick powders and sprays should never be combined with each other or with a flea collar, because you may overdose your pet with these chemicals. This is especially true of small breed dogs. Please don't take a chance.

• Cedar shavings or pine needles will repel fleas from animal bedding and doghouses. Salt also repels fleas, so washing your dog's doghouse periodically with salt water is a good prevention.

• Fleas are attracted to light. Make a flea trap with a light-colored, shallow pan, and a 25-watt lamp, without shade:

1. Every night for several weeks, fill the pan with soapy water and set it on the floor.
2. Position the lamp next to the pan so that the bulb is a foot or so above the water. (This should be the only source of light in the area.)
     When the light is turned on, fleas will jump toward the heat and fall into the water.
3. Rinse out the pan in the morning.

• To help keep fleas off you, bathe daily with soaps containing green dyes.

• Fleas spend only a short time on your pet; most of the time they are happily breeding in carpets, bedding, and your yard. To prevent reinfestation, you must treat your home and yard as well as your pet.

While each flea control product has its own set of instructions, the basic principles of eliminating fleas from your and your pet's environment are as follows:

1. In the yard, use a commercial spray with a garden hose hook-up.
2. Inside, clean and vacuum the house, and immediately dispose of the vacuum bag. Then use a room fogger and spray hard-to-reach areas with a kennel spray.

• Remove all pets and cover fish tanks and exposed food before you use a fogger.

• Close exterior doors and windows, and turn off the furnace or air conditioner to allow insecticide to disperse.

• Put a fogger in each room and position it in the center of the room on newspapers to protect the floor or carpet from droplets.

• Do not reenter the home for two hours and then when you do, open doors and windows to ventilate for at least 30 minutes.

Traveling with Your Pet

Like some people, some pets are not good travelers and are best left with a sitter or in a boarding kennel. If the trip is short, perhaps a neighbor could look in on your pet while you are gone. Often older pets fare better when kept at home in familiar surroundings instead of in a kennel.

Your vet or local Humane Society can recommend safe, well-run kennels in which to board your pet.

• You will need a veterinarian's exam to get the legal documents needed for transporting animals interstate and internationally. In addition to examining your animal to determine general health, the veterinarian should provide any inoculations your pet requires, such as for rabies, distemper, infectious hepatitis, and leptospirosis.

• A veterinarian can prescribe a sedative or tranquilizer for jittery traveling pets, but you should never give your human medicines to pets. Some human medications can, at the least, make them ill and, at worst, damage the pet's internal organs or be poisonous.

• If you take along familiar food and even water from your hometown supply, stop frequently to give your pets water and exercise, and check ahead to make sure the hotel or motel you've reserved will accept pets, you'll make traveling with them easier.

Legal Requirements for Transporting Pets

Dogs and cats crossing state lines need to be accompanied by a valid health certificate and a certificate of rabies inoculation.

(While state pet travel health restrictions are rarely enforced, having the proper documents avoids the risk of having your pet quarantined or refused entry into a state.)

• Within the United States, pet travel is generally unrestricted, with the exception of travel to Hawaii, where there is an unwaivable 120-day mandatory quarantine for all dogs and cats.

• To enter Canada, cats don't need special documents if they are healthy. Dogs must have a certificate of rabies vaccination issued within the previous 12 months. Also, a definitive description of the traveling dog is required.

• Before taking a pet to Mexico, a health certificate, prepared in duplicate, should be mailed to the Mexican consulate with a fee. The certificate must include a description of your pet, the rabies vaccine used, proof of distemper vaccine, and a veterinarian's statement verifying the animal is free from infectious or contagious diseases. You may proceed with your trip when the certificate has been certified and returned, which can take some time, possibly months.

How to Select a Pet Carrier

• The carrier should have opaque sides, several venting holes on all sides, a grille door, and be durable, with enough space to allow your pet to stand, sit or lie down. A secure door handle is a must. Most domestic airlines sell pet carriers that meet travel standards.

CAUTION: Zinc nuts used to secure some types of dog cages can be toxic to dogs if the dogs swallow the nuts. If the cage you've bought has zinc nuts, substitute stainless steel or nylon nuts, often sold for car license plates in automobile supply stores.

When Your Pet Is a Car Passenger

• Expose your pets to car travel gradually with short trips before you attempt a cross-country journey with a pet.

- Dog harnesses that attach to seat belts are available in pet stores. It's not safe to have pets crawling on your lap or around your feet while driving.

- Cats, because they tend to move erratically, should be in carriers. It saves them from getting injured by closing doors and getting lost if they make a panic leap from the car when you make a rest stop.

- Put two collars with identification on your pet when it is traveling, just in case one falls off. And please include an area code and phone number of someone who can be reached.

Birds

My two cockatiels and Rocky, a Military Macaw, keep everybody who visits me entertained. I keep them in my office so that they can see my staff and visitors all day long.

- All birds need companionship, either with other birds or people. They've been known to pull out their feathers when lonely or bored. Give them toys, bells, and mirrors so that they can keep themselves amused and give them attention, too, just like you do with dogs and cats.

- You really shouldn't keep your bird cage in the kitchen. If a non-stick pan accidentally burns dry, it will give off toxic fumes that can cause polymer-fume fever and that can be fatal, especially to small birds.

- Small birds, such as canaries, finches, and parakeets, have delicate respiratory systems and are sensitive to fumes of all kinds—hair sprays, deodorants, and flea powders and sprays.

- A bird cage should be placed out of drafts, away from air-conditioning or heating ducts, and not near a window where the sun will shine directly on it for long periods of time, especially in the summer. Place the cage where the bird can have plenty of light and circulating air and cover the bird when the sun goes down.

- To teach your bird how to talk, repetition is the key. You can put the word (repeated many times) on cassette tape and then play it for your bird when you don't have time to chat or when you go away on a trip and don't want your bird to forget.

- Birds need exercise and attention. A lonely parakeet can actually get "love-sick" and act strangely. If your bird begins to preen before a mirror or plastic cage toy (some birds may even regurgitate food onto the mirror or toy), it is practicing courting and nesting behavior, which is usually reserved for mates and offspring. The cure for "lovesickness" is to remove the "love object" from the cage for two to three weeks and give your bird more exercise and attention.

• NOTE: Regurgitation by parakeets and other birds can also be a symptom of digestive ailments. If your bird regurgitates frequently but has no other "lovesick" symptoms, check with your vet.

• CAUTION: When you buy an imported pet bird, be sure that it has entered this country legally. Many birds are smuggled in without the benefit of quarantine, a practice that endangers birds in the United States. Outbreaks of exotic Newcastle disease, a devastating bird disease, have occurred in the past because of illegal importation of pet birds.

On a recent trip to a Mexican border town, I saw some parrots, wild cardinals, and other birds offered for sale, and when I asked about a yellow-headed parrot, the salesman offered me a price reduced from $25 to $15 that included taking the birds across the border and delivering them to me. I refused, of course, because not only is such a practice illegal, it's a way of smuggling in bird diseases along with birds.

• Buy a bird only from a reputable dealer. All imported birds must have stainless steel leg bands, which are put on when they enter quarantine.

Cats

Cats are affectionate pets. Who can resist their purrs?

One reason for their increased popularity these days is that cats are such practical pets for apartment dwellers. However, cat owners should know that even if Tabby never goes outdoors, it should be inoculated annually against many diseases.

• Outdoor cats may be better off without a collar, unless the collar is elastic and can slip off if your cat gets caught on something while climbing trees and rooftops. You can still attach a bell and rabies tag on the elastic collar.

Disciplining a Cat

There are ways to train a cat to stay off furniture and out of house plants.

• Spritz the cat with water from a spray bottle each time the cat does something wrong or goes to a place it doesn't belong while you sternly say, "No!"

He'll soon associate it with what he was doing and will eventually stop. You have to be consistent; cats can learn the word "no" just as well as a dog.

• If your cat has decided that water won't deter it from certain places, try this: Each time the cat goes to the forbidden place, dab a cotton ball moistened with vinegar on the cat's lips . . . just a dab, you don't have to rub or hurt the animal. If you are consistent, kitty will learn that going to the forbidden place means touching that nasty vinegar smell and give up. You can leave the saturated cotton ball in the forbidden place as an added deterrent.

• Keep cats out of your plants by covering the soil with wads of nylon net or a layer of pine cones. You can water plants through the net or cones.

• Keep cats out of newly seeded plant beds by laying rolled or crumpled lengths of chicken wire on the beds.

Cat Toys

Cats like to bat around just about anything.

• Put a few pebbles or a tiny bell into a small plastic pill bottle and close it tightly.

• Roll up a sock into a ball.

• Toss your cat a tennis ball, or even a wad of crumpled paper.

• Hang a fishing float on a string from a door knob and watch kitty bat it around.

• CAUTION: Don't give your cat a ball of yarn. He can become entangled and strangle himself while playing.

Cat Scratchers

• Play a game with your cat by getting it to chase a scratchable toy that you dangle from a fishing rod; you can reel in the toy while kitty chases it. Then, use this game to lead kitty to using its scratching post by dangling the toy over and on the post. Soon kitty will play and scratch on the post whenever the mood strikes.

• You don't need to buy a scratching post. Cover a length of log (cat-length high and about six inches in diameter) with carpet and nail its end to a flat board base.

• Some cats—those that are used to scratching the wooden fences they walk on—will be happy scratching on a 2″ × 4″ wooden wall stud that's about twice the cat's body length. Just saw off a piece and let it lie on the floor. Kitty will stand on it and scratch at the same time.

• Sprinkles of catnip can lure a cat to a scratching post, but don't be surprised if your cat ignores catnip; not all cats like it.

Cat Health

• Cats that look malnourished even though well fed and have frequent loose stools, a lackluster coat, and bloated stomach could have worms. See a vet quickly.

• When a cat's membranous eyelids half-cover its eyes, it's generally a sign of intestinal illness. Consult the vet immediately.

• Constant discharge from a cat's eye can be a symptom of local infection or systemic disease—another case for the vet.

• If a cat stops urinating normally or seems to have trouble urinating, get it to a vet quickly. A cat with urinary problems may stop using the litter pan because it associates the litter pan with pain. Treating the problem will help get the cat to use its litter again. Cats really are clean animals and prefer to use their litter.

• Cats build up tartar on their teeth, and while a little dry food helps prevent tartar buildup, it doesn't replace an annual vet checkup and cleaning.

Neutering and Spaying

• Even a neutered male cat will sometimes "spray" in the house, particularly if it perceives a threat to the status of its environment (such as the appearance of a new baby). Such spraying normally stops after the cat has adjusted to the change. Some cats will spray their own images in the mirror, thinking the image is an enemy. Try the "forbidden place" discipline if your cat is spraying a certain mirror.

• A female cat that hasn't been either spayed or bred will come into heat for two to three weeks twice a year. If you want to avoid living with a cat that periodically acts like she's insane, either have her spayed or let her have kittens. But if you let her have kittens, be sure you can find homes for them. Stray kittens abandoned on the road meet the same sad fate as abandoned dogs.

Cat Litter Boxes

• Pregnant women should avoid changing or handling cat litter boxes. Toxoplasmosis, a disease transmitted from cats to pregnant women, is responsible for about three thousand birth defects annually, according to the March of Dimes Birth Defects Foundation.

This disease, caused by passing of parasites from cats to humans, also causes brain damage and death in people with poor immune systems. About two million people are infected each year. As this book is being written, a vaccine can be administered to cats but not humans and may be years away from general use.

• Wear rubber gloves and wash your hands carefully when you change that litter pan!

• Baking soda sprinkled on the bottom of a litter pan before the litter is added helps deodorize the litter.

• A newspaper section placed on the bottom of the litter pan makes it easier to dump out the litter.

• Avoid mess by putting the whole pan into a large plastic garbage bag before you tip it to empty it. Tap the back of the pan while it's still inside the bag to get any stuck litter off, then hose off the litter tray, and, if you can, leave it in the sun for a while to air.

• Tape newspapers to the wall behind the litter pan with masking tape to protect the wall from flying litter if you have an especially enthusiastic cat.

• For a quickie temporary deodorizer for litter, sprinkle baking soda or carpet or litter freshener powder on top of the litter and give it a bit of a stir with your "pooper scooper." It'll stay reasonably fresh for a few hours until you can change the litter.

• Keeping an air freshener in the room with the litter box helps, but nothing works as well to keep odors down as frequent changing of the litter.

• If you change litter brands, to one with a different texture or odor, your cat might develop "litter phobia." The cat may refuse to use the new litter and actually suffer from urine retention and constipation.

To avoid this, add new litter in increments of one-fourth new litter to three-fourths old brand of litter, increasing the increment of new litter gradually as you change the litter pans so that your cat can get used to the new brand.

• Some cat owners train their cats to use newspaper sections instead of litter in the litter pan. It's easier to lift out a newspaper section than to dump messy litter, and you don't have litter tracked around in the "litter room." However, you have to believe that the cat won't use your newspapers before they get put into the litter pan—you could be forever uninformed about what's going on in the world.

Cat Carriers

With newspapers on the bottom, the following can be used to transport a cat.

• A bird cage will hold a small kitten en route to a new home.

• Two small laundry or storage baskets, one right side up and the other upside down, laced or tied together will serve as an emergency cat carrier in the car.

• A sturdy case from bottled beer, tied shut with rope, will serve as a cat carrier. The handgrip spaces provide air and see-through windows.

Dogs

Bringing a Puppy Home

• On puppy's first night home, if you place a ticking clock wrapped in a soft towel near him in his bed at night, it will help him think he still hears his mother's heartbeat. Being allowed to sleep on a hot water bottle wrapped in a towel will comfort a puppy too.

Housebreaking a Puppy

• To create a bed, cover the bottom of an old plastic wading pool or playpen with a plastic shower curtain or drop cloths and then layers of newspapers. The puppy will soon get used to such a new home and enjoy it until he is too big to confine.

• When you take a puppy outside to "outside-break" it, don't just plop the puppy on your porch, patio, or doorstep—he will use those places to relieve himself. Instead, place him where you prefer to have him perform his duties.

• It helps to take a rag you've used to clean up a mess and place it where you prefer the puppy to relieve itself, and then always take the puppy to that area. A dog's acute sense of smell will tell him that is where he is to do his job.

• Be sure to praise the pup when he performs as you want him to. If your puppy relieves himself in the house, discipline the pup if you catch him in the act; a puppy has a short memory and will not understand why you are scolding him half an hour later.

• It helps if you confine your new puppy to one certain room, especially a room with a wipeable floor, until he is housebroken.

• You can use ready-cut 2' × 4' pegboards as temporary doorway barriers for small puppies. Prop the pegboards in place in the doorway with a chair or other furniture; there's no need to make holes in walls or woodwork. With only a "half door" in place, your puppy won't feel as isolated as he will with the door closed, and if he scratches up the pegboards it won't matter as much as if he scratches up a door.

The pegboards can be used to hang things in your garage after the puppy gets free reign in the house.

Some dogs get the idea that the pegboard means "no admittance," and then you can use the pegboards to bar your dog from any off-limits room (bookcase, chair) at any time by just using a pegboard piece as a "stop" sign.

• Crate-training a dog will also help to housebreak it. Animals don't soil their own environments, and if a crate (or cage) becomes a dog's inside doghouse/bed, he won't urinate or defecate in it.

While some people don't like the idea of a dog in a cage, a crate-trained dog is a happier dog at the vet's when he's ill or in a boarding kennel if you're on a trip. If you don't treat the crate as a "punishing place," the animal will soon look upon it as his secure home and will be content to sleep in it and be put in it when non-dog people are visiting your home.

• While it seems counterproductive to give your dog water while you are crate-training it and housebreaking it at the same time, the dog needs water at all times.

• Some crated dogs will step in and tip over their water bowls. The solution is to buy a "rabbit cage" bottle at the pet store. A rabbit-size bottle holds about a quart and comes with a wire holder that you can attach to the crate.

Heartworm Medication

This deadly disease can be avoided if you take your dog to the veterinarian for annual blood tests and give him the preventive pills. Heartworms are transmitted by mosquitoes and affect only dogs.

• Contrary to what some pet owners think, the preventive pills should be given year-round, whether you live in warm or cold climates, according to the American Heartworm Association. Call your vet for complete information on heartworm disease.

Feeding Your Dog

• If your dog always tips over his outdoor food dish or likes to carry it around, get a sturdy plastic bowl or dishpan, pound a wooden stake (like a tent stake) through its bottom, and anchor the dish to the ground.

• Use heavy old butter crocks (from junque shops) for food and water with small or medium-size dogs who aren't likely to tip them over. I have seen larger dogs carry crocks around.

• A clean plastic garbage can with a lid can be used to store large bags of dry dog food and to protect it from insects and rodents if you store it in a garage.

General Dog Care Tips

• Exercise your dog early in the morning or late at night during the summer. Midday heat can cause heat exhaustion. Remember, dogs are so eager to please they will run and keep going well beyond their capacity to tolerate heat.

• A newly clipped dog shouldn't be walked in the peak sunshine, because its skin could get burned.

• Salt and chemical de-icers can irritate and cause cracks in the skin on a dog's feet in wintery climates. Wash the dog's feet off when you bring him in from a walk.

• If the pads of your dog's feet become dry or cracked, rub a little petroleum jelly into them. Wipe off the excess to protect your carpet. You can also put creamy lotion on them to help healing. This is a special treat for both Zinfandel and me in the wintertime.

• It's best not to keep your dog on a leash in the car. A leash can get caught on door handles and other projections and your dog could be injured.

• Leave your radio on if you have to leave your dog alone at home for several hours. The sound will reassure your pet and make him feel less abandoned. Dogs are pack animals, and since their humans become their pack when they are brought into a family, many dogs panic when left alone.

(A radio that's on also deters would-be housebreakers. They're likely to assume that someone's home.)

• Leave a rag or towel and old bathrobe or shirt that you have used with your dog when you go away, or, in the case of a new puppy, when you go to bed, and your scent will comfort him. Send along something with your scent on it or a rawhide bone that your dog's been chewing on when you board your dog, too, to make him feel at home.

• Wipe away the daily rheum that gathers at the corners of your dog's eyes with a dab of cotton dipped in a boric-acid solution.

• You don't have to get soaked when you wash your dog. Try making a coverall apron for yourself by cutting holes for your heads and arms in a plastic trash bag.

• Some dogs won't stay put when being washed out in the yard with a garden hose but will at least stand in one spot if you have them stand in a child's plastic wading pool or other large low-sided water holder. The advantage is that the dog's feet will be soaked clean while you lather and hose the rest of him.

Tropical Fish

Choosing Tropical Fish

Although fish don't require leash walking, litter changing, and regular trips to the vet for inoculations, they do require care and attention, and saltwater aquariums require even more attention than freshwater ones.

Whether or not hand-feeding many saltwater tank inhabitants, such as invertebrates (sea urchins, anemones), is fun or a chore is one factor to consider when you are choosing between saltwater and freshwater aquariums. The other is that saltwater aquariums require frequent testing to maintain the proper pH and salt concentration in the water, and the inhabitants are more sensitive to temperature changes.

If you just want to watch fish swim, you may prefer a freshwater tank.

An aquarium is a community of fish that functions best if the community is planned. Here's what to do when you are setting up a new aquarium community.

• If you are starting up a new saltwater tank, be aware that the water has to become "seasoned" for several days before you put any living creatures into it. Use your test kit to see if the pH and the salt content are suitable for fish. You will put invertebrates such as sea urchins, anemones, crabs, and starfish into the tank first, wait several days or weeks for the water to be seasoned again, and then add vertebrates—the actual finny fish.

• A fish tank is a "jungle."

1. Buy fish of similar size and maturity to keep them from becoming each other's dinner.
2. Select fish according to their natural characteristics. For example, although they eat their own young, peaceful platy will be compatible with other live-bearers and Mexican tetras. Tetras and barbels like to live in schools, so buy three to five of them at one time. The common angelfish we see in fish stores will live in pairs and with other peaceful species but need to have the cover of seaweed to swim in. However, regal angelfish are very aggressive and territorial; you can have only one in a large tank with other similarly sized fish. A lionfish can be kept in a tank only with fish its own size or larger; it will corner smaller fish and eat them. Tiger fish are so aggressive that they can be kept only with their own species. And so on. . . .
3. Choose the fish according to the aquarium level at which they prefer to live. Observe the fish in the store tanks and get advice from someone knowledgeable. For example, catfish breeds tend to live and feed at the bottom; tetras swim around in schools near the top, and angelfish and gouramies tend to stay around the middle of the aquarium. When fish have their own territories, they are more likely to leave each other alone.

• When you add new fish to an established aquarium community, disorient the "home" fish so that they "forget" which part of the tank they've claimed as their territories. Do this by rearranging the foliage, shells, ceramics, or other tank decorations at the same time that you add the new fish. All the fish will then have a chance to stake out their squatter's rights as if it were a new tank, and you'll have fewer fish fights and harassments.

• Prevent introducing fish diseases into your aquarium by having a "holding tank" for new fish. Quarantine new fish for about a month before putting them in with the rest unless you deal with an aquarium store that quarantines fish before selling them. (Sometimes, they'll have holding tanks in a back room if they quarantine new fish.)

• If your aquarium store has already quarantined the fish, you can add them to the tank from their plastic bags, but don't just dump the fish in, whether it's into the main or holding tank. Allow the bagged fish to float in the tank for about 15 to 20 minutes so that the new fish can become acclimated to your tank's temperature. After the waiting time, open the bag while it's still in the tank and allow the fish to swim into its new home.

Maintaining Aquariums

• A well-balanced aquarium with bottom-feeding and top-feeding fish and a properly functioning filter system needs less maintenance than most people think. In fact, too much fussing and water changing can disturb the pH and the bacteria balance in a tank, not to mention disturbing the fish, which will become disoriented if you change their scenery too often.

• Don't put things into your aquarium for decorations unless they are from an aquarium store. Souvenir shells from the ocean may be contaminated with bacteria or parasites; shells from a dime store could be lacquered, and some decorations could have poisonous paints or other chemicals on them.

• Always dechlorinate water before adding it to a fish tank and always return some of the "seasoned water" to the tank when you clean it. Dechlorinate water by letting it stand for several hours or by using commercial preparations that dechlorinate water with a certain number of drops per gallon.

• A large plastic wastebasket or small plastic garbage can can be used to mix up your salt water or dechlorinated water for the aquarium. If you don't keep a container specifically for this purpose, avoid getting harmful substances into the tank by lining the wastebasket or garbage can with a clean, sturdy plastic garbage bag, which you can use for garbage after you've mixed the water and put it into the tank.

• Move aquarium decorations (shells, ceramic things) with plastic salad tongs instead of contaminating the water with your hands. A plastic "spaghetti grabber" also helps you move things around in the tank.

• Anchor plastic vegetation to the bottom of the tank with the weight of glass marbles.

- A kitchen baster (used only for the fish tank) makes a good vacuum for the bottom of the tank. Just be sure not to wave it around as you remove it or you'll splatter fish gunk everywhere.

- Non-saltwater aquarium water is good for your plants.

- Putting a fish tank in front of a window may seem like a good decorating idea, but sunlight makes algae grow. Note that aquarium stores keep their tanks in the dark and use the tank lights to display fish.

- Leaving your tank light on too many hours during the day also will make algae grow. How many hours depends upon how light or dark your room is naturally—experiment with light and dark to see how many hours your tank can be lit without growing excess algae.

- Allow some of the green algae that form under your tank lid to fall to the bottom and feed invertebrates in a saltwater tank. Then you won't have to buy green algae from the pet store freezer compartment.

- If a lot of algae have turned white coral or other tank decorations murky gray, you don't have to throw these expensive decorations away. Make them white again by soaking them overnight in a solution of one part liquid chlorine bleach to four parts water.

CAUTION: You must remove the bleach before returning the decorations to the tank. Do this by soaking the items in water to which you've added at least five times the normal amount of dechlorinating chemicals. Soak them until you can't smell any chlorine in them at all.

Aquarium Equipment

- Don't buy your aquarium and fish at the same time. Even if you don't have to allow the water to season, as you do for saltwater fish, having the tank set up for a few days gives you a chance to make sure the filters and motors work properly and that the tank doesn't leak. It's no fun to move fish around when you find defects in your aquarium setup, and it can harm the fish.

- Always have a lid on the aquarium to keep things from falling in and to keep fish from jumping out. Yes, even some very small fish are "jumpers" and will land belly-up on the floor!

- When your usually quiet aquarium motor starts to hum loudly, it's probably getting ready to die; better buy a spare.

• Unplug mineral deposits from aquarium tubing with wooden shish kabob sticks. Also, keep extra tubing on hand in case you can't unplug some tubes.

• Make a long-handled cotton swab to clean algae out of a tube by wetting the end of a shish kebab stick and twirling the wet end in an appropriately sized wad of cotton.

• If the room in which you keep your aquarium has a constant temperature, you may not need to heat your aquarium and, in fact, you may tend to overheat the water. Check water temperature frequently with an aquarium thermometer. Most fish live well at 68 to 72 degrees Fahrenheit. Fish are healthier if they aren't submitted to too many changes of water and temperature, and they will be most active at moderate temperatures. Too cold or too warm water makes them sluggish and can encourage growth of harmful bacteria in the tank.

Fish Nutrition

Fish suffering from dietary deficiencies can lose weight, have cloudy eyes, pale color, scoliosis (twisted spine), or a bloated appearance known as ascites.

Although dried commercial fish foods are formulated to be nutritionally balanced, they can lose their nutrients during processing or while sitting on the shelf.

• Boost your fish feedings with this homemade supplement once or twice a week: Mix nine parts of minced, partially cooked beef liver and one part commercial food, plus 400 mg vitamin C, in a blender and process until combined. This mixture can be frozen for future use.

• When you buy fresh shrimp, save a few pieces (raw) for your fish. Cut finely and drop the pieces into the tank, but feed only the amount that can be totally consumed in five minutes. You can buy a fish feeder that holds individual pieces of shrimp or other fish food and lets you hand-feed invertebrates like anemones or sea urchins. Freeze the leftover shrimp for future fish treats.

• Uneaten food can spoil and pollute the tank; that's why you should feed only the amount your fish will consume in a single feeding frenzy, which usually lasts five to ten minutes. Feed enough food so that the top and bottom feeders get their share.

Gerbils, Hamsters, Guinea Pigs

These little animals can be wonderful pets for apartment dwellers. They live in self-contained environments; are clean; odor-free if their cages are kept clean; and don't bark, claw the carpet, or otherwise annoy landlords.

Also, they make especially entertaining pets for children who are bedridden or confined to wheelchairs, because they are always busy exploring, chewing, and climbing.

• A ten-gallon aquarium with a wire screen or mesh cover over it is a perfect home for gerbils and hamsters. (Guinea pigs need a bit more space.) There is no mess from litter coming through, as with a regular cage.

• Many plastic aquarium/tunnel homes can be bought for gerbils and hamsters, and, if you are handy, you can make a habitat from plexiglass panels bolted together (much larger and wider than, but similar to, an "ant farm" container); then, fill it with cedar shavings and other critter bedding so the gerbil or hamster can make its own tunnels and hideaways. If you make your own, don't forget the air holes and a secure place to hold a water bottle.

• Small rodents need to adjust to handling. They should be handled for increasing periods of time to "tame" them. They like to burrow in pockets and sleeves, and if they are gently and frequently handled, they become pleasant, cuddly pets.

• The females will become very restless when they are in heat and if they can, they may find a way to escape from their homes. Always be certain that lids and tunnels are properly fastened, especially during the females' restless periods. Males are generally more docile than females.

• An exercise wheel or ball will help your guinea pig, gerbil, or hamster get rid of excess energy and will entertain you too. Just don't forget that your pet is "at the ball" and leave it without food and water for too long.

• An exercise ball is a good carrier for a gerbil or hamster if you have to return it to the pet store or take it to a new home.

• Small rodents will eat carrots, lettuce, and many other foods in addition to store-bought pet food. They like to take their food from the food dish and hide it as if they were in the wild and had to stock up for the winter. They also eat live insects that might get into their cages.

• Metal jar lids can be used to hold seeds and other food. These small rodent pets will often eat plastic items, so it's best to use judgment about what you put into their cages. Small (nonedible) ceramic food bowls can be bought at pet stores.

• Rodents, and that includes tiny gerbils and hamsters, need to chew, so provide them with chew sticks and carrots to satisfy their needs; otherwise they will chew on their cages.

• Don't try to keep a gerbil, hamster, or guinea pig in a cardboard box "home." Cardboard is just another munchie, and they will chew their way out in no time at all. Many chew holes in the boxes they are put in for transport to their new owners' homes before they get carried through the doorway!

• These animals also are very supple; a grown hamster can squeeze out through a hole the size of a quarter. So inspect their homes often to make sure they can't escape.

• Gerbils don't usually climb straight, smooth sides well, so if you have a number of babies, a deep plastic dishpan will hold them until you can get a covered cage.

• A bird cage will hold a gerbil or hamster, but be sure to tie the lift-up door shut, because they are smart enough to get out through such an escape hatch.

• Although they don't drink much water and they get some of their water needs met by eating lettuce and other vegetables, these animals need to have a supply of fresh water in a stopper bottle at all times.

• Most pet stores have inexpensive booklets on raising gerbils, hamsters, and guinea pigs, and you can get information from the library to help you too.

Wild Animals

• If you find a featherless baby bird that is completely helpless and unable to keep its head up, you should try to help. As in the case of any helpless wild animal, call your Humane Society for help.

Loss of a Pet

Much is written about the love that binds people to their pets, and recent medical research has shown the mental and physical health benefits of having a pet. For most of us, losing a cherished pet is like losing a member of the family—consolation is difficult and mere words can't totally describe the grief. However, here is an excerpt from "The Last Will and Testament of an Extremely Distinguished Dog," written by Eugene O'Neill (published by Yale University Press, 1956, Copyright 1956, Carlotta O'Neill), which I have found to be comforting and which I've sent to others who have lost pets to comfort them:

The dog "writes" of his love for his Master and Mistress, asks them to remember him but tells them not to grieve too long, and then makes one last request:

> One last request I earnestly make. I have heard my Mistress say, "When Blemie dies we must never have another dog. I love him so much I could never love another one." Now I would ask her for love of me, to have another. It would be a poor tribute to my memory never to have a dog again. What I would like to feel is that, having once had me in the family, now she cannot live without a dog! I have never had a narrow jealous spirit. I have always held that most dogs are good . . . some dogs, of course, are better than others.

As I always say about the small zoo at our home, they own us, we don't own them, and I wouldn't have it any other way! A pet is more than a watchdog, attack cat, or alarm bird; they are members of the family. Think about how little they ask for—food, water, a scratch or two behind the ears, and a pat on the head. Isn't it amazing that they usually give love and attention so unconditionally? Boy, I sure wouldn't "speak," or do a flip, or sit up for a dog bone, but we ask them to. Please remember, our animal friends may not be able to talk in human terms, but they sure can speak to us in many other ways, so take the time to listen when they say "I love you."

CHAPTER 12

Entertaining

Having Fun at Your Own Party

T rust me; it's possible to have fun at your own party, even if you are doing all of the cooking yourself.

• Do as much as possible ahead of time and, above all, make a list of things to do and what to serve so that you don't have to clutter your mind with details on the day of the party. Also, if some of your guests are helping you serve, lists enable them to help you more easily.

I've listed some pre-party chores below. As you complete your party preparations, check them off on the list so that you have a feeling of accomplishment.

• It's hard to host and parent at the same time. The best tip to parents of small children who are having a party is to hire a baby-sitter to entertain them, either in your home or at one of your guests' houses. School-age children can sleep over at friends' houses and you can return the favor to their friends' parents when they have a party.

• To avoid possible messes, pretest the capacity of serving pieces by filling them with water measured according to the anticipated recipe amount.

• If you are having your party catered, book the caterer as soon as you know when you're entertaining. Whether you are having the party in your home or elsewhere, don't assume anything. Have all details about food, beverages, and serving them spelled out in the contract so that on party day nobody says, "I assumed you were doing that." This is especially important if you are having food brought into your home.

• Make a detailed list of who will provide:

1. All food on the menu, from entrées to nuts and mints, and if serving dishes for these items will be yours or the caterer's.
2. All beverages, including soft drinks, wine, mixers, coffee, ice, coolers, and glasses or cups in which to serve them.
3. All tableware, including napkins, plates, cups, flatware—disposable or not.
4. Table linens and centerpiece.

Also agree upon in writing:

5. Time the food will be served.
6. Fees for bartending and food service.
7. Price per person and variations of the price if you furnish the wine, a special dessert, or cheeses or whatever else you will take responsibility for.
8. And, are the leftovers yours, or does the caterer get to take them with him or her?

Here's what to do two weeks before a big party if you are doing the cooking:

• Plan your menu and make a two-part shopping list.

1. First list nonperishables to buy ahead of time, such as bottled beverages, canned and bottled food items, spices, and paper plates and napkins if you'll be using them. Buying these things as soon as you know you'll need them eases the last-minute scramble before the party and ensures you're having exactly the products you need.

   It's a good idea to order special cuts of meat ahead of time, too, even if your supermarket "always has that," because Murphy's Law will prevail; the day before your party will be the first day that your supermarket doesn't have those special brands and items.

2. Make a second shopping list, of the perishables to be bought the day before or on the day of the party—such as salad veggies, coffee cream, baked goods.

• Post a copy of your menu on the refrigerator door; it's the best way to make sure you serve everything you've cooked or bought for the party.

• On the day before your party:

1. Review your lists to make sure you have everything.
2. Check out your serving trays and bowls to make sure they are clean and ready for use.
   Make some tentative arrangements on the table and make sure that you have enough trivets and so forth to protect your table from hot dishes and that the centerpiece fits.
3. Check out your table linens to see if they need ironing (or, with some permanent-press, a spin in the dryer with a damp towel) to make them look right.
4. Cut, chop, slice, marinate, cook, and do anything else to the food that can be done the day before.

• On the day of the party:

1. If you haven't bought your perishables, do it in the morning when you are still calm.
2. Cook what needs cooking.
3. Set up what needs setting up.
4. Take a break for yourself.

• Notice that I didn't schedule any housecleaning. That's because we all have different standards for cleaning before a party.

Some people clean every nook and cranny with a toothbrush before a party and even wash their windows for a nighttime event held indoors with all the draperies closed. Others think top cleaning is good enough and focus on the food and fun.

One of the best party givers I ever knew never did heavy cleaning before a party. She just fluffed around with a feather duster, shined the bathroom sinks, and then went through the house on the day of the party replacing all light bulbs with colored or very dim-wattage bulbs on the premise that nobody who matters cares about the house anyway and that the time to clean up is AFTER the party.

• If you can't afford to pay for help with a party, make a trade-off deal with a friend in similar circumstances.

• Date and keep your party lists and menus for reference. If you entertain a lot, it's easy to forget what you've served, how you served it, and to whom. Having a record helps you to remember such things as:

1. What amounts of food you prepared for how many people, and if you ran out or had too many leftovers.
2. How much longer you had to bake four casseroles than it usually takes to bake one in your oven.
3. If you served shrimp to Eunice and then found out that she is so allergic to them that she stops breathing.
    (It's not bad manners to ask a guest, "Do you have any allergies?" when they respond to your invitation.)
4. If Albert is totally wild about your kumquats au gratin you should serve them again.
    (If at all possible, always invite one guest who really loves all food. It's good for your ego.)

Food Planning

• The amounts of food necessary depend upon the occasion, how early the food is served, and which guests you invite.

• A buffet is the easiest way to feed large groups in your home.

• Always offer non-alcoholic beverages when you're serving alcoholic ones so that everyone can have something.

• When you need to cool a lot of canned beverages, use your washing machine as a large cooler. Fill it with cans and dump ice over them. You might want to put a towel in the bottom to prevent chipping enameled washers.

A family-size washing machine holds approximately four cases of soda water plus a few more. Guests can help themselves. The cover opens and closes easily, the cans stay nice and cold, and it sure saves wear and tear on your freezer or bothering with a cooler that never seems to stay shut properly. In the morning, simply take out any remaining cans and spin the water out of the washing machine using the spin cycle.

Here are some tips for estimating amounts of food needed.

• If you are having a "come and go" reception, tea or coffee for adults, plan about three small sandwiches, two small finger foods, and two beverages per person. If you are serving children and teenagers, plan more food, especially cookies.

• A gallon of punch makes about 40 punch cups.

• A pound of coffee brews 50 cups.

• A 20- to 24-ounce loaf of sandwich bread has about 25 slices and will make 52 small, triangular, closed sandwiches.

• One pound of cooked lean meat will provide 32 ½-ounce slices for small sandwiches.

• A ½-ounce slice of cheese is enough for a small sandwich.

• A 3½- to 4-pound chicken will make chicken salad for about 70 small triangular sandwiches.

• A quart of dip, such as crab or broccoli, will make about 150 teaspoon-size servings.

• A 12-ounce can of nuts should serve 20 to 25.

• One-half pound of small candies serves 25.

Using Your Freezer for Parties

• Freeze fruit juice punch in gallon milk jugs or cartons. Remove from freezer several hours ahead of time to thaw to a "mush" and then add cold ginger ale when ready to serve.

(If you can't get the mush out of the plastic milk jug, just take a serrated knife and saw off the top section. Always cut away from yourself, even when you're rushed at a party!)

• When baking cakes ahead of time, layers may be lightly glazed and frozen, leaving the final frosting and decorating until later, or they can be completely decorated and then frozen.

• Pies can be frozen either baked or ready-to-bake.

• Freeze frosted cupcakes for children's parties.

• Such foods as spaghetti sauce, lasagna, chili, or sloppy Joes can be frozen and just reheated for spontaneous parties, especially for teens.

• You can whip and freeze individual "toppers" of sweetened, flavored whipped cream to dress up warm cobblers, puddings, or shortcakes.

• Roll scoops of ice cream in tinted coconut or finely chopped nuts, then serve with fruit, fudge, or caramel sauce or liqueurs.

(Ice-cream balls or scoops can be put into barware cocktail glasses or small, clear or holiday-decorated old-fashioned-style plastic tumblers ready to be topped with fruit, fudge sauce, or liqueurs.)

• Freeze individual fruit salads.

• Cookies, fruit and nut breads, party sandwiches, canapés, some dips, cheese balls, and other appetizers can be frozen and then heated on party day.

• Cream puffs can be filled with ice cream or whipped cream and frozen until needed.

• Meringue shells frozen in airtight containers can be filled with ice cream, sherbet, fresh or frozen fruit, or lemon sauce.

• Freeze coffee cakes, rolls, and muffins for company breakfasts or coffee.

(Layer a store-bought angel food cake with your favorite ice cream so that you have three layers of cake to two layers of ice cream and then keep it in the freezer so that you can top it with appropriate liqueurs or sauces for an easy, always-ready dessert.)

• Make double batches of your favorite recipes; eat one and have one on hand for unexpected guests or expected ones, for that matter.

• Most cookbooks have information on how best to freeze foods. Just remember that fresh, crisp vegetables get limp in frozen sandwiches. Egg whites toughen and become rubbery, so they must be chopped very finely or put through a sieve or food processor if egg salad is to be frozen.

• If such fillings are to be frozen, use salad dressing instead of mayonnaise, and if you must use mayo, use it only sparingly.

The "Good China, Crystal, and Linens"

How you store your china, crystal, good linens, and other items used mainly for special occasions and entertaining has a lot to do with how often and how exhausting it is to use these things.

If your "good things" are stored where they get dusty, you'll be washing and wiping before and after using them.

If they are stored so that you have to move heaven and earth to get at them, the chances are they won't get used at all.

My personal philosophy is that you should use your good china, crystal, silverware, and so forth, as often as possible. Now obviously, if you have small children in your household that are capable of dropping things, I wouldn't use them every day; however, set them on a shelf that you can reach and use them when you fix yourself a sandwich, a glass of tea, or the like. And as my mother used to always say, "If you don't use them, the second or third wife will."

Tableware

Storing China, Crystal, Serving Pieces

• Dishes and serving pieces that are stored in the back of lower kitchen cupboards will be easier to slide in and out if they are in a box, small plastic storage baskets, or dishpans. You won't have to crawl into the cupboard to get them. The other advantage of having them in a box or other covered container is that they will stay clean.

• If you have extra cupboard drawer space, try storing flat baking dishes and platters in drawers instead of on cupboard shelves. You can just pull them out easily when you need them.

• Protect your china from chips and surface scratches by placing cushions between plates, cups, or other stacked pieces. Use coffee filters, napkins (paper or cloth), paper towels, paper plates, cloth remnants cut into handkerchief-size pieces, clean handkerchiefs, clean foam meat trays. If you have some spare time and want to spend some money, buy flannel, felt, or nonwoven interfacing at fabric shops when it's on sale and make custom-size pads to go between china pieces.

• Store the padded stacks of pieces you use only a few times a year in plastic bags or just cover them with plastic bags the way people cover kitchen appliances with ready-made covers.

• Store larger items in plastic bags closed with a twistie or in boxes to keep them clean. Silver items can be wrapped in tarnish-preventing cloth or bags, not with light plastic and rubber bands. However, a heavy plastic bag that you can close is sufficient.

• Instead of wrapping each piece or stack of seldom used china or crystal, you can make a "tarp" or "drapery" of plastic wrap over a whole cupboard shelf of items. The construction of some cupboards will allow you to tape a "window" of plastic wrap over the shelf face. This is especially effective for that top cupboard shelf that seems to attract greasy dust like a magnet.

• If you are moving, you can pad your breakables with clean old clothing or towels.

• If you live alone, you may find that you use only the top one or two plates of a stack, while the bottom ones gather dust. Rotating your dishes occasionally will give them all a turn at being used and washed.

• When you don't have a full dishwasher load, you can fill up the space with seldom-used tableware so that it gets a bath between uses.

• If you've stacked glasses or other similarly shaped items and find that you've got two stuck together, don't reach for a hammer and don't despair: Try filling the top glass or cup with cold water or ice cubes and then put the bottom glass or cup into warm or hot water. The cold water in the top piece should shrink it slightly and the warm water around the bottom piece should expand it just enough to let you separate the two pieces.

Also, dribbling mineral oil around the stuck parts and allowing it to seep through will often do the trick.

Next time, put a pad of something in between pieces or don't stack them!

• You don't have to stack glasses to save shelf space if you put them in rows, alternating one glass right side up and the next upside down. Alternate right side up and upside down with the rows, too, and you'll be surprised at how many more glasses can be put on a shelf. This method works very well with slanted water glasses and many shapes of stemware.

Tableware Tricks

• If your china has dark scratches on it from being stacked, you may be able to remove these marks by rubbing them with baking soda.

• When a favorite dish or plate gets a slight crack, try putting it in a pan of milk, then bring to a boil and simmer for 45 minutes at low heat. In many cases, this method makes the crack disappear and you can use your dish again.

• Old ironstone items that are crazed and stained from food and oven heating can sometimes be reclaimed if you soak them in liquid bleach, diluted by half with water. If you can't submerge an item, such as a platter, in bleach because it's too large, try wrapping paper towels around it before putting it into a plastic bag. Put the bagged item in a bathtub or sink where it will be safe from children or pets and then pour bleach over the paper toweling. The paper will keep the bleach on the platter's surfaces and edges and you'll use less bleach than if you try to submerge a large item. Close up the bag and let the bleach do its job for 24 or more hours. Some badly burned plates can't be recovered, but most stains will come out with this method. You may have to do this in two steps, bleaching the top side of a platter or bowl the first time and then the bottom with the second application.

• In some cases, you can remove stains from china by "painting" the item with liquid dishwasher detergent and waiting several hours or a day.

• A "poultice" of baking soda or powdered dishwasher detergent will also remove some stains.

Here are a few tips on clean-up which are included in Chapter 1, but which bear repeating:

CAUTION: Wear rubber gloves when you work with strong bleach or dishwasher detergent to protect your skin.

• If you spray glass baking dishes with oven cleaner, let them stand for about 30 minutes; you'll get the burned-on grease off and have sparkling clean dishes again. This is especially important if the glass dishes are used with silver holders, where burned-on gunk looks doubly bad.

• Soak dirty dishes in hot, soapy water as you are preparing a meal for family or guests and you won't have as much scraping to do during the final cleanup. Just fill the sink with water and then add utensils and dishes as you work.

CAUTION: Don't bury knives in this dishwater. What you can't see in the suds can hurt you!

• Soak dishes and pans with dried egg or milk on them in cold water. Hot water actually cooks these foods onto their containers and makes cleaning more work.

• Dip washed dishes in vinegar water bath to rinse them clean.

• When you wash fragile china or glass in the sink, line the bottom with a washcloth or small towel to prevent chips and scrapes and a case of nerves, too!

• If you break a glass, let the water drain out and use a paper towel to retrieve it so you don't cut your hand.

• Have an extra sink strainer handy to accommodate the extra dishes you use when you have company. If you have people drying dishes as you wash, you can put one strainer on each side of the sink and ease the traffic congestion in the kitchen. (With two strainers, you can also give the more fragile pieces to the more careful dish dryers, especially if you have children helping you!)

• Make a spare strainer and avoid clutter in your cupboards: Cover several layers of newspapers with a clean towel, and the newspaper will absorb the dripping water and keep it from flowing across your countertops.

• If you are washing stacks of dishes, put the whole stack into the dishwater at one time so that the bottom ones soak while you swish off the top ones. This is much easier than putting a stack of dishes beside the sink and putting dishes one at a time into the dishwater for washing.

• When you are loading the dishwasher after a party, it may be easier to wash a whole load of just saucers and plates of various sizes, and then a load of cups, glasses, and odd-size pieces. Then, if you have to stack cups or odd serving pieces on the plates for storage, the plates will have been washed first and will already be in place in the cupboard and you won't have as much shifting around of heavy china.

• Save TV dinner plates and/or have paper plates (especially those with compartments) handy when you have a party and you can give your guests leftovers to take home. Then, if you are dieting, you won't be tempted to eat "for shame," as in "it's a shame to waste that."

Heating Plates

• If you have a gas stove, you'll find that the pilot light will heat your dishes if you put them into the oven for several minutes before serving.

• Heat plates by running them through the rinse cycle of your dishwasher.

• Your microwave oven will heat plates too, but remember, not all dishes are microwave safe. For a quick test from the Association of Home Appliance Manufacturers that will help you determine whether or not a dish is safe, see Chapter 1, "Saving Time in the Kitchen," page 43.

Linens

Table Setting

• Here's a terrific tip for parents of small children who like to entertain and use tablecloths instead of place mats:

As any toddler parent knows, a dangling tablecloth says, "Pull me" to any toddler. To keep small children from giving the tablecloth a disastrous yank after you've set the table for guests, just open the table's groove, as you would to insert an extra table leaf (about an inch), then crease the tablecloth into the groove and close it up. If you are adding a leaf to the table, insert the tablecloth on either side of the leaf.

A slight line across the table is certainly more attractive than the pile of broken china and crystal that can result when little fingers and curious minds operate in a dining room! And your peace of mind is the bonus!

Linen Laundering

• Protect a lace tablecloth by laundering it in a mesh bag.

• Save yourself a lot of anguish: DON'T launder a crocheted tablecloth with long fringes in the washer, not even in a mesh bag. Believe me, the result is the worst tangle you'll ever cuss at. Hand wash such items!

• Shaping a lace tablecloth after washing it is easy if you just drape it over the protected dining room table to dry. If it's starched, you'll need to pin it in place on a clean bedsheet using nonrust pins. But remember that water is an enemy of tabletops! Protect the table surface with a flannel-backed plastic cloth, a shower curtain, or a painter's drop cloth.

• Here is a way to iron a tablecloth, even a large Irish linen cloth, without really ironing it:

1. Place a large sheet on the floor.
2. Straight pin the wet tablecloth to the sheet with nonrust pins, smoothing out wrinkles as you pin.
3. Let it dry while you read a book or do something else that's more fun than ironing a large tablecloth.

• When ironing tablecloths on an ironing board, reverse the board so that you are ironing on the wider end. Iron curtains on the wider end too. (If you sew and have a padded cutting table, that's the place to iron any large items the easiest way!)

• You can also iron a large tablecloth (and curtains or bed cover) right on the bed.

• Hopelessly stained or yellowed white linen damask cloths can be dyed commercially and given a new life.

• It may be possible to cover up an unremovable coffee stain on a white tablecloth by dyeing the whole cloth with coffee to get a champagne-colored cloth.

Brew a big pot of strong coffee, pour it into a large plastic pail or tub, and then slosh the stained tablecloth around until the color is evenly distributed.
(See the clothing chapter's spot removal chart for tips on removing stains from fabric.)

Repairing Linens

• Small cuts or slits in lacy tablecloths (and sheer or lacy curtains too) can be repaired as follows:

1. Place a piece of wax paper under the cut.
2. Apply a little clear nail polish across the threads.

After the nail polish dries, the mend should be nearly invisible.

Storing Linens

• ALWAYS clean linens before storing them. Spots and stains will set if left in the fabric. With fine linens, you'll be saving money in the long run if you have them professionally cleaned. And tell your dry cleaner what those spots and stains are so that they can be properly treated before cleaning.

• If you store your fine linens in a cedar chest, the fumes from cedar oil may yellow them.

Instead, store them in a dry place where they won't mildew or get musty-smelling. You can prevent yellowing of white linens that will be stored for a long time by wrapping them first in white tissue paper, then in blue tissue paper.

• Hang linens on hangers that you can cover with dry cleaners' bags or garbage bags. Before putting tablecloths on the hangers, fold as described below.

• Here's how to fold a tablecloth so that the creases look as neat as hotel banquet cloths:

1. Make the first fold down the middle with the right side out.
2. Then fold each side back toward and slightly beyond the center.
   When the tablecloth is opened, the side creases will be alike and you won't have a dust streak down the center.

• Having such even folds helps you center the cloth when you are putting it on the table.

• An adjustable tension curtain rod installed in the back of a small closet will also hold table linens neatly and out of your way.

• If you have a round table and several round tablecloths but very little storage space, store all of the tablecloths right on the table—two, three, or four deep. Put a plastic tablecloth under the one currently in use to keep the bottom layers clean. The best bonus of this is that all of your round tablecloths will be stored without wrinkles. You know how difficult it is to fold or hang a round cloth neatly!

Miscellaneous Tips

Not everything has to be used according to its original purpose.

• Use covered bonbon dishes for serving grated cheese or jelly.

• Any stemmed drinking glass can be a holder for a short candle at Christmas time. Turn it upside down so that you have the candle on the bottom of the stem; then you can put an ornament into the glass and then set up rows of pretty Christmas candles. Melted candle wax or floral clay will stick the candles to the glass-stem bottoms.

   CAUTION: Don't let candles burn too low; the glasses can get too hot and may crack.

• Serve company salad in a glass punch bowl.

• Ice down wine or champagne in a silver punch bowl.

• Serve coffee to a crowd in glass punch cups.

Most people would rather have coffee in a mug or real cup instead of paper or foam ones, even if the mugs and cups don't match. At a casual buffet, just put the mugs and small paper cocktail napkins beside the coffee urn and let guests serve themselves. I have set out mugs with different sayings on them that were gifts from friends, and guests have enjoyed laughing at the messages and pictures printed on them. Saucers for cups are optional if yours is a casual group. Just make sure there are a lot of coasters distributed throughout the house to protect your furniture.

• Make mulled cider in your party-size coffee percolator. Or heat it in the microwave oven in a heat-safe glass punch bowl (or pitcher) and then serve it in the same container.

• Those long French bread baskets or other appropriately sized ones will hold silverware on a buffet table.

• If your buffet requires only forks, use an appropriately sized vase as a holder. It will save space on a small table.

• Use a clean, new clay flowerpot to hold silverware on a casual buffet table and also in your kitchen as a drain for newly washed silverware and cutlery. In either case, it won't tip.

• An ice bucket is a handy mini-cooler for radishes, carrot and celery sticks, or other crispy raw veggie munchies at your tailgate picnic.

• Ice down your picnic jug of wine in a deep plastic tub.

• Chill canned beverages in your washer or laundry room sink when you're having a party. The melted ice will drain away!

• Sugar cube tongs will pick up tiny pickles and things on a relish tray.

• Use a sentimental silver baby cup for a sugar bowl and baby's spoon for the sugar.

• Small, fringed terry-cloth towels make colorful place mats for casual settings. And for families, terry catches spills before they drip to the floor.

• Washcloths can be super family table napkins, especially when you find them on sale by the dozen!

• A spa-size bath towel can be a picnic table cloth.

• If you sew, twin or double permanent press sheets, depending upon the size of your table, can be cut and trimmed so that you can make a tablecloth and matching napkins. If you don't sew, a twin sheet will fit some tables as is.

• A thin flannel sheet or blanket can be a good table pad.

• Four dinner-size napkins stitched together could cover a card table.

• For a novelty party tablecloth, spread a clear plastic drop cloth or tablecloth over anything flat and colorful, such as fall leaves or dime store paper decorations for Saint Patrick's Day, Valentine's Day, Easter, Christmas, or a birthday. You can even put a plastic cloth over a decorated paper cloth when you have a child's birthday party so that the first spill doesn't totally destroy the whole table decor.

• Spread a solid-color tablecloth or sheet on the table and have everyone at the party autograph it with felt-tip pens or liquid embroidery paint. (Make sure that there's a pad beneath the cloth to protect the table.)

• Your centerpiece need not come from the florist. Pick any greenery from your backyard to serve as a base and add fruit, flowers, peppers, pine cones, candles, figurines, wood carvings, or anything else that looks right to you. Even pot plants set in a pretty bowl can be a centerpiece.

• If you are serving a decorated cake or other pretty dessert or salad, especially fruit, that is the centerpiece.

• No space for a centerpiece? Cut a few strands of any kind of ivy and use as runners down the center length of the table. A fat candle or single flower in a bud vase in the center will be the finishing touch.

• Confetti on the tablecloth at a New Year's party will decorate a small table so that you don't need a centerpiece.

Bridal/Groom Showers and Weddings

Since many newlyweds already have fully equipped apartments and are in enough of a quandary about what to do with "his and hers" everything, personal items or pantry food items may be more appreciated than such traditional shower and wedding gifts as toasters, blenders, and silver. Shower invitations can say that it will be a "kitchen," "pantry," or "personal" shower. Many showers now include the groom, too. Often the bridesmaids pitch in together to buy the bride a negligee or some item for the couple that none of them could afford to buy alone.

Here are a few suggestions for gifts you can make or assemble that may not only save the day but save you some money if you're on a tight budget.

• A personal shower: For the nondomestic bride (and groom), a few trousseau items: negligee, lacy underwear, favorite bath product or cologne, leisure clothing. For the groom: a robe, wallet, pocket knife, or shirt.

• Toys: Games such as word games, banking games, board games, and puzzles. (Remember the saying that "you can tell the age of the boys by the price of their toys"?)

• Books, craft supplies: If the couple has hobbies or special interests, buy books and items related to them. If you buy cookbooks, add some of the spices used in the recipes to the top of the package as a decoration.

• A honeymoon kit: Include headache pills, antacids, adhesive bandages, a small tube of antiseptic or spray that can be used on sunburn if the couple is going to the shore, hand cream, tweezers and clippers for hangnails and splinters, and maybe a couple of granola bars for emergency middle-of-the-night hunger pangs.

• A home-warming kit: Scissors, gauze, tape, cotton, thermometer, heating pad, hot water bottle, upset-stomach remedies, pain relievers, and other accessories for a home first-aid cabinet, including a first-aid book.

• A fix-it kit: Include a hammer, set of screwdrivers, pliers, nails, picture hooks. You can also add a gas can, oil or silicon spray, garden hose, and any other home-aid items.

• A cupboard kit: Grocery staples and boxed mixes such as cake mix, corn bread mix, meat helper mix, pastas, basic spices, flavorings and colorings, and other food items that are nice to keep on hand. You can also include casserole dishes or baking pans and wooden spoons or spatulas to go with the mixes.

• Recipe kit: A recipe box with your favorite recipes, and if you're the mother of the bride or groom, her or his favorite recipes. You can ask each shower guest to bring her favorite recipes to add to the box. Also, if it's a kitchen shower, favorite recipes could be accompanied by nonperishable ingredients and the proper pan (cookie cutter or other utensil) needed to prepare the recipe.

• You could "theme" the kits so that you provide the staples and spices for making Italian, Cajun, Tex-Mex, or other ethnic foods.

Tuck in a few store coupons with food kits.

• A munchies/picnic kit: A picnic cooler filed with disposable plates, cups, napkins, and flatware and some munchies, ranging from bean dip and a six-pack to caviar and champagne, depending upon the taste of the couple.

• A sewing kit: A supply of different-color thread, a sewing box or basket, measuring tape, mending tape (fusible, iron-on), scissors, needles, straight and safety pins, a few assorted buttons, snaps, hooks, fabric glue, pin cushion, and anything else that catches your eye at the store that will help a couple keep themselves and their clothing out of tatters and tears.

(If you like, ask each shower guest to put a spool of colored thread on the gift as a decoration.)

• Happy memory quilt: If the shower guests sew, each can bring a quilt square embroidered with the guest's name, so that all the squares can be sewn together for a treasured keepsake.

• A reality kit: Include a bucket, broom, mop, cleaning supplies, sponges, and other facts of life.

• You can attach small kitchen items (potato peelers, can opener, wooden spoons) to a clothesline and then put them into a laundry basket; as the line is pulled out, so are the utensils.

• A Heloise kit: A copy of this book and some of my favorite "do-alls," such as white vinegar, lemon juice, salt, candles, baking soda, dental floss, and any of the other ordinary items used in my hints to do many extraordinary things.

Shower Memories

• Make a copy of the guest list with names and addresses to help the honoree send out thank-you notes. Leave about three lines of space so that a description of the gift can be noted after the name as the gifts are opened.

• Have each guest write her name, address, and the gift on a slip of paper or index card to be used for a door-prize drawing at the shower and by the honoree for writing thank-you notes after the shower. Index cards can be put into a permanent address file for Christmas cards.

• Have each guest write her name, address, and her hint for a happy, successful marriage on an index card, which can be read by the bride during the shower and, as noted above, kept in a permanent address file. Reviewing friends' hints for a happy marriage in the address file is a cure for the monotony of addressing Christmas cards.

• Take instant pictures during the shower and put them into an album for the honoree.

• Mothers of the bride and groom could assemble photo albums of precious shots from birth to adulthood and present them to the couple, or friends could call the mothers and ask for the photos so that they can assemble them. (This is a good idea for a baby shower, too. Everyone wants to know "who the baby looks like," and so such an album can be a reference after baby is born.)

• Have shower (and wedding) guests sign a guest book, which the couple can use in their home. The custom of guest books comes and goes, but anyone who's been married a long time and has kept one through the years knows how nice it is to remember good times, not to mention how nice it is to be able to find the answer to "What was Harry's first wife's name?"

• Autograph a plain tablecloth with laundry pens or liquid embroidery/fabric paint and give it to the honoree. Or have guests autograph a wooden rolling pin, tray, or cutting board with a felt-tip marker, then shellac it and present it to the couple after the shellac has dried, for a lasting memory.

• Have the wedding invitation matted and framed professionally for a gift or, if the couple have written their own vows or have a special poem or biblical text read at the wedding, have the words done in calligraphy and framed for a keepsake gift. We were lucky enough to receive three of our wedding invitations mounted, matted, and framed, and it's such a delight I have one in each area of the house. There is one exceptionally beautiful one hung in my bathroom, and each morning when I brush my teeth I look at it and smile.

• Cut a hole in the center of a paper plate and, as each gift is opened, poke the ribbons through the hole, leaving the bows on top. By the end of the gift opening, the bride will have a bouquet to save or to throw as she chooses.

Baby Showers

Buying baby gifts is fun, but what do you buy a mother of several children who already has equipment and lots of leftover clothing? Here are some tips that could also be given a first-time mother.

• A baby shower tree: Attach coupons for "Three Hours of Baby-sitting in Your Home or Mine," interspersed with store discount coupons for baby supplies, to a small, squatty end of a tree branch that has been spray painted white and weighted in a flower pot so that it won't tip. Multicolored bows can be attached in between the coupons so that this table centerpiece can be a decoration in baby's room after the shower and after all the coupons have been redeemed and used.

• A hospital kit for Mom: Include toiletries, comb, brush, instant "dry" shampoo, regular shampoo, lotion, mascara, lip gloss, and a bag of change so that Mom can use a pay telephone or vending machines once she's up and about in the hospital or birthing center. A nice bed jacket, robe, or nightgown is a help too. Make sure these open conveniently in the front if Mom plans to breast-feed. Breast pads could be included in this kit if you feel very practical.

• A certificate for a manicure and pedicure to be used during those last months of pregnancy when Mom-to-be can't even see her feet, much less give them a pedicure.

• A certificate for a haircut and/or set by a hairdresser who makes house calls if your city has these services. Very new mothers often need such a boost in the first week or two after baby comes and may have trouble getting out of the house, especially if breast-feeding.

• A frozen casserole shower: Food that's ready to thaw, heat and eat is a blessing to new mothers, especially those with other children at home. Just make sure to put the food in disposable containers so that there's no chore of returning dishes.

• A gift certificate for a cleaning service day, to be used when the mom-to-be gets a frantic "nesting" urge to "have everything nice and clean for the baby" or a couple of weeks after baby is born, when the house has been neglected for more important things—like enjoying the baby.

I especially like these ideas, as it seems to be Mom who has done all the work needs to be pampered.

Other Help for Mom

• If the person who hosts the baby shower buys thank-you notes and envelopes and has each guest address the envelopes, the envelopes can be used to draw for a door prize and by the mom-to-be when she sends out thank-you cards. Some etiquette experts may say this is not proper, but I think it's certainly a help to the mom-to-be.

• Have guests address birth announcements to themselves at the shower and save Mom (or Dad) a lot of energy.

Long-Distance Bridal and Baby Showers

Being separated by miles doesn't necessarily mean families and friends can't have the traditional showers that mean so much to brides and moms-to-be. The shower tradition just needs to be carried out in some untraditional ways. Here's how to hold a shower for someone far from home.

• For a surprise shower: Tell the honoree to call home (or elsewhere) at a specific time and day. When the call comes through, have all the guests shout "surprise" and then take turns wishing the bride or mom-to-be good thoughts and love. If you don't want to make it a surprise shower, just tell the honoree that you will be having a long-distance shower and that you will call her at a certain time on that day.

• While the honoree is on the phone, have each guest describe the gift brought to the shower. These gifts need not be wrapped; just have cards attached to them for identification. The host can just pack up all the gifts and send them to the honoree.

• If you can, photograph, cassette-tape, or videotape the event, including the shower games and some of the guest conversations.

Long-Distance Birthday Party

• College students need love and remembering too. Send photos of the family, including pets, along with gifts, paper plates, napkins, decorations, and money for cake, ice cream, and other refreshments to a responsible roommate so that your student can have a really happy birthday. Make plans to call wherever the party is held so that the family can sing "Happy Birthday" too, and have the roommate take pictures for a remembrance.

• You can mail a whole party to someone. Just enclose non-perishable favorite foods, party paper plates and napkins, and anything else your imagination tells you to include.

Some of the "memories" tips from showers can be used for other party occasions. Here are some tips for a farewell party.

• Put a sheet of paper in some easily accessible place, and then have guests sign their names, addresses, and phone numbers so that the person leaving won't lose touch.

Instead of a list, have them sign an appropriate poster, menu from a favorite restaurant hangout, program from a special event shared by the honoree and guests, an address book, or any other meaningful or sentimental item. Put one of the guests in charge of this list if you're too busy with the party to make sure everyone signs.

• Take instant photos of the party and mount them in an album, leaving space for each guest to write a personal message beside the picture.

General Party Tips

Organizing a Co-Hosted Party

Here's when you really need to make a list and keep all information handy, because these events, often held by church, school, and office groups, are often potluck and cost-sharing.

Usually, in these parties, the co-hosting agreement is that those who bring less expensive foods or those who bring nothing will contribute cash to the party fund for reimbursing those who brought more expensive items and to contribute toward paying other expenses, such as hall rental and entertainment.

• Make a sheet of paper with columns so that each column is headed with certain information and so that you can enter this information as you receive it.

You need to record names, addresses, phone numbers, and descriptions of potluck dishes brought and gifts (to avoid duplications). Record each guest's cost for the potluck foods or beverages (and contributed cash amounts) so that all costs and contributions are in black and white and can easily be prorated.

Keep all receipts for your expenses, too, and note your expenses as contributions.

Where's the Party?

• Whether the party is for adults or children, identify the house with a "you are here" sign, ribbons, or a bunch of inflated balloons tied to a porch, mailbox, or whatever will hold them without breaking them.

• Inside the house, place small signs directing people to bathrooms so that they won't always have to be asking directions. Put a sign on the bathroom door too.

• If your house is the kind that keeps you from hearing the doorbell or if your doorbell rings too softly to be heard above the chatter, either assign a friend to stay near the door to let guests in or put a sign on the door telling them to "walk in" or "go around to the back patio," because "we can't hear the bell." Put up signs with arrows directing guests to the backyard gate.

CAUTION: If you and your guests are all out in your backyard, it's a good idea to lock your front door so that you don't get any unwelcome guests in the house.

Traffic Flow

At a buffet dinner where guests will fill their plates and then seat themselves at different tables, here's how you can have the guests move smoothly to their places without asking where to sit.

• Be traditional and make up place cards.

• If you have seating at two tables in two different rooms and don't want to suggest who is to eat with whom, try this: Use two sets of china and linen colors and designate "blue cornflowers" to the "blue table" and "green bamboo" to the "beige table." Then, set the plates for the table farthest from the buffet service at the top of the plate pile.

Breaking the Ice

Sometimes, when your guests are strangers to each other, you need something to get them comfortable and in a party mood.

• If you can afford to hire a musician who knows how to entertain at your type of party, music really does soothe the savage breast and stranger guest. A guitar player from the church choir can lead Christmas carol singing in your home as well as in church; a restaurant fiddler can serenade guests in a home as well as in a restaurant. Such musicians need not perform more than an hour or so, because your guests can't converse well in a home if music is too loud.

• If you have a lot of musicians in your circle of friends, even amateur ones, ask them all to bring their instruments and jam for about an hour at your party.

• If you have a player piano, provide vaudeville-style straw hats, kazoos, and other noninstruments for guests to wear and play while they are both the entertainers and the entertained.

• If you have a pool table, have a tournament and give silly prizes.

• If you have yard space, and it's a casual party, set up a horseshoe game, badminton net, and/or a croquet set. Again, offer silly prizes to winners.

• If you have a swimming pool party, don't be offended if only a few people actually swim. For reasons that I can't figure out, people tend to stand around and admire pools at pool parties but seldom actually bring their suits and swim.

• Make fortune balloons instead of fortune cookies. On small pieces of paper, write out "fortunes" that pertain to the particular group of people you've invited and then put the papers into balloons before inflating them and tying them securely. Let each person pop a balloon to find a prediction. This could be especially fun at a New Year's Eve party, where you could make predictions for the upcoming year.

• For a Valentine's Day party, cut inexpensive valentines in half with different zigzag cuts for each one, and then have guests find their matching halves to meet each other or to be dinner or bridge partners.

• Cut cartoons from newspapers and use them the same way suggested for valentines.

• One of the best tips I can give for enjoying your own party is to make sure that you get at least 15 to 20 minutes of rest at some point on party day. It's hard to smile when your feet are killing you, you are exhausted, and you are wishing that you had never even thought of having a party.

Entertaining can be as easy and simple as you want it to be or a full-blown black-tie dinner. Do what you're the most comfortable with, and make no excuses. If you don't say that the dessert didn't turn out as good as it usually does, no one will really know, so don't tell on yourself! Take a few minutes to write everything out, do the best that you can, and when someone asks, "May I help?" for heaven's sake say yes if you need someone to pitch in.

CHAPTER 13

Leaving the Home Behind

Work for many people means carrying a suitcase along with a briefcase and accumulating frequent-flyer bonuses.

I travel so much that I don't ever completely unpack my suitcases. My toiletries and the other "security blanket" comfies that make my hotel room my home away from home are always kept replenished and in their places, already packed for the next trip. And I know that I'm not the only working gypsy, because my mail has all sorts of tips from "frequent flyers" and "frequent roadies."

I also know that I'm not the only traveler who carries all my luggage onto the plane. I have to do this because I frequently travel to a different city each day and my luggage, if lost, might never catch up to me. Because I carry it all on, I have to pack very efficiently; *lightweight* and *coordinated* are my buzzwords.

Traveling around the country for business and fun has been a real learning experience for me. I've learned a lot about doing and "making do" when you're on the road, which I've included in this chapter.

Planning Your Trip

Buying Airline Tickets

• With so many discounted fares available, it's time-consuming to call different airlines to get the best fare for your trip. Travel agents have all this information on their computers, at the touch of a finger.

When you are deciding to buy discounted tickets, you need to consider which is more important to you: Price or scheduling? Will you fly at a less convenient time to save $25? Can you change your reservation without a penalty? What will the airline do for you if your flight is canceled?

• Always make reservations several months in advance if you plan to fly on a holiday.

• In large metropolitan areas your fare may vary, depending upon which airport you use.

• Remember, the cost of the ticket is the price in effect when you pay for your ticket, not the price in effect when you make your reservation.

• If you travel a lot, collecting frequent-flyer bonuses is really a bonus. You can use your accumulated business travel benefits to take a vacation—which you'll probably need desperately if you've accumulated lots of bonuses.

• Always phone to confirm your flight a day or so before it's scheduled.

International flights need to be confirmed at least 72 hours before flight time. No confirmation can result in a canceled reservation on international flights.

• If your flight is delayed and you have a full-fare ticket, check with other airlines to find out if there are available seats on flights to your destination. Many airlines honor other airlines' tickets. If the second airline won't honor your ticket, you can request a refund from the first airline. If you have a discounted ticket, however, you may get only a partial refund or no refund at all.

• If you arrive early and find that the airline on which you are booked has available seats on an earlier flight, you may be able to switch to the earlier flight. This is another instance where carrying on your bags comes in handy.

Dealing with Travel Agents

• The best way to find a travel agent is to get recommendations from friends who travel. They'll know if the agent takes time to answer your questions, knows the intricate details about getting you to your destination, is efficient, and has full computer service so that you get the most current information about rates and changes in tours or tickets. A good agent will ask about your trip after you've returned to check on the tour, accommodations, and so forth.

An agent should belong to some professional organizations, such as the American Society of Travel Agents, the International Airlines Travel Agent Network, or the Airlines Reporting Corporation. If your agent displays evidence of membership in the ASTA, IATAN, or ARC, it generally means that the agency meets professional standards. If your agent is not meeting professional standards, you can complain to these professional organizations. You can also complain to your state government's Consumer Protection Division and to the Better Business Bureau in your area.

How to Complain About Poor Travel Service

• Whenever you complain, provide a daytime phone number where you can be called, and when you write to complain, always include a return address. If you don't properly identify yourself, you can't get results!

• Complain about travel agents to ASTA Consumer Affairs Department, 4400 MacArthur Blvd., N.W., Washington, D.C. 20007.

• When you have any type of travel service problem (with airlines, buses, trains), complain to the U.S. Department of Transportation, Consumer Affairs. The phone number is 202-366-2220. Or write to: U.S. Department of Transportation, Office of Community and Consumer Affairs, 400 Seventh St., S.W., Room 10405, Washington, D.C. 20590.

This department will usually contact the airline (bus or train service) to find out if your complaint was properly handled and get back to you. It will also provide information about your rights under federal laws. Consumer complaints are kept in the department's records and used to document the need for changes in consumer protection regulations.

At the time this book was being written, the U.S. Department of Transportation was offering a free booklet entitled "Fly Rights" to those who call and request it.

• The airline needs to know what you want before it can take any action at all, so if you write exactly what you want the airline to do: settle the claim with money, have the rude employees send an apology note, or do something else to compensate for your inconvenience. The airline may offer to settle your claim with a check or other compensation, such as a free trip.

• To complain about safety hazards, write to the Federal Aviation Administration, Community and Consumer Liaison Division, APA-400, Federal Aviation Administration, 800 Independence Avenue, S.W., Washington, D.C. 20591, or call 202-267-3481.

Lost Luggage

• The only real way to preserve valuables is to keep them on your person. Never check anything of great value, such as money, jewelry, cameras, medicine, liquids, glass, negotiable securities, or anything else that is irreplaceable, is very fragile, or has sentimental value.

• Double-check all destination tags put on your checked baggage and always take off old tags before you check the bags to avoid confusion.

• Some airlines have a ceiling of $1,250 on delayed, lost, or damaged bags on domestic flights. If your luggage or contents are worth more than that, you may want to buy "excess valuation" coverage if it is available. On international flights the liability is 250 French gold francs (you need to get current conversion for this to United States dollars) for each kilo (about 2.2 pounds) of checked baggage. Your baggage should be weighed for international flights to ensure your being able to claim the right amount. If your bags aren't weighed, your claim will be based on the assumption that your bag weighed 32 kilos (about 70 pounds)

• Keep records of everyone you speak to about your lost baggage and never throw away any travel documents or receipts for money spent in connection with the baggage loss. If you give your baggage tags to the airline when you fill out a loss form, the form should note that you did give up those claim tags when it was filled out.

• Generally, airlines will pay for a reasonable amount of inconvenience due to the lost bag, but this amount must be negotiated. Some airlines have emergency funds for purchases and will give you cash; others will pay later. Save those receipts! (Delayed luggage is delivered to you at no charge.)

• If your bag is really lost and not just delayed, you may have to fill out a second claim form; check with the airline.

• Airlines usually pay "depreciated," not "replacement," costs. Keep receipts for the clothing and other items as well as for the bags, so that if your luggage is lost, you have a better chance of settling your claim without too much bargaining with the airline.

CAUTION: Don't exaggerate your claim values. The airlines can completely deny claims they believe to be inflated or fraudulent!

Vacation Information Sources

• If you are planning to visit a major city, call that city's tourist or convention office to get information about what's to see and do when you get there. Knowing what you might do helps you plan your time and finances so that you can enjoy as much as you want and can afford.

• If you plan to travel by train, Amtrak sends a free travel planner for traveling in the United States, complete with maps and money-saving hotel and tour packages. Call 1-800-USA-RAIL. This is a very busy line; don't be discouraged if you are on hold for a minute or so. You can also write to Travel Planner, Dept. N, Amtrak Distribution Center, P.O. Box 7717, Itasca, Ill. 60143. It takes about eight days for the packet to reach you if you call for it.

Travel for Handicapped People

• A nonprofit organization, Society for the Advancement of Travel for the Handicapped (SATH), sends information about travel to handicapped people. Send a stamped, self-addressed envelope and $1 for postage and handling for general travel information, or $2 if you also want the "U.S. Welcome for Handicapped Visitors" booklet. It's important to send the postage, because this society receives no funding other than membership fees for its services. Members (dues in 1988 were $40 per year for adults and $25 for students and retired persons) receive a quarterly newsletter and other helpful publications for handicapped travelers. Write to SATH, Penthouse Suite, 26 Court St., Brooklyn, N.Y. 11242.

Deciding on Vacation Ideas

Here's a tip for getting everyone's frank opinion on where to go and what to do.

Write down, on a secret ballot, all the activities that are possible during the vacation, such as: visit the zoo; white-water rafting; charter a fishing boat; sleep all day; and so forth.

Beside each activity, draw a row of boxes in which to rate the activity according to: want to do very much; would like to do; wouldn't mind doing it if everyone else does it; rather not.

Give a ballot to each person going on the trip with instructions not to talk about it until all the ballots are in. The official trip planner can then pick the activities accordingly, so that everyone gets a turn at doing the "want to do very much" activities at least once.

Everyone doesn't have to be together every minute of the vacation time. You may want to split up to cover more activities.

Finding a Place to Stay

• Have a travel agent make all the phone calls. I still meet people who think they have to pay for travel agent services. Travel agents are paid by their travel industry clients and can save you money in phone calls and by finding low travel and accommodations rates, not to mention a lot of time. Often, the agent has been in the area on a "fam tour" (familiarization tour) and can give you tips on time, financial, and wardrobe needs.

• Most hotel chains have 800 numbers, so you can call to find out whether they accept children or pets, and what kind of facilities they offer. To get 800 number information, dial 1-800-555-1212 and then ask for the 800 number for the hotel/motel chain you want to call.

Cruises

If you've been in a high-speed mode at work and need a rest, try a cruise. Most cruise ships offer optional side trips off the ship every other day or so, alternating with days to sleep and relax.

• If you are on a fixed income or budget, a cruise may be the kind of vacation you can enjoy without worrying your wallet and heating up your credit cards. All your meals and lodging are paid for. Extra expenses are for drinks, tours, and souvenirs. Often plane tickets are included in the package.

• Picking the right cabin for your cruise can make you more comfortable physically and financially. The most expensive cabins are on the top decks, but most people prefer to be at the water line of the ship, because that's the most stable level of the ship. Cabins in the center of the ship are more expensive than those at either end, and outside cabins are more expensive than inside ones, but if you need a porthole to prevent claustrophobia, the extra price is worth it.

• If you tend to get motion sickness, see your doctor for some of the newer medications that don't make you sleepy. Also, get a room mid-ship at the water line for best stability and the least rocking and rolling.

• You can save money by traveling off-season. For example, May and June are off-season for Caribbean vacations. Prices drop 25 to 60 percent on air fare, hotels, and rental cars. Even the stores have sales on resort clothing during these off months.

• Travel "standby." Often special tours or cruise ships have cancellations or vacancies, and since they want to have a full roster of clients, they will offer huge discounts to people who can travel with a few days' notice. Check with your travel agent.

• Save all travel brochures until after the trip. They are the proof of what was offered to you, in case you have to take legal action against a travel company for not providing what it advertised.

• Don't forget time-share vacations. For some people, they offer the perfect alternatives.

The American Resorts and Residential Development Association offers general information about time-share accommodations in a booklet entitled "Consumer's Guide to Timesharing." Send $2 and a No. 10 envelope to ARRDA, 1220 L Street, N.W., Suite 510, Washington, D.C. 20005.

Boating

• If you want a sailing vacation but don't own a boat, check with your travel agent about sailing vacations in which you can rent a sailboat (usually with crew), just like renting an RV (recreational vehicle).

• When equipping your own boat, it's safety first!

Many people who die in boating accidents do so because they have no lifesaving gear aboard. The U.S. Coast Guard requires personal flotation devices (PFDs) on all boats. The number, type, and sizes required for each boat depend upon the number of people per boat and size of the craft. Generally, at least one PFD is required per person.

• Be cautious when using inflatable mattresses, toys, and rafts. They aren't true safety flotation devices and shouldn't be used for that purpose. They can take you into deep water, slip away, or develop leaks and leave you in serious trouble far from shore.

• The best safety rule is to learn how to swim and to administer lifesaving techniques just in case.

• If you have too much boat and not enough garage, the trailer tongues and wiring will be exposed to the rain. To keep the wiring from shorting out, put a sandwich bag over the wires and tie it shut with twisties.

• Ever-faithful nylon net helps boaters too. Use it to remove dirt and scum from the bottom and sides of a fiberglass boat. David usually wipes his boat while it's still in the water and then all he has to do when he gets home is to rinse it off with a garden hose.

• You'll never have to worry about losing or getting your keys, driver's license, glasses, makeup, or whatever wet when you're on water in any kind of boat (canoe, raft, whatever) if you put such items in a plastic travel jar or, if you have many items and a big boat, into a cooler. Well-sealed jars will float for a while and so will some coolers; you can retrieve them if they fall overboard. (Do this at the beach, too, to keep sand and water away from cameras and other items.)

• Wide, flat-bottomed coffee cups designed to be set on car dashboards are really useful on boats.

• Most camping, kitchen, and trailer tips apply to boating—using tight-fitting lids on containers and putting them into plastic bags prevent spills, and anything that conserves space is a blessing. (See camping hints later in this chapter.)

Traveling by Car

• If you are driving alone, take a break at least every two hours to prevent dozing off after being mesmerized by the road.

• Get your car tuned up, checked, and serviced before a long trip to prevent trouble on the road. And especially, check those tires and belts! (But you knew that, right?)

• Keep duct tape in your trunk. It will seal and hold many broken car parts together long enough for you to get to a service station.

- Also keep a large towel or blanket in the trunk to lie on in case you have to look under the car, or to place in front of or behind tires for traction in snow or ice.

- A couple of containers of cat litter, gravel, or sand also come in handy for ice emergencies.

- Check out an automobile shop for aerosol tire inflation products, which will fill a leaky (not seriously damaged) tire with enough air to get you to a service station. It's probably a good idea to replace the aerosol product from time to time to make sure it won't be outdated and will work when you have an emergency.

- Don't forget the universal signal for car trouble is a raised hood. It helps, too, to have one of those cardboard sunscreens that has a picture on one side and HELP, CALL POLICE printed on the other side.

- If you are driving in Europe, you are required to put a danger signal on the road or shoulder a short distance behind your car to warn motorists that a stalled car is ahead. Red triangle signs on a stand are sold there for this purpose. (That's what that thing in your rental car trunk was!)

- When you rent a car, before driving off take some time to find out how to turn on the headlights, windshield wipers, flashers, air conditioner, or heater, even if the type of car seems familiar to you. Also check to see if there is a spare tire, jack, and operating manual in the car.

If you should have an auto accident:

1. Get the name, address, phone number, and license number of the other person involved and names, addresses, and phone numbers of any passengers in the other car or of witnesses.
   Make a note if any injuries occurred, to whom, and if everyone was wearing seat belts.
   If possible, while you are still at the scene, make a rough diagram of the street or intersection, positions of the cars and point of impact, including compass points and car colors and makes, so that you won't have to rely on memory when you fill out insurance forms or tape-record a report on the phone, as is required by some companies.
2. Call the police as soon as possible. Some cities have designated off-the-road places to go in case of an accident; in others, you have to wait for the police to arrive before moving. In most cases you can pull off the road to let traffic flow, if your car can be moved.

3. Notify your insurance company. Most larger national companies have an 800 number to call, which you should keep in your wallet. Write your policy number on the note card with the phone number so that you can refer to it when you call. Your insurance company can also advise you if your policy covers a rental car to use while your car is being fixed.
4. If you have an accident while driving a rental car, call the rental office. You'll find the number on your rental contract.

Renting a Car

On the surface, renting a car seems expensive, but according to Tom Brosnahan's book *How to Beat the High Cost of Travel,* no rental fees are carved in stone.

Don't just pay the fee without asking about the many hidden savings, such as discounts for longer rentals, weekend rates, unlimited mileage or number of free miles, free return and delivery, discounts for belonging to certain groups, and frequent-flyer car rental bonuses.

Calculating Expenses of Car Travel

Many people erroneously think traveling by car is the least expensive way. Travel writer Brosnahan says four or more people sharing a car is "budget travel," but one or two people sharing a car is "luxury travel." When you add up the costs realistically, you may find that air or train travel is less expensive.

• When you calculate the cost of travel in your own car, add up fuel, oil, tires, maintenance, wear and tear, insurance, parking and tolls, highway food, and overnight hotel/motel costs.

• When you calculate the cost of rental cars, add up the daily or weekly rental charge, mileage charge (this and fuel are the biggest expenses), plus taxes, fuel, parking and tolls, pickup and delivery charges (if you use those services), and various other stamp taxes, "document fees," or "execution fees."

• If you are staying in the downtown part of a city, it may cost less to use cabs if you don't really need to have a car every moment. You won't need a rental car if most places you'll go are close enough for low taxi fares, if you'll be walking part of the time, or if you can use public transportation.

• If you are older than 21 and have a driver's license and references, you may be able to drive someone else's car from one point to another for a "drive-away firm." These firms arrange for people's cars to be delivered to various parts of the United States. You will have to sign a contract, and pay a deposit and fuel costs, but repairs are paid by the owner. You'll have to meet the car owner's schedule, but some owners may allow you to spend a day in a tourist city en route.

• Often colleges offer driver services that enable you to share driving with a car owner who doesn't want to drive alone on a long trip. Find out by calling the largest university in your area.

Eating Out While on Vacation

• Don't just go to the first restaurant recommended to you. Ask several people for recommendations. If the same name comes up often, you'll know you have a winner.

• You'll save money if you select in-season and regional foods from the menu, such as strawberries in early summer, seafood in coastal cities, and beef in Kansas City or Texas.

• You'll get better meals if you choose the chef's daily specials. This is based on the idea that the chef gets bored with the regular menu and puts more effort into daily specials. Specials are more likely to be made with fresh, perishable ingredients than regular menu items, which may come from the freezer in some restaurants.

• Ask how menu items are prepared and if the appetizer you are ordering goes with the entrée. In a good restaurant, waiters or waitresses should be able to help you order complementary foods and select wines if there is no sommelier.

• Be aware that dining customs in foreign countries or even different parts of the United States may be different from yours, so don't get annoyed if you don't get whatever you are used to having. For example, coffee is served with meals in some Midwestern states, whereas it's served after dinner in other areas. In some foreign countries, coffee drinking is a breakfast and mid-afternoon activity, not always with or after meals.

In Southern states, asking for "tea" will bring iced tea automatically unless you specify "hot tea." And asking for iced tea in early May in Maine will get you a look of horror.

You're not likely to get an automatic glass of water in foreign countries, and in some third-world countries that's good, because the water isn't safe to drink.

Tipping

• When you are on tour in a foreign country, it's best to ask your guide about appropriate tipping.

• On most cruise ships, you will tip at the end of the cruise, and the suggested tip will be noted in the ship's daily newsletter. Most provide special envelopes on the last day for you to use, which are printed to indicate tips for cabin or dining room and bar personnel.

• In a restaurant, read the menu or bill to find out if the tip is added automatically. If so, you can still tip anyone who has given you special service if you wish.

• Generally, 15 percent is the normal tip to waiters and waitresses in a "modest restaurant," and 20 percent of the total bill in an expensive restaurant.

In an expensive restaurant, divide the 20 percent of the total bill into 75 percent to the waiter and 25 percent to the captain of the table (the person who supervises waiters and table busing or attends to special requests).

If you can't figure 15 percent of anything in your head, buy a tip card, sold at greeting card stores, or just compute 10 percent of the total amount, which is easy; add it to one-half of whatever is 10 percent; and you'll get a total of 15 percent.

• Tip the maitre'd $5, $10, or more for a table, depending upon the type of restaurant and the size of the city, and if you are getting special consideration, such as a best-located table.

• Tip the wine steward, or sommelier, $3 to $5 per bottle. In an expensive restaurant, tip 15 percent of the wine bill.

• Bartenders usually get 15 percent or the change, if it's a reasonable amount.

• Ladies' room attendants can be tipped $1 per woman using the facilities.

• Hotel bellhops get $1 or $2 per bag in most cases.

• Tip the doorman who summons a cab or your car $1; the garage attendant who brings your car up front $1 or $2.

• I've learned that if you are going to be staying in a hotel or frequent a restaurant a lot, tip early on, instead of waiting till the very end of your stay, and you will get great service.

• If you are in doubt, ask about local customs and then tip the concierge a dollar or two for providing the information. Ask for restaurant and entertainment recommendations, and for directions while you're at it, and get more info for your tip!

While You Are Gone

• Make arrangements for someone to keep your house looking "lived in." Rather than canceling newspaper subscriptions and having your mail held for you (which alerts a lot of people whom you don't know and tells them exactly how long you'll be gone), ask a reliable friend or relative, or pay someone to house-sit.

• Most major cities have house-sitting services in which bonded people check your house daily; pick up newspapers, flyers, and mail; water your house plants; feed your fish; and take care of your cat and/or dog. The fee you pay is worth it if you get peace of mind. Always ask for references and check them out when you hire a sitter service for anything.

• Set lights on timers so that lights go on and off instead of staying on 24 hours a day (which advertises that somebody is gone and is trying to make the house look occupied).

• If you are going on an extended trip of several months, and you want to rent out your house or condominium apartment, check with your insurance agent about your policy's coverage.

• If you have an automatic garage door, unplug it to avoid having the door opened by someone with an opener on your frequency. Most people who have automatic garage doors report occasional mysterious openings due to others having the same-frequency openers.

Getting Packed

Carry-On Luggage or Checked Luggage

• If you plan to carry on or check unusually shaped or very large items, call the airline ahead of time to make sure it'll permit it. For example, most airlines will provide a box for a bicycle, but you'll probably have to dismantle the bike and pay an extra fee for shipping it. On international flights, a bicycle counts as one of your two free pieces of luggage, so if you already have two pieces of luggage, you'll have to pay a substantial fee for shipping it.

(You'll probably need to furnish your own box for a bike when traveling by bus.)

• Always put your name and address on all your possessions when you travel. Stick-on address labels can be stuck on cameras, binoculars, and anything plastic (they peel off some fabrics).

• Tape business cards inside your bags for identification in case luggage tags get ripped off.

• When you carry on baggage, be among the first to board in your section and you won't be left "holding the bag"—literally—when all the compartments are full.

Travel Wardrobes

Whether you are a woman or a man, the best way to pick out a travel wardrobe is to stick to a basic color scheme. Mine is black, but yours could be navy, brown, or whatever is your favorite basic, neutral color. I plan what I will wear when I go on public-relations tours and actually write up a "menu" of the combinations of separates and accessories I will wear and then tape the menu on one of the hangers.

Here's my favorite on-the-road combination, which could be anyone's menu, with some additions and subtractions. Believe it or not, by mixing and matching and changing accessories, I can and have lived comfortably for as long as two weeks with what's listed here.

• A black suit; a gray skirt in the same fabric as the suit; a topper (blazer, jacket, or vest); three blouses in white, red, gray, or a print that has these three colors (I don't like to travel with busy-printed dresses, because you get tired of them when you have to wear them over and over again—I'd rather save the prints for a blouse or scarves to flash some color); and a sweater for cool weather (turtleneck or pullover).

• Accessories include belts in gold, black, and/or gray or red; a couple of scarves with black, red, gray, and white patterns to dress up blouses, tie up my hair, and use as belts or hat bands; panty hose in black, gray, or white, depending upon the season; a pair of gray shoes and black shoes, including a pair of comfy walking shoes; a handbag that holds everything I need en route.

In addition to the above, I pack the following things for evening wear.

• A pair of black dressy slacks; a black or white overshirt of fabric similar to the dressy slacks that I can wear alone, belted, or over a camisole or tube top; a camisole or tube top to wear under the overshirt or with my black suit, with or without a dressy belt; a pair of dressy sandals and a lightweight evening bag.

Men's Wardrobes Need Coordinating Too

A man's wardrobe for traveling is similar and also depends upon what kinds of business events are connected with the trip.

• Generally, a dark suit, worn with a white shirt and a coordinated tie, will take a man anywhere.

• Add a sport coat and slacks (one or two pairs), and shirts in colors that go with the dark suit and the sport coat and slacks combination, plus ties that are also interchangeable with the suit and sport coat. It helps if the suit pants can also be worn with the sport coat in case of spills or stains.

• Add a sweater or sweater vest for cool weather, and then this wardrobe is versatile. An extra pair of shoes rounds out the male travel wardrobe for business.

General Tips on Selecting Travel Clothes

• In both women's and men's suits, you'll find that year-round fabrics such as lightweight wool, wool blends, and silk and wool blends are the best travelers. If you take a sweater and a lightweight raincoat, you can keep warm by layering and keep cool by unlayering.

• Denim is always a good casual traveling fabric.

• A sweater or sweater vest is a good cover-up if you have a spot on your last clean blouse or shirt and still want to look respectable on the return flight!

• Check out fabric stores. You'll find many new spot removers and wrinkle-removing sprays to help you keep your wardrobe in reasonably good shape while you are traveling.

• If you are going to a resort, or on a tour or cruise, note how the people are dressed in the brochure's photos. Then you'll have a clue whether you'll need casual, dressy, or even formal clothing.

• If you are going on a vacation trip, you'll need play clothes according to what play you've planned and how hard you play! Some folks can play 18 holes of golf in the noonday sun and still look like they just came out of the club-house; others get as rumpled as an unmade bed just walking from the hotel door to the tour bus.

How to Pack

Unless your trip is an emergency, pack more than a couple of hours before you leave so that you have time to organize your wardrobe and accessories. I honestly find that, as my trip progresses, I become a better packer each time I repack. Here are some ways to pack so that you don't crush and smash things.

• Some luggage comes with packing instructions; don't throw these away, especially if you've bought any of the newer hanging, folding, and generally innovative travel gear. Between trips, it's easy to forget the manufacturer's carefully devised "goesintas." (As in: "This goesinta this pocket" and "That goesinta that zipper compartment.")

• Heavy things should be packed at the bottom of your suitcase so they won't squash everything when the suitcase is picked up. And, when I say "bottom of your suitcase," I mean whatever will be the bottom when the case is picked up.

• When you put shoes into a standard suitcase, put them sole to sole with the heel of one shoe touching the toe of the other. Stuff small light things into your shoes to save space and to help keep their shapes. I stuff my shoes with slips, underwear, panty hose (especially if the hose matches that pair of shoes), and even small bags of vitamins or pill bottles.

• Fill empty spaces with softies, such as socks, underwear, T-shirts. Put large clothing items on the top.

• Fold skirts once and keep them flat. You can pad the fold with another garment.

• You can match pants cuff to cuff, then fold in half (over each other if you have several pairs) or roll them.

• This idea of folding clothes over other clothes can be carried out with almost all of your garments if you alternate large garments with smaller ones until everything fits in. For example: You can lay an unfolded pair of trousers horizontally in your suitcase, with the top of the pants placed against the suitcase's edge and the pants' bottom hanging out over the side. Then, place a smaller garment, such as a shirt, vertically in the suitcase, with the top placed at the suitcase's edge and the bottom hanging over the edge. If you alternate garment with garment, each placed in the opposite direction in the suitcase, you can then flip up all the ends of the garments that have been hanging over the edges and close your suitcase. All garments will have padded the others and you'll have fewer wrinkles.

• To pack a dress in a standard suitcase, hold up the dress by its shoulders and lay it in the suitcase so that the top of the dress is in the suitcase and the skirt is draped over the edge. Then fold the sleeves across the front of the dress, and fold the skirt up across the dress top. If the dress has a very full skirt, fold the sides inward first and then fold up the skirt.

• I hate to bring up panty hose again, but here's yet another use for them. If you roll garments for packing, you can make tubes from panty hose legs that have the tops and toes cut off. These tubes will hold your clothing rolls neatly in the suitcase.

• In fact, you can even pack panty hose in panty hose! Use the leg of an old pair to hold all your new ones and then use the "panty hose sausage" you've created to pack folds in folded garments. Rolled-up underwear can also pad sleeves and folded garments and will stay in a roll if you pack it in a panty hose leg.

• Stuff clothing or tissue into folds of clothing to prevent pressing in the creases and button up, zip up, or belt clothing so it stays in shape.

• I use a lightweight hanging-type garment bag so that I don't have to fold up clothing. If you use a heavy-duty bag, you can tuck shoes, hair dryers, and other bulky things into the top two corners above the "shoulders" of your clothing; then you save the pockets for other things.

• If your dress is too long for a garment bag, slit a cardboard tube and put it over the hanger so that you can fold your dress over the tube, in half or at the waist, so that the dress is only half as long and won't get a crumpled hemline.

• If you keep clothing in plastic dry-cleaners' bags and then put them into the hanging bag, they don't get as crushed. I don't know why—they just seem to slip around and stay unwrinkled.

• Hang-up cosmetic bags that have small, clear plastic compartments for your personal items are nice travel aids, because you can hang them on the back of the door of the hotel bathroom and see all of what you need at a glance. I imagine they are a blessing for hotel maids, because your stuff isn't strewn all over the bathroom. They certainly keep you from forgetting personal items when you leave. I've seen these bags in department stores and in some catalogs.

• Find a packing system that works for you. We all have ways of doing things that work for us and not for others. For example, some people don't ever get all the way unpacked when they travel; others, like me, like to get partially unpacked because they feel more "at home" in the hotel when they have their things in view and easier to get at.

Don't Forget Your Comfies

• If you carry on luggage, a collapsible luggage carrier is a real source of comfort.

• If your travel is a series of "one-nighters," it's easy to get disoriented when you wake up in the middle of the night. Carry a small plug-in night-light or keep a pocket flashlight on the nightstand; neither weighs much, and being able to figure out where you are in the middle of the night is worth adding another thing to your travel kit.

• Tea bags and individual packets of instant coffee, cider, cocoa, or whatever beverage makes you happy can be a godsend when you are on the road and don't feel like waiting for room service or if you feel wanton and guilty when you order a $7 cup of coffee.

• There's no rule that says you can't pick up individual juice portions at a convenience store near the hotel, take them up to your room, and pour the juice over ice for a pick-me-up drink. More and more hotels are putting fridge hospitality in their rooms, but many times the markup on the beverages makes room service seem a bargain!

• People with special dietary restrictions can often get special diet foods on meal-serving flights if the airline knows in advance. I always special-order a vegetarian or fruit platter. It seems that everyone who is eating mystery meat or gray roast beef often wonders how I was lucky enough to receive a special meal. All you have to do is call in advance.

• On flights that don't serve food, you may want to bring your favorite nutritious snack to eat on the plane.

• On long flights, consider tossing some "footies" or sport socks into your carry-on bag so that you can slip off your shoes and walk around the plane in comfort.

• You may also want to carry a sleep mask if you're the kind of person who needs absolute darkness before you can nod off.

LEAVING THE HOME BEHIND

• Soft foam ear plugs are an absolute must for me; I carry one set in my makeup case in my purse and another in my carry-on travel bag. It makes all the difference in the world when you want to close your eyes and shut out the airplane noise for a few minutes.

Packing the Essentials

I keep my "essentials" packed all the time because I travel so much. The general categories on my mental checklist are: makeup, hair-care items, body-care items, medications, clothing, accessories, and business supplies.

You can make your own mental list by going from head down or from feet up (e.g., shoes, stockings, lingerie, clothes, makeup, jewelry, coat, purse, briefcase.)

• Buy the little sample sizes of shampoo, creme rinse, deodorant, hand lotion, baby oil, and so forth, that you see in the drugstores, just in case the hotel's hospitality corner doesn't have these items. I have even found sample sizes of eye drops and nasal spray.

• Remember that shampoo can double as laundry soap, and creme rinse can double as shaving cream.

Travel Checklist

My checklist may differ from yours, but here it is.

• Makeup and something to remove eye makeup.

• Toothbrush, toothpaste.

(Save the smidgens at the end of a big tube and use that for travel or get the smallest-size tube.)

• Bath powder, deodorant, perfume in small sizes.

• Facial tissues, individual packets of "wipes," a few cotton balls and swabs.

• Shaving equipment, a pair of tweezers, small scissors (folding embroidery scissors are nice 'cause they don't poke holes), safety pins, and a small sewing kit.

• A few adhesive bandages and/or felt adhesive pads in case a shoe rubs you the wrong way and place.

• Eyeglasses and/or contacts (and an extra pair), plus any of the "extras" you need to care for your contacts. You can buy eyeglass-cleaning tissues for plastic or glass lenses, and these can be a real aid to sightseeing.

• Credit cards, traveler's checks, tip change—single dollars or loose change. If you don't have a credit card for phones, you need an assortment of dimes and quarters. And boy, does this loose change come in handy when you want a soft drink, fruit juice, or snack in the middle of the night, and normally you don't have any change.

• Small notebook, pen or pencil, to keep track of phone numbers, expenses, people's names, any other information. Include a few of your address labels in case you need to identify a package. The free suitcase tags from the airport ticket counter can come in handy if you go shopping on your trip and buy something that has to be checked. Tuck a marker, twine, or packaging tape into your luggage if you are a dedicated traveling shopper.

• Something to read.

(In my case, it's usually column or book printouts, but occasionally, I like to read a novel or catch up on my magazine reading.)

• Take your own travel alarm clock, unless you are extremely optimistic and can go to sleep with total trust in whoever at the hotel desk took the message about your wake-up call. I also prefer the sound of MY alarm. It's too much of a jolt to hear different buzzes, beeps, and strange radio stations when you are in the twilight zone in a strange city.

• Here's an important tip from a traveling friend of mine who once got startled out of a sound sleep at 2 A.M. If your hotel has them, check the clocks and clock radios before your turn in for the night to make sure they aren't set and to make sure you know how to turn them off.

• I have cut down on the weight of my "essentials" by calling the 800 number of the hotel where I'll stay to find out if they provide hair dryers, irons and boards, and so on. Some hotels even have curlers and electric razors available on request. Some hotels charge for use of such items and some don't; ask when you call. Don't forget that if you are traveling in Europe, your electric things must work on 220 voltage and have adapter plugs.

Crushed Clothing

• The old "hang it in the bathroom when you take a shower so the steam loosens wrinkles" still is the best tip.

• If you have stubborn creases and don't have a travel iron, you can some-times "iron" them out by sliding the creases over a well-dusted hot light bulb. Just remember to put the lamp shade back on the lamp when you are finished!

• If you have a travel iron, you can make an ironing board by putting a pile of towels on the floor and ironing away. If the nap of the towels is too thick (meaning you stay at better hotels), put the towel "pad" into a pillowcase. When you are finished, put the pillowcase back on your pillow and dream away. Using makeshift ironing boards on the floor usually works better for me, but you may want to use the bed.

• Some new aerosol de-wrinkle sprays are sold at fabric and other stores; read the labels to make sure these sprays are compatible with your clothing fabrics.

Other Hints

• Tuck in some spring clothespins to clip skirts and slippery fabric garments to hangers and to clip things you've rinsed out to whatever you've hung them on. Most hotels have retractable drying lines in the shower.

• Avoid laundry. Travel with disposables. I know women who make dispos-able panties by cutting off panties from panty hose that have runs. You can have other disposables, too, such as those bras you've never liked, panty hose that has nailpolish mends in the foot where it doesn't show, any underwear that has semi–stretched-out elastic, or any other garment you want to get rid of anyway. Wear 'em and leave 'em behind!

• Instead of toting around brochures and other papers, mail them to yourself in large, brown self-addressed mailing envelopes. If you are in a foreign country, don't forget that you have to buy the stamps of that country! Which is especially nice if you are a stamp collector or know one.

• If you don't want to carry a folding umbrella, a one-yard square of plastic, like the kind paint drop cloths are made of, folded and kept in a plastic sandwich bag can be your umbrella, rain cap, or coat, and something to sit on when you need a rest. Cut a face-size hole in the middle if you want it to be a hood.

• Zipper-sealed plastic sandwich bags are a must when you travel. I put any-thing that might leak into bags. The bags also keep your hose from getting snagged, your underwear in easy-to-find clusters, and so forth.

388 _____ ALL-NEW HINTS FROM HELOISE

• Some parents, when traveling with children, pack each day's change of clothing in a large bag and then use the bag from fresh clothing to hold the previous day's laundry.

When You Travel Outside the United States

• Always take all medications and hygienic items with you, especially if you travel to third-world countries or the Soviet Union. This includes aspirin, allergy and cold medicines, and those for upset stomach.

• Take along a flat rubber sink stopper if you like to take baths. These stoppers are also handy when you are traveling with children and stopping in camping facilities that have only shower stalls. You can get at least two to four inches of water stopped up in a shower stall to bathe a small child or at least give yours or a child's feet a soothing soak.

• Don't forget soap, washcloth, and small towel; not all guest facilities in other countries provide these things.

• I like to carry a quick-drying sponge instead of a washcloth, when I travel anywhere, and I know a lot of people who like to wash with the soaps their skins are used to instead of those provided in hotels, no matter what designer labels are on them.

• Check with the Centers for Disease Control (CDC) in Atlanta, Foreign Travel Department, to find out which, if any, immunizations are needed for the country you will visit. The number to call is 1-404-639-2572. The main switchboard number for the CDC is 1-404-639-3311. Often local agencies and doctors don't have current information, so it's better to call the CDC.

• It takes several weeks to get a passport. You need proof of citizenship, such as a birth certificate or a voter registration card, and four small pictures from a place that specifies "passport photos." If you have an outdated passport, you can renew by mail. Get your passport forms and instructions at federal or state courthouses or post offices. Passports are good for ten years.

• When you are traveling abroad, remember that some countries have special customs. For example, in the Middle East, a woman needs to be more covered up—no shorts, halters, sleeveless tops, and so forth.

• When you travel, always take your best patience and your sense of humor and remember that you are the guest/visitor/outsider in foreign countries. It's their country and their rules prevail!

As a wise traveler once told a complaining one, if you want everything to be just like you have it at home, stay at home!

Camping and Hiking

The National Park Service has information on campsites and trails, but remember that Park Service campsites and cabins, when they are available, are very popular and therefore booked well in advance. You can't just decide to go to Yellowstone National Park next week and expect to get space if it's the peak of summer travel season.

To get information about the National Park Service facilities, look in the federal government section of your phone book under "Interior, Department of" and then National Park Service Administrative Office.

Hiking

• A small lightweight book on plants makes hiking more fun. It's like going to a party and knowing the other guests' names instead of going to a party where you don't know a soul. And nature's beauty is certainly a party!

• Also, even the clearest streams can contain Giardia and other parasites that will turn your walk into a run when you get gas, diarrhea, and stomach pains. If you are going to an area where you will have to drink from rivers, lakes, streams, and yes, even springs, buy water purification products or devices from stores that sell camping supplies.

• You can purify water by boiling it for at least 15 minutes, or you can use commercial purifiers.

• You can pack oranges in your backpack to quench your thirst. Put the peels into the plastic litter bag you tucked into your backpack. You did take a litter bag, didn't you?

• Raisins and other dried fruit, nuts, and granola all make good snacks on the trail, because they give you energy without being heavy to carry. If you like it, beef jerky is also a lightweight snack.

What to Wear

• Remember that if you go hiking during hunting season, be sure to wear brightly colored clothing or, better yet, wear a bright orange hunter's vest so that you are very obviously not game! Wearing brightly colored clothing is a must for children so that, if they do wander off, they can be seen more easily.

• When you think about comfort in the wilderness, "the right stuff" means the right clothes. Hypothermia, or what used to be called exposure, can happen to anyone while backpacking or camping.

• Bring a set of "sweats" on long hikes or camping trips to put on when you get wet.

• Always bring extras for children, who, bless their little curious hearts, tend to fall into water and mud puddles as naturally as breathing.

Trudging On

• Make sure your shoes fit properly so that their heels don't rub and cause blisters. Wearing cushiony terry or wool socks helps protect your feet. Hiking is supposed to be fun, not pain! If you plan to do serious hiking on rough terrain, you will need hiking shoes that support your ankles and have treaded soles to prevent your slipping down hills. New hiking shoes are as light and are made of the same materials as tennis-type sport shoes.

Insects—Unwelcome Outdoor Companions

• Insect repellent is a must in the great outdoors, and you'll find some repellents in individual packets that can be tucked into a pocket. Insects carry many diseases, so their stings and bites can be more than just annoying and itchy! To be less appealing to the insects don't wear your favorite perfume, scented hand lotion, hair spray, or aftershave cologne, which will only let the little buggers know exactly where you are.

• The traditional way of killing chiggers is still the quickest. Paint their bites with clear nail polish (or red, if you're itchy and that's all you have).

• If the area in which you travel is known to have disease-bearing ticks, wear long pants and long-sleeved shirts, and use insect repellent. Remember it's necessary to remove a tick's head when you remove the tick. If you just pull off the body, you risk infection. The best way to remove a tick is to gently pull it with tweezers until it releases its grasp; then you'll get the whole tick out. Put a pair of tweezers in your first-aid kit and it will be handy for stickers too.

• Treat insect bites with alcohol, witch hazel, or antibiotic preparations.

• Ant bites can be made wet and sprinkled with meat tenderizer to neutralize the venom. The same technique works for many other stinging insects.

- Ammonia or vinegar dabbed on with a cotton ball can also help itchy stings.

- Baking soda mixed in water will help itchy stings as well.

- Remember what Mom told you about scratching bites. Don't! They will leave scars if they get infected from dirty fingers. Cleanse, disinfect, and then keep the area clean until it heals! If you must scratch, scratch on either side of the bite, and it will psychologically help relieve the itching.

Hiking with Pets

- Hiking with your faithful dog companion can be a wonderful experience, but keep him controlled on a leash.

- Carry a small plastic bowl for giving your pet water.

- Don't forget to tick proof and bug proof your pet, and when you check for insects and ticks on yourself, don't forget your faithful little friend.

Sleeping Bags

- If you are cold, sleeping in a sweat/jogging suit is one way to add keep-warm layers. Layers are the key, because they keep more warm air trapped in the bag.

- Most campers prefer man-made fibers for sleeping bag insulation, because they are lighter in weight and when wet still keep you warm. When goose or duck down sleeping bags get wet, they no longer hold air to insulate you.

- Children can sleep in adult bags. Just fold up the empty bottom flat to cover the child or fold it under to make a softer "mattress" for the child.

- Remember that you can freeze from the ground up, so always put a mat, some plastic, or an air mattress under your sleeping bag.

Disposable and Homemade Camping Aids

- A "hand washer" can be made from a gallon jug, which can be hung from a tree limb or tent rope by its handle. Poke a small hole in the bottom and insert a stick or piece of twig for a plug. If you make the hole no bigger than your "pinkie" finger, you won't have a mess under the "hand washer" from excess water. Most of the time you only need a "spritz," not enough to shower or wash your hair!

• Hang a bar of hand-washing soap that is tied in the foot of a panty hose leg nearby, unless you have one of those soaps-on-a-rope that people give as gifts. I guess you could call this camping aid "soap in a sock."

• You can also put a mixture of regular liquid detergent and water into a detergent bottle that has a plug/squirt cap and use it to wash hands, dishes, whatever.

• If you have old terry "footies," use them as camping washcloths; they can be tossed into the dumpster when you're finished with them.

• You can hang a roll of paper towels up on a tree branch if you open one side of a cardboard-tubed pants hanger, slip on the roll of towels, and put the hanger back together again. If the cardboard breaks, you can just bend the wire ends so that they hold the paper towels.

• An inflatable plastic wading pool can be a portable bathtub, and it won't take much space in your camper but will be a blessing if you camp at a site with no bathing facilities. If you need privacy, hook a shower curtain to a plastic hula hoop and balance the curtain between a couple of tree branches or above swing-out camper back doors.

• You can also put a garbage bag inside a clothes basket or clean trash can for a makeshift bathtub/foot soaker when you're camping where there aren't any bathing facilities.

• Tent ropes can be clotheslines; if you have a camper, bring along a folding ironing caddy to hang things on.

• When you set up your camp table, putting its feet into tuna cans filled with water will give each table leg its own moat to trap hungry, pesty ants.

• A painter's drop cloth can be an emergency raincoat, something to sit on so that your "sitter" doesn't get damp from the ground, and something to put under your sleeping bag as a barrier between the damp ground and you.

• If you think it's hard to make the beds of your camper, just use sleeping bags.

• You can make a totable "cushion" for sitting on if you put something flat (newspapers, your towel) into a handled plastic shopping bag, especially the kind that can be snapped shut at the top.

• Get a bunch of super-long, super-strong shoelaces and hang a whistle and your utility "army" knife around your neck. The whistle is a signal in case you get lost and/or injured and need to call for help. Having the "army" folding knife around your neck just makes it easier to find it when you need it.

• To make ice for your cooler, freeze water in quart or gallon jugs; you can drink this water as it thaws.

• Cold-natured campers who want some warmth at night can take a hot rock that was close to the fire and warm up like folks did before central heating was invented. Handling the hot rock with oven mitts, wrap it in a couple of layers of heavy foil, then place it next to your feet. It will generate enough heat to keep your feet warm and cozy.

• If you want to cushion the benches on a picnic table while camping, use foam rubber that's about 1½ to 2 inches thick. Cut it into four strips (10 inches by 4 feet).

Cover each pad with permanent-press denim or any other sturdy fabric. Sew it on the machine, leaving one seam open to hand stitch closed once the foam pad is inserted. When you're finished, you can sew elastic to each side of the pad's end so you can anchor it to the bench.

• When camping and traveling, carry two extra pillowcases for the dirty laundry—one for white clothes only, the other for colors. When the clothes are dirty, into the proper pillowcase they go. Let everyone do their own wash, so the work isn't left to just one person.

• Toss a couple of fabric softener sheets into the soiled clothes bag to keep odors under control and to make dumping them into the wash more pleasant for whoever ends up with this chore.

• This is a hint for campers who use a tent with a center pole: If you will invert a tin funnel over the center pole before inserting it to raise the tent, you won't tear the ring out.

Eating in the Wilderness

The two keys to camp cookery and cook's convenience are: planning to ensure that you have everything you need to cook and clean up, and the scouting motto "KISS" (Keep it simple, stupid).

• If you want to grill hot dogs on a stick, be sure you know what kind of stick you are using if you've cut it from a tree or bush. Oleander is poisonous, for example, so don't cook a hot dog on an oleander branch! You can make disposable hot dog and marshmallow roasting sticks from unbent wire coat hangers.

• Take along a block of frozen chili or stew and use that for your first meal at the campsite.

• You don't need a colander if you cook noodles in a coffeepot that has holes in the spout.

• Wrap diced potatoes, a hot dog cut in one-inch pieces, some sliced carrots, and a dab or two of water, wine, or beer in a heavy-duty foil pouch and cook about 20 minutes on coals. The time on this depends upon how big the food pieces are and how hot your fire is, so 20 minutes is just an estimate. Eat out of the foil to save mess.

• Beer is a good liquid to add to a camp stew pot because it makes a rich sauce without adding a lot of ingredients that aren't likely to be handy when you are camping.

• Measure the spices needed for a favorite camping meal, put them into a plastic bag or envelope, and label it "chicken dish" or "good stew," and then it will be ready to sprinkle on the food when you start cooking at the camp fire.

• When traveling in a camper, put opened milk cartons or juice cans in a plastic bread bag and tie with a twist tie before you put them back into the cooler or camper fridge to prevent spills.

• If you coat the bottoms and sides of pots and pans with liquid detergent or rub with a bar of soap before you set them on the open camp fire, they won't get black from soot and smoke, and cleanup time will be quick and easy.

Camping with Children

Believe it or not, avid camping families say that camping or backpacking with babies younger than one year old is easy. They nap often, are not too heavy to carry on a hike, and don't complain about having "nothing to do." Also, feeding is simple, and a small child can sleep with Mom or Dad in a sleeping bag.

• Even disposable diapers are light, but be sure to carry along a plastic bag to hold used ones until you can dispose of them properly.

• Do cover a child's head with a hat or light blanket and use sunscreen on all of baby's exposed skin. Baby skin is tender and will get redder than you think just from reflected sun, and that includes sun reflected on a cloudy day, too.

• If you are hiking or camping with a toddler, be sure to pack a lot of patience and do some advance planning to deal with children at this active age.

• Camp with other toddler parents. Not only will the children enjoy each other, but you'll have more helping hands and feet to keep up with them. (Many families take along a friend or cousin of older children, too, so that their children will have the company of someone their own age.)

• Taking along favorite toys, or that special blanket or other "life-preserving" necessity, helps a toddler adjust to different surroundings. Many toddlers don't like to have their nap or bedtime routines disrupted and will be difficult all day if they haven't slept well.

• Small children have short attention spans. Scenery doesn't thrill them for long. Bring lightweight, plastic "pretend" camping gear so that a small child can mimic your activities—cooking, chopping wood, and so on.

• Get your toddler a small backpack and use it to carry crayons, paper, scissors, and so forth. When you are settling down to prepare a meal, small children can draw things they've seen on the trail.

• A diary is a good idea for older children, so they can record their feelings and whatever they have seen. Children who can't write can draw in their diaries, which can be simple, lightweight notebooks. Paste a picture from a travel brochure or magazine on the front.

• When you travel with a baby who is still drinking from a bottle, you may want to put the 2 A.M. feeding into an insulated carrier so that it's ready when baby is. It's no fun to stoke up a fire or fiddle around with a camp stove at that hour to heat up formula or juice.

• If you're not sure how good a traveler your baby or child is, you might try some "training sessions."

Camp overnight in your backyard, take a hike in a nearby park, go to the zoo or a botanical center. Let your child "help" with the planning so that it's your child's trip, too, even if it's just deciding what toy to take along.

In addition to conditioning your child to dealing with outdoor trips, these pre-trip events will help you know what sort of food, clothing, and equipment you need.

• If the children go away to camp without you, give them prepaid addressed postcards so they won't have any excuses for not writing home.

• Most send-away camps provide lists of what children should bring with them, and it's best to stick to the list so your child will have the same things the others have and feel more like "one of the guys/gals."

• First-aid kits should include syrup of ipecac to induce vomiting in case a budding gourmet does some forbidden tasting of the flora on the path. If you have space, you might want to carry an "instant ice compress." These light-weight plastic bags of chemical crystals are activated if struck and can be applied to painful sprains and bruises.

The Heloise Survival Kit

Through the years, certain things have become absolutely essential to life in a Heloise Home.

Vinegar, baking soda, and nylon net have had the most press, but there are many others. I've listed them here, from A (ammonia) to V (vinegar). You'll find them used throughout this book, sometimes in unorthodox fashion. For example, in Chapter 3, "In and Around the House," you'll find vinegar used at least 11 times. Here's the Heloise Survival Kit:

Ammonia
Baking Soda
Bleach
Borax
Candles
Cat Litter
Clothespins
Coffee Cans
Coffee Grounds
Cornstarch
Crayons
Cream of Tartar
Dental Floss
Dryer Lint
Fabric Softener Sheets
Fishing Line
Hair Spray
Innertubes (old, used)
Nail Polish
Nail Polish Remover

Newspapers
Nylon Net
Old Gloves and Socks
Oven Cleaner
Panty Hose
Petroleum Jelly
Plastic Squeeze Bottles
Prewash Spray
Rubbing Alcohol
Salt
Sandpaper
Silicon Spray
Shoeboxes
Steel Wool
Tackle Box
Toothbrushes
Toothpaste
Typewriter Correction Fluid
Vinegar

INDEX

Kitchen appliances, *see* Appliances
Kitchens:
  cleaning, 49–51
  decoration of, 127
  design of, 29–30
  pest control in, 56–59
Kitchen sinks, 50–51
Kitchen utensils, 51–56, 67–69
  for microwave ovens, 43
  storing, 67, 69
  wooden, 64
  See also Cookware; *and specific items*
Kiwis (kiwifruit), 76
Knickknacks, 106, 123
Knob celery, 80
Knobs, loose, 110
Kumquats, 77

Ladders, 141–42
Lamps, cleaning, 106–7
Laundromats, 220–21
Laundry, 211, 217–21
  baby's, 191–92
  linens, 353–54
  See also Dryers, Clothes; Washers,
    Clothes
Lawn mowers, 31
  storing, 148, 154
Lawns, 171–72
Leases, 266–67
Leather
  storing, 236
  upholstery, 115
Leaves, 165, 166, 171
Leftovers, 38–39, 62–63, 67, 90
Legumes, 247–48
Letters:
  computers and, 281
  taping, 294
  writing, 241–42
Lettuce, 75, 89
  indoor growing of, 161
Lights:
  outdoor, 176
  underwater, 177

Linens, 353–55
  "good," when to use, 348–49
  repairing, 354–55
  storing, 354–55
Linoleum, 118, 119
Lint, 218, 220
Lipstick stains, 215
Litter boxes, 331–32
Locks, 137, 147
Loquats, 77
Luggage
  for air travel, 379–80
  lost, 370–71
  See also Packing

Macaroni necklaces, 202
Mangoes, 77
  growing, 156
Margarine stains, 215
Marigolds, 166
Marjoram, 66, 167
Mattress stains, 217
Mayonnaise, 89
Meat, 247
  for babies, 186–87
  buying, 75
  ground, 64
  kitchen shears and, 68
  quantities of, for parties, 347
  refreezing, 90
  storing, 86–89
Medications:
  for children, 192, 197–98
  disposal of, 262
  poisoning by, 262
Memo books, 239–40
Menu planning, 71
  for parties, 344
Message center, family, 207, 264
Mexico, taking pets to, 326
Microwave ovens, 31, 42–45
  baby's bottle and, 44, 183, 184
  children and, 197
  cleaning, 45
  coffee and, 44, 59–61